The American Intellectual Tradition

The American Intellectual Tradition

A Sourcebook

Volume II: 1865 to the Present

Edited by
DAVID A. HOLLINGER
University of Michigan
and
CHARLES CAPPER
University of North Carolina at Chapel Hill

New York Oxford
OXFORD UNIVERSITY PRESS
1989

Oxford University Press

Oxford New York Toronto
Delhi Bombay Calcutta Madras Karachi
Petaling Jaya Singapore Hong Kong Tokyo
Nairobi Dar es Salaam Cape Town
Melbourne Auckland
and associated companies in
Berlin Ibadan

Published by Oxford University Press, Inc.,
200 Madison Avenue, New York, New York 10016

Library of Congress Cataloging-in-Publication Data

The American intellectual tradition.
Contents: v. 1. 1620–1865 — v. 2. 1865 to the present.
1. United States—Intellectual life—Sources.
I. Hollinger, David A. II. Capper, Charles
E169.1.A47218 1989 973 88-12632
ISBN 0-19-505774-0 (set)
ISBN 0-19-504461-4 (v. 1: pbk.)
ISBN 0-19-504462-2 (v. 2: pbk.)

2 4 6 8 9 7 5 3 1

Printed in the United States of America
on acid-free paper

For
Henry F. May

Preface

If a tradition is a family of disagreements, the American intellectual tradition is a very extended family. Its members include arguments inspired by the interests and ideals of a variety of communities within the United States as well as arguments concerned with the national community itself. The family also embraces arguments responsive to Western, if not universal, issues in philosophy, science, religion, politics, literature, and the arts. Some of the most influential members of this family are highly conscious of their European ancestry, whereas others have married into European families and still others remain always preoccupied with the family's Americanness. The family is currently quite content with its extended state; it is happy to count among its many arguments those voiced against the Unitarians by Ralph Waldo Emerson, against Booker T. Washington by W.E.B. Du Bois, and against John Stuart Mill by B. F. Skinner. But the family is vague on just what makes it a family to begin with. And the family is divided, if not confused, over exactly which of its members ought to supervise the education of its young. What disagreements are primary? How should the tradition be structured for the purposes of its continuation and critical revision? What specific artifacts of discourse have played the greatest role historically in developing the American intellectual tradition?

Answers to these questions are necessarily implied by any sourcebook for the study of American intellectual history. In deciding what to include in this collection, we have been aware of the dynamism and diversity of our subject as well as highly conscious of the differing constructions of it offered by various scholars. We have sought the advice of numerous colleagues and have designed *The American Intellectual Tradition* to make easily available to students many of the documents now routinely assigned—often through photocopies of uncertain legality—by teachers of this subject in American colleges and universities. Hence these volumes are chiefly practical devices, not outlines of a systematic, comprehensive interpretation of American intellectual history. Yet certain priorities have shaped these volumes, and it is appropriate to make them explicit.

The American Intellectual Tradition is frankly intellectual in orientation. Most of the documents collected herein are the result of someone's effort to perform an analysis and to persuade others of the correctness of that analysis. Although these documents express "attitudes" and embody "ideas," we have been more sensitive to their status as *arguments.* Hence most of our selections are of the genres classically associated with purposive discourse: sermon, address, letter, treatise, and essay. We have sought to identify pieces of argumentation that became prominent points of reference for contemporaries or for Americans of later generations. In so doing, we have necessarily been drawn again and again to the work of men and women normally regarded as intellectual leaders: people who were relatively effective at making arguments.

Arguments can be addressed to an infinite number of issues, but the writings collected herein respond to issues that have persistently generated extensive intellectual discussion. The bulk of our selections concern the theoretical basis for religious, scientific, artistic, political, social, and economic practice. Because the United States is above all a polity, the American family of disagreements includes a high proportion of arguments about the basis of politics. Because the public culture of America has often been caught up in the distinctive ethos of Protestant Christianity, many of our selections—especially in volume I—are directed at religious issues. Because modern America has been a peculiarly science-preoccupied civilization, many of the selections in volume II address the character of the scientific enterprise and debate the implications of scientific knowledge.

In order to give these issues historical shape, we have organized the documents around general themes or movements, which we address briefly in introductions preceding each main section. Were this a textbook rather than a sourcebook, we would have sought more consistently to indicate the entire structure of discourse surrounding the texts we discuss; here we can do no more than hint at this, leaving it to the instructor to fill in the missing arguments and counterarguments. In framing our selections, we have also sought to avoid what seems to us a failing in many previous anthologies: the packaging of each source as an example of a particular doctrine or movement. Throughout we have tried to promote the recognition that most intellectual works are dynamic and multifaceted and therefore have meaning in more than one frame of reference. With this in mind, we have written headnotes that emphasize the dense interiority of each document as well as the setting in which it was produced.

Wherever possible we have sought to include countervailing voices in this anthology, along with newer voices just beginning to be heard—or heard again—by historians. Yet one could easily list a fair number of creative American intellectuals whose names do not appear in our contents. The obvious solution would have been to expand our list. We have resisted this temptation for two reasons. First, not all formulations and figures were equally original or influential in the American intellectual tradition. Second, to have included a large number of individuals would have required reproducing only snippets. But reducing these texts to snippets would have all but eliminated their complexity and integrity, or the very qualities that define their character as intellectual sources. Also, because their complexity opens them to varying interpretations, reducing them to brief excerpts would have diminished their value as practical teaching devices. Hence, whenever we have been obliged to choose between reflecting the social and cultural diversity of American intellectual life and giving students an opportunity to confront a substantial piece of argumentation by a major thinker, we have most often chosen the second of these alternatives. Occasionally we have selected sections from a book or a letter, but most of the documents in these volumes are complete or nearly complete essays, addresses, or chapters.

The American Intellectual Tradition appears at a time when the study of intellectual history in American colleges and universities has recently been enlivened by vigorous methodological debate and conceptual innovation. We want to call attention to three especially cogent discussions of the state of the art: John E. Toews, "Intellectual History After the Linguistic Turn: The Autonomy of Meaning and the Irreducibility of Experience," *American Historical Review,* 92 (October 1987), 879–907; Donald R. Kelley, "Horizons of Intellectual History: Retrospect, Circumspect, Prospect," *Journal of the History of Ideas,* 48 (January–March 1987), 143–69; and Michael

Ermarth, "Mindful Matters: The Empire's New Codes and the Plight of Modern European Intellectual History," *Journal of Modern History,* 57 (1985), 506–27. Students interested in the ongoing discussions of intellectual historians can consult the *Intellectual History Newsletter,* published at Boston University under the editorship of David D. Hall.

For advice in relation to this sourcebook, we wish to thank the following individuals: Robert C. Bannister of Swarthmore College; Thomas Bender of New York University; Ruth H. Bloch of the University of California, Los Angeles; Paul Boyer of the University of Wisconsin–Madison; Charles Lloyd Cohen of the University of Wisconsin–Madison; George Cotkin of California State Polytechnic University at San Luis Obispo; David Brion Davis of Yale University; John P. Diggins of the University of California, Irvine; Richard Wightman Fox of Reed College; George M. Fredrickson of Stanford University; James B. Gilbert of the University of Maryland; Samuel Haber of the University of California, Berkeley; Thomas L. Haskell of Rice University; Hugh Hawkins of Amherst College; E. Brooks Holifield of Emory University; James Hoopes of Babson College; Daniel Walker Howe of the University of California, Los Angeles; David Johnson of Portland State University; John F. Kasson of the University of North Carolina at Chapel Hill; Linda K. Kerber of the University of Iowa; James T. Kloppenberg of Brandeis University; Bruce Kuklick of the University of Pennsylvania; Henry F. May of the University of California, Berkeley; Donald B. Meyer of Wesleyan University; Robert Moates Miller of the University of North Carolina at Chapel Hill; Lewis Perry of Vanderbilt University; Daniel T. Rodgers of Princeton University; Dorothy Ross of the University of Virginia; Joan Shelly Rubin of the State University College of New York at Brockport; Barbara Sicherman of Trinity University; Daniel Singal of Hobart and William Smith Colleges; Wilson Smith of the University of California, Davis; James Turner of the University of Michigan; and Daniel Wilson of Muhlenberg College. Some of these colleagues would have preferred a somewhat different contents ("An anthology for American intellectual history without Henry Adams? . . . a contradiction in terms!"), but without their counsel *The American Intellectual Tradition* would be less representative than it is of current teaching practice.

For assistance in the preparation of this sourcebook we wish to thank Thomas Baker, Martin Burke, James Jennings, and Brian Lloyd. The project was supported by grants from the University Research Council and the College of Arts and Sciences of the University of North Carolina at Chapel Hill. We also wish to express our appreciation for the advice and assistance of Nancy Lane of Oxford University Press.

The editors have worked closely at every stage of the preparation of *The American Intellectual Tradition,* but responsibility for volume I belongs to Charles Capper and for volume II to David Hollinger.

Ann Arbor, Mich. D.A.H.
Chapel Hill, N.C. C.C.
June 1988

Contents

Part One: Toward a Secular Culture

Part Two: Social Progress and the Power of Intellect

Part Three: To Formulate the Modern

Part One

Toward a Secular Culture

Introduction

William James recognized that the life of the mind during his own time was becoming increasingly secular. The Bible, which had for so long been uniquely privileged as a foundation for knowledge and morals, came to be approached more critically, especially in the light of modern science. James did not lament this historic transformation; on the contrary, he welcomed it. Yet he was concerned that the scientific spirit of the age would intimidate people into giving up cherished beliefs about God which might, after all, remain plausible even in the wake of such discoveries as evolution, thermodynamics, and the multiple authorship of various books of the Bible. When James wrote "The Will to Believe" in 1897, he sought to vindicate the individual soul's right to retain aspects of the Protestant heritage not actually proven false by the advancement of secular learning. James himself was an eminent man of science; his defense of religious belief can remind us that many late-nineteenth-century American intellectuals were extremely conscious of a tension between religious tradition and scientific innovation.

Not all the documents in Part One manifest this tension as vividly as does James's "The Will to Believe," but these documents do display a tendency, if not a determination, to ground argument in naturalistic and humanistic premises. Even Josiah Royce's overtly biblical "The Problem of Job" did not suggest that scriptural authority enhances an idea's claim to truth. Rather, it was to logical analysis and humane instincts that Royce appealed in arguing for the justness of God's decision to permit the suffering of innocent persons.

Although the persistence of religious concern amid secular initiatives is a vital theme in the intellectual history of the United States during the late nineteenth century, these secular initiatives themselves are properly central to Part One of this collection. The most general of these initiatives was the effort to install "scientific method" as the chief agency by which culture was to be constituted. In recognition of the vigor and enthusiasm with which contemporaries of James and Royce advanced this program, Part One begins with Charles Peirce's argument for the supreme utility of scientific method. Because realism in literature and the arts was allied with the movement for a more scientific culture, Peirce is followed in these pages by William Dean Howells's plea for a literature that would tell the truth about people's actual lives rather than idealize them to suit a parochial moral agenda.

Gilded Age thinkers often hoped that social science might provide a new, solid foundation for organizing and governing their society, but they disagreed radically about just what principles were "scientific." The selections from William Graham Sumner and Lester Frank Ward—both of whom were adamant critics of inherited religious ideas—encapsule the debate between conservative and liberal assessments of the political implications of Darwinian science. Sumner and Ward also partook of the period's interest in explaining social phenomena historically, often with reference to the operation of putative natural laws. This interest is more fully represented in the selection from Charlotte Perkins Gilman that follows Ward's essay. Gilman tried to explain in terms of evolutionary history the subordinate social position of women.

Gilman's contribution is a convenient stepping-stone to the initiatives on behalf of blacks and women represented here by W.E.B. Du Bois and Elizabeth Cady Stanton. Du Bois attacked what he saw as the mistakenly passive and accommodationist program for black progress developed by Booker T. Washington; Stanton indicted an entire social order for its patent violation of the rights of human beings who happened to be women. Although some advocates of the rights of women and of blacks spoke within the old Protestant cultural consensus, Du Bois and Stanton drew more deeply—sometimes defiantly—from the Enlightenment tradition of universal natural rights.

The intellectual initiatives for which historians remember the several decades immediately following the Civil War are thus largely secular, but Part One closes with Royce and James in order that we remember the intensity with which Protestant Christianity could still be defended at the turn of the twentieth century even by the most sophisticated of American intellectuals.

Recommendations for Further Reading

Laurence R. Veysey, *The Emergence of the American University* (Chicago, 1965); Howard Mumford Jones, *The Age of Energy: Varieties of American Experience, 1865–1915* (New York, 1973); and *The Incorporation of America: Culture & Society in the Gilded Age* (New York, 1982); T. J. Jackson Lears, *No Place of Grace: Antimodernism and the Transformation of American Culture, 1880–1920* (New York, 1981); William R. Hutchinson, *The Modernist Impulse in American Protestantism* (Cambridge, Mass., 1976); James Turner, *Without God, Without Creed: The Origins of Unbelief in America* (Baltimore, 1985); Bruce Kuklick, *Churchmen and Philosophers: From Jonathan Edwards to John Dewey* (New Haven, Conn., 1985); R. Jackson Wilson, *In Quest of Community: Social Philosophy in the United States, 1860–1920* (New York, 1968); Thomas Bender, *New York Intellect: A History of Intellectual Life in New York City, from 1750 to the Beginnings of Our Own Time* (New York, 1987); Alexandra Oleson and John Voss, eds., *The Organization of Knowledge in America, 1860–1920* (Baltimore, 1979); Larzer Ziff, *The American 1890s: Life and Times of a Lost Generation* (New York, 1966); Daniel Walker Howe, ed., *Victorian America* (Philadelphia, 1976); Lewis Perry, *Intellectual Life in America: A History* (New York, 1984), 261–316.

CHARLES PEIRCE

"The Fixation of Belief"
1877

With this essay of 1877, Charles Peirce (1839–1914) began a series of articles on which much of his fame as a philosopher came to be based. Here he only introduced the topic of this series—"the logic of science"—but in so doing managed to (a) articulate a largely *social* vision of the scientific enterprise, according to which the community rather than the individual knower is the primary agent of cognitive progress; (b) direct the method of science against not only beliefs about nature, but against the entire panorama of inherited beliefs, especially and explicitly *religious* beliefs; (c) assert that open, honest inquiry is decidedly superior *morally* to pious loyalty to an inherited faith; and (d) argue, in what would eventually be recognized as a "pragmatic" mode, that true belief is simply a *habit* that can remain stable, a "fixed opinion." Peirce's life and work are discussed cogently by R. Jackson Wilson, "Charles Sanders Peirce: The Community of Inquiry," in Wilson's *In Quest of Community: Social Philosophy in the United States, 1860–1920* (New York, 1968), 32–59. For a more technical, philosophically rigorous study, see Murray G. Murphey, *The Development of Peirce's Philosophy* (Cambridge, Mass., 1961). For a lucid account of Peirce's work in relation to his contemporaries in the Harvard milieu, see Bruce Kuklick, *The Rise of American Philosophy: Cambridge, Massachusetts, 1960–1930* (New Haven, 1977), esp. 104–26.

Few persons care to study logic, because everybody conceives himself to be proficient enough in the art of reasoning already. But I observe that this satisfaction is limited to one's own ratiocination, and does not extend to that of other men.

We come to the full possession of our power of drawing inferences the last of all our faculties, for it is not so much a natural gift as a long and difficult art. The history of its practice would make a grand subject for a book. The medieval schoolman, following the Romans, made logic the earliest of a boy's studies after grammar, as being very easy. So it was as they understood it. Its fundamental principle, according to them, was, that all knowledge rests on either authority or reason; but that whatever is deduced by reason depends ultimately on a premise derived from authority. Accordingly, as soon as a boy was perfect in the syllogistic procedure, his intellectual kit of tools was held to be complete.

To Roger Bacon, that remarkable mind who in the middle of the thirteenth century was almost a scientific man, the schoolmen's conception of reasoning appeared only an obstacle to truth. He saw that experience alone teaches anything—a proposition which to us seems easy to understand, because a distinct conception of experience has been handed down to us from former generations; which to him also seemed perfectly clear, because its difficulties had not yet unfolded themselves. Of all kinds of experience, the best, he thought, was interior illumination, which teaches many things about Nature which the external senses could never discover such as the transubstantiation of bread.

Four centuries later, the more celebrated Bacon, in the first book of his "Novum Organum," gave his clear account of experience as something which must be open to verification and re-examination. But, superior as Lord Bacon's conception is to earlier notions, a modern reader who is not in awe of his grandiloquence is chiefly struck by the inadequacy of his view of scientific procedure. That we have only to make some crude experiments, to draw up briefs of the results in certain blank forms, to go through these by rule, checking off everything disproved and setting down the alternatives, and that thus in a few years physical science would be finished up—what an idea! "He wrote on science like a Lord Chancellor," indeed.

The early scientists, Copernicus, Tycho Brahe, Kepler, Galileo, and Gilbert, had methods more like those of their modern brethren. Kepler undertook to draw a curve through the places of Mars; and his greatest service to science was in impressing on men's minds that this was the thing to be done if they wished to improve astronomy; that they were not to content themselves with inquiring whether one system of epicycles was better than another but that they were to sit down by the figures and find out what the curve, in truth, was. He accomplished this by his incomparable energy and courage, blundering along in the most inconceivable way (to us), from one irrational hypothesis to another, until, after trying twenty-two of these, he fell, by the mere exhaustion of his invention, upon the orbit which a mind well furnished with the weapons of modern logic would have tried almost at the outset.

In the same way, every work of science great enough to be remembered for a few generations affords some exemplification of the defective state of the art of reasoning of the time when it was written; and each chief step in science has been a lesson in logic. It was so when Lavoisier and his contemporaries took up the study of Chemistry. The old chemist's maxim had been, "Lege, lege, lege, labora, ora, et relege." Lavo-

Source: Popular Science Monthly, 12 (November 1877), 1–15.

isier's method was not to read and pray, not to dream that some long and complicated chemical process would have a certain effect, to put it into practice with dull patience, after its inevitable failure to dream that with some modification it would have another result, and to end by publishing the last dream as a fact: his way was to carry his mind into his laboratory, and to make of his alembics and cucurbits instruments of thought, giving a new conception of reasoning as something which was to be done with one's eyes open, by manipulating real things instead of words and fancies.

The Darwinian controversy is, in large part, a question of logic. Mr. Darwin proposed to apply the statistical method to biology. The same thing has been done in a widely different branch of science, the theory of gases. Though unable to say what the movement of any particular molecule of gas would be on a certain hypothesis regarding the constitution of this class of bodies, Clausius and Maxwell were yet able, by the application of the doctrine of probabilities, to predict that in the long run such and such a proportion of the molecules would, under given circumstances, acquire such and such velocities; that there would take place, every second, such and such a number of collisions, etc.; and from these propositions they were able to deduce certain properties of gases, especially in regard to their heat-relations. In like manner, Darwin, while unable to say what the operation of variation and natural selection in every individual case will be, demonstrates that in the long run they will adapt animals to their circumstances. Whether or not existing animal forms are due to such action, or what position the theory ought to take, forms the subject of a discussion in which questions of fact and questions of logic are curiously interlaced.

The object of reasoning is to find out, from the consideration of what we already know, something else which we do not know. Consequently, reasoning is good if it be such as to give a true conclusion from true premises, and not otherwise. Thus, the question of validity is purely one of fact and not of thinking. A being the premises and B being the conclusion, the question is, whether these facts are really so related that if A is B is. If so, the inference is valid; if not, not. It is not in the least the question whether, when the premises are accepted by the mind, we feel an impulse to accept the conclusion also. It is true that we do generally reason correctly by nature. But that is an accident; the true conclusion would remain true if we had no impulse to accept it; and the false one would remain false, though we could not resist the tendency to believe in it.

We are, doubtless, in the main logical animals, but we are not perfectly so. Most of us, for example, are naturally more sanguine and hopeful than logic would justify. We seem to be so constituted that in the absence of any facts to go upon we are happy and self-satisfied; so that the effect of experience is continually to counteract our hopes and aspirations. Yet a lifetime of the application of this corrective does not usually eradicate our sanguine disposition. Where hope is unchecked by any experience, it is likely that our optimism is extravagant. Logicality in regard to practical matters is the most useful quality an animal can possess, and might, therefore, result from the action of natural selection; but outside of these it is probably of more advantage to the animal to have his mind filled with pleasing and encouraging visions, independently of their truth; and thus, upon unpractical subjects, natural selection might occasion a fallacious tendency of thought.

That which determines us, from given premises, to draw one inference rather than another, is some habit of mind, whether it be constitutional or acquired. The habit is good or otherwise, according as it produces true conclusions from true premises or not; and an inference is regarded as valid or not, without reference to the truth or falsity of its conclusion specially, but according as the habit which determines it is such as to produce true conclusions in general or not. The particular habit of mind which governs this or that inference may be formulated in a proposition whose truth depends on the validity of the inferences which the habit determines; and such a formula is called a *guiding principle* of inference. Suppose, for example, that we observe that a rotating disk of copper quickly comes to rest when placed between the poles of a magnet, and we infer that this will happen with every disk of copper. The guiding principle is, that what is true of one piece of copper is true of another. Such a guiding principle with regard to copper would be much safer than with regard to many other substances—brass, for example.

A book might be written to signalize all the most important of these guiding principles of reasoning. It would probably be, we must confess, of no service to a person whose thought is directed wholly to practical subjects, and whose activity moves along thoroughly beaten paths. The problems which present themselves to such a mind are matters of routine which he has learned once for all to handle in learning his business. But let a man venture into an unfamiliar field, or where his results are not continually checked by experience, and all history shows that the most masculine intellect will ofttimes lose his orientation and waste his efforts in directions which bring him no nearer to his goal, or even carry him entirely astray. He is like a ship on the open sea, with no one on board who understands the rules of navigation. And in such a case some general study of the guiding principles of reasoning would be sure to be found useful.

The subject could hardly be treated, however, without being first limited; since almost any fact may serve as a guiding principle. But it so happens that there exists a division among facts, such that in one class are all those which are absolutely essential as guiding principles, while in the other are all those which have any other interests as object of research. This division is between those which are necessarily taken for granted in asking whether a certain conclusion follows from certain premises, and those which are not implied in that question. A moment's thought will show that a variety of facts are already assumed when the logical question is first asked. It is implied, for instance, that there are such states of mind as doubt and belief—that a passage from one to the other is possible, the object of thought remaining the same, and that this transition is subject to some rules which all minds are alike bound by. As these are facts which we must already know before we can have any clear conception of reasoning at all, it cannot be supposed to be any longer of much interest to inquire into their truth or falsity. On the other hand, it is easy to believe that those rules of reasoning which are deduced from the very idea of the process are the ones which are the most essential; and, indeed, that so long as it conforms to these it will, at least, not lead to false conclusions from true premises. In point of fact, the importance of what may be deduced from the assumptions involved in the logical question turns out to be greater than might be supposed, and this for reasons which it is difficult to exhibit at the outset. The only one which I shall here mention is, that conceptions which are really products of logical reflections, without being readily seen to be so, mingle with our ordinary thoughts, and are frequently the causes of great confusion. This is the case, for example, with the conception of quality. A quality as such is never an object of observation. We can see that a thing is blue or green, but the quality of being blue and the quality of being green are not things which we see; they are products of logical reflections. The truth is, that common-sense, or thought as it first emerges above the level of the narrowly practical, is deeply imbued with that bad logical quality to which the epithet *metaphysical* is commonly applied; and nothing can clear it up but a severe course of logic.

We generally know when we wish to ask a question and when we wish to pronounce a judgment, for there is a dissimiliarity between the sensation of doubting and that of believing.

But this is not all which distinguishes doubt from belief. There is a practical difference. Our beliefs guide our desires and shape our actions. The Assassins, or followers of the Old Man of the Mountain, used to rush into death at his least command, because they believed that obedience to him would insure everlasting felicity. Had they doubted this, they would not have acted as they did. So it is with every belief, according to its degree. The feeling of believing is a more or less sure indication of there being established in our nature some habit which will determine our actions. Doubt never has such an effect.

Nor must we overlook a third point of difference. Doubt is an uneasy and dissatisfied state from which we struggle to free ourselves and pass into the state of belief; while the latter is a calm and satisfactory state which we do not wish to avoid, or to change to a belief in anything else. On the contrary, we cling tenaciously, not merely to believing, but to believing just what we do believe.

Thus, both doubt and belief have positive effects upon us, though very different ones. Belief does not make us act at once, but puts us into such a condition that we shall behave in a certain way, when the occasion arises. Doubt has not the least effect this sort, but stimulates us to action until it is destroyed. This reminds us of the irritation of a nerve and the reflex action produced thereby; while for the analogue of belief, in the nervous system, we must look to what are called nervous associations—for example, to that habit of the nerves in consequence of which the smell of a peach will make the mouth water.

The irritation of doubt causes a struggle to attain a state of belief. I shall term this struggle *inquiry,* though it must be admitted that this is sometimes not a very apt designation.

The irritation of doubt is the only immediate motive for the struggle to attain belief. It is certainly best for us that our beliefs should be such as may truly guide our actions so as to satisfy our desires; and this reflection will make us reject any belief which does not seem to have been so formed as to insure this result. But it will only do so by creating a doubt in the place of that belief. With the doubt, therefore, the struggle begins, and with the cessation of doubt it ends. Hence, the sole object of inquiry is the settlement of opinion. We may fancy that this is not enough for us, and that we seek not merely an opinion, but a true opinion. But put this fancy to the test, and it proves groundless; for as soon as a firm belief is reached we are entirely satisfied, whether the belief be false or true. And it is clear that nothing out of the sphere of our knowledge can be our object, for nothing which does not affect the mind can be a motive for a mental effort. The most that can be maintained is, that we seek for a belief that we shall *think* to be true. But we think each one of our beliefs to be true, and, indeed, it is mere tautology to say so.

That the settlement of opinion is the sole end of inquiry is a very important proposition. It sweeps away, at once, various vague and erroneous conceptions of proof. A few of these may be noticed here.

1. Some philosophers have imagined that to start an inquiry it was only necessary to utter or question or set it down on paper, and have even recommended us to begin our studies with questioning everything! But the mere putting of a proposition into the interrogative form does not stimulate the mind to any struggle after belief. There must be a real and living doubt, and without all this discussion is idle.

2. It is a very common idea that a demonstration must rest on some ultimate and absolutely indubitable propositions. These, according to one school, are first principles of a general nature; according to another, are first sensations. But, in point of fact, an inquiry, to have that completely satisfactory result called demonstration, has only to start with propositions perfectly free from all actual doubt. If the premises are not in fact doubted at all, they cannot be more satisfactory that they are.

3. Some people seem to love to argue a point after all the world is fully convinced of it. But no further advance can be made. When doubt ceases, mental action on the subject comes to an end; and, if it did go on, it would be without a purpose.

If the settlement of opinion is the sole object of inquiry, and if belief is of the nature of a habit, why should we not attain the desired end, by taking any answer to a question, which we may fancy, and constantly reiterating it to ourselves, dwelling on all which may conduce to that belief, and learning to turn with contempt and hatred from anything which might disturb it? This simple and direct method is really pursued by many men. I remember once being entreated not to read a certain newspaper lest it might change my opinion upon free-trade. "Lest I might be entrapped by its fallacies and misstatements," was the form of expression. "You are not," my friend said, "a special student of political economy. You might, therefore, easily be deceived by fallacious arguments upon the subject. You might, then, if you read this paper, be led to believe in protection. But you admit that free-trade is the true doctrine; and you do not wish to believe what is not true." I have often known this system to be deliberately adopted. Still oftener, the instinctive dislike of an undecided state of mind, exaggerated into a vague dread of doubt, makes men cling spasmodically to the views they already take. The man feels that, if he only holds to his belief without wavering, it will be entirely satisfactory. Nor can it be denied that a steady and immovable faith yields great peace of mind. It may, indeed, give rise to inconveniences, as if a man should resolutely continue to believe that fire would not burn him, or that he would be eternally damned if he received his *ingesta* otherwise than through a stomach-pump. But then the man who adopts this method will not allow that its inconveniences are greater than its advantages. He will say, "I hold steadfastly to the truth and the truth is always wholesome." And in many cases it may very well be that the pleasure he derives from his calm faith overbalances any inconveniences resulting from its deceptive character. Thus, if it be true that death is annihilation, then the man who believes that he will certainly go straight to heaven when he dies, provided he have fulfilled certain simple observances in this life, has a cheap pleasure which will not be followed by the least disappointment. A similar consideration seems to have weight with many persons in religious topics, for we frequently hear it said, "Oh, I could not believe so-and-so, because I should be wretched if I did." When an ostrich buries its head in the sand as danger approaches, it very likely takes the happiest course. It hides the danger, and then calmly says there is no danger; and, it feels perfectly sure there is none, why should it raise its head to see? A man may go through life, systematically keeping out of view all that might cause a change in his opinions, and if he only succeeds—basing his method, as he does, on two fundmental psychological laws—I do not see what can be said against his doing so. It would be an egotistical impertinence to object that his procedure is irrational, for that only amounts to saying that his method of settling belief is not ours. He does not propose to himself to be rational, and indeed, will often talk with scorn of man's weak and illusive reason. So let him think as he pleases.

But this method of fixing belief, which may be called the method of tenacity, will be unable to hold its ground in practice. The social impulse is against it. The man who adopts it will find that other men think differently from him, and it will be apt to occur to him in some saner moment that their opinions are quite as good as his own, and this will shake his confidence in his belief. This conception, that another man's thought or sentiment may be equivalent to one's own, is a distinctly new step, and a highly important one. It arises from an impulse too strong in man to be suppressed, without danger of destroying the human species. Unless we make ourselves hermits, we shall necessarily influence each other's opinions; so that the problem becomes how to fix belief, not in the individual merely, but in the community.

Let the will of the state act, then, instead of that of the individual. Let an institution be created which shall have for its object to keep correct doctrines before the attention of the people, to reiterate them perpetually, and to teach them to the young; having at the same time power to prevent contrary doctrines from being taught, advocated, or expressed. Let all possible causes of a change of mind be removed from men's apprehensions. Let them be kept ignorant, lest they should learn of some reason to think otherwise than they do. Let their passions be enlisted, so that they may regard private and unusual opinions with hatred and horror. Then, let all men who reject the established belief be terrified into silence. Let the people turn out and tar-and-feather such men, or let inquisitions be made into the manner of thinking of suspected persons, and, when they are found guilty of forbidden beliefs, let them be subjected to some signal punishment. When complete agreement could not otherwise be reached, a general massacre of all who have not thought in a certain way has proved a very effective means of settling opinion in a country. If the power to do this be wanting, let a list of opinions be drawn up, to which no man of the least independence of thought can assent, and let the faithful be required to accept all these propositions, in order to segregate them as radically as possible from the influence of the rest of the world.

This method has, from the earliest times, been one of the chief means of upholding correct theological and political doctrines, and of preserving their universal or catholic character. In Rome, especially, it has been practiced from the days of Numa Pompilius to those of Pius Nonus. This is the most perfect example in history; but wherever there is a priesthood—and no religion has been without one—this method has been more or less made use of. Wherever there is artistocracy, or a guild, or any association of a class of men whose interests depend or are supposed to depend on certain propositions, there will be inevitably found some traces of this natural product of social feeling. Cruelties always accompany this system; and when it is consistently carried out, they become atrocities of the most horrible kind in the eyes of any rational man. Nor should this occasion surprise, for the officer of a society does not feel justified in surrendering the interests of that society for the sake of mercy, as he might his own private interests. It is natural, therefore, that sympathy and fellowship should thus produce a most ruthless power.

In judging this method of fixing belief, which may be called the method of authority, we must, in the first place, allow its immeasurable mental and moral superiority to the method of tenacity. Its success is proportionally greater; and in fact it has over and over again worked the most majestic results. The mere structures of stone which it has caused to be put together—in Siam, for example, in Egypt, and in Europe—have many of them a sublimity hardly more than rivaled by the greatest works of Nature. And, except the geological epochs, there are no periods of time so vast as those which are measured by some of these organized faiths. If we scrutinize the matter closely, we shall find that there has not been one of their creeds which has remained always the same; yet the change is so slow as to be imperceptible during one person's life, so that individual belief remains sensibly fixed. For the mass of mankind, then, there is perhaps no better method than this. If it is their highest impulse to be intellectual slaves, then slaves they ought to remain.

But no institution can undertake to regulate opinions upon every subject. Only the most important ones can be attended to, and on the rest men's minds must be left to the action of natural causes. This imperfection will be no source of weakness so long as men are in such a state of culture that one opinion does not influence another—that is, so long as they cannot put two and two together. But in the most priest-ridden states some individuals will be found who are raised above that conditon. These men possess a wider sort of social feeling; they see that men in other countries and in other ages have held to very different doctrines from those which they themselves have been brought up to believe; and they cannot help seeing that it is the mere accident of their having been taught as they have, and of their having been surrounded with the manners and associations they have, that has caused them to believe as they do and not far differently. And their candor cannot resist the reflection that there is no reason to rate their own views at a higher value than those of other nations and other centuries; and this gives rise to doubts in their minds.

They will further perceive that such doubts as these must exist in their minds with reference to every belief which seems to be determined by the caprice either of themselves or of those who originated the popular opinions. The willful adherence to a belief, and the arbitrary forcing of it upon others, must, therefore, both be given up and a new method of settling opinons must be adopted, which shall not only produce an impulse to believe, but shall also decide what proposition it is which is to be believed. Let the action of natural preferences be unimpeded, then, and under their influence let men conversing together and regarding matters in diffeent lights, gradually develop beliefs in harmony with natural causes. This method resembles that by which conceptions of art have been brought to maturity. The most perfect example of it is to be found in the history of metaphysical philosophy. Systems of this sort have not usually rested upon observed facts, at least not in any great degree. They have been chiefly adopted because their fundamental propositions seemed "agreeable to reason." This is an apt expression; it does not mean that which agrees with experience, but that which we find ourselves inclined to believe. Plato, for example, finds it agreeable to reason that the distances of the celestial spheres from one another should be proportional to the different lengths of strings which produce harmonious chords. Many philosophers have been led to their main conclusions by considerations like this;

but this is the lowest and least developed form which the method takes, for it is clear that another man might find Kepler's [earlier] theory, that the celestial spheres are proportional to the inscribed and circumscribed spheres of the different regular solids, more agreeable to *his* reason. But the shock of opinions will soon lead men to rest on preferences of a far more universal nature. Take, for example, the doctrine that man only acts selfishly—that is, from the consideration that acting in one way will afford him more pleasure than acting in another. This rests on no fact in the world, but it has had a wide acceptance as being the only reasonable theory.

This method is far more intellectual and respectable from the point of view of reason than either of the others which we have noticed. But its failure has been the most manifest. It makes of inquiry something similar to the development of taste; but taste, unfortunately, is always more or less a matter of fashion, and accordingly, metaphysicians have never come to any fixed agreement, but the pendulum has swung backward and forward between a more material and a more spiritual philosophy, from the earliest times to the latest. And so from this, which has been called the *a priori* method, we are driven, in Lord Bacon's phrase, to a true induction. We have examined into this *a priori* method as something which promised to deliver our opinions from their accidental and capricious element. But development, while it is a process which eliminates the effect of some casual circumstances, only magnifies that of others. This method, therefore, does not differ in a very essential way from that of authority. The government may not have lifted its finger to influence my convictions; I may have been left outwardly quite free to choose, we will say, between monogamy and polygamy, and appealing to my conscience only, I may have concluded that the latter practice is in itself licentious. But when I come to see that the chief obstacle to the spread of Christianity among a people of as high culture as the Hindoos has been a conviction of the immorality of our way of treating women, I cannot help seeing that, though governments do not interfere, sentiments in their development will be very greatly determined by accidental causes. Now, there are some people, among whom I must suppose that my reader is to be found, who, when they see that any belief of theirs is determined by any circumstance extraneous to the facts, will from that moment not merely admit in words that that belief is doubtful, but will experience a real doubt of it, so that it ceases to be a belief.

To satisfy our doubts, therefore, it is necessary that a method should be found by which our beliefs may be caused by nothing human, but by some external permanency—by something upon which our thinking has no effect. Some mystics imagine that they have such a method in a private inspiration from on high. But that is only a form of the method of tenacity, in which the conception of truth as something public is not yet developed. Our external permanency would not be external, in our sense, if it was restricted in its influence to one individual. It must be something which affects, or might affect, every man. And, though these affections are necessarily as various as are individual conditions, yet the method must be such that the ultimate conclusion of every man shall be the same. Such is the method of science. Its fundamental hypothesis, restated in more familiar language, is this: There are real things, whose characters are entirely independent of our opinions about them; whose realities affect our senses according to regular laws, and, though our sensations are as different as our relations to the objects, yet, by taking advantage of the laws of perception, we can ascertain by reasoning how things really are, and any man, if he have sufficient experience and reason enough about it, will be led to the one true conclusion. The new conception here involved is that of reality. It may be asked how I know that there are any realities. If this hypothesis is the sole support of my method of inquiry, my method of inquiry must not be used to support my hypothesis. The reply is this: 1. If investigation cannot be regarded as proving that there are real things, it at least does not lead to a contrary conclusion; but the method and the conception on which it is based remain ever in harmony. No doubts of the method, therefore, necessarily arise from its practice, as is the case with all the others. 2. The feeling which gives rise to any method of fixing belief is a dissatisfaction at two repugnant propositions. But here already is a vague concession that there is some *one* thing to which a proposition should conform. Nobody, therefore, can really doubt that there are realities, or, if he did, doubt would not be a source of dissatisfaction. The hypothesis, therefore, is one which every mind admits. So that the social impulse does not cause me to doubt it. 3. Everybody uses the scientific method about a great many things, and only ceases to use it when he does not know how to apply it. 4. Experience of the method has not led me to doubt it, but, on the contrary, scientific investigation has had the most wonderful triumphs in the way of settling opinion. These afford the explanation of my not doubting the method or the hypothesis which it supposes; and not having any doubt, nor believing that anybody else whom I could influence has, it would be the merest babble for me to say more about it. If there be anybody with a living doubt upon the subject, let him consider it.

To describe the method of scientific investigation is the object of this series of papers. At present I have only room to notice some points of contrast between it and other methods of fixing belief.

This is the only one of the four methods which presents any distinction of a right and a wrong way. If I adopt the method of tenacity and shut myself out from all influences, whatever I think necessary to doing this is necessary according to that method. So with the method of authority: the state may try to put down heresy by means which, from a scientific point of view, seems very ill-calculated to accomplish its purposes; but the only test *on that method* is what the state thinks, so that it cannot pursue the method wrongly. So with the *a priori* method. The very essence of it is to think as one is inclined to think. All metaphysicians will be sure to do that, however they may be inclined to judge each other to be perversely wrong. The Hegelian system recognizes every natural tendency of thought as logical, although it is certain to be abolished by counter-tendencies. Hegel thinks there is a regular system in the succession of these tendencies, in consequence of which, after drifting one way and the other for a long time, opinion will at last go right. And it is true that metaphysicians get the right ideas at last; Hegel's system of Nature represents tolerably the science of that day; and one may be sure that whatever scientific investigation has put out of doubt will presently receive *a priori* demonstration on the part of the metaphysicians. But with the scientific method the case is different. I may start with known and observed facts to proceed to the unknown; and yet the rules which I follow in doing so may not be such as investigation would approve. The test of whether I am truly following the method is not an immediate appeal to my feelings and purposes, but, on the contrary, itself involves the application of the method. Hence it is that bad reasoning as well as good reasoning is possible; and this fact is the foundation of the practical side of logic.

It is not to be supposed that the first three methods of settling opinion present no advantage whatever over the scientific method. On the contrary, each has some peculiar convenience of its own. The *a priori* method is distinguished for its comfortable conclusions. It is the nature of the process to adopt whatever belief we are inclined to, and there are certain flatteries to one's vanities which we all believe by nature, until we are awakened from our pleasing dream by rough facts. The method of authority will always govern the mass of mankind; and those who wield the various forms of organized force in the state will never be convinced that dangerous reasoning ought not to be suppressed in some way. If liberty of speech is to be untrammeled from the grosser forms of constraint, then uniformity of opinion will be secured by a moral terrorism to which the respectability of society will give its thorough approval. Following the method of authority is the path of peace. Certain non-conformities are permitted; certain others (considered unsafe) are forbidden. These are different in different countries and in different ages; but, wherever you are let it be known that you seriously hold a tabooed belief, and you may be perfectly sure of being treated with a cruelty no less brutal but more refined than hunting you like a wolf. Thus, the greatest intellectual benefactors of mankind have never dared, and dare not now, to utter the whole of their thought; and thus a shade of *prima facie* doubt is cast upon every proposition which is considered essential to the security of society. Singularly enough, the persecution does not all come from without; but a man torments himself and is oftentimes most distressed at finding himself believing propositions which he has been brought up to regard with aversion. The peaceful and sympathetic man will, therefore, find it hard to resist the temptation to submit his opinions to authority. But most of all I admire the method of tenacity for its strength, simplicity, and directness. Men who pursue it are distinguished for their decision of character, which becomes very easy with such a mental rule. They do not waste time in trying to make up their minds to what they want, but, fastening like lightning upon whatever alternative comes first, they hold to it to the end, whatever happens, without an instant's irresolution. This is one of the splendid qualities which generally accompany brilliant, unlasting success. It is impossible not to envy the man who can dismiss reason, although we know how it must turn out at last.

Such are the advantages which the other methods of settling opinions have over scientific investigation. A man should consider well of them; and then he should consider that, after all, he wishes his opinions to coincide with the fact, and that there is no reason why the results of these three methods should do so. To bring about this effect is the prerogative of the method of science. Upon such considerations he has to make his choice—a choice which is far more than the adoption of any intellectual opinion, which is one of the ruling decisions of his life, to which when once made he is bound to adhere. The force of habit will sometimes cause a man to hold on to old beliefs, after he is in a condition to see that they have no sound basis. But reflection upon the state of the case will overcome these habits, and he ought to allow reflection full weight. People sometimes shrink from doing this, having an idea that beliefs are wholesome which they cannot help feeling rest on nothing. But let such persons suppose an analogous though different case from their own. Let them ask themselves what they would say to a reformed Mussulman who should hesitate to give up his old notions in regard to the relations of the sexes; or to a reformed Catholic who should still shrink from the Bible. Would they not say that these persons ought to consider the matter fully, and clearly understand the new doctrine, and then ought to embrace it in its entirety? But, above all, let it be considered that what is more wholesome than any particular belief, is integrity of belief; and that to avoid looking into the support of any belief from a fear that it may turn out rotten is quite as immoral as it is disadvantageous. The person who confesses that there is such a thing as truth, which is distinguished from falsehood simply by this, that if acted on it will carry us to the point we aim at and not astray, and then though convinced of this, dares not know the truth and seeks to avoid it, is in a sorry state of mind, indeed.

Yes, the other methods do have their merits: a clear logical conscience does cost something—just as any virtue, just as all that we cherish, costs us dear. But, we should not desire it to be otherwise. The genius of a man's logical method should be loved and reverenced as his bride, whom he has chosen from all the world. He need not condemn the others; on the contrary, he may honor them deeply, and in doing so he only honors her the more. But she is the one that he has chosen, and he knows that he was right in making that choice. And having made it, he will work and fight for her, and will not complain that there are blows to take, hoping that there may be as many and as hard to give, and will strive to be the worthy knight and champion of her from the blaze of whose splendors he draws his inspiration and his courage.

WILLIAM DEAN HOWELLS

"Pernicious Fiction"
1887

Perhaps no single individual was more central to the literary culture of the United States of the late nineteenth and early twentieth centuries than William Dean Howells (1837–1920). Accomplished and supremely influential as novelist, critic, and editor, Howells was at once an old-fashioned moralist—a figure in what came to be patronized as "the genteel tradition"—and a "realist." The piece of 1887 reprinted here expresses both features of Howell's sensibility. Howells displays acute concern for the moral effects of literature on the reader, yet at the same time he insists, in the realist's mode, on "truth" as the ultimate standard for "any work of the imagination." Howells was not prepared to consider the possibility that truth might sometimes conflict with morality or with beauty, but his ideals of morality and beauty were liberal enough to enable him in good conscience to sponsor Mark Twain, Hamlin Garland, Frank Norris, and other writers whose challenge to gentility was deeper than Howells's own. This responsiveness on Howells's part is the focal point of a chapter ("Literary Hospitality") in Larzer Ziff, *The American 1890s: Life and Times of a Lost Generation* (New York, 1966), 24–49. A solid biography is Kenneth S. Lynn, *William Dean Howells: An American Life* (New York, 1971). For a splendid portrait of the literary culture of which Howells was the center, see Henry F. May, *The End of American Innocence: A Study of the First Years of Our Time, 1912–1917* (New York, 1959), 3–117.

It must have been a passage from Vernon Lee's *Baldwin*, claiming for the novel an indefinitely vast and subtle influence on modern character, which provoked the following suggestive letter from one of our readers:

—, — Co., Md., Sept. 18, 1886.

"Dear Sir,—With regard to article IV, in the Editor's Study in the September *Harper*, allow me to say that I have very grave doubts as to the whole list of magnificent things that you seem to think novels have done for the race, and can witness in myself many evil things which they have done for me. Whatever in my mental make-up is wild and visionary, whatever is untrue, whatever is injurious, I can trace to the perusal of some work of fiction. Worse than that, they beget such high-strung and supersensitive ideas of life that plain industry and plodding perseverance are despised, and matter-of-fact poverty, or everyday, commonplace distress, meets with no sympathy, if indeed noticed at all, by one who has wept over the impossibly accumulated sufferings of some gaudy hero or heroine.

"Hoping you will pardon the liberty I have taken in addressing you, I remain,

"Most respectfully yours,

———————

We are not sure that we have the controversy with the writer which he seems to suppose, and we should perhaps freely grant the mischievous effects which he says novel-reading has wrought upon him, if we were not afraid that he had possibly reviewed his own experience with something of the inaccuracy we find in his report of our opinions. By his confession he is himself proof that Vernon Lee is right in saying, "The modern human being has been largely fashioned by those who have written about him, and most of all by the novelist," and there is nothing in what he urges to conflict with her claim that "the chief use of the novel" is "to make the shrewd and tolerant a little less shrewd and tolerant, and to make the generous and austere a little more skeptical and easy-going." If he will look more closely at these postulates, we think he will see that in the one she deals with the effect of the novel in the past, and in the other with its duty in the future. We still think that there "is sense if not final wisdom" in what she says, and we are quite willing to acknowledge something of each in our correspondent.

But novels are now so fully accepted by every one pretending to cultivated taste—and they really form the whole intellectual life of such immense numbers of people, without question of their influence, good or bad, upon the mind—that it is refreshing to have them frankly denounced, and to be invited to revise one's ideas and feelings in regard to them. A little honesty, or a great deal of honesty, in this quest will do the novel, as we hope yet to have it, and as we have already begun to have it, no harm; and for our own part we will confess that we believe fiction in the past to have been largely injurious, as we believe the stage play to be still almost wholly injurious, through its falsehood, its folly, its wantonness, and its aimlessness. It may be safely assumed that most of the novel-reading which people fancy is an intellectual pastime is the emptiest dissipation, hardly more related to thought or the wholesome exercise of the mental faculties than opium-eating; in either case the brain is drugged, and left weaker and crazier for the debauch. If this may be called the negative result of the

Source: Harper's Magazine, 74 (April 1887), 824–26.

fiction habit, the positive injury that most novels work is by no means so easily to be measured in the case of young men whose character they help so much to form or deform, and the women of all ages whom they keep so much in ignorance of the world they misrepresent. Grown men have little harm from them, but in the other cases, which are the vast majority, they hurt because they are not true—not because they are malevolent, but because they are idle lies about human nature and the social fabric, which it behooves us to know and to understand, that we may deal justly with ourselves and with one another. One need not go so far as our correspondent, and trace to the fiction habit "whatever is wild and visionary, whatever is untrue, whatever is injurious," in one's life; bad as the fiction habit is, it is probbly not responsible for the whole sum of evil in its victims, and we believe that if the reader will use care in choosing from this fungus-growth with which the fields of literature teem every day, he may nourish himself as with the true mushroom, at no risk from the poisonous species.

The tests are very plain and simple, and they are perfectly infallible. If a novel flatters the passions, and exalts them above the principles, it is poisonous; it may not kill, but it will certainly injure; and this test will alone exclude an entire class of fiction, of which eminent examples will occur at all. Then the whole spawn of so-called unmoral romances, which imagine a world where the sins of sense are unvisited by the penalties following, swift or slow, but inexorably sure, in the real world, are deadly poison: these do kill. The novels that merely tickle our prejudices and lull our judgment, or that coddle our sensibilities, or pamper our gross appetite for the marvellous, are not so fatal, but they are innutritious, and clog the soul with un-wholesome vapors of all kinds. No doubt they too help to weaken the mental fibre, and make their readers indifferent to "plodding perseverance and plain industry," and to "matter-of-fact poverty and commonplace distress."

Without taking them too seriously, it still must be owned that the "gaudy hero and heroine" are to blame for a great deal of harm in the world. That heroine long taught by example, if not precept, that Love, or the passion or fancy she mistook for it, was the chief interest of a life which is really concerned with a great many other things; that it was lasting in the way she knew it; that it was worthy of every sacrifice, and was altogether a finer thing than prudence, obedience, reason; that love alone was glorious and beautiful, and these were mean and ugly in comparison with it. More lately she has begun to idolize and illustrate Duty, and she is hardly less mischievous in this new rôle, opposing duty, as she did love, to prudence, obedience, and reason. The stock hero, whom, if we met him, we could not fail to see was a most deplorable person, has undoubtedly imposed himself upon the victims of the fiction habit as admirable. With him, too, love was and is the great affair, whether in its old romantic phase of chivalrous achievement or manifold suffering for love's sake, or its more recent development of the "virile," the bullying, and the brutal, or its still more recent agonies of self-sacrifice, as idle and useless as the moral experiences of the insane asylums. With his vain posturings and his ridiculous splendor he is really a painted barbarian, the prey of his passions, and his delusions, full of obsolete ideals, and the motives and ethics of a savage, which the guilty author of his being does his best—or his worst—in spite of his own light and knowledge, to foist upon the reader as something generous and noble. We are not merely bringing this charge against that sort of fiction which is beneath literature and outside of it, "the shoreless lakes of ditch-water," whose miasms fill the air below the empyrean where the great ones sit; but we are accusing the work of some of the most famous, who have, in this instance or in that, sinned against the truth, which can alone exalt and purify men. We do not say that they have constantly done so, or even commonly done so; but that they have done so at all marks them as of the past, to be read with the due historical allowance for their epoch and their conditions. For we believe that, while inferior writers will and must continue to imitate them in their foibles and their errors, no one hereafter will be able to achieve greatness who is false to humanity, either in its facts or its duties. The light of civilization has already broken even upon the novel, and no conscientious man can now set about painting an image of life without perpetual question of the verity of his work, and without feeling bound to distinguish so clearly that no reader of his may be misled, between what is right and what is wrong, what is noble and what is base, what is health and what is perdition, in the actions and the characters he portrays.

The fiction that aims merely to entertain—the fiction that is to serious fiction as the opéra bouffe, the ballet, and the pantomime are to the true drama—need not feel the burden of this obligation so deeply; but even such fiction will not be gay or trivial to any reader's hurt, and criticism will hold it to account if it passes from painting to teaching folly.

More and more not only the criticism which prints its opinions, but the infinitely vaster and powerfuler criticism which thinks and feels them merely, will make this demand. For our own part we confess that we do not care to judge any work of the imagination without first of all applying this test to it. We must ask ourselves before we ask anything else, Is it true?—true to the motives, the impulses, the principles that shape the life of actual men and women? This truth, which necessarily includes the highest morality and the highest artistry—this truth given, the book *cannot* be wicked and cannot be weak; and without it all graces of style and feats of invention and cunning of construction are so many superfluities of naughtiness. It is well for the truth to have all these, and shine in them, but for falsehood they are merely meretricious, the bedizenment of the wanton; they atone for nothing, they count for nothing. But in fact they come naturally of truth, and grace it without solicitation; they are added unto it. In the whole range of fiction we know of no *true* picture of life—that is, of human nature—which is not also a masterpiece of literature, full of divine and natural beauty. It may have no touch or tint of this special civilization or of that; it had *better* have this local color well ascertained; but the truth is deeper and finer than aspects, and if the book is true to what men and women know of one another's souls it will be true enough, and it will be great and beautiful. It is the conception of literature as something apart from life, superfinely aloof, which makes it really unimportant to the great mass of mankind, without a message or a meaning for them; and it is the notion that a novel may be false in its portrayal of causes and effects that makes literary art contemptible even to those whom it amuses, that forbids them to regard the novelist as a serious or right-minded person. If they do not in some moment of indignation cry out against all novels, as our correspondent does, they remain besotted in the fume of the delusions purveyed to them, with no higher feeling for the author than such maudlin affection as the *habitué* of an opium-joint perhaps knows for the attendant who fills his pipe with the drug.

WILLIAM GRAHAM SUMNER

"Sociology"
1881

When William Graham Sumner (1840–1910) hailed sociology as a science of nature ready to stand next to physics and biology, he spoke for a host of nineteenth-century intellectuals eager to bring human affairs within the scope of science. But Sumner placed a politically conservative construction on the new science of society; this construction contrasted sharply with the outlook of some other enthusiasts for this new "science," including, for example, Lester Frank Ward, author of the essay that follows Sumner's selection. In this essay of 1881, Sumner interprets as scientific facts the doctrines of Thomas Malthus, David Ricardo, and other economists of the "classicial," laissez faire persuasion. Sumner attacks as scientifically naive the reformers of his own day who proposed to regulate in the public interest the economic activities of individuals. Arguing that "hard work and self-denial" are "the only two things" that really promote human progress, Sumner holds that one's chief mission in life ought to be "to accumulate capital." Although Sumner has often been called a social Darwinist, this term exaggerates Sumner's affinities with Darwin and minimizes his ties to the British discipline of political economy that was well developed before Darwin. For a detailed treatment, see Donald C. Bellomy, "'Social Darwinism' Revisited," *Perspectives in American History,* 1 n.s. (1984), 1–129. For a brief account of Sumner's intellectual development, see chapter 5 of Robert C. Bannister, *Social Darwinism: Science and Myth in Anglo-American Social Thought* (Philadelphia, 1979), 97–113.

. . . . . .

Let us . . . endeavor to define the field of sociology. Life in society is the life of a human society on this earth. Its elementary conditions are set by the nature of human beings and the nature of the earth. We have already become familiar, in biology, with the transcendent importance of the fact that life on earth must be maintained by a struggle against nature, and also by a competition with other forms of life. In the latter fact biology and sociology touch. Sociology is a science which deals with one range of phenomena produced by the struggle for existence, while biology deals with another. The forces are the same, acting on different fields and under different conditions. The sciences are truly cognate. Nature contains certain materials which are capable of satisfying human needs, but those materials must, with rare and mean exceptions, be won by labor, and must be fitted to human use by more labor. As soon as any number of human beings are struggling each to win from nature the material goods necessary to support life, and are carrying on this struggle side by side, certain social forces come into operation. The prime condition of this society will lie in the ratio of its numbers to the supply of materials within its reach. For the supply at any moment attainable is an exact quantity, and the number of persons who can be supplied is arithmetically limited. If the actual number present is very much less than the number who might be supported, the condition of all must be ample and easy. Freedom and facility mark all social relations under such a state of things. If the number is larger than that which can be supplied, the condition of all must be one of want and distress, or else a few must be well provided, the other being proportionately still worse off. Constraint, anxiety, possibly tyranny and repression, mark social relations. It is when the social pressure due to an unfavorable ratio of population to land becomes intense that the social forces develop increased activity. Division of labor, exchange, higher social organization, emigration, advance in the arts, spring from the necessity of contending against the harsher conditions of existence which are continually reproduced as the population surpasses the means of existence on any given status.

The society with which we have to deal does not consist of any number of men. An army is not a society. A man with his wife and his children constitutes a society, for its essential parts are all present, and the number more or less is immaterial. A certain division of labor between the sexes is imposed by nature. The family as a whole maintains itself better under an organization with division of labor than it could if the functions were shared so far as possible. From this germ the development of society goes on by the regular steps of advancement to higher organization, accompanied and sustained by improvements in the arts. The increase of population goes on according to biological laws which are capable of multiplying the species beyond any assignable limits, so that the number to be provided for steadily advances and the status of ease and abundance gives way to a status of want and constraint. Emigration is the first and simplest remedy. By winning more land the ratio of population to land is once more rendered favorable. It is to be noticed, however, that emigration is painful to all men. To the uncivilized man, to emigrate means to abandon a mass of experiences and traditions which have been won by suffering, and to go out to confront new hardships

Source: Collected Essays in Political and Social Science, William Graham Sumner (New York: Holt, 1885). Footnotes omitted.

and perils. To the civilized man migration means cutting off old ties of kin and country. The earth has been peopled by man at the cost of this suffering.

On the side of the land also stands the law of the diminishing return as a limitation. More labor gets more from the land, but not proportionately more, hence, if more men are to be supported, there is need not of a proportionate increase of labor, but of a disproportionate increase of labor. The law of population, therefore, combined with the law of the diminishing returns, constitutes the great underlying condition of society. Emigration, improvements in the arts, in morals, in education, in political organization, are only stages in the struggle of man to meet these conditions, to break their force for a time, and to win room under them for ease and enlargement. Ease and enlargement mean either power to support more men on a given stage of comfort or power to advance the comfort of a given number of men. Progress is a word which has no meaning save in view of the laws of population and the diminishing return, and it is quite natural that anyone who fails to understand those laws should fall into doubt which way progress points, whether towards wealth or poverty. The laws of population and the diminishing return, in their combination, are the iron spur which has driven the race on to all which it has ever achieved, and the fact that population ever advances, yet advances against a barrier which resists more stubbornly at every step of advance, unless it is removed to a new distance by some conquest of man over nature, is the guarantee that the task of civilization will never be ended, but that the need for more energy, more intelligence, and more virtue will never cease while the race lasts. If it were possible for an increasing population to be sustained by proportionate increments of labor, we should all still be living in the original home of the race on the spontaneous products of the earth. Let him, therefore, who desires to study social phenomena first learn the transcendent importance for the whole social organization, industrial, political, and civil, of the ratio of population to land.

We have noticed that the relations involved in the struggle for existence are twofold. There is first the struggle of individuals to win the means of subsistence from nature, and secondly there is the competition of man with man in the effort to win a limited supply. The radical error of the socialists and sentimentalists is that they never distinguish these two relations from each other. They bring forward complaints which are really to be made, if at all, against the author of the universe for the hardships which man has to endure in his struggle with nature. The complaints are addressed, however, to society; that is, to other men under the same hardships. The only social element, however, is the competition of life, and when society is blamed for the ills which belong to the human lot, it is only burdening those who have successfully contended with those ills with the further task of conquering the same ills over again for somebody else. Hence liberty perishes in all socialistic schemes, and the tendency of such schemes is to the deterioration of society by burdening the good members and relieving the bad ones. The law of the survival of the fittest was not made by man and cannot be abrogated by man. We can only, by interfering with it, produce the survival of the unfittest. If a man comes forward with any grievance against the order of society so far as this is shaped by human agency, he must have patient hearing and full redress; but if he addresses a demand to society for relief from the hardships of life, he asks simply that somebody else should get his living for him. In that case he ought to be left to find out his error from hard experience.

The sentimental philosophy starts from the first principle that nothing is true which is disagreeable, and that we must not believe anything which is "shocking," no matter what the evidence may be. There are various stages of this philosophy. It touches on one side the intuitional philosophy which proves that certain things must exist by proving that man needs them, and it touches on the other side the vulgar socialism which affirms that the individual has a right to whatever he needs, and that this right is good against his fellow men. To this philosophy in all its grades the laws of population and the diminishing return have always been very distasteful. The laws which entail upon mankind an inheritance of labor cannot be acceptable to any philosophy which maintains that man comes into the world endowed with natural rights and an inheritor of freedom. It is a death-blow to any intuitional philosophy to find out, as an historical fact, what diverse thoughts, beliefs, and actions man has manifested, and it requires but little actual knowledge of human history to show that the human race has never had any ease which it did not earn, or any freedom which it did not conquer. Sociology, therefore, by the investigations which it pursues, dispels illusions about what society is or may be, and gives instead knowledge of facts which are the basis of intelligent effort by man to make the best of his circumstances on earth. Sociology, therefore, which can never accomplish anything more than to enable us to make the best of our situation, will never be able to reconcile itself with those philosophies which are trying to find out how we may arrange things so as so satisfy any ideal of society.

The competition of life has taken the form, historically, of a struggle for the possession of the soil. In the simpler states of society the possession of the soil is tribal, and the struggles take place between groups, producing the wars and feuds which constitute almost the whole of early history. On the agricultural stage the tribal or communal possession of land exists as a survival, but it gives way to private property in land whenever the community advances and the institutions are free to mold themselves. The agricultural stage breaks up tribal relations and encourages individualization. This is one of the reasons why it is such an immeasurable advance over the lower forms of civilization. It sets free individual energy, and while the social bond gains in scope and variety, it also gains in elasticity, for the solidarity of the group is broken up and the individual may work out his own ends by his own means, subject only to the social ties which lie in the natural conditions of human life. It is only on the agricultural stage that liberty as civilized men understand it exists at all. The poets and sentimentalists, untaught to recognize the grand and world-wide cooperation which is secured by the free play of individual energy under the great laws of the social order, bewail the decay of early communal relations and exalt the liberty of the primitive stages of civilization. These notions all perish at the first touch of actual investigation. The whole retrospect of human history runs downwards towards beast-like misery and slavery to the destructive forces of nature. The whole history has been one series of toilsome, painful, and bloody struggles, first to find out where we were and what were the conditions of greater ease, and then to devise means to get relief. Most of the way the motives of advance have been experience of suffering and instinct. It is only in the most recent years that science has undertaken to teach without and in advance of suffering, and as yet science has to fight so hard against tradition that its authority is only slowly winning recognition. The institutions whose growth constitutes the advance of civilization have their guarantee in the very fact that they grew and became established. They suited man's purpose better than what went before. They are all imperfect, and all carry with them incidental ills, but each came to be because it was better than what went before, and each of which has perished, perished because a better one supplanted it.

It follows once and for all that to turn back to any defunct institution or organization because existing institutions are imperfect is to turn away from advance and is to retrograde. The path of improvement lies forwards. Private property in land, for instance, is an institution which has been developed in the most direct and legitimate manner. It may give way at a future time to some other institution which will grow up by imperceptible stages out of the efforts of men to contend successfully with existing evils, but the grounds for private property in land are easily perceived, and it is safe to say that no *a priori* scheme of state ownership or other tenure invented *en bloc* by any philosopher and adopted by legislative act will ever supplant it. To talk of any such thing is to manifest a total misconception of the facts and laws which it is the province of sociology to investigate. The case is less in magnitude but scarcely less out of joint with all correct principle when it is proposed to adopt a unique tax on land, in a country where the rent of land is so low that any important tax on land exceeds it, and therefore becomes indirect, and where also political power is in the hands of small landowners, who hold, without ever having formulated it, a doctrine of absolute property in the soil such as is not held by any other landowners in the world.

Sociology must exert a most important influence on political economy. Political economy is the science which investigates the laws of the material welfare of human societies. It is not its province to teach individuals how to get rich. It is a social science. It was the first branch of sociology which was pursued by man as a science. It is not strange that when the industrial organization of society was studied apart from the organism of which it forms a part it was largely dominated over by arbitrary dogmatism, and that it should have fallen into disrepute as a mere field of opinion, and of endless wrangling about opinions for which no guarantees could be given. The rise of a school of "historical" economists is itself a sign of a struggle towards a positive and scientific study of political economy, in its due relations to other social sciences, and this sign loses none of its significance in spite of the crudeness and extravagance of the opinions of the historical economists, and in spite of their very marked tendency to fall into dogmatism and hobby-riding. Political economy is thrown over-board by all groups and persons whenever it becomes troublesome. When it got in the way of Mr. Gladstone's land-bill he relegated it, by implication, to the planet Saturn, to the great delight of all the fair-traders, protectionists, soft-money men, and others who had found it in the way of their devices. What political economy needs in order to emerge from the tangle in which it is now involved, and to win a dignified and orderly development, is to find its field and its relations to other sciences fairly defined within the wider scope of sociology. Its laws will then take their place not as arbitrary or broken fragments, but in due relation to other laws. Those laws will win proof and establishment from this relation.

For instance, we have plenty of books, some of them by able writers, in which the old-fashioned Malthusian doctrine of population and the Ricardian law of rent are disputed because emigration, advance in the arts, etc., can offset the action of those laws or because those laws are not seen in action in the United States. Obviously no such objections ever could have been raised if the laws in question had been understood or had been put in their proper bearings. The Malthusian law of population and the Ricardian law of rent are cases in which by rare and most admirable acumen powerful thinkers perceived two great laws in particular phases of their action. With wider information it now appears that the law of population breaks the barriers of Malthus' narrower formulae and appears as a great law of biology. The Ricardian law of rent is only a particular application of one of the great conditions of production. We have before us not special dogmas of political economy, but facts of the widest significance for the whole social development of the race. To object that these facts may be set aside by migration or advance in the arts is nothing to the purpose, for this is only altering the constants in the equation, which does not alter the form of the curve, but only its position relatively to some standard line. Furthermore, the laws themselves indicate that they have a maximum point for any society, or any given stage of the arts, and a condition of under-population, or of an extractive industry below its maximum, is just as consistent with the law as a condition of over-population and increasing distress. Hence inferences as to the law of population drawn from the status of an under-populated country are sure to be fallacious. In like manner arguments drawn from American phenomena in regard to rent and wages, when rent and wages are as yet only very imperfectly developed here, lead to erroneous conclusions. It only illustrates the unsatisfactory condition of political economy, and the want of strong criticism in it, that such arguments can find admission to its discussions and disturb its growth.

It is to the pursuit of sociology and the study of the industrial organization in combination with the other organizations of society that we must look for the more fruitful development of political economy. We are already in such a position with sociology that a person who has gained what we now possess of that science will bring to bear upon economic problems a sounder judgment and a more correct conception of all social relations than a person who may have read a library of the existing treatises on political economy. The essential elements of political economy are only corollaries or special cases of sociological principles. One who has command of the law of the conservation of energy as it manifests itself in society is armed at once against socialism, protectionism, paper money, and a score of other economic fallacies. The sociological view of political economy also includes whatever is sound in the dogmas of the "historical school" and furnishes what that school is apparently groping after.

As an illustration of the light which sociology throws on a great number of political and social phenomena which are constantly misconstrued, we may notice the differences in the industrial, political, and civil organizations which are produced all along at different stages of the ratio of population to land.

When a country is under-populated newcomers are not competitors, but assistants. If more come they may produce not only new quotas, but a surplus besides, to be divided between themselves and all who were present before. In such a state of things land is abundant and cheap. The possession of it confers no power or privilege. No one will work for another for wages when he can take up new land and be his own master. Hence it will pay no one to own more land than he can cultivate by his own labor, or with such aid as his own family supplies. Hence, again, land bears little or no rent; there will be no landlords living on rent and no laborers living on wages, but only a middle class of yeoman farmers. All are substantially on an equality, and democracy becomes the political form, because this is the only state of society in which the dogmatic assumption of equality, on which democracy is based, is realized as a fact. The same effects are powerfully reenforced by other facts. In a new and under-populated country the industries which are most profitable are the extractive industries.

The characteristic of these, with the exception of some kinds of mining, is that they call for only a low organization of labor and small amount of capital. Hence they allow the workman to become speedily his own master, and they educate him to freedom, independence, and self-reliance. At the same time, the social groups being only vaguely marked off from each other, it is easy to pass from one class of occupations, and consequently from one social grade, to another. Finally, under the same circumstances education, skill, and superior training have but inferior value compared with what they have in densely populated countries. The advantages lie, in an under-populated country, with the coarser, unskilled, manual occupations, and not with the highest developments of science, literature, and art.

If now we turn for comparison to cases of over-population we see that the struggle for existence and the competition of life are intense where the pressure of population is great. This competition draws out the highest achievements. It makes the advantages of capital, education, talent, skill, and training tell to the utmost. It draws out the social scale upwards and downwards to great extremes and produces aristocratic social organizations in spite of all dogmas of equality. Landlords, tenants (i.e., capitalist employers), and laborers are the three primary divisions of any aristocratic order, and they are sure to be developed whenever land bears rent and whenever tillage requires the application of large capital. At the same time liberty has to undergo curtailment. A man who has a square mile to himself can easily do as he likes, but a man who walks Broadway at noon or lives in a tenement-house finds his power to do as he likes limited by scores of considerations for the rights and feelings of his fellowmen. Furthermore, organization with subordination and discipline is essential in order that the society as a whole may win a support from the land. In an over-populated country the extremes of wealth and luxury are presented side by side with the extremes of poverty and distress. They are equally the products of an intense social pressure. The achievements of power are highest, the rewards of prudence, energy, enterprise, foresight, sagacity, and all other industrial virtues is greatest; on the other hand, the penalties of folly, weakness, error, and vice are most terrible. Pauperism, prostitution, and crime are the attendants of a state of society in which science, art, and literature reach their highest developments. Now it is evident that over-population and under-population are only relative terms. Hence as time goes on any under-populated nation is surely moving forward towards the other status, and is speedily losing its natural advantages which are absolute, and also that relative advantage which belongs to it if it is in neighborly relations with nations of dense population and high civilization; viz., the chance to borrow and assimilate from them the products, in arts and science, of high civilization without enduring the penalties of intense social pressure.

We have seen that if we should try by any measures of arbitrary interference and assistance to relieve the victims of social pressure from the calamity of their position we should only offer premiums to folly and vice and extend them further. We have also seen that we must go forward and meet our problems. We cannot escape them by running away. If then it be asked what the wit and effort of man can do to struggle with the problems offered by social pressure, the answer is that he can do only what his instinct has correctly and surely led him to do without any artificial social organization of any kind, and that is, by improvements in the arts, in science, in morals, in political institutions, to widen and strengthen the power of man over nature. The task of dealing with social ills is not a new task. People set about it and discuss it as if the human race had hitherto neglected it, and as if the solution of the problem was to be something new in form and substance, different from the solution of all problems which have hitherto engaged human effort. In truth, the human race has never done anything else but struggle with the problem of social welfare. That struggle constitutes history, or the life of the human race on earth. That struggle embraces all minor problems which occupy attention here, save those of religion, which reaches beyond this world and finds it objects beyond this life. Every successful effort to widen the power of man over nature is a real victory over poverty, vice, and misery, taking things in general and in the long run. It would be hard to find a single instance of a direct assault by positive effort upon poverty, vice, and misery which has not either failed or, if it has not failed directly and entirely, has not entailed other evils greater than the one which it removed. The only two things which really tell on the welfare of man on earth are hard work and self-denial (in technical language, labor and capital), and these tell most when they are brought to bear directly upon the effort to earn an honest living, to accumulate capital, and to bring up a family of children to be industrious and self-denying in their turn. I repeat that this is the way to work for the welfare of man on earth; and what I mean to say is that the common notion that when we are going to work for the social welfare of man we must adopt a great dogma, organize for the realization of some great scheme, have before us an abstract ideal, or otherwise do anything but live honest and industrious lives, is a great mistake. From the standpoint of the sociologist pessimism and optimism are alike impertinent. To be an optimist one must forget the frightful sanctions which are attached to the laws of right living. To be a pessimist one must overlook the education and growth which are the product of effort and self-denial. In either case one is passing judgment on what is inevitably fixed, and on which the approval or condemnation of man can produce no effect. The facts and laws are, once and for all, so, and for us men that is the end of the matter. The only persons for whom there would be any sense in the question whether life is worth living are primarily the yet unborn children, and secondarily the persons who are proposing to found families. For these latter the question would take a somewhat modified form: Will life be worth living for children born of me? This question is, unfortunately, not put to themselves by the appropriate persons as it would be if they had been taught sociology. The sociologist is often asked if he wants to kill off certain classes of troublesome and burdensome persons. No such inference follows from any sound sociological doctrine, but it is allowed to infer, as to a great many persons and classes, that it would have been better for society, and would have involved no pain to them, if they had never been born.

In further illustration of the interpretation which sociology offers of phenomena which are often obscure, we may note the world-wide effects of the advances in the arts and sciences which have been made during the last hundred years. These improvements have especially affected transportation and communication; that is, they have lessened the obstacles of time and space which separate the groups of mankind from each other and have tended to make the whole human race a single unit. The distinction between over-populated and under-populated countries loses its sharpness, and all are brought to an average. Every person who migrates from Europe to America affects the comparative status of the two continents. He lessens the pressure in the country he leaves and increases it in the country to which he goes. If he goes to Minnesota and raises wheat there, which is carried back to the country he left as cheap food for those who have not emigrated, it is evident that the bearing upon social pressure is twofold. It is evident, also, that the problem of social pressure can no longer be correctly studied if the view is confined either to the country of immigration or the country of emigration, but that it must embrace both. It is easy to see, therefore, that the ratio of population to land with which we have to deal is only in peculiar and limited cases that ratio as it exists in England, Germany, or the United States. It is the ratio as it exists in the civilized world, and every year that passes, as our improved arts break down the barriers between different parts of the earth, brings us nearer to the state of things where all the population of Europe, America, Australasia, and South Africa must be considered in relation to all the land of the same territories, for all that territory will be available for all that population, no matter what the proportion may be in which the population is distributed over the various portions of the territory. The British Islands may become one great manufacturing city. Minnesota, Texas, and Australia may not have five persons to the square mile. Yet all will eat the meat of Texas and the wheat of Minnesota and wear the wool of Australia manufactured on the looms of England. That all will enjoy the maximum of food and raiment under that state of things is as clear as anything possibly can be which is not yet an accomplished fact. We are working towards it by all our instincts of profit and improvement. The greatest obstacles are those which come from prejudices, traditions, and dogmas, which are held independently of any observation of facts or any correct reasoning, and which set the right hand working against the left. For instance, the Mississippi Valley was, a century ago, as unavailable to support the population of France and Germany as if it had been in the moon. The Mississippi Valley is now nearer to France and Germany than the British Islands were a century ago, reckoning distance by the only true standard; viz., difficulty of communication. It is a fair way of stating it to say that the improvements in transportation of the last fifty years have added to France and Germany respectively a tract of land of the very highest fertility, equal in area to the territory of those states, and available for the support of their population. The public men of those countries are now declaring that this is a calamity, and are devising means to counteract it.

The social and political effects of the improvements which have been made must be very great. It follows from what we have said about the effects of intense social pressure and high competition that the effect of thus bringing to bear on the great centers of population the new land of outlying countries must be to relieve the pressure in the oldest countries and at the densest centers. Then the extremes of wealth and poverty, culture and brutality, will be contracted and there will follow a general tendency towards an average equality which, however, must be understood only within very broad limits. Such is no doubt the meaning of the general tendency towards equality, the decline of aristocratic institutions, the rise of the proletariat, and the ambitious expansion, in short, which is characteristic of modern civilized society. It would lead me too far to follow out of this line of speculation as to the future, but two things ought to be noticed in passing. (1) There are important offsets to the brilliant promise which there is for mankind in a period during which, for the whole civilized world, there will be a wide margin of ease between the existing population and the supporting power of the available land. These offsets consist in the effects of ignorance, error, and folly—the same forces which have always robbed mankind of half what they might have enjoyed on earth. Extravagant governments, abuses of public credit, wasteful taxation, legislative monopolies and special privileges, juggling with currency, restrictions on trade, wasteful armaments on land and sea, and other follies in economy and statecraft, are capable of wasting and nullifying all the gains of civilization. (2) The old classical civilization fell under an irruption of barbarians from without. It is possible that our new civilization may perish by an explosion from within. The sentimentalists have been preaching for a century notions of rights and equality, of the dignity, wisdom, and power of the proletariat, which have filled the minds of ignorant men with impossible dreams. The thirst for luxurious enjoyment has taken possession of us all. It is the dark side of the power to foresee a possible future good with such distinctness as to make it a motive of energy and persevering industry—a power which is distinctly modern. Now the thirst for luxurious enjoyment, when brought into connection with the notions of rights, of power, and of equality, and dissociated from the notions of industry and economy, produces the notion that a man is robbed of his rights if he has not everything that he wants, and that he is deprived of equality if he sees anyone have more than he has, and that he is a fool if, having the power of the State in his hands, he allows this state of things to last. Then we have socialism, communism, and nihilism; and the fairest conquests of civilization, with all their promise of solid good to man, on the sole conditions of virtue and wisdom, may be scattered to the winds in a war of classes, or trampled underfoot by a mob which can only hate what it cannot enjoy.

It must be confessed that sociology is yet in a tentative and inchoate state. All that we can affirm with certainty is that social phenomena are subject to law, and that the natural laws of the social order are in their entire character like the laws of physics. We can draw in grand outline the field of sociology and forsee the shape that it will take and the relations it will bear to other sciences. We can also already find the standpoint which it will occupy, and, if a figure may be allowed, although we still look over a wide landscape largely enveloped in mist, we can see where the mist lies and define the general features of the landscape, subject to further corrections. To deride or contemn a science in this state would certainly be a most unscientific proceeding. We confess, however, that so soon as we go beyond the broadest principles of the science we have not yet succeeded in discovering social laws, so as to be able to formulate them. A great amount of labor yet remains to be done in the stages of preparation. There are, however, not more than two or three other sciences which are making as rapid progress as sociology, and there is no other which is as full of promise for the welfare of man. That sociology has an immense department of human interests to control is beyond dispute. Hitherto this department has been included in moral science, and it has not only been confused and entangled by dogmas no two of which are consistent with each other, but also it has been without any growth, so that at this moment our knowledge of social science is behind the demands which existing social questions make upon us. We are face to face with an issue no less grand than this: Shall we, in our general social policy, pursue the effort to realize more completely that constitutional liberty for which we have been struggling throughout modern history, or shall we return to the mediaeval device of functionaries to regulate procedure and to adjust interests? Shall we try to connect with liberty an equal and appropriate responsibility as its essential complement and corrective, so that a man who gets his own way shall accept his own consequences, or shall we yield to the sentimentalism which, after preaching an unlimited liberty, robs those who have been wise out of pity for those who have been foolish? Shall we accept the inequalities which follow upon free competition as the definition of justice, or shall we suppress free competition in the interest of equality and to satisfy a baseless dogma of justice? Shall we try to solve the social entanglements which arise in a society where social ties are constantly becoming more numerous and more subtle, and where contract has only partly superseded custom and status, by returning to the latter, only hastening a more complete development of the former? These certainly are practical questions, and their scope is such that they embrace a great number of minor questions which are before us and which are coming up. It is to the science of society, which will derive true conceptions of society from the facts and laws of the social order, studied without prejudice or bias of any sort, that we must look for the correct answer to these questions. By this observation the field of sociology and the work which it is to do for society are sufficiently defined.

LESTER FRANK WARD

"Mind as a Social Factor"
1884

Lester Frank Ward (1841–1913) yielded to no one, including his great rival William Graham Sumner, in the degree of his devotion to science in general and to the particular task of developing a science of society. Ward associated such a science not with obedience to facts, but with the authority of human beings over their own destiny. In the essay of 1884 that follows, Ward insisted on the creative powers of the human mind. These powers, Ward declared, were ignored by the conservative laissez faire versions of social science that warned against meddling with nature. The order of nature is indeed dominated by natural selection, Ward granted, but our own species represents a new stage of evolution. Human beings make progress by protecting the weak rather than by a relentless competition in which only the fit survive; it is perfectly natural for human beings—with their distinctive mental powers—to cooperate, to reduce competition, and to alter through invention the setting in which they live. Let human beings be understood as active, Ward proposed, and the natural world as passive. For a recent and careful study of Ward that emphasizes his commitment to secular science, see Robert C. Bannister, *Sociology and Scientism: The American Quest for Objectivity, 1880–1940* (Chapel Hill, 1987), 13–34.

After many centurys of exclusive study of the soul the thinkers of the world turned their attention for some centuries more to the study of the intellect. During all this time, the true influence of mind as a social factor was left quite out of view. At last there rose up the scientific philosophy which essayed to explain the nature of mind. Its dependence upon organisation in general and upon brain in particular was proved by scientific experimentation, and the domain of metaphysics became that of psychology. Mind was shown to be a function of body and psychology became a department of biology. Man has now taken his true position in the animal world as a product of development. Brain, which alone raises him above other animals, has been developed in the same manner as the other anatomical characters. The brain is the organ of the mind, its physical seat and cause. Mind is therefore a natural product of evolution, and its achievements are to be classed and studied along with all other natural phenomena. Such is the scientific conception of mind.

The modern scientist places all objects in the midst of an infinite series of antecedents and consequents. Organic forms as well as inorganic must take their places in this series—the animal no less than the plant, the man no less than the beast. Mind itself is a link of this endless chain. Its activities consist in the transmission of the properties of its antecedents to its consequents. The quantity of force in the universe is constant. No power can increase or diminish it. All attempts on the part of the creatures of this constant and unchangeable force to modify its normal effects are not less vain because such creatures happen to have acquired the faculty of observing the changes going on in nature.

The protracted study of nature's processes leads to admiration of them, and the belief has become prevalent that they are not only unalterable but also in some way necessarily beneficent. Nature has made great progress in developing organised beings and is assumed to be still working in this direction. The natural method is always the true method, and to find it out is the aim of all scientific investigation. Out of this earnest and laudable strife to discover the true method of nature has grown, logically enough, the assumption that when found it must be something of great worth. It is commonly supposed that the highest wisdom of man is to learn and then to follow the ways of nature. Those dissatisfied people who would improve upon the natural course of events are rebuked as meddlers with the unalterable. Their systems are declared utopian, their laws *bruta fulmina*. All efforts in this direction are held to be trifling and are stigmatised as so many ignorant attempts to nullify the immutable laws of nature.

This general mode of reasoning is carried into all departments of human life.

In government every attempt to improve the condition of the state is condemned and denounced. Curiously enough, here the claim is illogically made that such measures are harmful. In fact, unfortunately for the whole theory, they have often been proved to be so. But this, of course, proves their efficacy. This glaring inconsistency is, however, overlooked, and government is implored, not to adopt wise and successful measures, but to refrain from adopting any, to let society alone, and thus allow the laws of nature to work out their beneficent results.

In commerce and trade absolute freedom is insisted upon. Free trade is the watchword of this entire school. The laws of trade, they maintain, are natural laws. As such they must be better than any human rules. And here again we find them insisting that regulation is injurious to trade, although it is at the same time declared to be nugatory.

Source: Mind, 4 (October 1884), 563–73.

In social affairs these doctrines are carried to their extreme logical outcome. The laws of nature as they manifest themselves in society must be left wholly untouched. The passions of men will neutralise and regulate themselves. Competition can be depended upon to correct abuses. The seller must be allowed to exaggerate and misstate the nature of his wares. This has the effect to sharpen the wits of the buyer, and this develops the brain. To dilute, adulterate, or even poison food and medicine for personal gain is not objectionable, since the destruction thereby of a few unwary consumers only proves their unfitness to survive in society. As in general commerce, so in private business, competition must be free. If a dealer, by selling at a loss, can hold out until all his competitors have been driven from the field, in order then to recover more than his losses by the monopoly he will enjoy, his right to do this must not be questioned. It is under such conditions and by the aid of such discipline that man and society have developed.

Education must be that of experience. Knowledge must be gained by efforts to avoid the consequences of ignorance already felt. The intellectual development of the child must be an epitome of that of the race. It is thus only that nature operates, and surely nature is greater and wiser than man.

All schemes of social reform are unscientific. Public charities tend to bolster up unworthy elements in society that nature has declared unfit to survive. Temperance reforms tend only to abridge individual liberty—for even the liberty to destroy one's self should be respected. Philanthropy is zeal without knowledge, while humanitarianism is fanaticism.

This general class of views antedated by many years the publication by Spencer and Darwin of their fomulated doctrines of the "survival of the fittest" and "natural selection." But it cannot be denied that these doctrines, supported as they were by facts fresh from nature, have greatly strengthened this habit of thought. Nature's method is now much better known than formerly, and it is now well understood that an utterly soulless competition constitutes its fundamental characteristic. Surely man cannot go astray in following in the footsteps of nature. Let him learn from the animal world. He has descended from some of the humble stocks which he is now studying. Nature's plan has raised him from the condition of a beast to that of a rational being. It has created and developed society and civilisation. Unless tampered with by "reformers" all the operations of society would be competitive. Competition is the law of nature out of which progress results. Sociology, as its founder insisted, must be based on biology, and the true sociologist must understand this biologic law. Those who propose to apply methods to society which are opposed to the methods of nature are supposed to be ignorant of these fundamental truths are called empiricists, "meddlers," and "tinkers."

Such, I way, is the tenor and tendency of modern scientific thought. I do not say that all scientific men hold these views. I merely maintain that leading ones have formulated and inculcated them a natural deductions from the established facts of science, and that the public mind is rapidly assimilating them, while scarcely any attempts are being made to check their advance.[1]

Is there any way of answering these arguments? Can the *laissez faire* doctrine be

1. The social philosophy of Mr. Herbert Spencer possesses this tone throughout, and his disciples, particularly in America, delight in going even farther than their master. The most extreme statement of the *laissez faire* doctrine known to me is that of Prof. W. G. Sumner, in his recent work *Social Classes*.

successfully met? That all attempts to do this have been timidly made cannot be denied. That these have been few and feeble is equally certain. While there has existed in the minds of many rational persons a vague sense of some hidden fallacy in all this reasoning, none have felt competent to formulate their objections with sufficient clearness and force to warrant pitting them against the resistless stream of concurrent science and philosophy of the nineteenth century. There has, however, been developing of late a more or less marked apprehension with regard to the possible consequences of this mode of thought. The feeling is distinct in the best minds, and to a large extent in the public mind, that the tendency of modern ideas is nihilistic. It is clear that if they become universally accepted they must work stagnation in society. The *laissez faire* doctrine is a gospel of inaction, the scientific creed is struck with sterility, the policy of resigning all into the hands of Nature is a surrender.

But this recognition is by no means proof that the prevalent opinions are false. At best it can only suggest this on the ground that true doctrines should be progressive. But this would be a *petitio principii*. Nature is not optimistic, still less anthropocentric. For aught we know, the laws of nature are such as make a recognition of strict scientific truth a positive barrier to social advancement. The argument we have been considering must be refuted, if at all, by legitimate counter-argument.

The present attempt to meet some parts of this argument is made in full consciousness of its strength as a factor in modern thought and with due deference to the great names that stand committed to it. The scientific facts which its defenders have brought to its support are, in the main, incontestable. To answer by denying these would be to abjure science and deserve contempt. The method of nature has been correctly interpreted. The doctrines of the survival of the fittest and natural selection are perfectly true doctrines. The law of competition is the fundamental law. It is unquestionably true that progress, not only in primary organic development, but also in society, has resulted from the action of this law.

After conceding all this, the attempt, notwithstanding, to stem the tide of modern scientific thought must, indeed, seem a hopeless one. At the outset it must be frankly acknowledged that if the current views are unsound the fault is not chargeable to science. If there is any defect it must lie in the inferences drawn from the facts and not in the facts themselves. To what extent, then, is the *laissez faire* doctrine, as defined and popularly accepted, an inference? If the method of nature is correctly formulated by that doctrine, wherein lies the fallacy when it is applied to man and to society?

In order to grapple at once with the whole problem let me answer these questions by the open charge that the modern scientific philosophers fail to recognise the true value of the *psychic factor*. Just as the metaphysicians lost their bearings by an empty worship of mind and made philosophy a plaything, so the modern evolutionists have missed their mark by degrading mind to a level with mechanical force. They seem thus about to fling away the grand results that the doctrine of evolution cannot otherwise fail to achieve. Far be it from me to appeal to the prejudices of the enemies of science by casting opprobrium upon scientific deductions, but when I consider the tendencies which are now so unmistakable, and which are so certainly the consequence of the protracted study, on the part of leading scientists, of the unquestionable methods of nature, I think I can, though holding precisely opposite opinions, fully sympathise with Carlyle in characterising the philosophy of evolution as a "gospel of dirt."

But I need not longer dwell upon the blighting influence of this construction of the known laws of nature. Let us approach the kernel of the problem.

The *laissez faire* doctrine fails to recognise that, in the development of mind, a virtually *new power* was introduced into the world. To say that this has been done is no startling announcement. It is no more than has taken place many times in the course of the evolution of living and feeling beings out of the tenuous nebulae of space. For, while it is true that nature makes no leaps, while, so long as we consider their beginning, all the great steps in evolution are due to minute increments repeated through vast periods, still, when we survey the whole field, as we must do to comprehend the scheme, and contrast the extremes, we find that nature has been making a series of enormous strides, and reaching from one plane of development of another. It is these independent achievements of evolution that the true philosopher must study.

Not to mention the great steps in the cosmical history of the solar system and of the earth, we must regard the evolution of protoplasm, the "physical basis of life," as one of those gigantic strides which thenceforth completely revolutionised the surface of our planet. The development of the cell as the unit of organisation was another such stride. The origin of vertebrate life introduced a new element, and the birth of man wrought still another transformation. These are only a few of nature's revolutions. Many more will suggest themselves. And although, in no single one of these cases can it be said at what exact point the new essence commenced to exist, although the development of all these several expessions of Nature's method of concentrating her hitherto diffused forces was accomplished through an unbroken series of minute transitional increments continued through eons of time, still, it is not a whit less true that each of these grand products of evolution, when at length fully formed, constituted a new cosmic energy, and proceeded to stamp all future products and processes with a character hitherto wholly unknown upon the globe.

It is in this sense, and in this only, that I claim the development of mind—of the thinking, reasoning, inventing faculty of the human brain—as another, and one of the best marked, of the great cosmic strides that have characterised the course of evolution and belong to the legitimate methods of nature.

It is, for example, only to a limited extent and in the most general way that we can apply the same canons to the organic as to the inorganic world. It is usually, but falsely, supposed that the student of biology need know nothing of physics, the assumption being that they have nothing in common. While this error is fatal to all fundamental acquaintance with the laws of life, it well illustrates the immensity of the advance from one realm to the other. The same could be said, in varying degrees of obviousness, of every one of the ascending steps to which reference has been made. I freely admit that the theologians and metaphysicians commit the most fatal error in treating the soul, or mind, as independent of the body, but this enormous fallacy is scarcely greater than that of the modern evolutionist, who, finding out their dependence, ignores the *magnitude* of the step by which mind was made a property of body, and proceeds as though no new factor had entered into the world.

But all this may be regarded as mere generality. Let us come to something more specific.

It has always been a marvel to my comprehension that wise men and philosophers, when smitten with the specious logic of the *laissez faire* school, can close their eyes to the most obtrusive fact that civilisation presents. In spite of the influence of philosophy, all forms of which have thus far been negative and nihilistic, the human animal, with his growing intellect, has still ever realised the power that is vouchsafed through mind, and has ever exercised that power. Philosophy would have long since robbed him of it and caused his early extermination from the earth but for the persistence, through heredity, of the impulse to exercise in self-preservation every power in his possession; by which practice alone he first gained his ascendancy ages before philosophy began.

The great fact, then, to which I allude is that, in spite of all philosophy, whether mythologic, metaphysical, or naturalistic, declaring that man must and can do nothing, he *has,* from the very dawn of his intelligence, been transforming the entire surface of the planet he inhabits. No other animal performs anything comparable to what man performs. This is solely because no other possesses the developed psychic faculty.

If we analyse mind into its two departments, sense and intellect, we shall see that it is through this latter faculty that these results are accomplished. If we inquire more closely into the mode by which intellect operates, we shall find that it serves as a guiding power to those natural forces with which it is acquainted (and no others), directing them into channels of human advantage. If we seek for a single term by which to characterise with precision the nature of this process, we find this in *Invention.* The essential characteristic of all intellectual action is invention.

Glancing now at the *ensemble* of human achievement, which may be collectively called civilisation, we readily see that it is all the result of this inventive process. All practical art is merely the product of successful invention, and it requires no undue expansion of the term, nor extraordinary power of generalisation, to see in all human institutions only modified forms of arts, and true products of the intellectual, or inventive, faculty.

But what is the general result of all this? An entirely new dispensation has been given to the world. All the materials and forces of nature have been thus placed completely under the control of one of the otherwise least powerful of the creatures inhabiting the earth. He has only to know them in order to become their master. Nature has thus been made the servant of man. Thus only has man succeeded in peopling the entire globe while all other animals are restricted to narrow faunal areas. He has also peopled certain portions far more densely than any other species could have done, and he seems destined to continue multiplying his numbers for a long time yet in the future. But this quantitative proof is even less telling than the qualitative. When we confine our attention to the *élite* of mankind we do not need to have the ways specified in detail by which the powers of mind have exalted the intellectual being above all other products of creation. At the present moment the most dense and the most enlightened populations of the globe occupy what are termed temperate latitudes, which means latitudes in which for from three to five months each year vegetation ceases entirely, the waters are locked in ice, and the temperature frequently sinks far below the zero of the Fahrenheit thermometer. Imagine the thin-skinned, furless animal man subsisting in such a climate. Extinguish his fires, banish his clothing, blot out the habitations that deck the civilised landscape. How long would the puny race survive? But these are not products of nature, they are products of *art,* the wages of thought—fruits of the intellect.

When a well-clothed philosopher on a bitter winter's night sits in a warm room well lighted for his purpose and writes on paper with pen and ink in the arbitrary characters of a highly developed language the statement that civilisation is the result of natural laws, and that man's duty is to let nature alone so that untrammeled it may work out a higher civilisation, he simply ignores every circumstance of his existence and deliberately closes his eyes to every fact within the range of his faculties. If man had acted upon his theory there would have been no civilisation, and our philosopher would have remained a troglodyte.

But how shall we distinguish this human, or anthropic, method from the method of nature? Simply by reversing all the definitions. Art is the antithesis of nature. If we call one the natural method we must call the other the artificial method. If nature's process is rightly named natural selection, man's process is artificial selection. The survival of the fittest is simply the survival of the strong, which implies, and might as well be called, the destruction of the weak. And if nature progresses through the destruction of the weak, man progresses through the *protection* of the weak. This is the essential distinction.

In human society the psychic power has operated to secure the protection of the weak in two distinct ways: first, by increasing the supply of the necessities of life, and, secondly, by preventing the destruction of life through the enemies of man. The immediate instrumentality through which the first of these processes is carried on is art, the product of invention. The second process takes place through the establishment of positive institutions.

It is difficult to say which of these agencies has been most effective. Both were always indispensable, and therefore all comparison is unprofitable.

Art operates to protect the weak against adverse surroundings. It is directed against natural forces, chiefly physical. By thus defeating the destructive influences of the elements and hostile forms of life, and by forcing nature to yield an unnatural supply of man's necessities, many who would have succumbed from inability to resist these adverse agencies—the feebler members of society—were able to survive, and population increased and expanded. While no one openly denies this, there is a tendency either to ignore it in politico-economic discussions, or to deny its application to them as an answer to naturalistic arguments.

If, on the other hand, we inquire into the nature of human institutions, we shall perceive that they are of three kinds, tending to protect the weak in three ways, or ascending degrees. These three successively higher means through which this end is attained are, first, Justice, second, Morality, and third, Charity. These forms of action have been reached through the development, respectively, of the three corresponding sentiments: Equity, Beneficence, and Benevolence.

All of these altruistic sentiments are wholly unknown, or known only in the merest embryo, to all animals below man, and therefore no such means of protection exist among them. They are strictly human, or anthropic. Many evolutionists fail to recognise this. Some sociologists refuse to admit it. They look about and see so much injustice, immorality and rapacity that they are led to suppose that only natural methods are in operation in society. This is a great mistake. In point of fact, the keener the sense of justice the more conspicuous the diminishing number of violations of it come to appear, and conversely, the obviousness of injustice proves the general prevalence of justice. It is the same with morality and philanthropy.

If we consider the effect of these three codes of human conduct in the direction of enabling the weaker ones to survive we shall see that it has been immense. Out of the first has arisen government, the chief value and function of which has always been and still is such protection. Great systems of jurisprudence have been elaborated, engrossing the attention of a large portion of the population of enlightened as well as of barbaric states. To say that these have been failures because often weighted with grave defects is to misinterpret history and misunderstand society. No one could probably be found to gainsay that the moral law of society has exerted a salutary influence, yet its aim is strictly altruistic, opposed to the law of the survival of the fittest, and wholly in the direction of enabling those to survive who would not survive without its protection. Finally, the last sentiment to be developed, and doubtless the highest, is so universally recognised as peculiar to man that his very name has been given to it—the sentiment of *humanity*. Yet the mode of protecting the weak arising out of this sentiment is the one that has been most seriously called in question by the naturalistic school. It must be admitted that humanitarian institutions have done far less good than either juridical or ethical institutions. The sentiment itself is of recent origin, the product only of highly developed and greatly refined mental organisation. It exists to an appreciable degree only in a minute fraction of the most enlightened populations. It is rarely directed with judgment; no fixed, self-enforcing code of conduct, as in the other cases, having had time to take shape. The institutions established to enforce it are for the most part poorly supported, badly managed, and often founded on a total misconception of human nature and of the true mode of attaining the end in view. Hence they are specially open to attack. But if ever humanitarian sentiments become diffused throughout the body politic, become the object of deep study, as have those of justice and right, it may be confidently predicted that society will prove itself capable of caring for the most unfortunate of its members in a manner that shall not work demoralisation.

In all these ways man, through his intelligence, has laboured successfully to resist the law of nature. His success is conclusively demonstrated by a comparison of his condition with that of other species of animals. No other cause can be assigned for his superiority. How can the naturalistic philosophers shut their eyes to such obvious facts? Yet, what is their attitude? They condemn all attempts to protect the weak, whether by private or public methods. They claim that it deteriorates the race by enabling the unfit to survive and transmit their inferiority. This is true only in certain cases of hereditary diseases or mental deficiencies, which should be taken account of by man because they are not by nature. Nothing is easier than to show that the unrestricted competition of nature does not secure the survival of the fittest possible, but only of the actually fittest, and in every attempt man makes to obtain something fitter than this actual fittest he succeeds, as witness improved breeds of animals and grafts of fruits. Now, the human method of protecting the weak deals in some such way with men. It not only increases the number but improves the quality.

But "government," at least, must *laisser faire*. It must not "meddle" with natural laws. The laws of trade, business, social intercourse, are natural laws, immutable and indestructible. All interference with them is vain. The fallacy here is a *non sequitur*. It may be readily granted that these laws are immutable and indestructible. Were this not the case it would certainly be hopeless to interfere with their action. But every mechanical invention proves that nothing is easier than to interfere successfully with the operation of these uniform natural forces. They have only to be first thoroughly understood and then they are easily *controlled*. To *destroy* a force is one thing, to control its action is quite another. Those who talk in this way involve themselves in the most palpable inconsistency. They must not be allowed to stop where they do. They must go on and carry their strictures to a logical conclusion. They must deny to government the right to protect its citizens from injustice. This is a clear interference with the natural laws of society. They must deny to society the right to enforce its code of morals. Nothing is more unnatural. They must suppress the healing art which keeps the sick from dying as they do among animals. Nor is this all. They must condemn all interference with physical laws and natural forces. To dam a stream must be characterised as a "vain" attempt to overcome a natural law. The wind must be left free to blow where it will, and not be forced against the fan of a wind-mill. The vapour of heated water must be allowed to float off naturally into the air and not be pent up in a steam-boiler and thence conducted into the cylinder of a steam-engine. All these things and every other device of inventive man are so many attempts to "violate" the laws of nature, which is declared impossible.

What then remains of the *laissez faire* doctrine? Nothing but this: That it is useless, and may be dangerous, to attempt to control natural forces until their character is first well understood. This is a proposition which is true for every department of force, and does not involve the surrender of the whole domain of sociology after it has been demonstrated that society is a theatre of forces.

The truth thus comes forth from a rational study of nature and human society that social progress has been due only in very slight degree to natural evolution as accomplished through the survival of the fittest, and its chief success has resulted from the reduction of competition in the struggle for existence and the protection of the weaker members. Such competition, in so far as it has been permitted to operate, has tended to lower the standard of the fittest and to check advancement. It is not, of course, claimed that the natural method has even been fully overcome. It has always operated, and still operates, powerfully in many ways. It has been chiefly in the simpler departments of physical and mechanical phenomena that the psychic, or anthropic, method has superseded it. The inventive arts have been the result. Vital forces have yielded to some extent to the infleunce of mind in bringing about improved stocks of animals and vegetables, and even certain social laws have come under rational control through the establishment of institutions. Still, every step in this progress has been contested. It was not enough that the intellect was feeble and ill-fitted to grapple with such problems. It was not enough that ignorance of nature's laws should cause unnumbered failures. A still stronger barrier was presented by the intellect itself in the form of positive error embodied in philosophy. As already remarked, philosophy has always been negative and nihilistic, and has steadily antagonised the common sense of mankind. It is only quite recently that there has come into existence anything like a truly *positive* philosophy, i.e., a philosophy of *action*. The intellectual power of enlightened man has at length become sufficient to grasp the problems of social life. A large body of truth has been accumulated by which to be guided in their solution. Positive error in the drawing of false conclusions from established facts is now the chief obstacle. Rational interpretation has come to prevail in all the lower departments of phenomena. It is chiefly in the complex departments of psychic and social action that error still holds sway. Nothing remains to be done but to apply the established canons of science to these higher fields of activity. Here there is still competition. Here the weaker still go to the wall. Here the strong are still the fittest to survive. Here Nature still practises her costly selection which always involves the destruction of the defenceless. The demand is for still further reduction of competition, still greater interference with the operations of natural forces, still more complete control of the laws of nature, and still more absolute supremacy of the psychic over the natural method of evolution.

These ends will be secured in proportion as the true nature of mind is understood. When nature comes to be regarded as passive and man as active, instead of the reverse as now, when human action is recognised as the most important of all forms of action, and when the power of the human intellect over vital, psychic and social phenomena is practically conceded, then, and then only, can man justly claim to have risen out of the animal and fully to have entered the human stage of development.

CHARLOTTE PERKINS GILMAN

Selection from *Women and Economics* 1898

So prominent in the history of feminist theory in America are the works of Charlotte Perkins Gilman (1860–1935) that she is often called the Marx and the Veblen of American feminism. The selection herein—from *Women and Economics,* 1898—displays the sweep and the conviction with which she addressed the evolutionary-historical matrix of women's condition. Gilman argues that women, once forced into relations of dependency by men, were "cut off from the direct action of natural selection, that mighty force which heretofore had acted on male and female alike with inexorable and beneficial effect," developing the strength, skill, endurance and courage that made the human species what it was to become. Gilman was not only an evolutionary theorist, but an accomplished writer of fiction and verse. A good sampling of her work is Ann Lane, ed., *Charlotte Perkins Gilman Reader* (New York, 1980). Because so many of Gilman's scattered writings remained undiscovered until recently, however, an essential tool in the study of Gilman's ideas is Gary Scharnhorst, ed., *Charlotte Perkins Gilman: A Bibliography* (Metuchen, N.J., 1985). For a study of Gilman's youth and early adulthood, see Mary A. Hill, *Charlotte Perkins Gilman: The Making of a Radical Feminist, 1860–1896* (Philadelphia, 1980). For a provocative interpretation of Gilman's story of 1892, "The Yellow Wallpaper," in relation to her *Women and Economics,* see Walter Benn Michaels, *The Gold Standard and the Logic of Naturalism: American Literature at the Turn of the Century* (Berkeley, 1987), 3–28.

Having seen the disproportionate degree of sex-distinction in humanity and its greater manifestation in the female than in the male, and having seen also the unique position of the human female as an economic dependant on the male of her species, it is not difficult to establish a relation between these two facts. The general law acting to produce this condition of exaggerated sex-development . . . is as follows: the natural tendency of any function to increase in power by use causes sex-activity to increase under the action of sexual selection. This tendency is checked in most species by the force of natural selection, which diverts the energies into other channels and developes race-activities. Where the female finds her economic environment in the male, and her economic advantage is directly conditioned upon the sex-relation, the force of natural selection is added to the force of sexual selection, and both together operate to develope sex-activity. In any animal species, free from any other condition, such a relation would have inevitably developed sex to an inordinate degree, as may be readily seen in the comparatively similar cases of those insects where the female, losing economic activity and modified entirely to sex, becomes a mere egg-sac, an organism with no powers of self-preservation, only those of race-preservation. With these insects the only race-problem is to maintain and reproduce the species, and such a condition is not necessarily evil; but with a race like ours, whose development as human creatures is but comparatively begun, it is evil because of its check to individual and racial progress. There are other purposes before us besides mere maintenance and reproduction.

It should be clear to any one accustomed to the working of biological laws that all the tendencies of a living organism are progressive in their development, and are held in check by the interaction of their several forces. Each living form, with its dominant characteristics, represents a balance of power, a sort of compromise. The size of earth's primeval monsters was limited by the tensile strength of their material. Sea monsters can be bigger, because the medium in which they move offers more support. Birds must be smaller for the opposite reason. The cow requires many stomachs of a liberal size, because her food is of low nutritive value; and she must eat large quantities to keep her machine going. The size of arboreal animals, such as monkeys or squirrels, is limited by the nature of their habitat: creatures that live in trees cannot be so big as creatures that live on the ground. Every quality of every creature is relative to its condition, and tends to increase or decrease accordingly; and each quality tends to increase in proportion to its use, and to decrease in proportion to its disuse. Primitive man and his female were animals, like other animals. They were strong, fierce, lively beasts; and she was as nimble and ferocious as he, save for the added belligerence of the males in their sex-competition. In this competition, he, like the other male creatures, fought savagely with his hairy rivals; and she, like the other female creatures, complacently viewed their struggles, and mated with the victor. At other times she ran about in the forest, and helped herself to what there was to eat as freely as he did.

There seems to have come a time when it occurred to the dawning intelligence of this amiable savage that it was cheaper and easier to fight a little female, and have it done with, than to fight a big male every time. So he instituted the custom of enslaving the female; and she, losing freedom, could no longer get her own food nor that of her young. The mother ape, with her maternal function well fulfilled, flees leaping through the forest,—plucks her fruits and nuts, keeps up with the movement of the tribe, her young one on her back or held in one strong arm. But the mother woman, enslaved,

Source: Women and Economics, Charlotte Perkins Gilman (Boston: Small, Maynard & Co., 1898), 58–75.

could not do this. Then man, the father, found that slavery had its obligations: he must care for what he forbade to care for itself, else it died on his hands. So he slowly and reluctantly shouldered the duties of his new position. He began to feed her, and not only that, but to express in his own person the thwarted uses of maternity: he had to feed the children, too. It seems a simple arrangement. When we have thought of it at all, we have thought of it with admiration. The naturalist defends it on the ground of advantage to the species through the freeing of the mother from all other cares and confining her unreservedly to the duties of maternity. The poet and novelist, the painter and sculptor, the priest and teacher, have all extolled this lovely relation. It remains for the sociologist, from a biological point of view, to note its effects on the constitution of the human race, both in the individual and in society.

When man began to feed and defend woman, she ceased proportionately to feed and defend herself. When he stood between her and her physical environment, she ceased proportionately to feel the influence of that environment and respond to it. When he became her immediate and all-important environment, she began proportionately to respond to this new influence, and to be modified accordingly. In a free state, speed was of as great advantage to the female as to the male, both in enabling her to catch prey and in preventing her from being caught by enemies; but, in her new condition, speed was a disadvantage. She was not allowed to do the catching, and it profited her to be caught by her new master. Free creatures, getting their own food and maintaining their own lives, develope an active capacity for attaining their ends. Parasitic creatures, whose living is obtained by the exertions of others, develope powers of absorption and of tenacity,—the powers by which they profit most. The human female was cut off from the direct action of natural selection, that mighty force which heretofore had acted on male and female alike with inexorable and beneficial effect, developing strength, developing skill, developing endurance, developing courage,—in a word, developing species. She now met the influence of natural selection acting indirectly through the male, and developing, of course, the faculties required to secure and obtain a hold on him. Needless to state that these faculties were those of sex-attraction, the one power that has made him cheerfully maintain, in what luxury he could, the being in whom he delighted. For many, many centuries she had no other hold, no other assurance of being fed. The young girl had a prospective value, and was maintained for what should follow; but the old woman, in more primitive times, had but a poor hold on life. She who could best please her lord was the favorite slave or favorite wife, and she obtained the best economic conditions.

With the growth of civilization, we have gradually crystallized into law the visible necessity for feeding the helpless female; and even old women are maintained by their male relatives with a comfortable assurance. But to this day—save, indeed, for the increasing army of women wage-earners, who are changing the face of the world by their steady advance toward economic independence—the personal profit of women bears but too close a relation to their power to win and hold the other sex. From the odalisque with the most bracelets to the débutante with the most bouquets, the relation still holds good,—woman's economic profit comes through the power of sex-attraction.

When we confront this fact boldly and plainly in the open market of vice, we are sick with horror. When we see the same economic relation made permanent, established by law, sanctioned and sanctified by religion, covered with flowers and incense and all accumulated sentiment, we think it innocent, lovely, and right. The transient trade we think evil. The bargain for life we think good. But the biological effect remains the same. In both cases the female gets her food from the male by virtue of her sex-relationship to him. In both cases, perhaps even more in marriage because of its perfect acceptance of the situation, the female of genus homo, still living under natural law, is inexorably modified to sex in an increasing degree.

Followed in specific detail, the action of the changed environment upon women has been in given instances as follows: in the matter of mere passive surroundings she has been immediately restricted in her range. This one factor has an immense effect on man and animal alike. An absolutely uniform environment, one shape, one size, one color, one sound, would render life, if any life could be, one helpless, changeless thing. As the environment increases and varies, the development of the creature must increase and vary with it; for he acquires knowledge and power, as the material for knowldege and the need for power appear. In migratory species the female is free to acquire the same knowledge as the male by the same means, the same development by the same experiences. The human female has been restricted in range from the earliest beginning. Even among savages, she has a much more restricted knowledge of the land she lives in. She moves with the camp, of course, and follows her primitive industries in its vicinity; but the war-path and the hunt are the man's. He has a far larger habitat. The life of the female savage is freedom itself, however, compared with the increasing constriction of custom closing in upon the woman, as civilization advanced, like the iron torture chamber of romance. Its culmination is expressed in the proverb: "A woman should leave her home but three times,—when she is christened, when she is married, and when she is buried." Or this: "The woman, the cat, and the chimney should never leave the house." The absolutely stationary female and the wide-ranging male are distinctly human institutions, after we leave behind us such low forms of life as the gypsy moth, whose female seldom moves more than a few feet from the pupa moth. She has aborted wings, and cannot fly. She waits humbly for the winged male, lays her myriad eggs, and dies,—a fine instance of modification to sex.

To reduce so largely the mere area of environment is a great check to race-development; but it is not to be compared in its effects with the reduction in voluntary activity to which the human female has been subjected. Her restricted impression, her confinement to the four walls of the home, have done great execution, of course, in limiting her ideas, her information, her thought-processes, and power of judgment; and in giving a disproportionate prominence and intensity to the few things she knows about; but this is innocent in action compared with her restricted expression, the denial of freedom to act. A living organism is modified far less through the action of external circumstances upon it and its reaction thereto, than through the effect of its own exertions. Skin may be thickened gradually by exposure to the weather; but it is thickened far more quickly by being rubbed against something, as the handle of an oar or of a broom. To be surrounded by beautiful things has much influence upon the human creature: to make beautiful things has more. To live among beautiful surroundings and make ugly things is more directly lowering than to live among ugly surroundings and make beautiful things. What we do modifies us more than what is done to us. The freedom of expression has been more restricted in women than the freedom of impression, if that be possible. Something of the world she lived in she has seen from her barred windows. Some air has come through the purdah's folds, some knowledge has filtered to her eager ears from the talk of men. Desdemona learned somewhat of Othello. Had she known more, she might have lived longer. But in the ever-growing human impulse to create, the power and will to make, to do, to express one's new spirit in new forms,—here she has been utterly debarred. She might work as she had worked from the begining,—at the primitive labors of the household; but in the inevitable expansion of even those industries to professional levels we have striven to hold her back. To work with her own hands, for nothing, in direct body-service to her own family,—this has been permitted,—yes, compelled. But to be and do anything further from this she has been forbidden. Her labor has not only been limited in kind, but in degree. Whatever she has been allowed to do must be done in private and alone, the first-hand industries of savage times.

Our growth in industry has been not only in kind, but in class. The baker is not in the same industrial grade with the house-cook, though both make bread. To specialize any form of labor is a step up: to organize it is another step. Specialization and organization are the basis of human progress, the organic methods of social life. They have been forbidden to women almost absolutely. The greatest and most beneficent change of this century is the progress of women in these two lines of advance. The effect of this check in industrial development, accompanied as it was by the constant inheritance of increased racial power, has been to intensify the sensations and emotions of women, and to develope great activity in the lines allowed. The nervous energy that up to present memory has impelled women to labor incessantly at something, be it the veriest folly of fancy work, is one mark of this effect.

In religious development the same dead-line has held back the growth of women through all the races and ages. In dim early times she was sharer in the mysteries and rites; but, as religion developed, her place receded, until Paul commanded her to be silent in the churches. And she had been silent until to-day. Even now, with all the ground gained, we have but the beginnings—the slowly forced and disapproved beginnings—of religious equality for the sexes. In some nations, religion is held to be a masculine attribute exclusively, it being even questioned whether women have souls. An early Christian council settled that important question by vote, fortunately deciding that they had. In a church whose main strength has always been derived from the adherence of women, it would have been an uncomfortable reflection not to have allowed them souls. Ancient family worship ran in the male line. It was the son who kept the sacred grandfathers in due respect, and poured libations to their shades. When the woman married, she changed her ancestors, and had to worship her husband's progenitors instead of her own. This is why the Hindu and the Chinaman and many others of like stamp must have a son to keep them in countenance,—a deep-seated sex-prejudice, coming to slow extinction as women rise in economic importance.

It is painfully interesting to trace the gradual cumulative effect of these conditions upon women: first, the action of large natural laws, acting on her as they would act on any other animal; then the evolution of social customs and laws (with her position as the active cause), following the direction of mere physical forces, and adding heavily to them; then, with increasing civilization, the unbroken accumulation of precedent, burnt into each generation by the growing force of education, made lovely by art, holy by religion, desirable by habit; and, steadily acting from beneath, the unswerving pressure of economic necessity upon which the whole structure rested. These are strong modifying conditions, indeed.

The process would have been even more effective and far less painful but for one important circumstance. Heredity has no Salic law. Each girl child inherits from her father a certain increasing percentage of human development, human power, human tendency; and each boy as well inherits from his mother the increasing percentage of sex-development, sex-power, sex-tendency. The action of heredity has been to equalize what every tendency of environment and education made to differ. This has saved us from such a female as the gypsy moth. It has held up the woman, and held down the man. It has set iron bounds to our absurd effort to make a race with one sex a million years behind the other. But it has added terribly to the pain and difficulty of human life,—a difficulty and a pain that should have taught us long since that we were living on wrong lines. Each woman born, re-humanized by the current of race activity carried on by her father and re-womanized by her traditional position, has had to live over again in her own person the same process of restriction, repression, denial; the smothering "no" which crushed down all her human desires to create, to discover, to learn, to express, to advance. Each woman has had, on the other hand, the same single avenue of expression and attainment; the same one way in which alone she might do what she could, get what she might. All other doors were shut, and this one always open; and the whole pressure of advancing humanity was upon her. No wonder that young Daniel in the apocryphal tale proclaimed: "The king is strong! Wine is strong! But women are stronger!"

To the young man confronting life the world lies wide. Such powers as he has he may use, must use. If he chooses wrong at first, he may choose again, and yet again. Not effective or successful in one channel, he may do better in another. The growing, varied needs of all mankind call on him for the varied service in which he finds his growth. What he wants to be, he may strive to be. What he wants to get, he may strive to get. Wealth, power, social distinction, fame,—what he wants he can try for.

To the young woman confronting life there is the same world beyond, there are the same human energies and human desires and ambition within. But all that she may wish to have, all that she may wish to do, must come through a single channel and a single choice. Wealth, power, social distinction, fame,—not only these, but home and happiness, reputation, ease and pleasure, her bread and butter,—all, must come to her through a small gold ring. This is a heavy pressure. It has accumulated behind her through heredity, and continued about her through environment. It has been subtly trained into her through education, till she herself has come to think it a right condition, and pours its influence upon her daughter with increasing impetus. Is it any wonder that women are over-sexed? But for the constant inheritance from the more human male, we should have been queen bees, indeed, long before this. But the daughter of the soldier and the sailor, of the artist, the inventor, the great merchant, has inherited in body and brain her share of his development in each generation, and so stayed somewhat human for all her femininity.

All morbid conditions tend to extinction. One check has always existed to our inordinate sex-development,—nature's ready relief, death. Carried to its furthest excess, the individual has died, the family has become extinct, the nation itself has perished, like Sodom and Gomorrah. Where one function is carried to unnatural excess, others are weakened, and the organism perishes. We are familiar with this in individual cases,—at least, the physician is. We can see it somewhat in the history of nations. From younger races, nearer savagery, nearer the healthful equality of pre-human creatures, has come each new start in history. Persia was older than Greece, and its highly differentiated sexuality had produced the inevitable result of enfeebling the racial qualities. The Greek commander stripped the rich robes and jewels from his

Persian captives, and showed their unmanly feebleness to his men. "You have such bodies as these to fight for such plunder as this," he said. In the country, among peasant classes, there is much less sex-distinction than in cities, where wealth enables the women to live in absolute idleness; and even the men manifest the same characteristics. It is from the country and the lower classes that the fresh blood pours into the cities, to be weakened in its turn by the influence of this unnatural distinction until there is none left to replenish the nation.

The inevitable trend of human life is toward higher civilization; but, while that civilization is confined to one sex, it inevitably exaggerates sex-distinction, until the increasing evil of this condition is stronger than all the good of the civiliation attained, and the nation falls. Civilization, be it understood, does not consist in the acquisition of luxuries. Social development is an organic development. A civilized State is one in which the citizens live in organic industrial relation. The more full, free, subtle, and easy that relation; the more perfect the differentiation of labor and exchange of product, with their correlative institutions,—the more perfect is that civilization. To eat, drink, sleep, and keep warm,—these are common to all animals, whether the animal couches in a bed of leaves or one of eiderdown, sleeps in the sun to avoid the wind or builds a furnace-heated house, lies in wait for game or orders a dinner at a hotel. These are but individual animal processes. Whether one lays an egg or a million eggs, whether one bears a cub, a kitten, or a baby, whether one broods its chickens, guards its litter, or tends a nursery full of children, these are but individual animal processes. But to serve each other more and more widely; to live only by such service; to develope special functions, so that we depend for our living on society's return for services that can be of no direct use to ourselves,—this is civilization, our human glory and race-distinction.

All this human progress has been accomplished by men. Women have been left behind, outside, below, having no social relation whatever, merely the sex-relation, whereby they lived. Let us bear in mind that all the tender ties of family are ties of blood, of sex-relationship. A friend, a comrade, a partner,—this is a human relative. Father, mother, son, daughter, sister, brother, husband, wife,—these are sex-relatives. Blood is thicker than water, we say. True. But ties of blood are not those that ring the world with the succeeding waves of progressive religion, art, science, commerce, education, all that makes us human. Man is the human creature. Woman has been checked, starved, aborted in human growth; and the swelling forces of race-development have been driven back in each generation to work in her through sex-functions alone.

This is the way in which the sexuo-economic relation has operated in our species, checking race-development in half of us, and stimulating sex-development in both.

W.E.B. DU BOIS

On Mr. Booker T. Washington and Others
1903

The idea that black Americans should press for political rights and educational opportunities equal to those of whites was radical when W.E.B. Du Bois (1868–1963) advanced it during the Progressive Era. Discussions on the part of blacks as well as whites concerning what was then called the Negro problem were dominated instead by the ideas of the most prominent black leader of the entire period between Reconstruction and World War I, Booker T. Washington. Washington doubted the value—for black Americans of his time—of liberal arts education and of organized political struggles for civil rights. He urged gradual improvement of the black's lot through training in agricultural and industrial skills. Hence Du Bois's argument, in the essay reprinted here, was cast in the form of a critique of Washington's leadership of black Americans. Du Bois's ideas were influential in the forming of the National Association for the Advancement of Colored People, of which Du Bois was an early leader. Du Bois wrote in a number of literary and scholarly genres. As a literary essayist, he was most known for *Souls of Black Folk: Essays and Sketches* (Chicago, 1903); as a professional historian, his major achievement was *Black Reconstruction* (New York, 1935). He moved to Africa in 1961 and died there, an expatriate. The classic study of Du Bois's early thought in relation to that of Washington is August Meier, *Negro Thought in America, 1880–1915* (New York, 1963).

From birth till death enslaved; in word, in deed,
unmanned!

. . . . . .

Hereditary bondsmen! Know ye not
Who would be free themselves must strike the blow?

BYRON

Easily the most striking thing in the history of the American Negro since 1876 is the ascendancy of Mr. Booker T. Washington. It began at the time when war memories and ideals were rapidly passing; a day of astonishing commercial development was dawning; a sense of doubt and hesitation overtook the freedmen's sons,—then it was that his leading began. Mr. Washington came, with a single definite programme, at the psychological moment when the nation was a little ashamed of having bestowed so much sentiment on Negroes, and was concentrating its energies on Dollars. His programme of industrial education, conciliation of the South, and submission and silence as to civil and political rights, was not wholly original; the Free Negroes from 1830 up to wartime had striven to build industrial schools, and the American Missionary Association had from the first taught various trades; and Price and others had sought a way of honorable alliance with the best of the Southerners. But Mr. Washington first indissolubly linked these things; he put enthusiasm, unlimited energy, and perfect faith into this programme, and changed it from a by-path into a veritable Way of Life. And the tale of the methods by which he did this is a fascinating study of human life.

It startled the nation to hear a Negro advocating such a programme after many decades of bitter complaint; it startled and won the applause of the South, it interested and won the admiration of the North; and after a confused murmur of protest, it silenced if it did not convert the Negroes themselves.

To gain the sympathy and coöperation of the various elements comprising the white South was Mr. Washington's first task; and this, at the time Tuskegee was founded, seemed, for a black man, well-nigh impossible. And yet ten years later it was done in the word spoken at Atlanta: "In all things purely social we can be as separate as the five fingers, and yet one as the hand in all things essential to mutual progress." This "Atlanta Compromise" is by all odds the most notable thing in Mr. Washington's career. The South interpreted it in different ways: the radicals received it as a complete surrender of the demand for civil and politcal equality; the conservatives, as a generously conceived working basis for mutual understanding. So both approved it, and today its author is certainly the most distinguished Southerner since Jefferson Davis, and the one with the largest personal following.

Source: The Souls of Black Folk: Essays and Sketches, by W. E. Burghardt Du Bois (Chicago, 1903).

Next to this achievement comes Mr. Washington's work in gaining place and consideration in the North. Others less shrewd and tactful had formerly essayed to sit on these two stools and had fallen between them; but as Mr. Washington knew the heart of the South from birth and training, so by singular insight he intuitively grasped the spirit of the age which was dominating the North. And so thoroughly did he learn the speech and thought of triumphant commercialism, and the ideals of material prosperity that the picture of a lone black boy poring over a French grammar amid the weeds and dirt of a neglected home soon seemed to him the acme of absurdities. One wonders what Socrates and St. Francis of Assisi would say to this.

And yet this very singleness of vision and thorough oneness with his age is a mark of the successful man. It is as though Nature must needs make men narrow in order to give them force. So Mr. Washington's cult has gained unquestioning followers, his work has wonderfully prospered, his friends are legion, and his enemies are confounded. To-day he stands as the one recognized spokesman of his ten million fellows, and one of the most notable figures in a nation of seventy millions. One hesitates, therefore, to criticise a life which, beginning with so little has done so much. And yet the time is come when one may speak in all sincerity and utter courtesy of the mistakes and shortcomings of Mr. Washington's career, as well as of his triumphs, without being thought captious or envious, and without forgetting that it is easier to do ill than well in the world.

The criticism that has hitherto met Mr. Washington has not always been of this broad character. In the South especially has he had to walk warily to avoid the harshest judgments,—and naturally so, for he is dealing with the one subject of deepest sensitiveness to that section. Twice—once when at the Chicago celebration of the Spanish-American War he alluded to the color-prejudice that is "eating away the vitals of the South," and once when he dined with President Roosevelt—has the resulting Southern criticism been violent enough to threaten seriously his popularity. In the North the feeling has several times forced itself into words, that Mr. Washington's counsels of submission overlooked certain elements of true manhood, and that his educational programme was unnecessarily narrow. Usually, however, such criticism has not found open expression, although, too, the spiritual sons of the Abolitionists have not been prepared to acknowledge that the schools founded before Tuskegee, by men of broad ideals and self-sacrificing spirit, were wholly failures or worthy of ridicule. While, then, criticism has not failed to follow Mr. Washington, yet the prevailing public opinion of the land has been but too willing to deliver the solution of a wearisome problem into his hands, and say, "If that is all you and your race ask, take it."

Among his own people, however, Mr. Washington has encountered the strongest and most lasting opposition, amounting at times to bitterness, and even to-day continuing strong and insistent even though largely silenced in outward expression by the public opinion of the nation. Some of this opposition is, of course, mere envy; the disappointment of displaced demagogues and the spite of narrow minds. But aside from this, there is among educated and thoughtful colored men in all parts of the land a feeling of deep regret, sorrow, and apprehension at the wide currency and ascendancy which some of Mr. Washington's theories have gained. These same men admire his sincerity of purpose, and are willing to forgive much to honest endeavor which is doing something worth the doing. They coöperate with Mr. Washington as far as they conscientiously can; and, indeed, it is no ordinary tribute to this man's tact and power that, steering as he must between so many diverse interests and opinions, he so largely retains the respect of all.

But the hushing of the criticism of honest opponents is a dangerous thing. It leads some of the best of the critics to unfortunate silence and paralysis of effort, and others to burst into speech so passionately and intemperately as to lose listeners. Honest and earnest criticism from those whose interests are most nearly touched,—criticism of writers by readers, of government by those governed, of leaders by those led,—this is the soul of democracy and the safeguard of modern society. If the best of the American Negroes receive by outer pressure a leader whom they had not recognized before, manifestly there is here a certain palpable gain. Yet there is also irreparable loss,—a loss of that peculiarly valuable education which a group receives when by search and criticism it finds and commissions its own leaders. The way in which this is done is at once the most elementary and the nicest problem of social growth. History is but the record of such group-leadership; and yet how infinitely changeful is its type and character! And of all types and kinds, what can be more instructive than the leadership of a group within a group?—that curious double movement where real progress may be negative and actual advance be relative retrogression. All this is the social student's inspiration and despair.

Now in the past the American Negro has had instructive experience in the choosing of group leaders, founding thus a peculiar dynasty which in the light of present conditions is worth while studying. When sticks and stones and beasts form the sole environment of a people, their attitude is largely one of determined opposition to and conquest of natural forces. But when to earth and brute is added an environment of men and ideas, then the attitude of the imprisoned group may take three main forms,—a feeling of revolt and revenge; an attempt to adjust all thought and action to the will of the greater group; or, finally, a determined effort at self-realization and self-development despite environing opinion. The influence of all of these attitudes at various times can be traced in the history of the American Negro, and in the evolution of his successive leaders.

Before 1750, while the fire of African freedom still burned in the veins of the slaves, there was in all leadership or attempted leadership but the one motive of revolt and revenge,—typified in the terrible Maroons, the Danish blacks, and Cato of Stono, and veiling all the Americas in fear of insurrection. The liberalizing tendencies of the latter half of the eighteenth century brought, along with kindlier relations between black and white, thoughts of ultimate adjustment and assimilation. Such aspiration was especially voiced in the earnest songs of Phyllis, in the martyrdom of Attucks, the fighting of Salem and Poor, the intellectual accomplishments of Banneker and Derham, and the political demands of the Cuffes.

Stern financial and social stress after the war cooled much of the previous humanitarian ardor. The disappointment and impatience of the Negroes at the persistence of slavery and serfdom voiced itself in two movements. The slaves in the South, aroused undoubtedly by vague rumors of the Haitian revolt, made three fierce attempts at insurrection,—in 1800 under Gabriel in Virginia, in 1822 under Vesey in Carolina, and in 1831 again in Virginia under the terrible Nat Turner. In the Free States, on the other hand, a new and curious attempt at self-development was made. In Philadelphia and New York color-prescription led to a withdrawal of Negro communicants from white churches and the formation of a peculiar socio-religious institution among the

Negroes known as the African Church,—an organization still living and controlling in its various branches over a million of men.

Walker's wild appeal against the trend of the times showed how the world was changing after the coming of the cotton-gin. By 1830 slavery seemed hopelessly fastened on the South, and the slaves thoroughly cowed into submission. The free Negroes of the North, inspired by the mulatto immigrants from the West Indies, began to change the basis of their demands; they recognized the slavery of slaves, but insisted that they themselves were freemen, and sought assimilation and amalgamation with the nation on the same terms with other men. Thus, Forten and Purvis of Philadelphia, Shad of Wilmington, Du Bois of New Haven, Barbadoes of Boston, and others, strove singly and together as men, they said, not as slaves; as "people of color," not as "Negroes." The trend of the times, however, refused them recognition save in individual and exceptional cases, considered them as one with all the despised blacks, and they soon found themselves striving to keep even the rights they formerly had of voting and working and moving as freemen. Schemers of migration and colonization arose among them; but these they refused to entertain, and they eventually turned to the Abolition movement as a final refuge.

Here, led by Remond, Nell, Wells-Brown, and Douglass, a new period of self-assertion and self-development dawned. To be sure, ultimate freedom and assimilation was the ideal before the leaders, but the assertion of the manhood rights of the Negro by himself was the main reliance, and John Brown's raid was the extreme of its logic. After the war and emancipation, the great form of Frederick Douglass, the greatest of American Negro leaders, still led the host. Self-assertion, especially in political lines, was the main programme, and behind Douglass came Elliot, Bruce, and Langston, and the Reconstruction politicians, and, less conspicuous but of greater social significance Alexander Crummell and Bishop Daniel Payne.

Then came the Revolution of 1876, the suppression of the Negro votes, the changing and shifting of ideals, and the seeking of new lights in the great night. Douglass, in his old age, still bravely stood for the ideals of his early manhood,—ultimate assimilation *through* self-assertion, and no other terms. For a time Price arose as a new leader, destined, it seemed, not to give up, but to re-state the old ideals in a form less repugnant to the white South. But he passed away in his prime. Then came the new leader. Nearly all the former ones had become leaders by the silent suffrage of their fellows, had sought to lead their own people alone, and were usually, save Douglass, little known outside their race. But Booker T. Washington arose as essentially the leader not of one race but of two,—a compromiser between the South, the North, and the Negro. Naturally the Negroes resented, at first bitterly, signs of compromise which surrendered their civil and political rights, even though this was to be exchanged for larger chances of economic development. The rich and dominating North, however, was not only weary of the race problem, but was investing largely in Southern enterprises, and welcomed any method of peaceful coöperation. Thus, by national opinion, the Negroes began to recognize Mr. Washington's leadership; and the voice of criticism was hushed.

Mr. Washington represents in Negro thought the old attitude of adjustment and submission; but adjustment at such a peculiar time as to make his programme unique. This is an age of unusual economic development, and Mr. Washington's programme naturally takes an economic cast, becoming a gospel of Work and Money to such an extent as apparently almost completely to overshadow the higher aims of life. Moreover, this is an age when the more advanced races are coming in closer contact with the less developed races, and the race-feeling is therefore intensified; and Mr. Washington's programme practically accepts the alleged inferiority of the Negro races. Again, in our own land, the reaction from the sentiment of war time has given impetus to race-prejudice against Negroes, and Mr. Washington withdraws many of the high demands of Negroes as men and American citizens. In other periods of intensified prejudice all the Negro's tendency to self-assertion has been called forth; at this period a policy of submission is advocated. In the history of nearly all other races and peoples the doctrine preached at such crises has been that manly self-respect is worth more than lands and houses, and that a people who voluntarily surrender such respect, or cease striving for it, are not worth civilizing.

In answer to this, it has been claimed that the Negro can survive only through submission. Mr. Washington distinctly asks that black people give up, at least for the present, three things,—

First, political power,

Second, insistence on civil rights,

Third, higher education of Negro youth,—

and concentrate all their energies on industrial education, the accumulation of wealth, and the conciliation of the South. This policy has been courageously and insistently advocated for over fifteen years, and has been triumphant for perhaps ten years. As a result of this tender of the palm-branch, what has been the return? In these years there have occurred:

1. The disfranchisement of the Negro.
2. The legal creation of a distinct status of civil inferiority for the Negro.
3. The steady withdrawal of aid from institutions for the higher training of the Negro.

These movements are not, to be sure, direct results of Mr. Washington's teachings; but his propaganda has, without a shadow of doubt, helped their speedier accomplishment. The question then comes: Is it possible, and probable, that nine millions of men can make effective progress in economic lines if they are deprived of political rights, made a servile caste, and allowed only the most meagre chance for developing their exceptional men? If history and reason give any distinct answer to these questions, it is an emphatic *No*. And Mr. Washington thus faces the triple paradox of his career:

1. He is striving nobly to make Negro artisans business men and property-owners; but it is utterly impossible, under modern competitive methods, for workingmen and property-owners to defend their rights and exist without the right of suffrage.
2. He insists on thrift and self-respect, but at the same time counsels a silent submission to civic inferiority such as is bound to sap the manhood of any race in the long run.
3. He advocates common-school and industrial training, and depreciates institutions of higher learning; but neither the Negro common-schools, nor Tuskegee itself, could remain open a day were it not for teachers trained in Negro colleges, or trained by their graduates.

This triple paradox in Mr. Washington's position is the object of criticism by two classes of colored Americans. One class is spiritually descended from Toussaint the Savior, through Gabriel, Vesey, and Turner, and they represent the attitude of revolt and revenge; they hate the white South blindly and distrust the white race generally, and so far as they agree on definite action, think that the Negro's only hope lies in emigration beyond the borders of the United States. And yet, by the irony of fate, nothing has more effectually made this programme seem hopeless than the recent course of the United States toward weaker and darker peoples in the West Indies, Hawaii, and the Philippines,—for where in the world may we go and be safe from lying and brute force?

The other class of Negroes who cannot agree with Mr. Washington has hitherto said little aloud. They deprecate the sight of scattered counsels, of internal disagreement; and especially they dislike making their just criticism of a useful and earnest man an excuse for a general discharge of venom from small-minded opponents. Nevertheless, the questions involved are so fundamental and serious that it is difficult to see how men like the Grimkes, Kelly Miller, J.W.E. Bowen, and other representatives of this group, can much longer be silent. Such men feel in conscience bound to ask of this nation three things.

1. The right to vote.
2. Civic equality.
3. The education of youth according to ability.

They acknowledge Mr. Washington's invaluable service in counselling patience and courtesy in such demands; they do not ask that ignorant black men vote when ignorant whites are debarred, or that any reasonable restrictions in the suffrage should not be applied; they know that the low social level of the mass of the race is responsible for much discrimination against it, but they also know, and the nation knows, that relentless color-prejudice is more often a cause than a result of the Negro's degradation; they seek the abatement of this relic of barbarism, and not its systematic encouragement and pampering by all agencies of social power from the Associated Press to the Church of Christ. They advocate, with Mr. Washington, a broad system of Negro common schools supplemented by thorough industrial training; but they are surprised that a man of Mr. Washington's insight cannot see that no such educational system ever has rested or can rest on any other basis than that of the well-equipped college and university, and they insist that there is a demand for a few such institutions throughout the South to train the best of the Negro youth as teachers, professional men, and leaders.

This group of men honor Mr. Washington for his attitude of conciliation toward the white South; they accept the "Atlanta Compromise" in its broadest interpretation; they recognize, with him, many signs of promise, many men of high purpose and fair judgment, in this section; they know that no easy task has been laid upon a region already tottering under heavy burdens. But, nevertheless, they insist that the way to truth and right lies in straightforward honesty, not in indiscriminate flattery; in praising those of the South who do well and criticising uncompromisingly those who do ill; in taking advantage of the opportunities at hand and urging their fellows to do the same, but at the same time in remembering that only a firm adherence to their higher ideals and aspirations will ever keep those ideals within the realm of possibility. They do not expect that the free right to vote, to enjoy civic rights, and to be educated, will come in a moment; they do not expect to see the bias and prejudices of years disappear at the blast of a trumpet; but they are absolutely certain that the way for a people to gain their reasonable rights is not by voluntarily throwing them away and insisting that they do not want them; that the way for a people to gain respect is not by continually belittling and ridiculing themselves; that, on the contrary, Negroes must insist continually, in season and out of season, that voting is necessary to modern manhood, that color discrimination is barbarism, and that black boys need education as well as white boys.

In failing thus to state plainly and unequivocally the legitimate demands of their people, even at the cost of opposing an honored leader, the thinking classes of American Negroes would shirk a heavy responsibility,—a responsibility to themselves, a responsibility to the struggling masses, a responsibility to the darker races of men whose future depends so largely on this American experiment, but especially a responsibility to this nation,—this common Fatherland. It is wrong to encourage a man or a people in evil-doing; it is wrong to aid and abet a national crime simply because it is unpopular not to do so. The growing spirit of kindliness and reconciliation between the North and South after the frightful difference of a generation ago ought to be a source of deep congratulation to all, and especially to those whose mistreatment caused the war; but if that reconciliation is to be marked by the industrial slavery and civic death of those same black men, with permanent legislation into a position of inferiority, then those black men, if they are really men, are called upon by every consideration of patriotism and loyalty to oppose such a course by all civilized methods, even though such opposition involves disagreement with Mr. Booker T. Washington. We have no right to sit silently by while the inevitable seeds are sown for a harvest of disaster to our children, black and white.

First, it is the duty of black men to judge the South discriminatingly. The present generation of Southerners are not responsible for the past, and they should not be blindly hated or blamed for it. Furthermore, to no class is the indiscriminate endorsement of the recent course of the South toward Negroes more nauseating than to the best thought of the South. The South is not "solid"; it is a land in the ferment of social change, wherein forces of all kinds are fighting for supremacy; and to praise the ill the South is to-day perpetrating is just as wrong as to condemn the good. Discriminating and broad-minded criticism is what the South needs,—needs it for the sake of her own white sons and daughters, and for the insurance of robust, healthy mental and moral development.

To-day even the attitude of the Southern whites toward the blacks is not, as so many assume, in all cases the same; the ignorant Southerner hates the Negro, the workingmen fear his competition, the money-makers wish to use him as a laborer, some of the educated see a menace in his upward development, while others—usually the sons of the masters—wish to help him to rise. National opinion has enabled this last class to maintain the Negro common schools, and to protect the Negro partially in property, life, and limb. Through the pressure of the money-makers, the Negro is in danger of being reduced to semi-slavery, especially in the country districts; the workingmen, and those of the educated who fear the Negro, have united to disfranchise him, and some have urged his deportation; while the passions of the ignorant are easily aroused to lynch and abuse any black man. To praise this intricate whirl of thought and prejudice is nonsense; to inveigh indiscriminately against "the South" is unjust; but to use the same breath in praising Governor Aycock, exposing Senator Morgan, arguing with Mr. Thomas Nelson Page, and denouncing Senator Ben Tillman, is not only sane, but the imperative duty of thinking black men.

It would be unjust to Mr. Washington not to acknowledge that in several instances he has opposed movements in the South which were unjust to the Negro; he sent memorials to the Louisiana and Alabama constitutional conventions, he has spoken against lynching, and in other ways has openly or silently set his influence against sinister schemes and unfortunate happenings. Notwithstanding this, it is equally true to assert that on the whole the distinct impression left by Mr. Washington's propaganda is, first, that the South is justified in its present attitude toward the Negro because of the Negro's degradation; secondly, that the prime cause of the Negro's failure to rise more quickly is his wrong education in the past; and, thirdly, that his future rise depends primarily on his own efforts. Each of these propositions is a dangerous half-truth. The supplementary truths must never be lost sight of: first, slavery and race-prejudice are potent if not sufficient causes of the Negro's position; second, industrial and common-school training were necessarily slow in planting because they had to await the black teachers trained by higher institutions,—it being extremely doubtful if any essentially different development was possible, and certainly a Tuskegee was unthinkable before 1880; and, third, while it is a great truth to say that the Negro must strive and strive mightily to help himself, it is equally true that unless his striving be not simply seconded, but rather aroused and encouraged, by the initiative of the richer and wiser environing group, he cannot hope for great success.

In his failure to realize and impress this last point, Mr. Washington is especially to be criticised. His doctrine has tended to make the whites, North and South, shift the burden of the Negro problem to the Negro's shoulders and stand aside as critical and rather pessimistic spectators; when in fact the burden belongs to the nation, and the hands of none of us are clean if we bend not our energies to righting these great wrongs.

The South ought to be led, by candid and honest criticism, to assert her better self and do her full duty to the race she has cruelly wronged and is still wronging. The North—her co-partner in guilt—cannot salve her conscience by plastering it with gold. We cannot settle this problem by diplomacy and suaveness, by "policy" alone. If worse comes to worst, can the moral fibre of this country survive the slow throttling and murder of nine millions of men?

The black men of America have a duty to perform, a duty stern and delicate,—a forward movement to oppose a part of the work of their greatest leader. So far as Mr. Washington preaches Thrift, Patience, and Industrial Training for the masses, we must hold up his hands and strive with him, rejoicing in his honors and glorying in the strength of this Joshua called of God and of man to lead the headless host. But so far as Mr. Washington apologizes for injustice, North or South, does not rightly value the privilege and duty of voting, belittles the emasculating effects of caste distinctions, and opposes the higher training and ambition of our brighter minds,—so far as he, the South, or the Nation, does this,—we must unceasingly and firmly oppose them. By every civilized and peaceful method we must strive for the rights which the world accords to men, clinging unwaveringly to those great words which the sons of the Fathers would fain forget: "We hold these truths to be self-evident: That all men are created equal; that they are endowed by their Creater with certain unalienable rights; that among these are life, liberty, and the pursuit of happiness."

ELIZABETH CADY STANTON

"The Solitude of Self"
1892

When the seventy-seven-year old Elizabeth Cady Stanton (1815–1902) stepped down from the presidency of the National American Woman Suffrage Association in 1892, she sought to vindicate the rights of women on the grounds of "the solitude and personal responsibility" of each woman's "individual life." Stanton made other arguments as well—in "The Solitude of Self" and throughout her career—but in treating the political significance and psychological resources of the "self" she produced one of the most vivid and prophetic testimonials in the entire discourse of modern feminism. Stanton demanded equality for women in the life of the mind as well as the life of politics. She was a distinctively intellectual exemplar for American women and spoke beyond as well as within feminist circles on many issues of her time. Stanton gained notoriety as a freethinker and was openly critical of Christianity. In *The Woman's Bible* (1895), she boldly evaluated sections of the Old Testament in terms of the attitudes toward women promoted by these texts. For Stanton's career and thought, see Lois W. Banner, *Elizabeth Cady Stanton: A Radical for Women's Rights* (Boston, 1980), and the extensive introductory and editorial comments of Ellen Carol Du Bois, ed., *Elizabeth Cady Stanton and Susan B. Anthony: Correspondence, Writings, Speeches* (New York, 1981). The version of "The Solitude of Self," reprinted herein, follows Du Bois's editing of the text.

The point I wish plainly to bring before you on this occasion is the individuality of each human soul; our Protestant idea, the right of individual conscience and judgment; our republican idea, individual citizenship. In discussing the rights of woman, we are to consider, first, what belongs to her as an individual, in a world of her own, the arbiter of her own destiny, an imaginary Robinson Crusoe, with her woman, Friday, on a solitary island. Her rights under such circumstances are to use all her faculties for her own safety and happiness.

Secondly, if we consider her as a citizen, as a member of a great nation, she must have the same rights as all others members, according to the fundamental principles of our Government.

Thirdly, viewed as a woman, an equal factor in civilization, her rights and duties are still the same—individual happiness and development.

Fourthly, it is only the incidental relations of life, such as mother, wife, sister, daughter, which may involve some special duties and training. . . .

The strongest reason for giving woman all the opportunities for higher education, for the full development of her faculties, her forces of mind and body; for giving her the most enlarged freedom of thought and action; a complete emancipation from all forms of bondage, of custom, dependence, superstition; from all the crippling influences of fear—is the solitude and personal responsibility of her own individual life. The strongest reason why we ask for woman a voice in the government under which she lives; in the religion she is asked to believe; equality in social life, where she is the chief factor; a place in the trades and professions, where she may earn her bread, is because of her birthright to self-sovereignty; because, as an individual, she must rely on herself. No matter how much women prefer to lean, to be protected and supported, nor how much men desire to have them do so, they must make the voyage of life alone, and for safety in an emergency, they must know something of the laws of navigation. To guide our own craft, we must be captain, pilot, engineer; with chart and compass to stand at the wheel; to watch the winds and waves, and know when to take in the sail, and to read the signs in the firmament over all. It matters not whether the solitary voyager is man or woman; nature, having endowed them equally, leaves them to their own skill and judgment in the hour of danger, and, if not equal to the occasion, alike they perish.

To appreciate the importance of fitting every human soul for independent action, think for a moment of the immeasurable solitude of self. We come into the world alone, unlike all who have gone before us, we leave it alone, under circumstances peculiar to ourselves. No mortal ever has been, no mortal ever will be like the soul just launched on the sea of life. There can never again be just such a combination of prenatal influences; never again just such environments as make up the infancy, youth and manhood of this one. Nature never repeats herself, and the possibilities of one human soul will never be found in another. No one has ever found two blades of ribbon grass alike, and no one will ever find two human beings alike. Seeing, then, what must be the infinite diversity in human character, we can in a measure appreciate the loss to a nation when any class of the people is uneducated and unrepresented in the government.

We ask for the complete development of every individual, first, for his own benefit and happiness. In fitting out an army, we give each soldier his own knapsack,

Source: Woman's Column, 1892.

arms, powder, his blanket, cup, knife, fork and spoon. We provide alike for all their individual necessities; then each man bears his own burden.

Again, we ask complete individual development for the general good; for the consensus of the competent on the whole round of human interests, on all questions of national life; and here each man must bear his share of the general burden. It is sad to see how soon friendless children are left to bear their own burdens, before they can analyze their feelings; before they can even tell their joys and sorrows, they are thrown on their own resources. The great lesson that nature seems to teach us at all ages in self-dependence, self-protection, self-support. . . .

In youth our most bitter disappointments, our brightest hopes and ambitions, are known only to ourselves. Even our friendship and love we never fully share with another; there is something of every passion, in every situation, we conceal. Even so in our triumphs and our defeats. . . .

We ask no sympathy from others in the anxiety and agony of a broken friendship or shattered love. When death sunders our nearest ties, alone we sit in the shadow of our affliction. Alike amid the greatest triumphs and darkest tragedies of life, we walk alone. On the divine heights of human attainment, eulogized and worshipped as a hero or saint, we stand alone. In ignorance, poverty and vice, as a pauper or criminal, alone we starve or steal; alone we suffer the sneers and rebuffs of our fellows; alone we are hunted and hounded through dark courts and alleys, in by-ways and high-ways; alone we stand in the judgment seat; alone in the prison cell we lament our crimes and misfortunes; alone we expiate them on the gallows. In hours like these we realize the awful solitude of individual life, its pains, its penalties, its responsibilities, hours in which the youngest and most helpless are thrown on their own resources for guidance and consolation. Seeing, then, that life must ever be a march and a battle that each soldier must be equipped for his own protection, it is the height of cruelty to rob the individual of a single natural right.

To throw obstacles in the way of a complete education is like putting out the eyes; to deny the rights of property is like cutting off the hands. To refuse political equality is to rob the ostracized of all self-respect; of credit in the market place; of recompense in the world of work, of a voice in choosing those who make and administer the law, a choice in the jury before whom they are tried, and in the judge who decides their punishment. [Think of] . . . woman's position! Robbed of her natural rights, handicapped by law and custom at every turn, yet compelled to fight her own battles, and in the emergencies of life to fall back on herself for protection. . . .

The young wife and mother, at the head of some establishment, with a kind husband to shield her from the adverse winds of life, with wealth, fortune and position, has a certain harbor of safety, secure against the ordinary ills of life. But to manage a household, have a desirable influence in society, keep her friends and the affections of her husband, train her children and servants well, she must have rare common sense, wisdom, diplomacy, and a knowledge of human nature. To do all this, she needs the cardinal virtues and the strong points of character that the most successful statesman possesses. An uneducated woman trained to dependence, with no resources in herself, must make a failure of any position in life. But society says women do not need a knowledge of the world, the liberal training that experience in public life must give, all the advantages of collegiate education; but when for the lack of all this, the woman's happiness is wrecked, alone she bears her humiliation; and the solitude of the weak and the ignorant is indeed pitiable. In the wild chase for the prizes of life, they are ground to powder.

In age, when the pleasures of youth are passed, children grown up, married and gone, the hurry and bustle of life in a measure over, when the hands are weary of active service, when the old arm chair and the fireside are the chosen resorts, then men and women alike must fall back on their own resources. If they cannot find companionship in books, if they have no interest in the vital questions of the hour, no interest in watching the consummation of reforms with which they might have been identified, they soon pass into their dotage. The more fully the faculties of the mind are developed and kept in use, the longer the period of vigor and active interest in all around us continues. If, from a life-long participation in public affairs, a woman feels responsible for the laws regulating our system of education, the discipline of our jails and prisons, the sanitary condition of our private homes, public buildings and thoroughfares, an interest in commerce, finance, our foreign relations, in any or all these questions, her solitude will at least be respectable, and she will not be driven to gossip or scandal for entertainment.

The chief reason for opening to every soul the doors to the whole round of human duties and pleasures is the individual development thus attained, the resources thus provided under all circumstances to mitigate the solitude that at times must come to everyone.

. . . Inasmuch, then, as woman shares equally the joys and sorrows of time and eternity, is it not the height of presumption in man to propose to represent her at the ballot box and the throne of grace, to do her voting in the state, her praying in the church, and to assume the position of high priest at the family altar?

Nothing strengthens the judgment and quickens the conscience like individual responsibility. Nothing adds such dignity to character as the recognition of one's self-sovereignty; the right to an equal place, everywhere conceded—a place earned by personal merit, not an artificial attainment by inheritance, wealth, family and position. Conceding, then, that the responsibilities of life rest equally on man and woman, that their destiny is the same, they need the same preparation for time and eternity. The talk of sheltering woman from the fierce storms of life is the sheerest mockery, for they beat on her from every point of the compass, just as they do on man, and with more fatal results, for he has been trained to protect himself, to resist, and to conquer. Such are the facts in human experience, the responsibilities of individual sovereignty. Rich and poor, intelligent and ignorant, wise and foolish, virtuous and vicious, man and woman; it is ever the same, each soul must depend wholly on itself.

Whatever the theories may be of woman's dependence on man, in the supreme moments of her life, he cannot bear her burdens. Alone she goes to the gates of death to give life to every man that is born into the world; no one can share her fears, no one can mitigate her pangs; and if her sorrow is greater than she can bear, alone she passes beyond the gates into the vast unknown.

From the mountain-tops of Judea long ago, a heavenly voice bade his disciples, "Bear ye one another's burdens"; but humanity has not yet risen to that point of self-sacrifice; and if ever so willing, how few the burdens are that one soul can bear for another! . . .

So it ever must be in the conflicting scenes of life, in the long, weary march, each one walks alone. We may have many friends, love, kindness, sympathy and charity, to smooth our pathway in everyday life, but in the tragedies and triumphs of human experience, each mortal stands alone.

But when all artificial trammels are removed, and women are recognized as individuals, responsible for their own environments, thoroughly educated for all positions in life they may be called to fill; with all the resources in themselves that liberal thought and broad culture can give; guided by their own conscience and judgment, trained to self-protection, by a healthy development of the muscular system, and skill in the use of weapons and defence; and stimulated to self-support by a knowledge of the business world and the pleasure that pecuniary independence must ever give; when women are trained in this way, they will in a measure be fitted for those hours of solitude that come alike to all, whether prepared or otherwise. As in our extremity we must depend on ourselves, the dictates of wisdom point to complete individual development.

In talking of education, how shallow the argument that each class must be educated for the special work it proposes to do, and that all those faculties not needed in this special work must lie dormant and utterly wither for want of use, when, perhaps, these will be the very faculties needed in life's greatest emergencies! Some say, "Where is the use of drilling girls in the languages, the sciences, in law, medicine, theology. As wives, mothers, housekeepers, cooks, they need a different curriculum from boys who are to fill all positions. The chief cooks in our great hotels and ocean steamers are men. In our large cities, men run the bakeries; they make our bread, cake and pies. They manage the laundries; they are now considered our best milliners and dressmakers. Because some men fill these departments of usefulness, shall we regulate the curriculum in Harvard and Yale to their present necessities? If not, why this talk in our best colleges of a curriculum for girls who are crowding into the trades and professions, teachers in all our public schools, rapidly filling many lucrative and honorable positions in life?"

. . . Women are already the equals of men in the whole realm of thought, in art, science, literature and government. . . . The poetry and novels of the century are theirs, and they have touched the keynote of reform, in religion, politics and social life. They fill the editor's and professor's chair, plead at the bar of justice, walk the wards of the hospital, speak from the pulpit and the platform. Such is the type of womanhood that an enlightened public sentiment welcomes to-day, and such the triumph of the facts of life over the false theories of the past.

Is it, then, consistent to hold the developed woman of this day within the same narrow political limits as the dame with the spinning wheel and knitting needle occupied in the past? No, no! Machinery has taken the labors of woman as well as man on its tireless shoulders; the loom and the spinning wheel are but dreams of the past; the pen, the brush, the easel, the chisel, have taken their places, while the hopes and ambitions of women are essentially changed.

We see reason sufficient in the outer conditions of human beings for individual liberty and development, but when we consider the self-dependence of every human soul, we see the need of courage, judgment and the exercise of every faculty of mind and body, strengthened and developed by use, in woman as well as man.

Whatever may be said of man's protecting power in ordinary conditions, amid all the terrible disasters by land and sea, in the supreme moments of danger, alone woman must ever meet the horrors of the situation. The Angel of Death even makes no royal pathway for her. Man's love and sympathy enter only into the sunshine of our lives. In that solemn solitude of self, that links us with the immeasurable and the eternal, each soul lives alone forever. A recent writer says: "I remember once, in crossing the Atlantic, to have gone upon the deck of the ship at midnight, when a dense black cloud enveloped the sky, and the great deep was roaring madly under the lashes of demoniac winds. My feeling was not of danger or fear (which is a base surrender of the immortal soul) but of utter desolation and loneliness; a little speck of life shut in by a tremendous darkness. . . ."

And yet, there is a solitude which each and every one of us has always carried with him, more inaccessible than the ice-cold mountains, more profound than the midnight sea; the solitude of self. Our inner being which we call ourself, no eye nor touch of man or angel has ever pierced. It is more hidden than the caves of the gnome; the sacred adytum of the oracle; the hidden chamber of Eleusinian mystery, for to it only omniscience is permitted to enter.

Such is individual life. Who, I ask you, can take, dare take on himself the rights, the duties, the responsibilities of another human soul?

JOSIAH ROYCE

"The Problem of Job"
1898

During most of the twentieth century the Idealist philosopher Josiah Royce (1855–1916) has been remembered in the terms proposed by his critics, especially his two great anti-Idealist colleagues at Harvard, William James and George Santayana. To these earthier-than-thou thinkers, Royce was a tender soul, looking always on the bright side, complacently aloof from the strivings and sufferings of real men and women. "The Problem of Job" (1898) lends credibility to this view of Royce, as it justifies the ghastliest of evils as part of God's perfect plan for the universe. But the piece also displays the directness, the relentlessness, and the vigor that led Royce's admirers to compare him to the reigning heavyweight champion of the world: He was the John L. Sullivan of philosophy. And it is the willingness of Job to argue with God, to demand rational answers, that most endears Job to Royce. Although Royce himself does not draw the comparison, his answer to the problem of evil is, in fact, widely at variance with the response provided in the Book of Job. There, God convinces Job that he deserves no answer at all. But Royce, voicing the more rationalist faith characteristic of the liberal Protestantism of his milieu, believes he can give good reasons why a loving and just God allowed Job to suffer and allowed Armenians to be massacred by Turks. Royce's work as a whole is addressed in Bruce Kuklick, *Josiah Royce: An Intellectual Biography* (Indianapolis, Ind. 1972). A briefer, more accessible overview can be found in R. Jackson Wilson, *In Quest of Community: Social Philosophy in the United States, 1860–1920* (New York, 1968), 144–70.

Job's world, as he sees it, is organized in a fashion extremely familiar to us all. The main ideas of this cosmology are easy to be reviewed. The very simplicity of the scheme of the universe here involved serves to bring into clearer view the mystery and horror of the problem that besets Job himself. The world, for Job, is the work of a being who, in the very nature of the case, ought to be intelligible (since he is wise), and friendly to the righteous, since according to tradition, and by virtue of his divine wisdom itself, this God must know the value of a righteous man. But—here is the mystery—this God, as his works get known through our human experiences of evil, appears to us not friendly, but hopelessly foreign and hostile in his plans and his doings. The more, too, we study his ways with man, the less intelligible seems his nature. Tradition has dwelt upon his righteousness, has called him merciful, has magnified his love towards his servants, has described his justice in bringing to naught the wicked. One has learned to trust all these things, to conceive God in these terms, and to expect all this righteous government from him. Moreover, tradition joins with the pious observation of nature in assuring us of the omnipotence of God. Job himself pathetically insists that he never doubts, for an instant, God's power to do whatever in heaven or earth he may please to do. Nothing hinders God. No blind faith thwarts him. Sheol is naked before him. The abyss has no covering. The earth hangs over chaos because he orders it to do so. His power shatters the monsters and pierces the dragons. He can, then, do with evil precisely what he does with Rahab or with the shades, with the clouds or with the light or with the sea, namely, exactly what he chooses. Moreover, since he knows everything, and since the actual value of a righteous man is, for Job, an unquestionable and objective fact, God cannot fail to know this real worth of righteousness in his servants, as well as the real hatefulness and mischief of the wicked. God knows worth, and cannot be blind to it, since it is as real a fact as heaven and earth themselves.

Yet despite all these unquestioned facts, this God, who can do just what he chooses, "deprives of right" the righteous man, in Job's own case, and "vexes his soul," becomes towards him as a "tyrant," "persecutes" him "with strong hand," "dissolves" him "into storm," makes him a "byword" for outcasts, "casts" him "into the mire," renders him "a brother to jackals," deprives him of the poor joy of his "one day as a hireling," of the little delight that might come to him as a man before he descends hopelessly to the dark world of the shades, "watches over" him by day to oppress, by night to "terrify" him "with dreams and with visions"—in brief, acts as his enemy, "tears" him "in anger," "gnashes upon" him "with his teeth." All these are the expressions of Job himself. On the other hand, as, with equal wonder and horror the righteous Job reports, God on occasion does just the reverse of all this to the notoriously and deliberately wicked, who "grow old," "wax mighty in power," "see their offspring established," and their homes "secure from fear." If one turns from this view of God's especially unjust dealings with righteous and with wicked individuals to a general survey of his providential government of the world, one sees vast processes going on, as ingenious as they are merciless, as full of hints of a majestic wisdom as they are of indifference to every individual right.

A mountain that falleth is shattered,
And a rock is removed from its place;

Source: Studies of Good and Evil, Josiah Royce (New York: Appleton, 1898), 1–28.

The waters do wear away stones,
Its floods sweep the earth's dust away;
And the hope of frail man thou destroyest.
Thou subdu'st him for aye, and he goes;
Marring his face thou rejectest him.

Here is a mere outline of the divine government as Job sees it. To express himself thus is for Job no momentary outburst of passion. Long days and nights he has brooded over these bitter facts of experience, before he has spoken at all. Unweariedly, in presence of his friends' objections, he reiterates his charges. He has the right of the sufferer to speak, and he uses it. He reports the facts that he sees. Of the paradox involved in all this he can make nothing. What is clear to him, however, is that this paradox is a matter for reasoning, not for blind authority. God ought to meet him face to face, and have the matter out in plain words. Job fears not to face his judge, or to demand his answer from God. God knows that Job has done nothing to deserve this fury. The question at issue between maker and creature is therefore one that demands a direct statement and a clear decision. "Why, since you can do precisely as you choose, and since you know, as all-knower, the value of a righteous servant, do you choose, as enemy, to persecute the righteous with this fury and persistence of hate?" Here is the problem.

The human interest of the issue thus so clearly stated by Job lies, of course, in the universality of just such experiences of undeserved ill here upon earth. What Job saw of evil we can see ourselves to-day whenever we choose. Witness Armenia. Witness the tornadoes and earthquakes. Less interesting to us is the thesis mentioned by Job's friends, in the antiquated form in which they state it, although to be sure, a similar thesis, in altered forms, is prevalent among us still. And of dramatic significance only is the earnestness whith which Job defends his own personal righteousness. So naïve a self-assurance as is his is not in accordance with our modern conscience, and it is seldom indeed that our day would see any man sincerely using this phraseology of Job regarding his own consciousness of rectitude. But what is to-day as fresh and real to us as it was to our poet is the fact that all about us, say in every child born with an unearned heredity of misery, or in every pang of the oppressed, or in every arbitrary coming of ill-fortune, some form of innocence is beset with an evil that the sufferer has not deserved. Job wins dramatic sympathy as an extreme, but for the purpose all the more typical, case of this universal experience of unearned ill-fortune. In every such case we therefore still have the interest that Job had in demanding the solution of this central problem of evil. Herein, I need not say, lies the permanent significance of the problem of Job,—a problem that wholly outlasts any ancient Jewish controversy as to the question whether the divine justice always does or does not act as Job's friends, in their devotion to tradition, declare that it acts. Here, then is the point where our poem touches a question, not merely of an older religion, but of philosophy, and of all time.

The general problem of evil has received, as is well known, a great deal of attention from the philosophers. Few of them, at least in European thought, have been as fearless in stating the issue as was the original author of Job. The solutions offered have, however, been very numerous. For our purposes they may be reduced to a few.

First, then, one may escape Job's paradox by declining altogether to view the world in teleological terms. Evils, such as death, disease, tempests, enemies, fires, are not, so one may declare, the works of God or of Satan, but are natural phenomena. Natural, too, are the phenomena of our desires, of our pains, sorrows and failures. No divine purpose rules or overrules any of these things. That happens to us, at any time, which must happen, in view of our natural limitations and of our ignorance. The way to better things is to understand nature better than we now do. For this view—a view often maintained in our day—there is no problem of evil, in Job's sense, at all. Evil there indeed is, but the only rational problems are those of natural laws. I need not here further consider this method, not of solving but of abolishing the problem before us, since my intent is, in this paper, to suggest the possibility of some genuinely teleological answer to Job's question. I mention this first view only to recognize, historically, its existence.

In the second place, one may deal with our problem by attempting any one, or a number, of those familiar and popular compromises between the belief in a world of natural law and the belief in a teleological order, which are all, as compromises, reducible to the assertion that the presence of evil in the creation is a relatively insignificant, and an inevitable, incident of a plan that produces sentient creatures subject to law. Writers who expound such compromises have to point out that, since a burnt child dreads the fire, pain is, on the whole, useful as a warning. Evil is a transient discipline whereby finite creatures learn their place in the system of things. Again, a sentient world cannot get on without some experience of suffering, since sentience means tenderness. Take away pain (so one still again often insists), take away pain, and we should not learn our share of natural truth. Pain is the pedagogue to teach us natural science. The contagious diseases, for instance, are useful in so far as they lead us in the end to study Bacteriology, and thus to get an insight into the life of certain beautiful creatures of God whose presence in the world we should otherwise blindly overlook! Moreover (to pass to still another variation of this sort of explanation), created beings obviously grow from less to more. First the lower, then the higher. Otherwise there could be no Evolution. And were there no evolution, how much of edifying natural science we should miss! But if one is evolved, if one grows from less to more, there must be something to make the stages of growth. Now evil is useful to mark the lower stages of evolution. If you are to be, first an infant, then a man, or first a savage, then a civilized being, there must be evils attendant upon the earlier stages of your life—evils that make growth welcome and conscious. Thus, were there no colic and croup, were there no tumbles and crying-spells in infancy, there would be no sufficient incentives to loving parents to hasten the growing robustness of their children, and no motives to impel the children to long to grow big! Just so, cannibalism is valuable as a mark of a lower grade of evolution. Had there been no cannibalism, we should realize less joyously than we do what a respectable thing it is to have become civilized! In brief, evil is, as it were, the dirt of the natural order, whose value is that, when you wash it off, you thereby learn the charm of the bath of evolution.

The foregoing are mere hints of familiar methods of playing about the edges of our problem, as children play barefoot in the shallowest reaches of the foam of the sea. In our poem, . . . the speeches ascribed to Elihu contain the most hints of some such way of defining evil, as a merely transient incident of the discipline of the individual. With many writers explanations of this sort fill much space. They are even not without their proper place in popular discussion. But they have no interest for whoever has once come into the presence of Job's problem as it is in itself. A moment's thought reminds us of their superficiality. Pain is useful as a warning of danger. If we did not suffer, we should burn our hands off. Yes, but this explanation of one evil presupposes another, and a still unexplained and greater evil, namely, the existence of the danger of which we need to be thus warned. No doubt it is well that the past sufferings of the Armenians should teach the survivors, say the defenseless women and children, to have a wholesome fear in future of Turks. Does that explain, however, the need for the existence, or for the murderous doings of the Turks? If I can only reach a given goal by passing over a given road, say of evolution, it may be well for me to consent to the toilsome journey. Does that explain why I was created so far from my goal? Discipline, toil, penalty, surgery, are all explicable as means to ends, if only it be presupposed that there exists, and that there is quite otherwise explicable, the necessity for the situations which involve such fearful expenses. One justifies the surgery, but not the disease; the toil, but not the existence of the need for the toil; the penalty, but not the situation which has made the penalty necessary, when one points out that evil is in so many cases medicinal or disciplinary or prophylactic—an incident of imperfect stages of evolution, or the price of a distant good attained through misery. All such explanations, I insist, trade upon borrowed capital. But God, by hypothesis, is no borrower. He produces his own capital of ends and means. Every evil is explained on the foregoing plan only by presupposing at least an equal, and often a greater and a preëxistent evil, namely, the very state of things which renders the first evil the only physically possible way of reaching a given goal. But what Job wants his judge to explain is not that evil A is a physical means of warding off some other greater evil B, in this cruel world where the waters wear away even the stones, and where hopes of man are so much frailer than the stones; but why a God who can do whatever he wishes chooses situations where such a heaped-up mass of evil means become what we should call physical necessitites to the ends now physically possible.

No real explanation of the presence of evil can succeed which declares evil to be a merely physical necessity for one who desires, in this present world, to reach a given goal. Job's business is not with physical accidents, but with the God who chose to make this present nature; and an answer to Job must show that evil is not a physical but a logical necessity—something whose non-existence would simply contradict the very essence, the very perfection of God's own nature and power. This talk of medicinal and disciplinary evil, perfectly fair when applied to our poor fate-bound human surgeons, judges, jailors, or teachers, becomes cruelly, even cynically trivial when applied to explain the ways of a God who is to choose, not only the physical means to an end, but the very *Physis* itself in which path and goal are to exist together. I confess, as a layman, that whenever, at a funeral, in the company of mourners who are immediately facing Job's own personal problem, and who are sometimes, to say the least, wide enough awake to desire not to be stayed with relative comforts, but to ask that terrible and uttermost question of God himself, and to require the direct answer—that whenever I say, in such company I have to listen to these half-way answers, to these superficial plashes in the wavelets at the water's edge of sorrow, while the black, unfathomed ocean of finite evil spreads out before our wide-opened eyes—well, at such times this trivial speech about useful burns and salutary medicines makes me, and I fancy others, simply and wearily heartsick. Some words are due to children at school, to peevish patients in the sick-room who need a little temporary quieting. But quite other speech is due to men and women when they are wakened to the higher reason of Job by the fierce anguish of our mortal life's ultimate facts. They deserve either our simple silence, or, if we are ready to speak, the speech of people who ourselves inquire as Job inquired.

A third method of dealing with our problem is in essence identical with the course which, in a very antiquated form, the friends of Job adopt. This method takes its best known expression in the doctrine that the presence of evil in the world is explained by the fact that the value of free will in moral agents logically involves, and so explains and justifies, the divine permission of the evil deeds of those finite beings who freely choose to sin, as well as the inevitable fruits of the sins. God creates agents with free will. He does so because the existence of such agents has of itself an infinite worth. Were there no free agents, the highest good could not be. But such agents, because they are free, can offend. The divine justice of necessity pursues such offenses with attendant evils. These evils, the result of sin, must, logically speaking, be permitted to exist, if God once creates the agents who have free will, and himself remains, as he must logically do, a just God. How much ill thus results depends upon the choice of the free agents, not upon God, who wills to have only good chosen, but of necessity must leave his free creatures to their own devices, so far as concerns their power to sin.

This view has the advantage of undertaking to regard evil as a logically necessary part of a perfect moral order, and not as a mere incident of an imperfectly adjusted physical mechanism. So dignified a doctrine, by virtue of its long history and its high theological reputation, needs here no extended exposition. I assume it as familiar, and pass at once to its difficulties. It has its share of truth. There is, I doubt not, moral free will in the universe. But the presence of evil in the world simply cannot be explained by free will alone. This is easy to show. One who maintains this view asserts, in substance, "All real evils are the results of the acts of free and finite moral agents." These agents may be angels or men. If there is evil in the city, the Lord has *not* done it, except in so far as his justice has acted in readjusting wrongs already done. Such ill is due to the deeds of his creatures. But hereupon one asks at once, in presence of any ill, "Who did this?" Job's friends answer: "The sufferer himself; his deed wrought his own undoing. God punishes only the sinner. Every one suffers for his own wrongdoing. Your ill is the result of your crime."

But Job, and all his defenders of innocence, must at once reply: "Empirically speaking, this is obviously, in our visible world, simply not true. The sufferer may suffer innocently. The ill is often undeserved. The fathers sin; the child, diseased from birth, degraded, or a born wretch, may pay the penalty. The Turk or the active rebel sins. Armenia's helpless women and babes cry in vain unto God for help."

Hereupon the reply comes, although not indeed from Job's friends: "Alas! it is so. Sin means suffering; but the innocent may suffer *for* the guilty. This, to be sure, is God's way. One cannot help it. It is so." But therewith the whole effort to explain evil as a logically necessary result of free will and of divine justice alone is simply abandoned. The unearned ills are not justly due to the free will that indeed partly caused them, but to God who declines to protect the innocent. God owes the Turk and the rebel their due. He also owes to his innocent creatures, the babes and the women, his shelter. He owes to the sinning father his penalty, but to the son, born in our visible world a lost soul from the womb, God owes the shelter of his almighty wing, and no penalty. Thus Job's cry is once more in place. The ways of God are not thus justified.

But the partisan of free will as the true explanation of ill may reiterate his view in a new form. He may insist that we see but a fragment. Perhaps the soul born here as if lost, or the wretch doomed to pangs now unearned, sinned of old, in some previous state of existence. Perhaps Karma is to blame. You expiate to-day the sins of your own former existences. Thus the Hindoos varied the theme of our familiar doctrine. This is what Hindoo friends might have said to Job. Well, admit even that, if you like; and what then follows? Admit that here or in former ages the free deed of every present sufferer earned as its penalty every ill, physical or moral, that appears as besetting just this sufferer to-day. Admit that, and what logically follows? It follows, so I must insist, that the moral world itself, which this free-will theory of the source of evil, thus abstractly stated, was to save, is destroyed in its very heart and center.

For consider. A suffers ill. B sees A suffering. Can B, the onlooker, help his suffering neighbor, A? Can he comfort him in any true way? No, a miserable comforter must B prove, like Job's friends, so long as B, believing in our present hypothesis, clings strictly to the logic of this abstract free-will explanation of the origin of evil. T A he says: "Well, you suffer for your own ill-doing. I therefore simply cannot relieve you. This is God's world of justice. If I tried to hinder God's justice from working in your case, I should at best only postpone your evil day. It would come, for God is just. You are hungry, thirsty, naked, sick, in prison. What can I do about it? All this is your own deed come back to you. God himself, although justly punishing, is not the author of this evil. You are the sole originator of the ill." "Ah!" so A may cry out, "but can you not give me light, insight, instruction, sympathy? Can you not at least teach me to become good?" "No," B must reply, if he is a logical believer in the sole efficacy of the private free will of each finite agent as the one source, under the divine justice, of that agent's ill: "No, if you deserved light or any other comfort, God, being just, would enlighten you himself, even If I absolutely refused. But if you do not deserve light, I should preach to you in vain, for God's justice would harden your heart against any such good fortune as I could offer you from without, even if I spoke with the tongues of men and of angels. Your free will is yours. No deed of mine could give you a good free will, for what I gave you from without would not be *your* free will at all. Nor can any one but you cause your free will to be this or that. A great gulf is fixed between us. You and I, as sovereign free agents, live in God's holy world in sin-tight compartments and in evil-tight compartments too. I cannot hurt you, nor you me. You are damned for your own sins, while all that I can do is to look out for my own salvation." This, I say, is the logically inevitable result of asserting that every ill, physical or moral, that can happen to any agent, is solely the result of that agent's own free will acting under the government of the divine justice. The only possible consequence would indeed be that we live, every soul of us, in separate, as it were absolutely fire-proof, free-will compartments, so that real coöperation as to good and ill is excluded. What more cynical denial of the reality of any sort of moral world could be imagined than is involved in this horrible thesis, which no sane partisan of the abstract and traditional free-will explanation of the source of evil will to-day maintain, precisely because no such partisan really knows or can know what his doctrine logically means, while still continuing to maintain it. Yet whenever one asserts with pious obscurity that "No harm can come to the righteous," one in fact implies, with logical necessity, just this cynical consequence.

There remains a fourth doctrine as to our problem. This doctrine is in essence the thesis of philosophical idealism, a thesis which I myself feel bound to maintain, and, so far as space here permits, to explain. The theoretical basis of this view, the philosophical reasons for the notion of the divine nature which it implies, I cannot here explain. That is another argument. But I desire to indicate how the view in question deals with Job's problem.

This view first frankly admits that Job's problem is, upon Job's presuppositions, simply and absolutely insoluble. Grant Job's own presupposition that God is a being other than this world, that he is its external creator and ruler, and then all solutions fail. God is then either cruel or helpless, as regards all real finite ill of the sort that Job endures. Job, moreover, is right in demanding a reasonable answer to his question. The only possible answer is, however, one that undertakes to develop what I hold to be the immortal soul of the doctrine of the divine atonement. The answer to Job is: God is not in ultimate essence another being than yourself. He is the Absolute Being. You truly are one with God, part of his life. He is the very soul of your soul. And so, here is the first truth: When you suffer, *your sufferings are God's sufferings,* not his external work, not his external penalty, not the fruit of his neglect, but identically his own personal woe. In you God himself suffers, precisely as you do, and has all your concern in overcoming this grief.

The true question then is: Why does God thus suffer? The sole possible, necessary, and sufficient answer is, Because without suffering, without ill, without woe, evil, tragedy, God's life could not be perfected. This grief is not a physical means to an external end. It is a logically necessary and eternal constituent of the divine life. It is logically necessary that the Captain of your salvation should be perfect through suffering. No outer nature compels him. He chooses this because he chooses his own perfect selfhood. He is perfect. His world is the best possible world. Yet all its finite regions know not only of joy but of defeat and sorrow, for thus alone, in the completeness of his eternity, can God in his wholeness be triumphantly perfect.

This I say, is my thesis. In the absolute oneness of God with the sufferer, in the concept of the suffering and therefore triumphant God, lies the logical solution of the problem of evil. The doctrine of philosophical idealism is, as regards its purely theoretical aspects, a fairly familiar metaphysical theory at the present time. One may, then, presuppose here as known the fact that, for reasons which I have not now to expound, the idealist maintains that there is in the universe but one perfectly real being, namely, the Absolute, that the Absolute is self-conscious, and that his world is essentially in its wholeness the fulfillment *in actu* of an all-perfect ideal. We ourselves exist as fragments of the absolute life, or better, as partial functions in the unity of the absolute and conscious process of the world. On the other hand, our existence and our individuality are not illusory, but are what they are in an organic unity with the whole life of the Absolute Being. This doctrine once presupposed, our present task is to inquire what case idealism can make for the thesis just indicated as its answer to Job's problem.

In endeavoring to grapple with the theoretical problem of the place of evil in a world that, on the whole, is to be conceived, not only as good, but as perfect, there is happily one essentially decisive consideration concerning good and evil which falls directly within the scope of our own human experience, and which concerns matters at once familiar and momentous as well as too much neglected in philosophy. When we use such words as good, evil, perfect, we easily deceive ourselves by the merely abstract meanings which we associate with each of the terms taken apart from the other. We forget the experiences from which the words have been abstracted. To these experiences we must return whenever we want really to comprehend the words. If we take the mere words, in their abstraction, it is easy to say, for instance, that if life has any evil in it at all, it must needs not be so perfect as life would be were there no evil in it whatever. Just so, speaking abstractly, it is easy to say that, in estimating life, one has to set the good over against the evil, and to compare their respective sums. It is easy to declare that, since we hate evil, wherever and just so far as we recognize it, our sole human interest in the world must be furthered by the removal of evil from the world. And thus viewing the case, one readily comes to say that if God views as not only good but perfect a world in which we find so much evil, the divine point of view must be very foreign to ours, so that Job's rebellious pessimism seems well in order, and Prometheus appears to defy the world-ruler in a genuinely humane spirit. Shocked, however, by the apparent impiety of this result, some teachers, considering divine matters, still misled by the same one-sided use of words, have opposed one falsely abstract view by another, and have strangely asserted that the solution must be in proclaiming that since God's world, the real world, in order to be perfect, must be without evil, what we men call evil must be a mere illusion—a mirage of the human point of view—a dark vision which God, who sees all truth, sees not at all. To God, so this view asserts, the eternal world in its wholeness is not only perfect, but has merely the perfection of an utterly transparent crystal, unstained by any color of ill. Only mortal error imagines that there is any evil. There is no evil but only good in the real world, and that is why God finds the world perfect, whatever mortals dream.

Now neither of these abstract views is my view. I consider them both the result of a thoughtless trust in abstract words. I regard evil as a distinctly real fact, a fact just as real as the most helpless and hopeless sufferer finds it to be when he is in pain. Furthermore, I hold that God's point of view is not foreign to ours. I hold that God willingly, freely, and consciously suffers in us when we suffer, and that our grief is his. And despite all this I maintain that the world from God's point of view fulfills the divine ideal and is perfect. And I hold that when we abandon the one-sided abstract ideas which the words good, evil, and perfect suggest, and when we go back to the concrete experiences upon which these very words are founded, we can see, even within the limits of our own experience, facts which make these very paradoxes perfectly intelligible, and even commonplace.

As for that essentially pernicious view, nowadays somewhat current amongst a certain class of gentle but inconsequent people—the view that all evil is *merely* an illusion and that there is no such thing in God's world—I can say of it only in passing that it is often advanced as an idealistic view, but that, in my opinion, it is false idealism. Good idealism it is to regard all finite experience as an appearance, a hint, often a very poor hint, of deeper truth. Good idealism it is to admit that man can err about truth that lies beyond his finite range of experience. And very good idealism it is to assert that all truth, and so all finite experience, exists in and for the mind of God, and nowhere outside of or apart from God. But it is not good idealism to assert that any facts which fall within the range of finite experience are, even while they are experienced, mere illusions. God's truth is inclusive, not exclusive. What you experience God experiences. The difference lies only in this, that God sees in unity what you see in fragments. For the rest, if one said, "The source and seat of evil is only the error of mortal mind," one would but have changed the name of one's problem. If the evil were but the error, the error would still be the evil, and altering the name would not have diminished the horror of the evil of this finite world.

But I hasten from the false idealism to the true; from the abstractions to the enlightening insights of our life. As a fact, idealism does not say: The finite world is, as such, a mere illusion. A sound idealism says, whatever we experience is a fragment, and, as far as it goes, a genuine fragment of the truth of the divine mind. With this principle before us, let us consider directly our own experiences of good and of evil, to see whether they are as abstractly opposed to each other as the mere words often suggest. We must begin with the elementary and even trivial facts. We shall soon come to something deeper.

By good, as we mortals experience it, we mean something that, when it comes or is expected, we actively welcome, try to attain or keep, and regard with content. By evil in general, as it is in our experience, we mean whatever we find in any sense repugnant and intolerable. I use the words repugnant and intolerable because I wish to indicate that words for evil frequently, like the words for good, directly refer to our actions as such. Commonly and rightly, when we speak of evil, we make reference to acts of resistance, of struggle, of shrinking, of flight, of removal of ourselves from a source of mischief—acts which not only follow upon the experience of evil, but which serve to define in a useful fashion what we mean by evil. The opposing acts of pursuit and of welcome define what we mean by good. By the evil which we experience we mean precisely whatever we regard as something to be gotten rid of, shrunken from, put out of sight, of hearing, or of memory, eschewed, expelled, assailed, or otherwise directly or indirectly resisted. By good we mean whatever we regard as something to be welcomed, pursued, won, grasped, held, persisted in, preserved. And we show all this in our acts in presence of any grade of good or evil, sensuous, aesthetic, ideal, moral. To shun, to flee, to resist, to destroy, these are our primary attitudes towards ill; the opposing acts are our primary attitudes towards the good; and whether you regard us as animals or as moralists, whether it is a sweet taste, a poem, a virtue, or God that we look to as good, and whether it is a burn or a temptation, an outward physical fore, or a stealthy, inward, ideal enemy, that we regard as evil. In all our organs of voluntary movement, in all our deeds, in a turn of the eye, in a sigh, a groan, in a hostile gesture, in an act of silent contempt, we can show in endlessly varied ways the same general attitude of repugnance.

But man is a very complex creature. He has many organs. He performs many acts at once, and he experiences his performance of these acts in one highly complex life of consciousness. As the next feature of his life we all observe that he can at the same time shun one object and grasp at another. In this way he can have at once present to him a consciousness of good and a consciousness of ill. But so far in our account these sorts of experience appear merely as facts side by side. Man loves, and he *also* hates, loves this, and hates that, assumes an attitude of repugnance towards one object, while he welcomes another. So far the usual theory follows man's life, and calls it an experience of good and ill as mingled but exclusively and abstractly opposed facts. For such a view the final question as to the worth of a man's life is merely the question whether there are more intense acts of satisfaction and of welcome than of repugnance and disdain in his conscious life.

But this is by no means an adequate notion of the complexity of man's life, even as an animal. If every conscious act of hindrance, of thwarting, of repugnance, means just in so far an awareness of some evil, it is noteworthy that men can have and can show just such tendencies, not only towards external experiences, but towards their own acts. That is, men can be seen trying to thwart and to hinder even their own acts themselves, at the very moment when they note the occurrence of these acts. One can consciously have an impulse to do something, and at that very moment a conscious disposition to hinder or to thwart as an evil that very impulse. If, on the other hand, every conscious act of attainment, of pursuit, of reinforcement, involves the awareness of some good, it is equally obvious that once can show by one's acts a disposition to reinforce or to emphasize or to increase, not only the externally present gifts of fortune, but also one's own deeds, in so far as one observes them. And in our complex lives it is common enough to find ourselves actually trying to reinforce and to insist upon a situation which involves for us, even at the moment of its occurrence, a great deal of repugnance. In such cases we often act as if we felt the very thwarting of our own primary impulses to be so much of a conscious good that we persist in pursuing and reinforcing the very situation in which this thwarting and hindering of our own impulses is sure to arise.

In brief, as phenomena of this kind show, man is a being who can to a very great extent find a sort of secondary satisfaction in the very act of thwarting his own desires, and thus of assuring for the time his own dissatisfactions. On the other hand, man can to an indefinite degree find himself dissatisfied with his satisfaction and disposed to thwart, not merely his external enemies, but his own inmost impulses themselves. But I now affirm that in all such cases you cannot simply say that man is preferring the less of two evils, or the greater of two goods, as if the good and evil stood merely side by side in his experience. On the contrary, in such cases, man is not merely setting his acts or his estimates of good and evil side by side and taking the sum of each; but he is making his own relatively primary acts, impulses, desires, the objects of all sorts of secondary impulses, desires, and reflective observations. His whole inner state is one of tension: and he is either making a secondary experience of evil out of his estimate of a primary experience of good, as is the case when he at once finds himself disposed to pursue a given good and to thwart this pursuit as being an evil pursuit; or else he is making a secondary experience of good out of his primary experience of evil, as when he is primarily dissatisified with his situation, but yet secondarily regards this very dissatisfaction as itself a desirable state. In this way man comes not only to love some things and also to hate other things, he comes to love his own hates and to hate his own loves in an endlessly complex hierarchy of superposed interests in his own interests.

Now it is easy to say that such states of inner tension, where our conscious lives are full of a warfare of the self with itself, are contradictory or absurd states. But it is easy to say this only when you dwell on the words and fail to observe the facts of experience. As a fact, not only our lowest but our highest states of activity are the ones which are fullest of this crossing, conflict, and complex interrelation of loves and hates, of attractions and repugnances. As a merely physiological fact, we begin no muscular act without at the same time initiating acts which involve the innervation of opposing sets of muscles, and these opposing sets of muscles hinder each other's freedom. Every sort of control of movement means the conflicting play of opposed muscular impulses. We do nothing simple, and we will no complex act without willing what involves a certain measure of opposition between the impulses or partial acts which go to make up the whole act. If one passes from single acts to long series of acts, one finds only the more obviously this interweaving of repugnance and of acceptance, of pursuit and of flight upon which every complex type of conduct depends.

One could easily at this point spend time by dwelling upon numerous and relatively trivial instances of this interweaving of conflicting motives as it appears in all our life. I prefer to pass such instances over with a mere mention. There is, for instance, the whole marvelous consciousness of play, in its benign and in its evil forms. In any game that fascinates, one loves victory and shuns defeat, and yet as a loyal supporter of the game scorns anything that makes victory certain in advance; thus as a lover of fair play preferring to risk the defeat that he all the while shuns, and partly thwarting the very love of victory that from moment to moment fires his hopes. There are, again, the numerous cases in which we prefer to go to places where we are sure to be in a considerable measure dissatisfied; to engage, for instance, in social functions that absorbingly fascinate us despite or even in view of the very fact that, as long as they continue, they keep us in a state of tension which makes us, amongst other things, long to have the whole occasion over. Taking a wider view, one may observe that the greater part of the freest products of the activity of civilization, in ceremonies, in formalities, in the long social drama of flight, of pursuit, of repartee, of contest and of courtesy, involve an elaborate and systematic delaying and hindering of elemental human desires, which we continually outwit, postpone and thwart, even while we nourish them. When students of human nature assert that hunger and love rule the social world, they recognize that the elemental in human nature is trained by civilization into the service of the highest demands of the Spirit. But such students have to recognize that the elemental rules the higher world only in so far as the elemental is not only cultivated, but endlessly thwarted, delayed, outwitted, like a constitutional monarch, who is said to be a sovereign, but who, while he rules, must not govern.

But I pass from such instances, which in all their universality are still, I admit, philosophically speaking trivial, because they depend upon the accidents of human nature. I pass from these instances to point out what must be the law, not only of human nature, but of every broader form of life as well. I maintain that this organization of life by virtue of the tension of manifold impulses and interests is not a mere accident of our imperfect human nature, but must be a type of the organization of every rational life. There are good and bad states of tension, there are conflicts that can only be justified when resolved into some higher form of harmony. But I insist that, in general, the only harmony that can exist in the realm of the spirit is the harmony that we possess when we thwart the present but more elemental impulse for the sake of the higher unity of experience; as when we rejoice in the endurance of the tragedies of life, because they show us the depth of life, or when we know that it is better to have loved and lost than never to have loved at all, or when we possess a virtue in the moment of victory over the tempter. And the reason why this is true lies in the fact that the more one's experience fulfills ideals, the more that experience presents to one, not of ignorance, but of triumphantly wealthy acquaintance with the facts of manifold, varied and tragic life, full of tension and thereby of unity. Now this is an universal and not merely human law. It is not those innocent of evil who are fullest of the life of God, but those who in their own case have experienced the triumph over evil. It is not those naturally ignorant of fear, or those who, like Siegfried, have never shivered, who possess the genuine experience of courage; but the brave are those who have fears, but control their fears. Such know the genuine virtues of the hero. Were it otherwise, only the stupid could be perfect heroes.

To be sure it is quite false to say, as the foolish do, that the object of life is merely that we may "know life" as an irrational chaos of experiences of good and evil. But knowing the good in life is a matter which concerns the form, rather than the mere content of life. One who knows life wisely knows indeed much of the content of life; but he knows the good of life in so far as, in the unity of his experience, he finds the evil of his experience not abolished, but subordinated, and in so far relatively thwarted by a control which annuls its triumph even while experiencing its existence.

Generalizing the lesson of experience we may then say: It is logically impossible that a complete knower of truth should fail to know, to experience, to have present to his insight, the fact of actually existing evil. On the other hand, it is equally impossible for one to know a higher good than comes from the subordination of evil to good in a total experience. When one first loving, in an elemental way, whatever you please, himself hinders, delays, thwarts his elemental interest in the interest of some larger whole of experience, he not only knows more fact, but he possesses a higher good than would or could be present to one who was aware neither of the elemental impulse, nor of the thwarting of it in the tension of a richer life. The knowing of the good, in the higher sense, depends upon contemplating the overcoming and subordination of a less significant impulse, which survives even in order that it should be subordinated. Now this law, this form of the knowledge of the good, applies as well to the existence of moral as to that of sensuous ill. If moral evil were simply destroyed and wiped away from the external world, the knowledge of moral goodness would also be destroyed. For the love of moral good is the thwarting of lower loves for the sake of the higher organization. What is needed, then, for the definition of the divine knowledge of a world that in its wholeness is perfect, is not devine knowledge that shall ignore, wipe out and utterly make naught the existence of any ill, whether physical or moral, but a divine knowledge to which shall be present that love of the world as a whole which is fulfilled in the endurance of physical ill, in the subordination of moral ill, in the thwarting of impulses which survive even when subordinated, in the acceptance of repugnances which are still eternal, in the triumph over an enemy that endures even through its eternal defeat, and in the discovery that the endless tension of the finite world is included in the contemplative consciousness of the repose and harmony of eternity. To view God's nature thus is to view his nature as the whole idealistic theory views him, not as the Infinite One beyond the finite imperfections, but as the being whose unity determines the very constitution, the lack, the tension, and relative disharmony of the finite world.

The existence of evil, then, is not only consistent with the perfection of the universe, but is necessary for the very existence of that perfection. This is what we see when we no longer permit ourselves to be deceived by the abstract meanings of the words good and evil into thinking that these two opponents exist merely as mutually exclusive facts side by side in experience, but when we go back to the facts of life and perceive that all relatively higher good, in the trivial as in the more truly spiritual realm, is known only in so far as, from some higher reflective point of view, we accept as good the thwarting of an existent interest that is even thereby declared to be a relative ill, and love a tension of various impulses which even thereby involves, as the object of our love, the existence of what gives us aversion or grief. Now if the love of God is more inclusive than the love of man, even as the divine world of experience is richer than the human world, we can simply set no human limit to the intensity of conflict, to the tragedies of existence, to the pangs of finitude, to the degree of moral ill, which in the end is included in the life that God not only loves, but finds the fulfillment of the perfect ideal. If peace means satisfaction, acceptance of the whole of an experience as good, and if even we, in our weakness, can frequently find rest in the very presence of conflict and of tension, in the very endurance of ill in a good cause, in the hero's triumph over temptation, or in the mourner's tearless refusal to accept the lower comforts of forgetfulness, or to wish that the lost one's preciousness had been less painfully revealed by death—well, if even we know our little share of this harmony in the midst of the wrecks and disorders of life, what limit shall we set to the divine power to face this world of his own sorrows, and to find peace in the victory over all its ills.

But in the last expression I have pronounced the word that serves to link this theory as to the place of evil in a good world with the practical problem of every sufferer. Job's rebellion came from the thought that God, as a sovereign, is far off, and that, for his pleasure, his creature suffers. Our own theory comes to the mourner with the assurance: "Your suffering, just as it is in you, is God's suffering. No chasm divides you from God. He is not remote from you even in his eternity. He is here. His eternity means merely the completeness of his experience. But that completeness is inclusive. Your sorrow is one of the included facts." I do not say: "God sympathizes with you from without, would spare you if he could, pities you with helpless external pity merely as a father pities his children." I say: "God here sorrows, not *with* but *in* your sorrow. Your grief is identically his grief, and what you know as your loss, God knows as his loss, just in and through the very moment when you grieve."

But hereupon the sufferer perchance responds: "If this is God's loss, could he not have prevented it? To him are present in unity all the worlds; and yet he must lack just this for which I grieve." I respond: "He suffers here that he may triumph. For the triumph of the wise is no easy thing. Their lives are not light, but sorrowful. Yet they rejoice in their sorrow, not, to be sure, because it is mere experience, but because, for them, it becomes part of a strenuous whole of life. They wander and find their home even in wandering. They long, and attain through their very love of longing. Peace they find in triumphant warfare. Contentment they have most of all in endurance. Sovereignty they win in endless service. The eternal world contains Gethsemane."

Yet the mourners may still insist: "If my sorrow is God's, his triumph is not mine. Mine is the woe. His is the peace." But my theory is a philosophy. It proposes to be coherent. I must persist: "It is your fault that you are thus sundered from God's triumph. His experience in its wholeness cannot now be yours, for you just as you—this individual—are now but a fragment, and see his truth as through a glass darkly. But if you see his truth at all, through even the dimmest light of a glimmering reason, remember, that truth is in fact your own truth, your own fulfillment, the whole from which your life cannot be divorced, the reality that you mean even when you most doubt, the desire of your heart even when you are most blind, the perfection that you unconsciously strove for even when you were an infant, the complete Self apart from whom you mean nothing, the very life that gives your life the only value which it can have. In thought, if not in the fulfillment of thought, in aim if not in attainment of aim, in aspiration if not in the presence of the revealed fact, you can view God's triumph and peace as your triumph and peace. Your defeat will be no less real than it is, nor will you falsely call your evil a mere illusion. But you will see not only the grief but the truth, your truth, your rescue, your triumph."

Well, to what ill-fortune does not just such reasoning apply? I insist: our conclusion is essentially universal. It discounts any evil that experience may contain. All the horrors of the natural order, all the concealments of the divine plan by our natural ignorance, find their general relation to the unity of the divine experience indicated in advance by this account of the problem of evil.

"Yes," one may continue, "ill-fortune you have discovered, but how about moral evil? What if the sinner now triumphantly retorts: 'Aha! So my will is God's will. All then is well with me.'" I reply: What I have said disposes of moral ill precisely as definitely as of physical ill. What the evil will is to the good man, whose goodness depends upon its existence, but also upon the thwarting and the condemnation of its aim, just such is the sinner's will to the divine plan. God's will, we say to the sinner, is your will. Yes, but it is your will thwarted, scorned, over-come, defeated. In the eternal world you are seen, possessed, present, but your damnation is also seen including and thwarting you. Your apparent victory in this world stands simply for the vigor of your impulses. God will you not to triumph. And that is the use of you in the world—the use of evil generally—to be hated but endured, to be triumphed over through the very fact of your presence, to be willed down even in the very life of which you are a part.

But to the serious moral agent we say: What you mean when you say that evil in this temporal world ought not to exist, and ought to be suppressed, is simply what God means by seeing that evil ought to be and is endlessly thwarted, endured, but subordinated. In the natural world you are the minister of God's triumph. Your deed is his. You can never clean the world of evil: but you can subordinate evil. The justification of the presence in the world of the morally evil becomes apparent to us mortals only in so far as this evil is overcome and condemned. It exists only that it may be cast down. Courage, then, for God works in you. In the order of time you embody in outer acts what is for him the truth of his eternity.

WILLIAM JAMES

"The Will to Believe"
1897

Of the host of late-nineteenth-century American intellectuals preoccupied with the relation of religion to science, William James (1842–1910) was uniquely creative and influential. This preoccupation informed his work as a psychologist, a philosopher, and popular lecturer and essayist. Although "The Will to Believe" of 1897, which follows, was his most concentrated and widely quoted monument to this preoccupation with the destiny of religion in an age of science, his most probing and detailed exploration of religion was *The Varieties of Religious Experience* (New York, 1902). We also remember James for *The Principles of Psychology* (New York, 1890), and for *Pragmatism* (New York, 1907), a selection from which opens Part Two. For an interpretation of James's entire career as a response to the apparent conflict between religion and science, see David A. Hollinger, "William James and the Culture of Inquiry," in Hollinger's *In the American Province: Studies in the History and Historiography of Ideas* (Bloomington, Ind., 1985), 3–22. The most recent, comprehensive account of Jame's life and thought is Gerald Myers, *William James* (New Haven, 1986). A more thoroughly historical study—and one that takes full account of the professional and institutional matrix of James's work—is Bruce Kuklick, *The Rise of American Philosophy: Cambridge, Massachusetts, 1860–1930* (New Haven, 1977). Yet the single most valuable resource for studying James remains Ralph Barton Perry, *The Thought and Character of William James,* 2 vols. (Boston, 1935), in which an extensive selection from James's correspondence appears amid Perry's interpretive narrative of James's development as a thinker.

In the recently published *Life* by Leslie Stephen of his brother, Fitz-James, there is an account of a school to which the latter went when he was a boy. The teacher, a certain Mr. Guest, used to converse with his pupils in this wise: "Gurney, what is the difference between justification and sanctification?—Stephen, prove the omnipotence of God!" etc. In the midst of our Harvard freethinking and indifference we are prone to imagine that here at your good old orthodox College conversation continues to be somewhat upon this order; and to show you that we at Harvard have not lost all interest in these vital subjects, I have brought with me to-night something like a sermon on justification by faith to read to you,—I mean an essay in justification *of* faith, a defence of our right to adopt a believing attitude in religious matters, in spite of the fact that our merely logical intellect may not have been coerced. 'The Will to Believe,' accordingly, is the title of my paper.

I have long defended to my own students the lawfulness of voluntarily adopted faith; but as soon as they have got well imbued with the logical spirit, they have as a rule refused to admit my contention to the lawful philosophically, even though in point of fact they were personally all the time chock-full of some faith or other themselves. I am all the while, however, so profoundly convinced that my own position is correct, that your invitation has seemed to me a good occasion to make my statements more clear. Perhaps your minds will be more open than those with which I have hitherto had to deal. I will be as little technical as I can, though I must begin by setting up some technical distinctions that will help us in the end.

Let us give the name of *hypothesis* to anything that may be proposed to our belief; and just as the electricians speak of live and dead wires, let us speak of any hypothesis as either *live* or *dead*. A live hypothesis is one which appeals as a real possibility to him to whom it is proposed. If I ask you to believe in the Mahdi, the notion makes no electric connection with your nature,—it refuses to scintillate with any credibility at all. As an hypothesis it is completely dead. To an Arab, however (even if he be not one of the Mahdi's followers), the hypothesis is among the mind's possibilities: it is alive. This shows that deadness and liveness in an hypothesis are not intrinsic properties, but relations to the individual thinker. They are measured by his willingness to act. The maximum of liveness in an hypothesis means willingness to act irrevocably. Practically, that means belief; but there is some believing tendency wherever there is willingness to act at all.

Next, let us call the decision between two hypotheses an *option*. Options may be of several kinds. They may be—1, *living* or *dead;* 2, *forced* or *avoidable;* 3, *momentous* or *trivial;* and for our purposes we may call an option a *genuine* option when it is of the forced, living, and momentous kind.

1. A living option is one in which both hypotheses are live ones. If I say to you: "Be a theosophist or be a Mohammedan," it is probably a dead option, because for you neither hypothesis is likely to be alive. But if I say: "Be an agnostic or be a Christian," it is otherwise: trained as you are, each hypothesis makes some appeal, however small, to your belief.

2. Next, if I say to you: "Choose between going out with your umbrella or without it," I do not offer you a genuine option, for it is not forced. You can easily avoid it by not going out at all. Similarly, if I say, "Either love me or hate me," "Either call my theory true or call it false," your option is avoidable. You may remain indifferent to

Source: The Will to Believe, William James (New York: Longman's, 1897), 1–31.

me, neither loving nor hating, and you may decline to offer any judgment as to my theory. But if I say, "Either accept this truth or go without it," I put on you a forced option, for there is no standing place outside of the alternative. Every dilemma based on a complete logical disjunction, with no possibility of not choosing, is an option of this forced kind.

3. Finally, if I were Dr. Nansen and proposed to you to join my North Pole expedition, your option would be momentous; for this would probably be your only similar opportunity, and your choice now would either exclude you from the North Pole sort of immortality altogether or put at least the chance of it into your hands. He who refuses to embrace a unique opportunity loses the prize as surely as if he tried and failed. *Per contra,* the option is trivial when the opportunity is not unique, when the stake is insignificant, or when the decision is reversible if it later prove unwise. Such trivial options abound in the scientific life. A chemist finds an hypothesis live enough to spend a year in its verification: he believes in it to that extent. But if his experiments prove inconclusive either way, he is quit for his loss of time, no vital harm being done.

It will facilitate our discussion if we keep all these distinctions well in mind.

The next matter to consider is the actual psychology of human opinion. When we look at certain facts, it seems as if our passional and volitional nature lay at the root of all our convictions. When we look at others, it seems as if they could know nothing when the intellect had once said its say. Let us take the latter facts up first.

Does it not seem preposterous on the very face of it to talk of our opinions being modifiable at will? Can our will either help or hinder our intellect in its perceptions of truth? Can we, by just willing it, believe that Abraham Lincoln's existence is a myth, and that the portraits of him in *McClure's Magazine* are all of some one else? Can we, by any effort of our will, or by any strength of wish that it were true, believe ourselves well and about when we are roaring with rheumatism in bed, or feel certain that the sum of the two one-dollar bills in our pocket must be a hundred dollars? We can *say* any of these things, but we are absolutely impotent to believe them; and of just such things is the whole fabric of the truths that we do believe in made up,—matters of fact, immediate or remote, as Hume said, and relations between ideas, which are either there or not there for us if we see them so, and which if not there cannot be put there by any action of our own.

In Pascal's *Thoughts* there is a celebrated passage known in literature as Pascal's wager. In it he tries to force us into Christianity by reasoning as if our concern with truth resembled our concern with the stakes in a game of chance. Translated freely his words are these: You must either believe or not believe what God is—which will you do? Your human reason cannot say. A game is going on between you and the nature of things which at the day of judgment will bring out either heads or tails. Weigh what your gains and your losses would be if you should stake all you have on heads, or God's existence: if you win in such case, you gain eternal beatitude; if you lose, you lose nothing at all. If there were an infinity of chances, and only one for God in this wager, still you ought to stake your all on God; for though you surely risk a finite loss by this procedure, any finite loss is reasonable, even a certain one is reasonable, if there is but the possibility of infinite gain. Go, then, and take holy water, and have masses said; belief will come and stupefy your scruples,—*Cela vous fera croire et vous abêtira.* Why should you not? At bottom, what have you to lose?

You probably feel that when religious faith expresses itself thus, in the language of the gaming-table, it is put to its last trumps. Surely Pascal's own personal belief in masses and holy water had far other springs; and this celebrated page of his is but an argument for others, a last desperate snatch at a weapon against the hardness of the unbelieving heart. We feel that a faith in masses and holy water adopted willfully after such a mechanical calculation would lack the inner soul of faith's reality; and if we were ourselves in the place of the Deity, we would probably take particular pleasure in cutting off believers of this pattern from their infinite reward. It is evident that unless there be some pre-existing tendency to believe in masses and holy water, the option offered to the will by Pascal is not a living option. Certainly no Turk ever took to masses and holy water on its account; and even to us Protestants these means of salvation seem such foregone impossibilities that Pascal's logic, invoked for them specifically, leaves us unmoved. As well might the Mahdi write to us, saying, "I am the Expected One whom God has created in his effulgence. You shall be infinitely happy if you confess me; otherwise you shall be cut off from the light of the sun. Weigh, then, your infinite gain if I am genuine against your finite sacrifice if I am not!" His logic would be that of Pascal; but he would vainly use it on us, for the hypothesis he offers us is dead. No tendency to act on it exists in us to any degree.

The talk of believing by our volition seems, then, from one point of view, simply silly. From another point of view it is worse than silly, it is vile. When one turns to the magnificent edifice of the physical sciences, and sees how it was reared; what thousands of disinterested moral lives of men lie buried in its mere foundations; what patience and postponement, what choking down of preference, what submission to the icy laws of outer fact are wrought into its very stones and mortar; how absolutely impersonal it stands in its vast augustness,—then how besotted and contemptible seems every little sentimentalist who comes blowing his voluntary smoke-wreaths, and pretending to decide things from out of his private dream! Can we wonder if those bred in the rugged and manly school of science should feel like spewing such subjectivism out of their mouths? The whole system of loyalties which grow up in the schools of science go dead against its toleration; so that it is only natural that those who have caught the scientific fever should pass over to the opposite extreme, and write sometimes as if the incorruptibly truthful intellect ought positively to prefer bitterness and unacceptableness to the heart in its cup.

It fortifies my soul to know
That, though I perish, Truth is so—

sings Clough, while Huxley exclaims: "My only consolation lies in the reflection that, however bad our posterity may become, so far as they hold by the plain rule of not pretending to believe what they have no reason to believe, because it may be to their advantage so to pretend [the word 'pretend' is surely here redundant], they will not have reached the lowest depth of immorality." And that delicious *enfant terrible* Clifford writes: "Belief is desecrated when given to unproved and unquestioned statements for the solace and private pleasure of the believer. . . . Whoso would deserve well of his fellows in this matter will guard the purity of his belief with a very fanaticism of jealous care, lest at any time it should rest on an unworthy object, and catch a stain which can never be wiped away. . . . If [a] belief has been accepted on insufficient evidence [even though the belief be true, as Clifford on the same page explains] the pleasure is a stolen one. . . . It is sinful because it is stolen in defiance of our duty to mankind. That duty is to guard ourselves from such beliefs as from a pestilence which may shortly master our own body and then spread to the rest of the town. . . . It is wrong always, everywhere, and for every one, to believe anything upon insufficient evidence."

All this strikes one as healthy, even when expressed, as by Clifford, with somewhat too much of robustious pathos in the voice. Free-will and simple wishing do seem, in the matter of our credences, to be only fifth wheels to the coach. Yet if any one should thereupon assume that intellectual insight is what remains after wish and will and sentimental preference have taken wing, or that pure reason is what then settles our opinions, he would fly quite as directly in the teeth of the facts.

It is only our already dead hypotheses that our willing nature is unable to bring to life again. But what has made them dead for us is for the most part a previous action of our willing nature of an antagonistic kind. When I say 'willing nature,' I do not mean only such deliberate volitions as may have set up habits of belief that we cannot now escape from,—I mean all such factors of belief as fear and hope, prejudice and passion, imitation and partisanship, the circumpressure of our caste and set. As a matter of fact we find ourselves believing, we hardly know how or why. Mr. Balfour gives the name of 'authority' to all those influences, born of the intellectual climate, that make hypotheses possible or impossible for us, alive or dead. Here in this room, we all of us believe in molecules and the conservation of energy, in democracy and necessary progress, in Protestant Christianity and the duty of fighting for 'the doctrine of the immortal Monroe,' all for no reasons worthy of the name. We see into these matters with no more inner clearness, and probably with much less, than any disbeliever in them might possess. His unconventionality would probably have some grounds to show for its conclusions; but for us, not insight, but the *prestige* of the opinions, is what makes the spark shoot from them and light up our sleeping magazines of faith. Our reason is quite satisfied, in nine hundred and ninety-nine cases out of every thousand of us, if it can find a few arguments that will do to recite in case our credulity is criticised by some one else. Our faith is faith in some one else's faith, and in the greatest matters this is most the case. Our belief in truth itself, for instance, that there is a truth, and that our minds and it are made for each other,—what is it but a passionate affirmation of desire, in which our social system backs us up? We want to have a truth; we want to believe that our experiments and studies and discussions must put us in a continually better and better position towards it; and on this line we agree to fight out our thinking lives. But if a pyrrhonistic sceptic asks us *how we know* all this, can our logic find a reply? No! certainly it cannot. It is just one volition against another,—we willing to go in for life upon a trust or assumption which he, for his part, does not care to make.

As a rule we disbelieve all facts and theories for which we have no use. Clifford's cosmic emotions find no use for Christian feelings. Huxley belabors the bishops because there is no use for sacerdotalism in his scheme of life. Newman, on the contrary, goes over to Romanism, and finds all sorts of reasons good for staying there, because a priestly system is for him an organic need and delight. Why do so few 'scientists' even look at the evidence for telepathy, so called? Because they think, as a leading biologist, now dead, once said to me, that even if such a thing were true, scientists ought to band together to keep it suppressed and concealed. It would undo the uniformity of Nature and all sorts of other things without which scientists cannot carry on their pursuits. But if this very man had been shown something which as a scientist he might *do* with telepathy, he might not only have examined the evidence, but even have found it good enough. This very law which the logicians would impose upon us—if I may give the name of logicians to those who would rule out our willing nature here—is based on nothing but their own natural wish to exclude all elements for which they, in their professional quality of logicians, can find no use.

Evidently, then, our non-intellectual nature does influence our convictions. There are passional tendencies and volitions which run before and others which come after belief, and it is only the latter that are too late for the fair; and they are not too late when the previous passional work has been already in their own direction. Pascal's argument, instead of being powerless, then seems a regular clincher, and is the last stroke needed to make our faith in masses and holy water complete. The state of things is evidently far from simple; and pure insight and logic, whatever they might do ideally, are not the only things that really do produce our creeds.

Our next duty, having recognized this mixed-up state of affairs, is to ask whether it be simply reprehensible and pathological, or whether, on the contrary, we must treat it as a normal element in making up our minds. The thesis I defend is, briefly stated, this: *Our passional nature not only lawfully may, but must, decide an option between propositions, whenever it is a genuine option that cannot by its nature be decided on intellectual grounds; for to say, under such circumstances, "Do not decide, but leave the question open," is itself a passional decision,—just like deciding yes or no,—and is attended with the same risk of losing the truth.* The thesis thus abstractly expressed will, I trust, soon become quite clear. But I must first indulge in a bit more of preliminary work.

It will be observed that for the purposes of this discussion we are on 'dogmatic' ground,—ground, I mean, which leaves systematic philosophical scepticism altogether out of account. The postulate that there is truth, and that it is the destiny of our minds to attain it, we are deliberately resolving to make, though the sceptic will not make it. We part company with him, therefore, absolutely, at this point. But the faith that truth exists, and that our minds can find it, may be held in two ways. We may talk of the *empiricist* way and of the *absolutist* way of believing in truth. The absolutists in this matter say that we not only can attain to knowing truth, but we can *know when* we have attained to knowing it; while the empiricists think that although we may attain it, we cannot infallibly know when. To *know* is one thing, and to know for certain *that* we know is another. One may hold to the first being possible without the second; hence the empiricists and the absolutists, although neither of them is a sceptic in the usual philosophic sense of the term, show very different degrees of dogmatism in their lives.

If we look at the history of opinions, we see that the empiricist tendency has largely prevailed in science, while in philosophy the absolutist tendency has had everything its own way. The characteristic sort of happiness, indeed, which philosophies yield has mainly consisted in the conviction felt by each successive school or system that by it bottom-certitude had been attained. "Other philosophies are collections of opinions, mostly false; *my* philosophy gives standing-ground forever,"—who does not recognize in this the key-note of every system worthy of the name? A system, to be a system at all, must come as a *closed* system, reversible in this or that detail, perchance, but in its essential features never!

Scholastic orthodoxy, to which one must always go when one wishes to find perfectly clear statement, has beautifully elaborated this absolutist conviction in a doctrine which it calls that of 'objective evidence.' If, for example, I am unable to doubt that I now exist before you, that two is less than three, or that if all men are mortal then I am mortal too, it is because these things illumine my intellect irresistibly. The final ground of this objective evidence possessed by certain propositions is the *adaequatio intellectûs nostri cum rê*. The certitude it brings involves an *aptitudinem ad extorquendum certum assensum* on the part of the truth envisaged, and on the side of the subject a *quietem in cognitione*, when once the object is mentally received, that leaves no possibility of doubt behind; and in the whole transaction nothing operates but the *entitas ipsa* of the object and the *entitas ipsa* of the mind. We slouchy modern thinkers dislike to talk in Latin,—indeed, we dislike to talk in set terms at all; but at bottom our own state of mind is very much like this whenever we uncritically abandon ourselves: You believe in objective evidence, and I do. Of some things we feel that we are certain: we know, and we know that we do know. There is something that gives a click inside of us, a bell that strikes twelve, when the hands of our mental clock have swept the dial and meet over the meridian hour. The greatest empiricists among us are only empiricists on reflection: when left to their instincts, they dogmatize like infallible popes. When the Cliffords tell us how sinful it is to be Christians on such 'insufficient evidence,' insufficiency is really the last thing they have in mind. For them the evidence is absolutely sufficient, only it makes the other way. They believe so completely in an anti-christian order of the universe that there is no living option: Christianity is a dead hypothesis from the start.

But now, since we are all such absolutists by instinct, what in our quality of students of philosophy ought we to do about the fact? Shall we espouse and indorse it? Or shall we treat it as a weakness of our nature from which we must free ourselves, if we can?

I sincerely believe that the latter course is the only one we can follow as reflective men. Objective evidence and certitude are doubtless very fine ideals to play with, but where on this moonlit and dream-visited planet are they found? I am, therefore, myself a complete empiricist so far as my theory of human knowledge goes. I live, to be sure, by the practical faith that we must go on experiencing and thinking over our experience, for only thus can our opinions grow more true; but to hold any one of them—I absolutely do not care which—as if it never could be reinterpretable or corrigible, I believe to be a tremendously mistaken attitude, and I think that the whole history of philosophy will bear me out. There is but one indefectibly certain truth, and that is the truth that pyrrhonistic scepticism itself leaves standing,—the truth that the present phenomenon of consciousness exists. That, however, is the bare starting-point of knowledge, the mere admission of a stuff to be philosophized about. The various philosophies are but so many attempts at expressing what this stuff really is. And if we repair to our libraries what disagreement do we discover! Where is a certainly true answer found? Apart from abstract propositions of comparison (such as two and two are the same as four), propositions which tell us nothing by themselves about concrete reality, we find no proposition ever regarded by any one as evidently certain that has not either been called a falsehood, or at least had its truth sincerely questioned by some one else. The transcending of the axioms of geometry, not in play but in earnest, by certain of our contemporaries (as Zöllner and Charles H. Hinton), and the rejection of the whole Aristotelian logic by the Hegelians, are striking instances in point.

No concrete test of what is really true has ever been agreed upon. Some make the criterion external to the moment of perception, putting it either in revelation, the *consensus gentium*, the instincts of the heart, or the systematized experience of the race. Others make the perceptive moment its own test,—Descartes, for instance, with his clear and distinct ideas guaranteed by the veracity of God; Reid with his 'common-sense;' and Kant with his forms of synthetic judgment *a priori*. The inconceivability of the opposite; the capacity to be verified by sense; the possession of complete organic unity or self-relation, realized when a thing is its own other,—are standards which, in turn, have been used. The much lauded objective evidence is never triumphantly there; it is a mere aspiration or *Grenzbegriff*, marking the infinitely remote ideal of our thinking life. To claim that certain truths now possess it, is simply to say that when you think them true and they *are* true, then their evidence is objective, otherwise it is not. But practically one's conviction that the evidence one goes by is of the real objective brand, is only one more subjective opinion added to the lot. For what a contradictory array of opinions have objective evidence and absolute certitude been claimed! The world is rational through and through,—its existence is an ultimate brute fact; there is a personal God,— a personal God is inconceivable; there is an extra-mental physical world immediately known,—the mind can only know its own ideas; a moral imperative exists,—obligation is only the resultant of desires; a permanent spiritual principle is in every one,—there are only shifting states of mind; there is an endless chain of causes,—there is an absolute first cause; an eternal necessity,—a freedom; a purpose,—no purpose; a primal One,—a primal Many; a universal continuity,—an essential discontinuity in things; an infinity,—no infinity. There is this,—there is that; there is indeed nothing which some one has not thought absolutely true, while his neighbor deemed it absolutely false; and not an absolutist among them seems ever to have considered that the trouble may all the time be essential, and that the intellect, even with truth directly in its grasp, may have no infallible signal for knowing whether it be truth or no. When, indeed, one remembers that the most striking practical application to life of the doctrine of objective certitude has been the conscientious labors of the Holy Office of the Inquisition, one feels less tempted than ever to lend the doctrine a respectful ear.

But please observe, now, that when as empiricists we give up the doctrine of objective certitude, we do not thereby give up the quest or hope of truth itself. We still pin our faith on its existence, and still believe that we gain an ever better position towards it by systematically continuing to roll up experiences and think. Our great difference from the scholastic lies in the way we face. The strength of his system lies in the principles, the origin, the *terminus a quo* of his thought; for us the strength is in the outcome, the upshot, the *terminus ad quem*. Not where it comes from but what it leads to is to decide. It matters not to an empiricist from what quarter an hypothesis may come to him: he may have acquired it by fair means or by foul; passion may have whispered or accident suggested it; but if the total drift of thinking continues to confirm it, that is what he means by its being true.

One more point, small but important, and our preliminaries are done. There are two ways of looking at our duty in the matter of opinion,—ways entirely different, and yet ways about whose difference the theory of knowledge seems hitherto to have shown very little concern. *We must know the truth;* and *we must avoid error,*—these are our first and great commandments as would-be knowers; but they are not two ways of stating an identical commandment, they are two separable laws. Although it may indeed happen that when we believe the truth *A*, we escape as an incidental consequence from believing the falsehood *B*, it hardly ever happens that by merely disbelieving *B* we necessarily believe *A*. We may in escaping *B* fall into believing other falsehoods, *C* or *D*, just as bad as *B*; or we may escape *B* by not believing anything at all, not even *A*.

Believe truth! Shun error!—these, we see, are two materially different laws; and by choosing between them we may end by coloring differently our whole intellectual life. We may regard the chase for truth as paramount, and the avoidance of error as secondary; or we may, on the other hand, treat the avoidance of error as more imperative, and let truth take its chance. Clifford, in the instructive passage which I have quoted, exhorts us in the latter course. Believe nothing, he tells us, keep your mind in suspense forever, rather than by closing it on insufficient evidence incur the awful risk of believing lies. You, on the other hand, may think that the risk of being in error is a very small matter when compared with the blessings of real knowledge, and be ready to be duped many times in your investigation rather than postpone indefinitely the chance of guessing true. I myself find it impossible to go with Clifford. We must remember that these feelings of our duty about either truth or error are in any case only expressions of our passional life. Biologically considered, our minds are as ready to grind out falsehood as veracity, and he who says, "Better go without belief forever than believe a lie!" merely shows his own preponderant private horror of becoming a dupe. He may be critical of many of his desires and fears, but this fear he slavishly obeys. He cannot imagine any one questioning its binding force. For my own part, I have also a horror of being duped; but I can believe that worse things than being duped may happen to a man in this world: so Clifford's exhortation has to my ears a thoroughly fantastic sound. It is like a general informing his soldiers that it is better to keep out of battle forever than to risk a single wound. Not so are victories either over enemies or over nature gained. Our errors are surely not such awfully solemn things. In a world where we are so certain to incur them in spite of all our caution, a certain lightness of heart seems healthier than this excessive nervousness on their behalf. At any rate, it seems the fittest thing for the empiricist philosopher.

And now, after all this introduction, let us go straight at our question. I have said, and now repeat it, that not only as a matter of fact do we find our passional nature influencing us in our opinions, but that there are some options between opinions in which this influence must be regarded both as an inevitable and as a lawful determinant of our choice.

I fear here that some of you my hearers will begin to scent danger, and lend an inhospitable ear. Two first steps of passion you have indeed had to admit as necessary,—we must think so as to avoid dupery, and we must think so as to gain truth; but the surest path to those ideal consummations, you will probably consider, is from now onwards to take no further passional step.

Well, of course, I agree as far as the facts will allow. Wherever the option between losing truth and gaining it is not momentous, we can throw the chance of *gaining truth* away, and at any rate save ourselves from any chance of *believing falsehood*, by not making up our minds at all till objective evidence has come. In scientific questions, this is almost always the case; and even in human affairs in general, the need of acting is seldom so urgent that a false belief to act on is better than no belief at all. Law courts, indeed, have to decide on the best evidence attainable for the moment, because a judge's duty is to make law as well as to ascertain it, and (as a learned judge once said to me) few cases are worth spending much time over: the great thing is to have them decided on *any* acceptable principle, and got out of the way. But in our dealings with objective nature we obviously are recorders, not makers, of the truth; and decisions for the mere sake of deciding promptly and getting on to the next business would be wholly out of place. Throughout the breadth of physical nature facts are what they are quite independently of us, and seldom is there any such hurry about them that the risks of being duped by believing a premature theory need be faced. The questions here are always trivial options, the hypotheses are hardly living (at any rate not living for us spectators), the choice between believing truth or falsehood is seldom forced. The attitude of sceptical balance is therefore the absolutely wise one if we would escape mistakes. What difference, indeed, does it make to most of us whether we have or have not a theory of the Röntgen rays, whether we believe or not in mind-stuff, or have a conviction about the causality of conscious states? It makes no difference. Such options are not forced on us. On every account it is better not to make them, but still keep weighing reasons *pro et contra* with an indifferent hand.

I speak, of course, here of the purely judging mind. For purposes of discovery such indifference is to be less highly recommended, and science would be far less advanced than she is if the passionate desires of individuals to get their own faiths confirmed had been kept out of the game. See for example the sagacity which Spencer and Weismann now display. On the other hand, if you want an absolute duffer in an investigation, you must, after all, take the man who has no interest whatever in its results: he is the warranted incapable, the positive fool. The most useful investigator, because the most sensitive observer, is always he whose eager interest in one side of the question is balanced by an equally keen nervousness lest he become deceived. Science has organized this nervousness into a regular *technique,* her so-called method of verification; and she has fallen so deeply in love with the method that one may even say she has ceased to care for truth by itself at all. It is only truth as technically verified that interests her. The truth of truths might come in merely affirmative form, and she would decline to touch it. Such truth as that, she might repeat with Clifford, would be stolen in defiance of her duty to mankind. Human passions, however, are stronger than technical rules. "Le cœur a ses raisons," as Pascal says, "que la raison ne connaît pas;" and however indifferent to all but the bare rules of the game the umpire, the abstract intellect, may be, the concrete players who furnish him the materials to judge of are usually, each one of them, in love with some pet 'live hypothesis' of his own. Let us agree, however, that wherever there is no forced option, the dispassionately judicial intellect with no pet hypothesis, saving us, as it does, from dupery at any rate, ought to be our ideal.

The question next arises: Are there not somewhere forced options in our speculative questions, and can we (as men who may be interested at least as much in positively gaining truth as in merely escaping dupery) always wait with impunity till the coercive evidence shall have arrived? It seems *a priori* improbable that the truth should be so nicely adjusted to our needs and powers as that. In the great boarding-house of nature, the cakes and the butter and the syrup seldom come out so even and leave the plates so clean. Indeed, we should view them with scientific suspicion if they did.

Moral questions immediately present themselves as questions whose solution cannot wait for sensible proof. A moral question is a question not of what sensibly exists, but of what is good, or would be good if it did exist. Science can tell us what exists; but to compare the *worths,* both of what exists and of what does not exist, we must consult not science, but what Pascal calls our heart. Science herself consults her heart when she lays it down that the infinite ascertainment of fact and correction of false belief are the supreme goods for man. Challenge the statement, and science can only repeat it oracularly, or else prove it by showing that such ascertainment and correction bring man all sorts of other goods which man's heart in turn declares. The question of having moral beliefs at all or not having them is decided by our will. Are our moral preferences true or false, or are they only odd biological phenomena, making things good or bad for *us,* but in themselves indifferent? How can your pure intellect decide? If your heart does not *want* a world of moral reality, your head will assuredly never make you believe in one. Mephistophelian scepticism, indeed, will satisfy the head's play-instincts much better than any rigorous idealism can. Some men (even at the student age) are so naturally cool-hearted that the moralistic hypothesis never has for them any pungent life, and in their supercilious presence the hot young moralist always feels strangely ill at ease. The appearance of knowingness is on their side, of *naïveté* and gullibility on his. Yet, in the inarticulate heart of him, he clings to it that he is not a dupe, and that there is a realm in which (as Emerson says) all their wit and intellectual superiority is no better than the cunning of a fox. Moral scepticism can no more be refuted or proved by logic than intellectual scepticism can. When we stick to it that there *is* truth (be it of either kind), we do so with our whole nature, and resolve to stand or fall by the results. The sceptic with his whole nature adopts the doubting attitude; but which of us is the wiser. Omniscience only knows.

Turn now from these wide questions of good to a certain class of questions of fact, questions concerning personal relations, states of mind between one man and another. *Do you like me or not?*—for example. Whether you do or not depends, in countless instances, on whether I meet you half-way, am willing to assume that you must like me, and show you trust and expectation. The previous faith on my part in your liking's existence is in such cases what makes your liking come. But if I stand aloof, and refuse to budge an inch until I have objective evidence, until you shall have done something apt, as the absolutists say, *ad extorquendum assensum meum,* ten to one your liking never comes. How many women's hearts are vanquished by the mere sanguine insistence of some man that they *must* love him! he will not consent to the hypothesis that they cannot. The desire for a certain kind of truth here brings about that special truth's existence; and so it is in innumerable cases of other sorts. Who gains promotions, boons, appointments, but the man in whose life they are seen to play the part of live hypotheses, who discounts them, sacrifices other things for their sake before they have come, and takes risks for them in advance? His faith acts on the powers above him as a claim, and creates its own verification.

A social organism of any sort whatever, large or small, is what it is because each member proceeds to his own duty with a trust that the other members will simultaneously do theirs. Wherever a desired result is achieved by the co-operation of many independent persons, its existence as a fact is a pure consequence of the precursive faith in one another of those immediately concerned. A government, an army, a commercial system, a ship, a college, an athletic team, all exist on this condition, without which not only is nothing achieved, but nothing is even attempted. A whole train of passengers (individually brave enough) will be looted by a few highwaymen, simply because the latter can count on one another, while each passenger fears that if he makes a movement of resistance, he will be shot before any one else backs him up. If we believed that the whole car-full would rise at once with us, we should each severally rise, and train-robbing would never even be attempted. There are, then, cases where a fact cannot come at all unless a preliminary faith exists in its coming. *And where faith in a fact can help create the fact,* that would be an insane logic which should say that faith running ahead of scientific evidence is the 'lowest kind of immorality' into which a thinking being can fall. Yet such is the logic by which our scientific absolutists pretend to regulate our lives!

In truths dependent on our personal action, then, faith based on desire is certainly a lawful and possibly an indispensable thing.

But now, it will be said, these are all childish human cases, and have nothing to do with great cosmical matters, like the question of religious faith. Let us then pass on to that. Religions differ so much in their accidents that in discussing the religious question we must make it very generic and broad. What then do we now mean by the religious hypothesis? Science says things are; morality says some things are better than other things; and religion says essentially two things.

First, she says that the best things are the more eternal things, the overlapping things, the things in the universe that throw the last stone, so to speak, and say the final word. "Perfection is eternal,"—this phrase of Charles Secrétan seems a good way of putting this first affirmation of religion, an affirmation which obviously cannot yet be verified scientifically at all.

The second affirmation of religion is that we are better off even now if we believe her first affirmation to be true.

Now, let us consider what the logical elements of this situation are *in case the religious hypothesis in both its branches be really true.* (Of course, we must admit that possibility at the outset. If we are to discuss the question at all, it must involve a living option. If for any of you religion be a hypothesis that cannot, by any living possibility be true, then you need go no farther. (I speak to the 'saving remnant' alone.) So proceeding, we see, first, that religion offers itself as a *momentous* option. We are supposed to gain, even now, by our belief, and to lose by our non-belief, a certain vital good. Secondly, religion is a *forced* option, so far as that good goes. We cannot escape the issue by remaining sceptical and waiting for more light, because, although we do avoid error in that way *if religion be untrue,* we lose the good, *if it be true,* just as certainly as if we positively chose to disbelieve. It is as if a man should hesitate indefinitely to ask a certain woman to marry him because he was not perfectly sure that she would prove an angel after he brought her home. Would he not cut himself off from that particular angel-possibility as decisively as if he went and married some one else? Scepticism, then, is not avoidance of option; it is option of a certain particular kind of risk. *Better risk loss of truth than chance of error,*—that is your faith-vetoer's exact position. He is actively playing his stake as much as the believer is; he is backing the field against the religious hypothesis, just as the believer is backing the religious hypothesis against the field. To preach scepticism to us as a duty until 'sufficient evidence' for religion be found, is tantamount therefore to telling us, when in presence of the religious hypothesis, that to yield to our fear of its being error is wiser and better than to yield to our hope that it may be true. It is not intellect against all passions, then; it is only intellect with one passion laying down its law. And by what, forsooth, is the supreme wisdom of this passion warranted? Dupery for dupery, what proof is there that dupery through hope is so much worse than dupery through fear? I, for one, can see no proof; and I simply refuse obedience to the scientist's command to imitate his kind of option, in a case where my own stake is important enough to give me the right to choose my own form of risk. If religion be true and the evidence for it be still insufficient, I do not wish, by putting your extinguisher upon my nature (which feels to me as if it had after all some business in this matter), to forfeit my sole chance in life of getting upon the winning side,—that chance depending, of course, on my willingness to run the risk of acting as if my passional need of taking the world religiously might be prophetic and right.

All this is on the supposition that it really may be prophetic and right, and that, even to us who are discussing the matter, religion is a live hypothesis which may be true. Now, to most of us religion comes in a still further way that makes a veto on our active faith even more illogical. The more perfect and more eternal aspect of the universe is represented in our religions as having personal form. The universe is no longer a mere *It* to us, but a *Thou,* if we are religious; and any relation that may be possible from preson to person might be possible here. For instance, although in one sense we are passive portions of the universe, in another we show a curious autonomy, as if we were small active centres on our own account. We feel, too, as if the appeal of religion to us were made to our own active good-will, as if evidence might be forever withheld from us unless we met the hypothesis half-way. To take a trivial illustration: just as a man who in a company of gentlemen made no advances, asked a warrant for every concession, and believed no one's word without proof, would cut himself off by such churlishness from all the social rewards that a more trusting spirit would earn,—so here, one who should shut himself up in snarling logicality and try to make the gods extort his recognition willy-nilly, or not get it at all, might cut himself off forever from his only opportunity of making the gods' acquaintance. This feeling, forced on us we know not whence, that by obstinately believing that there are gods (although not to do so would be so easy both for our logic and our life) we are doing the universe the deepest service we can, seems part of the living essence of the religious hypothesis. If the hypothesis *were* true in all its parts, including this one, then pure intellectualism, with its veto on our making willing advances, would be an absurdity; and some participation of our sympathetic nature would be logically required. I, therefore, for one, cannot see my way to accepting the agnostic rules for truth-seeking, or wilfully agree to keep my willing nature out of the game. I cannot do so for this plain reason, that *a rule of thinking which would absolutely prevent me from acknowledging certain kinds of truth if those kinds of truth were really there, would be an irrational rule.* That for me is the long and short of the formal logic of the situation, no matter what the kinds of truth might materially be.

I confess I do not see how this logic can be escaped. But sad experience makes me fear that some of you may still shrink from radically saying with me, *in abstracto,* that we have the right to believe at our own risk any hypothesis that is live enough to tempt our will. I suspect, however, that if this is so, it is because you have got away from the abstract logical point of view altogether, and are thinking (perhaps without realizing it) of some particular religious hypothesis which for you is dead. The freedom to 'believe what we will' you apply to the case of some patent superstition; and the faith you think of is the faith defined by the schoolboy when he said, "Faith is when you believe something that you know ain't true." I can only repeat that this is misapprehension. *In concreto,* the freedom to believe can only cover living options which the intellect of the individual cannot by itself resolve; and living options never seem absurdities to him who has them to consider. When I look at the religious question as it really puts itself to concrete men, and when I think of all the possibilities which both practically and theoretically it involves, then this command that we shall put a stopper on our heart, instincts, and courage, and *wait*—acting of course meanwhile more or less as if religion were *not* true[1]—till doomsday, or till such time as our intellect and senses working together may have raked in evidence enough,—this command, I say, seems to me the queerest idol ever manufactured in the philosophic cave. Were we scholastic absolutists, there might be more excuse. If we had an infallible intellect with its objective certitudes, we might feel ourselves disloyal to such a perfect organ of knowledge in not trusting to it exclusively, in not waiting for its releasing word. But if we are empiricists, if we believe that no bell in us tolls to let us know for certain when truth is in our grasp, then it seems a piece of idle fantasticality to preach so solemnly our duty of waiting for the bell. Indeed we *may* wait if we will,—I hope you do not think that I am denying that,—but if we do so, we do so at our peril as much as if we believed. In either case we *act,* taking our life in our hands. No one of us ought to issue vetoes to the other, nor should we bandy words of abuse. We ought, on the contrary, delicately and profoundly to respect one another's mental freedom: then only shall we bring about the intellectual republic; then only shall we have that spirit of inner tolerance without which all our outer tolerance is soulless, and which is empiricism's glory; then only shall we live and let live, in speculative as well as in practical things.

I began by a reference to Fitz-James Stephen; let me end by a quotation from him. "What do you think of yourself? What do you think of the world? . . . These are questions with which all must deal as it seems good to them. They are riddles of the Sphinx, and in some way or other we must deal with them. . . . In all important transactions of life we have to take a leap in the dark. . . . If we decide to leave the riddles unanswered, that is a choice; if we waver in our answer, that, too, is a choice: but whatever choice we make, we make it at our peril. If a man chooses to turn his back altogether on God and the future, no one can prevent him; no one can show beyond reasonable doubt that he is mistaken. If a man thinks otherwise and acts as he thinks, I do not see that any one can prove that *he* is mistaken. Each must act as he thinks best; and if he is wrong, so much the worse for him. We stand on a mountain pass in the midst

1 Since belief is measured by action, he who forbids us to believe religion to be true, necessarily also forbids us to act as we should if we did believe it to be true. The whole defence of religious faith hinges upon action. If the action required or inspired by the religious hypothesis is in no way different from that dictated by the naturalistic hypothesis, then religious faith is a pure superfluity, better pruned away, and controversy about its legitimacy is a piece of idle trifling, unworthy of serious minds. I myself believe, of course, that the religious hypothesis gives to the world an expression which specifically determines our reactions, and makes them in a large part unlike what they might be on a purely naturalistic scheme of belief.

of whirling snow and blinding mist, through which we get glimpses now and then of paths which may be deceptive. If we stand still we shall be frozen to death. If we take the wrong road we shall be dashed to pieces. We do not certainly know whether there is any right one. What must we do? 'Be strong and of a good courage.' Act for the best, hope for the best, and take what comes. . . . If death ends all, we cannot meet death better."

Part Two

Social Progress and the Power of Intellect

Introduction

In an essay of 1917 reprinted herein, the young journalist Randolph Bourne denounced John Dewey for supporting American involvement in the Great War. The eminent philosopher had led contemporary American intellectuals to relinquish their independent critical voice, Bourne complained; no longer could these now-compromised intellectuals hope to be more than servants of the war administration of President Woodrow Wilson. This disagreement between Bourne and Dewey is one of the most famous episodes in the intellectual history of the first third of the twentieth century. This period—to which Part Two is devoted—is appropriately remembered for the fierceness of its conflicts over the proper responsibilities of intellectuals. And no one had done more than Dewey himself—two of whose contributions appear here—to convince men and women with intelligence and learning that the destiny of their society depended in large part on *them.* The systematic use of human intelligence and the proper education of the public could create, according to Dewey, a modern social order more responsive than any previous one to the vital needs of each and every individual. Bourne himself was something of a disciple of Dewey's and hence all the more troubled when Dewey himself interpreted differently than Bourne did the implications of ideals the two men shared. In a 1916 essay we find Bourne calling explicitly for the formation of a new "intelligentsia" with American society.

We often associate this confidence in the social value of intellect with the reform spirit that gave the Progressive Era its name. Edmund Wilson's 1931 plea to "progressive" intellectuals to lead political action illustrates the power of progressive ideals as late as the Great Depression. Yet not all believers in social progress made quite so much as Dewey and Bourne did of the powers of intellect, nor did all the early twentieth-century's celebrants of the latter find reform so promising an endeavor. Here in Part Two, Jane Addams represents those persistent reformers who placed more emphasis on moral than intellectual energies, and Thorstein Veblen represents those skilled analysts of society whose commitment to reform was ambiguous.

Although Margaret Mead was not inclined to theorize about the responsibilities of intellectuals, she was highly self-conscious about the role that intellectuals—especially social scientists like herself—could play in improving society. Although Mead's fellow social scientist Veblen had performed his critical role through an ironic and sarcastic description of the American leisure class, Mead herself, speaking in a frankly moralistic voice, contrasted the failings of her own modern, American culture to the apparent successes of some primitive societies studied by anthropologists. The enlargement of social science's space within American intellectual life is a prominent feature of the period.

Mead and Veblen represent also a relativistic perspective on social norms that became increasingly popular among educated Americans throughout the period covered by Part Two. This perspective is also evident in Dewey's work and in the strictures against natural law—included in Part Two—offered by Supreme Court Justice

Oliver Wendell Holmes, Jr. But perhaps the most powerful critic of absolute rules was William James, whose defense of pragmatism opens this Part.

James is a suitable choice to open "Social Progress and the Powers of Intellect" because he was both a social meliorist and an intellectual voluntarist. As a meliorist, he looked to the gradual improvement of the lives of human beings; as a voluntarist, he believed that truth was partly made by inquiring minds rather than merely uncovered when veils of illusion were removed. Both dispositions were manifest in James's pragmatism. James's specific philosophical doctrines were controversial, but in his devotion to active intellectual inquiry in the interests of human welfare, he was both an influence on and an emblem for the culture of educated Americans during the early decades of the twentieth century.

Recommendations for Further Reading

James T. Kloppenberg, *Uncertain Victory: Social Democracy and Progressivism in European and American Thought, 1870–1920* (New York, 1986); Morton G. White, *Social Thought in America: The Revolt Against Formalism* (New York, 2nd. ed., 1957); Henry F. May, *The End of American Innocence: A Study of the First Years of Our Own Time, 1912–1917* (New York, 1959); Jean B. Quandt, *From the Small Town to the Great Community: The Social Thought of Progressive Intellectuals* (New Brunswick, N.J., 1970); Robert Crunden, *Ministers of Reform: The Progressives' Achievement in American Civilization, 1889–1920* (New York, 1982); Christopher Lasch, *The New Radicalism in America, 1889–1963: The Emergence of the Intellectual as a Social Type* (New York, 1965); Rosalind Rosenberg, *Beyond Separate Spheres: Intellectual Roots of Modern Feminism* (New Haven, 1982); William E. Aiken, *Technocracy and the American Dream: The Technocrat Movement, 1900–1941* (Berkeley, 1977); Daniel J. Kevles, *In the Name of Eugenics: Genetics and the Uses of Human Heredity* (New York, 1985); Edward A. Purcell, Jr., *The Crisis of Democratic Theory* (Lexington, Ky., 1973); David A. Hollinger, *Morris R. Cohen and the Scientific Ideal* (Cambridge, Mass., 1975); Bruce Kuklick, *The Rise of American Philosophy: Cambridge, Massachusetts, 1860–1930* (New Haven, 1977); Alfred Kazin, *On Native Grounds: An Interpretation of Modern American Prose Literature,* 2nd ed. (New York, 1956); Lewis Perry, *Intellectual Life in America: A History* (New York, 1984), 317–78.

WILLIAM JAMES

"What Pragmatism Means"
1907

William James (1842–1910) opened *Pragmatism* (New York, 1907) with an account of the "present dilemma of philosophy" according to which individuals were asked to choose between two, obviously deficient alternatives: a "tender-minded" religious idealism, and a "tough-minded" scientific materialism. James offered pragmatism as a viable middle way. "What Pragmatism Means," which follows, is the second chapter of *Pragmatism*, following directly on James's characterization of philosophy's dilemma. Here, James projects his vision of an open, contingent universe within which people continually test and revise their store of "truths" against new experience. Although James's arguments were properly put to use by readers in many different secular contexts, James himself reminds readers of the religious preoccupations that render philosophy's dilemma so troubling to him: He returns to religion near the end of the essay and defends pragmatism as a means of widening the search for God. For additional information about James, including bibliography, see the headnote to "The Will to Believe," page 79.

Some years ago, being with a camping party in the mountains, I returned from a solitary ramble to find every one engaged in a ferocious metaphysical dispute. The *corpus* of the dispute was a squirrel—a live squirrel supposed to be clinging to one side of a tree-trunk; while over against the tree's opposite side a human being was imagined to stand. This human witness tries to get sight of the squirrel by moving rapidly round the tree, but no matter how fast he goes, the squirrel moves as fast in the opposite direction, and always keeps the tree between himself and the man, so that never a glimpse of him is caught. The resultant metaphysical problem is this: *Does the man go round the squirrel or not?* He goes round the tree, sure enough, and the squirrel is on the tree; but does he go round the squirrel? In the unlimited leisure of the wilderness, discussion had been worn threadbare. Every one had taken sides, and was obstinate; and the numbers on both sides were even. Each side, when I appeared, therefore appealed to me to make it a majority. Mindful of the scholastic adage that whenever you meet a contradiction you must make a distinction, I immediately sought and found one, as follows: "Which party is right," I said, "depends on what you *practically mean* by 'going round' the squirrel. If you mean passing from the north of him to the east, then to the south, and then to the west, and then to the north of him again, obviously the man does go round him, for he occupies these successive positions. But if on the contrary you mean being first in front of him, then on the right of him, then behind him, then on his left, and finally in front again, it is quite as obvious that the man fails to go round him, for by the compensating movements the squirrel makes, he keeps his belly turned towards the man all the time, and his back turned away. Make the distinction, and there is no occasion for any further dispute. You are both right and both wrong according as you conceive the verb 'to go round' in one practical fashion or the other."

Although one or two of the hotter disputants called my speech a shuffling evasion, saying they wanted no quibbling or scholastic hair-splitting, but meant just plain honest English "round," the majority seemed to think that the distinction had assuaged the dispute.

I tell this trivial anecdote because it is a pecularly simple example of what I wish now to speak of as *the pragmatic method*. The pragmatic method is primarily a method of settling metaphysical disputes that otherwise might be interminable. Is the world one or many?—fated or free?—material or spiritual?—here are notions either of which may or may not hold good of the world; and disputes over such notions are unending. The pragmatic method in such cases is to try to interpret each notion by tracing its respective practical consequences. What difference would it practically make to any one if this notion rather than that notion were true? If no practical difference whatever can be traced, then the alternatives mean practically the same thing, and all dispute is idle. Whenever a dispute is serious, we ought to be able to show some practical difference that must follow from one side or the other's being right.

A glance at the history of the idea will show you still better what pragmatism means. The term is derived from the same Greek word *κράγμα*, meaning action, from which our words "practice" and "practical" come. It was first introduced into philosophy by Mr. Charles Peirce in 1878. In an article entitled "How to Make Our Ideas Clear," in the *Popular Science Monthly* for January of that year Mr. Peirce, after pointing out that our beliefs are really rules for action, said that, to develop a thought's

Source: Pragmatism, William James (New York: Longman's 1907), 48–81.

meaning, we need only determine what conduct it is fitted to produce: that conduct is for us its sole significance. And the tangible fact at the root of all our thought-distinctions, however subtle, is that there is no one of them so fine as to consist in anything but a possible difference of practice. To attain perfect clearness in our thoughts of an object, then, we need only consider what conceivable effects of a practical kind the object may involve—what sensations we are to expect from it, and what reactions we must prepare. Our conception of these effects, whether immediate or remote, is then for us the whole of our conception of the object, so far as that conception has positive significance at all.

This is the principle of Peirce, the principle of pragmatism. It lay entirely unnoticed by any one for twenty years, until I, in an address before Professor Howison's Philosophical Union at the University of California, brought it forward again and made a special application of it to religion. By that date (1898) the times seemed ripe for its reception. The word "pragmatism" spread, and at present it fairly spots the pages of the philosophic journals. On all hands we find the "pragmatic movement" spoken of, sometimes with respect, sometimes with contumely, seldom with clear understanding. It is evident that the term applies itself conveniently to a number of tendencies that hitherto have lacked a collective name, and that it has "come to stay."

To take in the importance of Peirce's principle, one must get accustomed to applying it to concrete cases. I found a few years ago that Ostwald, the illustrious Leipzig chemist, had been making perfectly distinct use of the principle of pragmatism in his lectures on the philosophy of science, though he had not called it by that name.

"All realities influence our practice," he wrote me, "and that influence is their meaning for us. I am accustomed to put questions to my classes in this way: In what respects would the world be different if this alternative or that were true? If I can find nothing that would become different, then the alternative has no sense."

That is, the rival views mean practically the same thing, and meaning, other than practical, there is for us none. Ostwald in a published lecture gives this example of what he means. Chemists have long wrangled over the inner constitution of certain bodies called "tautomerous." Their properties seemed equally consistent with the notion that an instable hydrogen atom oscillates inside of them, or that they are instable mixtures of two bodies. Controversy raged, but never was decided. "It would never have begun," says Ostwald, "if the combatants had asked themselves what particualr experimental fact could have been made different by one or the other view being correct. For it would then have appeared that no difference of fact could possibly ensue; and the quarrel was as unreal as if, theorizing in primitive times about the raising of dough by yeast, one party should have invoked a 'brownie,' while another insisted on an 'elf' as the true cause of the phenomenon."

It is astonishing to see how many philosophical disputes collapse into insignificance the moment you subject them to this simple test of tracing a concrete consequence. There can *be* no difference anywhere that doesn't *make* a difference elsewhere—no difference in abstract truth that doesn't express itself in a difference in concrete fact and in conduct consequent upon that fact, imposed on somebody, somehow, somewhere, and somewhen. The whole function of philosophy ought to be to find out what definite difference it will make to you and me, at definite instants of our life, if this world-formula or that world-formula be the true one.

There is absolutely nothing new in the pragmatic method. Socrates was an adept at it. Aristotle used it methodically. Locke, Berkeley, and Hume made momentous contributions to truth by its means. Shadworth Hodgson keeps insisting that realities are only what they are "known as." But these forerunners of pragmatism used it in fragments: they were preluders only. Not until in our time has it generalized itself, become conscious of a universal mission, pretended to a conquering destiny. I believe in that destiny, and I hope I may end by inspiring you with my belief.

Pragmatism represents a perfectly familiar attitude in philosophy, the empiricist attitude, but it represents it, as it seems to me, both in a more radical and in a less objectionable form that it has ever yet assumed. A pragmatist turns his back resolutely and once for all upon a lot of inveterate habits dear to professional philosophers. He turns away from abstraction and insufficiency, from verbal solutions, from bad *a priori* reasons, from fixed principles, closed systems, and pretended absolutes and origins. He turns towards concreteness and adequacy, towards facts, towards action and towards power. That means the empiricist temper regnant and the rationalist temper sincerely given up. It means the open air and possibilities of nature, as against dogma, artificiality, and the pretence of finality in truth.

At the same time it does not stand for any special results. It is a method only. But the general triumph of that method would mean an enormous change in what I called in my last lecture the "temperament" of philosophy. Teachers of the ultra-rationalistic type would be frozen out, much as the courtier type is frozen out in republics, as the ultramontane type of priest is frozen out in Protestant lands. Science and metaphysics would come much nearer together, would in fact work absolutely hand in hand.

Metaphysics has usually followed a very primitive kind of quest. You know how men have always hankered after unlawful magic, and you know what a great part in magic *words* have always played. If you have his name, or the formula of incantation that binds him, you can control the spirit, genie, afrite, or whatever the power may be. Solomon knew the names of all the spirits, and having their names, he held them subject to his will. So the universe has always appeared to the natural mind as a kind of enigma, of which the key must be sought in the shape of some illuminating or power-bringing word or name. That word names the universe's *principle,* and to possess it is after a fashion to possess the universe itself. "God," "Matter," "Reason," "the Absolute," "Energy," are so many solving names. You can rest when you have them. You are at the end of your metaphysical quest.

But if you follow the pragmatic method, you cannot look on any such word as closing your quest. You must bring out of each word its practical cash-value, set it at work within the stream of your experience. It appears less as a solution, then, than as a program for more work, and more particularly as an indication of the ways in which existing realities may be *changed.*

Theories thus become instruments, not answers to enigmas, in which we can rest. We don't lie back upon them, we move forward, and, on occasion, make nature over again by their aid. Pragmatism unstiffens all our theories, limbers them up and sets each one at work. Being nothing essentially new, it harmonizes with many ancient philosophic tendencies. It agrees with nominalism, for instance, in always appealing to particulars; with utilitarianism in emphasizing practical aspects; with positivism in its disdain for verbal solutions, useless questions and metaphysical abstractions.

All these, you see, are *anti-intellectualist* tendencies. Against rationalism as a pretension and a method pragmatism is fully armed and militant. But, at the outset, at least, it stands for no particular results. It has no dogmas, and no doctrines save its method. As the young Italian pragmatist Papini has well said, it lies in the midst of our theories, like a corridor in a hotel. Innumerable chambers open out of it. In one you may find a man writing an atheistic volume; in the next some one on his knees praying for faith and strength; in a third a chemist investigating a body's properties. In a fourth a system of idealistic metaphysics is being excogitated; in a fifth the impossibility of metaphysics is being shown. But they all own the corridor, and all must pass through it if they want a practicable way of getting into or out of their respective rooms.

No particular results then, so far, but only an attitude of orientation, is what the pragmatic method means. *The attitude of looking away from first things, principles, "categories," supposed necessities; and of looking towards last things, fruits, consequences, facts.*

So much for the pragmatic method! You may say that I have been praising it rather than explaining it to you, but I shall presently explain it abundantly enough by showing how it works on some familiar problems. Meanwhile the word pragmatism has come to be used in a still wider sense, as meaning also a certain *theory of truth*. . . .

One of the most successfully cultivated branches of philosophy in our time is what is called inductive logic, the study of the conditions under which our sciences have evolved. Writers on this subject have begun to show a singular unanimity as to what the laws of nature and elements of fact mean, when formulated by mathematicians, physicists and chemists. When the first mathematical, logical, and natural uniformities, the first *laws,* were discovered, men were so carried away by the clearness, beauty and simplification that resulted, that they believed themselves to have deciphered authentically the eternal thoughts of the Almighty. His mind also thundered and reverberated in syllogisms. He also thought in comic sections, squares and roots and ratios, and geometrized like Euclid. He made Kepler's laws for the planets to follow; he made velocity increase proportionally to the time in falling bodies; he made the law of the sines for light to obey when refracted; he established the classes, orders, families and genera of plants and animals, and fixed the distances between them. He thought the archetypes of all things, and devised their variations; and when we rediscover any one of these his wondrous institutions, we seize his mind in its very literal intention.

But as the sciences have developed further, the notion has gained ground that most, perhaps all, of our laws are only approximations. The laws themselves, moreover, have grown so numerous that there is no counting them; and so many rival formulations are proposed in all the branches of science that investigators have become accustomed to the notion that no theory is absolutely a transcript of reality, but that any one of them may from some point of view be useful. Their great use is to summarize old facts and to lead to new ones. They are only a man-made language, a conceptual shorthand, as some one calls them, in which we write our reports of nature; and languages, as is well known, tolerate much choice of expression and many dialects.

Thus human arbitrariness has driven divine necessity from scientific logic. If I mention the names of Sigwart, Mach, Ostwald, Pearson, Milhaud, Poincaré, Duhem, Ruyssen, those of you who are students will easily identify the tendency I speak of, and will think of additional names.

Riding now on the front of this wave of scientific logic Messrs. Schiller and Dewey appear with the pragmatistic account of what truth everywhere signifies. Everywhere, these teachers say, "truth" in our ideas and beliefs means the same thing that it means in science. It means, they say, nothing but this, *that ideas (which themseles are but parts of our experience) become true just in so far as they help us to get into satisfactory relation with other parts of our experience,* to summarize them and get about among them by conceptual short-cuts instead of following the interminable succession of particular phenomena. Any idea upon which we can ride, so to speak; any idea that will carry us prosperously from any one part of our experience to any other part, linking things satisfactorily, working securely, simplifying, saving labor; is true for just so much, true in so far forth, true *instrumentally*. This is the "instrumental" view of truth taught so successfully at Chicago, the view that truth in our ideas means their power to "work," promulgated so brilliantly at Oxford.

Messrs. Dewey, Schiller, and their allies, in reaching this general conception of all truth, have only followed the example of geologists, biologists and philologists. In the establishment of these other sciences, the successful stroke was always to take some simple process actually observable in operation—as denudation by weather, say, or variation from parental type, or change of dialect by incorporation of new words and pronunciations—and then to generalize it, making it apply to all times, and produce great results by summating its effects thorugh the ages.

The observable process which Schiller and Dewey particularly singled out for generalization is the familiar one by which any individual settles into *new opinions*. The process here is always the same. The individual has a stock of old opinions already, but he meets a new experience that puts them to a strain. Somebody contradicts them; or in a reflective moment he discovers that they contradict each other; or he hears of facts with which they are incompatible; or desires arise in him which they cease to satisfy. The result is an inward trouble to which his mind till then had been a stranger, and from which he seeks to escape by modifying his previous mass of opinions. He saves as much of it as he can, for in this matter of belief we are all extreme conservatives. So he tries to change first this opinion, and then that (for they resist change very variously), until at last some new idea comes up which he can graft upon the ancient stock with a minimum of disturbance of the latter, some idea that mediates between the stock and the new experience and runs them into one another most felicitously and expediently.

This new idea is then adopted as the true one. It preserves the older stock of truths with a minimum of modification, stretching them just enough to make them admit the novelty, but conceiving that in ways as familiar as the case leaves possible. An *outrée* explanation, violating all our preconceptions, would never pass for a true account of a novelty. We should scratch round industriously till we found something less excentric. The most violent revolutions in an individual's beliefs leave most of his old order standing. Time and space, cause and effect, nature and history, and one's own biography remain untouched. New truth is always a go-between, a smoother-over of transitions. It marries old opinion to new fact so as ever to show a minimum of jolt, a maximum of continuity. We hold a theory true just in proportion to its success in solving this "problem of maxima and minima." But success in solving this problem is eminently a matter of approximation. We say this theory solves it on the whole more satisfactorily that that theory; but that means more satisfactorily to ourselves, and individuals will emphasize their points of satisfaction differently. To a certain degree, therefore, everything here is plastic.

The point I now urge you to observe particularly is the part played by the older truths. Failure to take account of it is the source of much of the unjust criticism levelled against pragmatism. Their influence is absolutely controlling. Loyalty to them is the first principle—in most cases it is the only principle; for by far the most usual way of handling phenomena so novel that they would make for a serious rearrangement of our preconception is to ignore them altogether, or to abuse those who bear witness for them.

You doubtless wish examples of this process of truth's growth, and the only trouble is their superabundance. The simplest case of new truth is of course the mere numerical addition of new kinds of facts, or of new single facts of old kinds, to our experience—an addition that involves no alteration in the old beliefs. Day follows day, and its contents are simply added. The new contents themselves are not true, they simple *come* and *are*. Truth is *what we say about* them, and when we say that they have come, truth is satisfied by the plain additive formula.

But often the day's contents oblige a rearrangment. If I should now utter piercing shrieks and act like a maniac on this platform, it would make many of you revise your ideas as to the probable worth of my philosophy. "Radium" came the other day as part of the day's content, and seemed for a moment to contradict our ideas of the whole order of nature, that order having come to be identified with what is called the conservation of energy. The mere sight of radium paying heat away indefinitely out of its own pocket seemed to violate that conservation. What to think? If the radiations from it were nothing but an escape of unsuspected "potential" energy, pre-existent inside of the atoms, the principle of conservation would be saved. The discovery of "helium" as the radiation's outcome, opened a way to this belief. So Ramsay's view is generally held to be true, because, although it extends our old ideas of energy, it causes a minimum of alteration in their nature.

I need not multiply instances. A new opinion counts as "true" just in proportion as it gratifies the individual's desire to assimilate the novel in his experience to his beliefs in stock. It must both lean on old truth and grasp new fact; and its success (as I said a moment ago) in doing this, is a matter for the individual's appreciation. When old truth grows, then, by new truth's addition, it is for subjective reasons. We are in the process and obey the reasons. That new idea is truest which performs most felicitously its function of satisfying our double urgency. It makes itself true, gets itself classed as true, by the way it works; grafting itself then upon the ancient body of truth, which thus grows much as a tree grows by the activity of a new layer of cambium.

Now Dewey and Schiller proceed to generalize this observation and to apply it to the most ancient parts of truth. They also once were plastic. They also were called true for human reasons. They also mediated between still earlier truths and what in those days were novel observations. Purely objective truth, truth in whose establishment the function of giving human satisfaction in marrying previous parts of experience with newer parts play no rôle whatever, is nowhere to be found. The reasons why we call things true is the reason why they *are* true, for "to be true" *means* only to perform this marriage-function.

The trail of the human serpent is thus over everything. Truth independent; truth that we *find* merely; truth no longer malleable to human need; truth incorrigible, in a word; such truth exists indeed superabundantly—or is supposed to exist by rationalistically minded thinkers; but then it means only the dead heart of the living tree, and its being there means only that truth also has its paleontology, and its "prescription," and may grow stiff with years of veteran service and petrified in men's regard by sheer antiquity. But how plastic even the oldest truths nevertheless really are has been vividly shows in our day by the transformation of logical and mathematical ideas, a transformation which seems even to be invading physics. The ancient formulas are reinterpreted as special expressions of much wider principles, principles that our ancestors never got a glimpse of in their present shape and formulation.

Mr. Schiller still gives to all this view of truth the name of "Humanism," but, for this doctrine too, the name of pragmatism seems fairly to be in the ascendant, so I will treat it under the name of pragmatism in these lectures.

Such then would be the scope of pragmatism—first, a method and second, a genetic theory of what is meant by truth.

. . . . . .

You will probably be surprised to learn . . . that Messrs. Schiller's and Dewey's theories have suffered a hailstorm of contempt and ridicule. All rationalism has risen against them. In influential quarters Mr. Schiller, in particular, has been treated like an impudent schoolboy who deserves a spanking. I should not mention this but for the fact that it throws so much sidelight upon that rationalistic temper to which I have opposed the temper of pragmatism. Pragmatism is uncomfortable away from facts. Rationalism is comfortable only in the presence of abstractions. This pragmatist talk about truths in the plural, about their utility and satisfactoriness, about the success with which they "work," etc., suggests to the typical intellectualist mind a sort of coarse lame second-rate makeshift article of truth. Such truths are not real truth. Such tests are merely subjective. As against this, objective truth must be something non-utilitarian, haughty, refined, remote, august, exalted. It must be an absolute reality. It must be what we *ought* to think unconditionally. The conditioned ways in which we *do* think are so much irrelevance and matter for psychology. Down with psychology, up with logic, in all this question!

See the exquisite contrast of the types of mind! The pragmatist clings to facts and concreteness, observes truth at its work in particular cases, and generalizes. Truth, for him, becomes a class-name for all sorts of definite working-values in experience. For the rationalist it remains a pure abstraction, to the bare name of which we must defer. When the pragmatist undertakes to show in detail just *why* we must defer, the rationalist is unable to recognize the concretes from which his own abstraction is taken. He accuses us of *denying* truth; whereas we have only sought to trace exactly why people follow it and always ought to follow it. Your typical ultra-abstractionist fairly shudders at concreteness: other things equal, he positively prefers the pale and spectral. If the two universes were offered, he would always choose the skinny outline rather than the rich thicket of reality. It is so much purer, clearer, nobler.

I hope that as these lectures go on, the concreteness and closeness to facts of the pragmatism which they advocate may be what approves itself to you as its most satisfactory pecularity. It only follows here the example of the sister-sciences, interpreting the unobserved by the observed. It brings old and new harmoniously together. It converts the absolutely empty notion of a static relation of "correspondence" (what that may mean we must ask later) between our minds and reality, into that of a rich and active commerce (that any one may follow in detail and understand) between particular thoughts of ours, and the great universe of other experiences in which they play their parts and have their uses.

But enough of this at present. The justification of what I say must be postponed.

I wish now to add a word in further explanation of the claim I made at our last meeting, that pragmatism may be a happy harmonizer of empiricist ways of thinking with the more religious demands of human beings.

Men who are strongly of the fact-loving temperament, you may remember me to have said, are liable to be kept at a distance by the small sympathy with facts which that philosophy from the present-day fashion of idealism offers them. It is far too intellectualistic. Old fashioned theism was bad enough, with its notion of God as an exalted monarch, made up of a lot of unintelligible or preposterous "attributes"; but, so long as it held strongly by the argument from design, it kept some touch with concrete realities. Since, however, Darwinsim has once for all displaced design from the minds of the "scientific," theism has lost that foothold; and some kind of an immanent or pantheistic deity working *in* things rather than above them is, if any, the kind recommended to our contemporary imagination. Aspirants to a philosophic religion turn, as a rule, more hopefully nowadays towards idealistic pantheism than towards the older dualistic theism, in spite of the fact that the latter still counts able defenders.

But, as I said in my first lecture, the brand of pantheism offered is hard for them to assimilate if they are lovers of facts, or empirically minded. It is the absolutistic brand, spurning the dust and reared upon pure logic. It keeps no connexion whatever with concreteness. Affirming the Absolute Mind, which is its substitute for God, to be the rational presupposition of all particulars of fact, whatever they may be, it remains supremely indifferent to what the particular facts in our world actually are. Be they what they may, the Absolute will father them. Like the sick lion in Esop's fable, all footprints lead into his den, but *nulla vestigia retrorsum*. You cannot redescend into the world of particulars by the Absolute's aid, or deduce any necessary consequences of detail important for your life from your idea of his nature. He gives you indeed the assurance that all is well with *Him*, and for his eternal way of thinking; but thereupon he leaves you to be finitely saved by your own temporal devices.

Far be it from me to deny the majesty of this conception, or its capacity to yield religious comfort to a most respectable class of minds. But from the human point of view, no one can pretend that it doesn't suffer from the faults of remoteness and abstractness. It is eminently a product of what I have ventured to call the rationalistic temper. It disdains empiricism's needs. It substitutes a pallid outline for the real world's richness. It is dapper, it is noble in the bad sense, in the sense in which to be noble is to be inapt for humble service. In this real world of sweat and dirt, it seems to me that when a view of things is "noble," that ought to count as a presumption against its truth, and as a philosophic disqualification. The prince of darkness may be a gentleman, as we are told he is, but whatever the God of earth and heaven is, he can surely be no gentleman. His menial services are needed in the dust of our human trials, even more than his dignity is needed in the empyrean.

Now pragmatism, devoted though she be to facts, has no such materialistic bias as ordinary empiricism labors under. Moreover, she has no objection whatever to the realizing of abstractions, so long as you get about among particulars with their aid and they actually carry you somewhere. Interested in no conclusions but those which our minds and our experiences work out together, she has no *a priori* prejudices against theology. *If theological ideas prove to have a value for concrete life, they will be true, for pragmatism, in the sense of being good for so much. For how much more they are true, will depend entirely on their relations to the other truths that also have to be acknowledged.*

What I said just now about the Absolute, of transcendental idealism, is a case in point. First, I called it majestic and said it yielded religious comfort to a class of minds, and then I accused it of remoteness and sterility. But so far as it affords such comfort, it surely is not sterile; it has that amount of value; it performs a concrete function. As a good pragmatist, I myself ought to call the Absolute true "in so far forth," then; and I unhesitatingly now do so.

But what does *true in so far forth* mean in this case? To answer, we need only apply the pragmatic method. What do believers in the Absolute mean by saying that their belief affords them comfort? They mean that since, in the Absolute finite evil is "overruled" already, we may, therefore, whenever we wish, treat the temporal as if it were potentially the eternal, be sure that we can trust its outcome, and, without sin, dismiss our fear and drop the worry of our finite responsibility. In short, they mean that we have a right ever and anon to take a moral holiday, to let the world wag in its own way, feeling that its issues are in better hands than ours and are none of our business.

The universe is a system of which the individual members may relax their anxieties occasionally, in which the don't-care mood is also right for men, and moral holidays in order—that, if I mistake not, is part, at least, of what the Absolute is "known-as," that is the great difference in our particular experiences which his being true makes, for us, that is his cash-value when he is pragmatically interpreted. Farther than that the ordinary lay-reader in philosophy who thinks favorably of absolute idealism does not venture to sharpen his conceptions. He can use the Absolute for so much, and so much is very precious. He is pained at hearing you speak incredulously of the Absolute, therefore, and disregards your criticism because they deal with aspects of the conception that he fails to follow.

If the Absolute means this, and means no more than this, who can possibly deny the truth of it? To deny it would be to insist that men should never relax, and that holidays are never in order.

I am well aware how odd it must seem to some of you to hear me say that an idea is "true" so long as to believe it is profitable to our lives. That it is *good*, for as much as it profits, you will gladly admit. If what we do by its aid is good, you will allow the idea itself to be good in so far forth, for we are the better for possessing it. But is it not a strange misuse of the word "truth," you will say, to call ideas also "true" for this reason?

To answer this difficulty fully is impossible at this stage of my account. You touch here upon the very central point of Messrs. Schiller's, Dewey's, and my own doctrine of truth, which I cannot discuss with detail until my sixth lecture. Let me now say only this, the truth is *one species of good*, and not, as is usually supposed, a category distinct from good, and co-ordinate with it. *The true is the name of whatever proves itself to be good in the way of belief, and good, too, for definite, assignable reasons.* Surely you must admit this, that if there were *no* good for life in true ideas, or if the knowledge of them were positively disadvantageous and false ideas the only useful ones, then the current notion that truth is divine and precious, and its pursuit a duty, could never have grown up or become a dogma. In a world like that, our duty would be to *shun* truth, rather. But in this world, just as certain foods are not only agreeable to our taste, but good for our teeth, our stomach, and our tissues; so certain ideas are not only agreeable to think about, or agreeable as supporting other ideas that we are fond of, but they are also helpful in life's practical struggles. If there be any life that it is really better we should lead, and if there be any idea which, if believed in, would help us to lead that life, then it would be really *better for us* to believe in that idea, *unless, indeed, belief in it incidentally clashed with other greater vital benefits.*

"What would be better for us to believe!" This sounds very like a definition of truth. It comes very near to saying "what we *ought* to believe"; and in *that* definition none of you would find any oddity. Ought we ever not to believe what it is *better for us* to believe? And can we then keep the notion of what is better for us, and what is true for us, permanently apart?

Pragmatism says no, and I fully agree with her. Probably you also agree, so far as the abstract statement goes, but with a suspicion that if we practically did believe everything that made for good in our own personal lives, we should be found indulging all kinds of fancies about this world's affairs, and all kinds of sentimental supersititions about a world hereafter. Your suspicion here is undoubtedly well founded, and it is evident that something happens when you pass from the abstract to the concrete that complicates the situation.

I said just now that what is better for us to believe is true *unless the belief incidentally clashes with some other vital benefit.* Now in real life what vital benefits is any particualr belief of our most liable to clash with? What ideed except the vital benefits yielded by *other beliefs* when these prove incompatible with the first ones? In other words, the greatest enemy of any one of our truths may be the rest of our truths. Truths have once for all this desperate instinct of self-preservation and of desire to extinguish whatever contradicts them. My belief in the Absolute, based on the good it does me, must run the gauntlet of all my other beliefs. Grant that it may be true in giving me a moral holiday. Nevertheless, as I conceive it—and let me speak now confidentially, as it were, and merely in my own private person—it clashes with other truths of mine whose benefits I hate to give up on its account. It happens to be associated with a kind of logic of which I am the enemy, I find that it entangles me in metaphysical paradoxes that are inacceptable, etc., etc. But as I have enough trouble in life already without adding the trouble of carrying these intellectual inconcistencies, I personally just give up the Absolute. I just *take* my moral holidays; or else as a professional philosopher, I try to justify them by some other principle.

If I could restrict my notion of the Absolute to its bare holiday-giving value, it wouldn't clash with my other truths. But we cannot easily thus restrict our hypotheses. They carry supernumerary features, and these it is that clash so. My disbelief in the Absolute means then disbelief in those other supernumerary features, for I fully believe in the legitimacy of taking moral holidays.

You see by this what I meant when I called pragmatism a mediator and reconciler and said, borrowing the word from Papini, that she "unstiffens" our theories. She has in fact no prejudices whatever, no obstructive dogmas, no rigid canons of what shall count as proof. She is completely genial. She will entertain any hypothesis, she will consider any evidence. It follows that in the religious field she is at a great advantage both over positivistic empiricism, with its anti-theological bias, and over religious rationalism, with its exclusive interest in the remote, the noble, the simple, and the abstract in the way of conception.

In short, she widens the field of search for God. Rationalism sticks to logic and the empyrean. Empiricism sticks to the external senses. Pragmatism is willing to take anything, to follow either logic or the senses and to count the humblest and most personal experiences. She will count mystical experiences if they have practical consequences. She will take a God who lives in the very dirt of private fact—if that should seem a likely place to find him.

Her only test of probable truth is what works best in the way of leading us, what fits every part of life best and combines with the collectivity of experience's demands, nothing being omitted. If theological ideas should do this, if the notion of God, in particular, should prove to do it, how could pragmatism possibly deny God's existence? She could see no meaning in treating as "not true" a notion that was pragmatically so successful. What other kind of truth could there be, for her, than all this agreement with concrete reality?

THORSTEIN VEBLEN

Selection from *The Theory of the Leisure Class* 1899

No evolutionary social theorist put Darwinian formulations to more slashingly critical uses than Thorstein Veblen (1857–1929). At once playful, angry, mordant, and ironic, Veblen etched in *The Theory of the Leisure Class: An Economic Study of Institutions* (New York, 1899) a picture of the turn-of-the-century "new rich" that endures in American literature as well as political economy. In our selections from this book reprinted below, Veblen depicts people of this class as social parasites who only "retard the adaptation of human nature to the exigencies of modern industrial life." Veblen went on to write a number of other influential books of social theory, including *The Engineers and the Price System* (New York, 1921) and an important collection of writings, *The Place of Science in Modern Civilisation and Other Essays* (New York, 1919). Eager as he was to see men and women of intellect lead society, he remained alienated from the prevailing academic culture of his time. He bounced from faculty to faculty and died in a tiny cabin in the hills above Stanford University. The most comprehensive study of his life and thought was written shortly after his death: Joseph Dorfmann, *Thorstein Veblen and His America* (New York, 1934). A more recent, highly provocative analysis is John P. Diggins, *The Bard of Savagery: Thorstein Veblen and Modern Social Theory* (New York, 1978). Perhaps the most succinct and penetrating introduction to Veblen's ideas is C. Wright Mills's introduction to the Mentor edition of *The Theory of the Leisure Class* (New York, 1953), vi–xix.

The life of man in society, just like the life of other species, is a struggle for existence, and therefore it is a process of selective adaptation. The evolution of social structure has been a process of natural selection of institutions. The progress which has been and is being made in human institutions and in human character may be set down, broadly, to a natural selection of the fittest habits of thought and to a process of enforced adaptation of individuals to an environment which has progressively changed with the growth of the community and with the changing institutions under which men have lived. Institutions are not only themselves the result of a selective and adaptive process which shapes the prevailing or dominant types of spiritual attitude and aptitudes; they are at the same time special methods of life and of human relations, and are therefore in their turn efficient factors of selection. So that the changing institutions in their turn make for a further selection of individuals endowed with the fittest temperament, and a further adaptation of individual temperament and habits to the changing environment through the formation of new institutions.

The forces which have shaped the development of human life and of social structure are no doubt ultimately reducible to terms of living tissue and material environment; but proximately, for the purpose in hand, these forces may best be stated in terms of an environment, partly human, partly non-human, and a human subject with a more or less definite physical and intellectual constitution. Taken in the aggregate or average, this human subject is more or less variable; chiefly, no doubt, under a rule of selective conservation of favourable variations. The selection of favourable variations is perhaps in great measure a selective conservation of ethnic types. In the life history of any community whose population is made up of a mixture of divers ethnic elements, one or another of several persistent and relatively stable types of body and of temperament rises into dominance at any given point. The situation, including the institutions in force at any given time, will favour the survival and dominance of one type of character in preference to another; and the type of man so selected to continue and to further elaborate the institutions handed down from the past will in some considerable measure shape these institutions in his own likeness. But apart from selection as between relatively stable types of character and habits of mind, there is no doubt simultaneously going on a process of selective adaptation of habits of thought within the general range of aptitudes which is characteristic of the dominant ethnic type or types. There may be a variation in the fundamental character of any population by selection between relatively stable types; but there is also a variation due to adaptation in detail within the range of the type, and to selection between specific habitual views regarding any given social relation or group of relations.

For the present purpose, however, the question as to the nature of the adaptive process—whether it is chiefly a selection between stable types of temperament and character, or chiefly an adaptation of men's habits of thought to changing circumstances—is of less importance than the fact that, by one method or another, institutions change and develop. Institutions must change with changing circumstances, since they are of the nature of an habitual method of responding to the stimuli which these changing circumstances afford. The development of these institutions is the development of society. The institutions are, in substance, prevalent habits of thought with respect to particular relations and particular functions of the individual and of

Source: The Theory of the Leisure Class: An Economic Study of Institutions, Thorstein Veblen (New York: Macmillan, 1899), 188–213, 233–444

the community; and the scheme of life, which is made up of the aggregate of institutions in force at a given time or at a given point in the development of any society, may, on the psychological side, be broadly characterised as a prevalent spiritual attitude or a prevalent theory of life. As regards its generic features, this spiritual attitude or theory of life is in the last analysis reducible to terms of a prevalent type of character.

The situation of to-day shapes the institutions of to-morrow through a selective, coercive process, by acting upon men's habitual view of things, and so altering or fortifying a point of view or a mental attitude handed down from the past. The institutions—that is to say the habits of thought—under the guidance of which men live are in this way received from an earlier time; more or less remotely earlier, but in any event they have been elaborated in and received from the past. Institutions are products of the past process, are adapted to past circumstances, and are therefore never in full accord with the requirements of the present. In the nature of the case, this process of selective adaptation can never catch up with the progressively changing situation in which the community finds itself at any given time; for the environment, the situation, the exigencies of life which enforce the adaptation and exercise the selection, change from day to day; and each successive situation of the community in its turn tends to obsolescence as soon as it has been established. When a step in the development has been taken, this step itself constitutes a change of situation which requires a new adaptation; it becomes the point of departure for a new step in the adjustment, and so on interminably.

It is to be noted then, although it may be a tedious truism, that the institutions of to-day—the present accepted scheme of life—do not entirely fit the situation of today. At the same time, men's present habits of thought tend to persist indefinitely, except as circumstances enforce a change. These institutions which have so been handed down, these habits of thought, points of view, mental attitudes and aptitudes, or what not, are therefore themselves a conservative factor. This is the factor of social inertia, psychological inertia, conservatism.

Social structure changes, develops, adapts itself to an altered situation, only through a change in the habits of thought of the several classes of the community; or in the last analysis, through a change in the habits of thought of the individuals which make up the community. The evolution of society is substantially a process of mental adaptation on the part of individuals under the stress of circumstances which will no longer tolerate habits of thought formed under and conforming to a different set of circumstances in the past. For the immediate purpose it need not be a question of serious importance whether this adaptive process is a process of selection and survival of persistent ethnic types or a process of individual adaptation and an inheritance of acquired traits.

Social advance, especially as seen from the point of view of economic theory, consists in a continued progressive approach to an approximately exact "adjustment of inner relations to outer relations"; but this adjustment is never definitively established, since the "outer relations" are subject to constant change as a consequence of the progressive change going on in the "inner relations." But the degree of approximation may be greater or less, depending on the facility with which an adjustment is made. A readjustment of men's habits of thought to conform with the exigencies of an altered situation is in any case made only tardily and reluctantly, and only under the coercion exercised by a situation which has made the accredited views untenable. The readjustment of institutions and habitual views to an altered environment is made in response to pressure from without; it is of the nature of a response to stimulus. Freedom and facility of readjustment, that is to say capacity for growth in social structure, therefore depends in great measure on the degree of freedom with which the situation at any given time acts on the individual members of the community—the degree of exposure of the individual members to the constraining forces of the environment. If any portion or class of society is sheltered from the action of the environment in any essential respect, that portion of the community, or that class, will adapt its views and its scheme of life more tardily to the altered general situation; it will in so far tend to retard the process of social transformation. The wealthy leisure class is in such a sheltered position with respect to the economic forces that make for change and readjustment. And it may be said that the forces which make for a readjustment of institutions, especially in the case of a modern industrial community, are, in the last analysis, almost entirely of an economic nature.

Any community may be viewed as an industrial or economic mechanism, the structure of which is made up of what is called its economic institutions. These institutions are habitual methods of carrying on the life process of the community in contact with the material environment in which it lives. When given methods of unfolding human activity in this given environment have been elaborated in this way, the life of the community will express itself with some facility in these habitual directions. The community will make use of the forces of the environment for the purposes of its life according to methods learned in the past and embodied in these institutions. But as population increases, and as men's knowledge and skill in directing the forces of nature widen, the habitual methods of relation between the members of the group, and the habitual method of carrying on the life process of the group as a whole no longer give the same result as before; nor are the resulting conditions of life distributed and apportioned in the same manner or with the same effect among the various members as before. If the scheme according to which the life process of the group was carried on under the earlier conditions gave approximately the highest attainable result—under the circumstances—in the way of efficiency or facility of the life process of the group; then the same scheme of life unaltered will not yield the highest result attainable in this respect under the altered conditions. Under the altered conditions of population, skill, and knowledge, the facility of life as carried on according to the traditional scheme may not be lower than under the earlier conditions; but the chances are always that it is less than might be if the scheme were altered to suit the altered conditions.

The group is made up of individuals, and the group's life is the life of individuals carried on in at least ostensible severalty. The group's accepted scheme of life is the consensus of views held by the body of these individuals as to what is right, good, expedient, and beautiful in the way of human life. In the redistribution of the conditions of life that comes of the altered method of dealing with the environment, the outcome is not an equable change in the facility of life throughout the group. The altered conditions may increase the facility of life for the group as a whole, but the redistribution will usually result in a decrease of facility or fulness of life for some members of the group. An advance in technical methods, in population, or in industrial organisation will require at least some of the members of the community to change their habits of life, if they are to enter with facility and effect into the altered industrial methods; and in doing so they will be unable to live up to the received notions as to what are the right and beautiful habits of life.

Any one who is required to change his habits of life and his habitual relations to his fellow-men will feel the discrepancy between the method of life required of him by the newly arisen exigencies, and the traditional scheme of life to which he is accustomed. It is the individuals placed in this position who have the liveliest incentive to reconstruct the received scheme of life and are most readily persuaded to accept new standards; and it is through the need of the means of livelihood that men are placed in such a position. The pressure exerted by the environment upon the group, and making for a readjustment of the group's scheme of life, impinges upon the members of the group in the form of pecuniary exigencies; and it is owing to this fact—that external forces are in great part translated into the form of pecuniary or economic exigencies—it is owing to this fact that we can say that the forces which count toward a readjustment of institutions in any modern industrial community are chiefly economic forces; or more specifically, these forces take the form of pecuniary pressure. Such a readjustment as is here contemplated is substantially a change in men's views as to what is good and right, and the means through which a change is wrought in men's apprehension of what is good and right is in large part the pressure of pecuniary exigencies.

Any change in men's views as to what is good and right in human life makes its way but tardily at the best. Especially is this true of any change in the direction of what is called progress; that is to say, in the direction of divergence from the archaic position—from the position which may be accounted the point of departure at any step in the social evolution of the community. Retrogression, reapproach to a standpoint to which the race has been long habituated in the past, is easier. This is especially true in case the development away from this past standpoint has not been due chiefly to a substitution of an ethnic type whose temperament is alien to the earlier standpoint.

The cultural stage which lies immediately back of the present in the life history of Western civilisation is what has here been called the quasi-peaceable stage. At this quasi-peaceable stage the law of status is the dominant feature in the scheme of life. There is no need of pointing out how prone the men of to-day are to revert to the spiritual attitude of mastery and of personal subservience which characterises that stage. It may rather be said to be held in an uncertain abeyance by the economic exigencies of to-day, than to have been definitively supplanted by a habit of mind that is in full accord with these later-developed exigencies. The predatory and quasi-peaceable stages of economic evolution seem to have been of long duration in the life history of all the chief ethnic elements which go to make up the populations of the Western culture. The temperament and the propensities proper to those cultural stages have, therefore, attained such a persistence as to make a speedy reversion to the broad features of the corresponding psychological constitution inevitable in the case of any class or community which is removed from the action of those forces that make for a maintenance of the later-developed habits of thought.

It is a matter of common notoriety that when individuals, or even considerable groups of men, are segregated from a higher industrial culture and exposed to a lower cultural environment, or to an economic situation of a more primitive character, they quickly show evidence of reversion toward the spiritual features which characterise the predatory type; and it seems probable that the dolicho-blond type of European man is possessed of a greater facility for such reversion to barbarism than the other ethnic elements with which that type is associated in the Western culture. Examples of such a reversion on a small scale abound in the later history of migration and colonisation. Except for the fear of offending that chauvinistic patriotism which is so characteristic a feature of the predatory culture, and the presence of which is frequently the most striking mark of reversion in modern communities, the case of the American colonies might be cited as an example of such a reversion on an unusually large scale, though it was not a reversion of very large scope.

The leisure class is in great measure sheltered from the stress of those economic exigencies which prevail in any modern, highly organised industrial community. The exigencies of the struggle for the means of life are less exacting for this class than for any other; and as a consequence of this privileged position we should expect to find it one of the least responsive of the classes of society to the demands which the situation makes for a further growth of institutions and a readjustment to an altered industrial situation. The leisure class is the conservative class. The exigencies of the general economic situation of the community do not freely or directly impinge upon the members of this class. They are not required under penalty of forfeiture to change their habits of life and their theoretical views of the external world to suit the demands of an altered industrial technique, since they are not in the full sense an organic part of the industrial community. Therefore these exigencies do not readily produce, in the members of this class, that degree of uneasiness with the existing order which alone can lead any body of men to give up views and methods of life that have become habitual to them. The office of the leisure class in social evolution is to retard the movement and to conserve what is obsolescent. This proposition is by no means novel; it has long been one of the commonplaces of popular opinion.

The prevalent conviction that the wealthy class is by nature conservative has been popularly accepted without much aid from any theoretical view as to the place and relation of that class in the cultural development. When an explanation of this class conservatism is offered, it is commonly the invidious one that the wealthy class opposes innovation because it has a vested interest, of an unworthy sort, in maintaining the present conditions. The explanation here put forward imputes no unworthy motive. The opposition of the class to changes in the cultural scheme is instinctive, and does not rest primarily on an interested calculation of material advantages; it is an instictive revulsion at any departure from the accepted way of doing and of looking at things—a revulsion common to all men and only to be overcome by stress of circumstances. All change in habits of life and of thought is irksome. The difference in this respect between the wealthy and the common run of mankind lies not so much in the motive which prompts to conservatism as in the degree of exposure to the economic forces that urge a change. The members of the wealthy class do not yield to the demand for innovation as readily as other men because they are not constrained to do so.

This conservatism of the wealthy class is so obvious a feature that it has even come to be recognised as a mark of respectability. Since conservatism is a characteristic of the wealthier and therefore more reputable portion of the community, it has acquired a certain honorific or decorative value. It has become prescriptive to such an extent that an adherence to conservative views is comprised as a matter of course in our notions of respectability; and it is imperatively incumbent on all who would lead a blameless life in point of social repute. Conservatism, being an upper-class characteristic, is decorous; and conversely, innovation, being a lower-class phenomenon, is vulgar. The first and most unreflected element in that instinctive revulsion and reprobation with which we turn from all social innovators is this sense of the essential vulgarity of the thing. So that even in cases where one recognises the substantial merits of the case for which the innovator is spokesman—as may easily happen if the evils which he seeks to remedy are sufficiently remote in point of time or space or personal contact—still one cannot but be sensible of the fact that the innovator is a person with whom it is at least distasteful to be associated, and from whose social contact one must shrink. Innovation is bad form.

The fact that the usages, actions, and views of the well-to-do leisure class acquire the character of a prescriptive canon of conduct for the rest of society, gives added weight and reach to the conservative influence of that class. It makes it incumbent upon all reputable people to follow their lead. So that, by virtue of its high position as the avatar of good form, the wealthier class comes to exert a retarding influence upon social development far in excess of that which the simple numerical strength of the class would assign it. Its prescriptive example acts to greatly stiffen the resistance of all other classes against any innovation, and to fix men's affections upon the good institutions handed down from an earlier generation.

There is a second way in which the influence of the leisure class acts in the same direction, so far as concerns hindrance to the adoption of a conventional scheme of life more in accord with the exigencies of the time. This second method of upper-class guidance is not in strict consistency to be brought under the same category as the instinctive conservatism and aversion to new modes of thought just spoken of; but it may as well be dealt with here, since it has at least this much in common with the conservative habit of mind that it acts to retard innovation and the growth of social structure. The code of proprieties, conventionalities, and usages in vogue at any given time and among any given people has more or less of the character of an organic whole; so that any appreciable change in one point of the scheme involves something of a change or readjustment at other points also, if not a reorganisation all along the line. When a change is made which immediately touches only a minor point in the scheme, the consequent derangement of the structure of conventionalities may be inconspicuous; but even in such a case it is safe to say that some derangement of the general scheme, more or less far-reaching, will follow. On the other hand, when an attempted reform involves the suppression or thorough-going remodelling of an institution of first-rate importance in the conventional scheme, it is immediately felt that a serious derangement of the entire scheme would result; it is felt that a readjustment of the structure to the new form taken on by one of its chief elements would be a painful and tedious, if not a doubtful process.

In order to realise the difficulty which such a radical change in any one feature of the conventional scheme of life would involve, it is only necessary to suggest the suppression of the monogamic family, or of the agnatic system of consanguinity, or of private property, or of the theistic faith, in any country of the Western civilisation; or suppose the suppression of ancestor worship in China, or of the caste system in India, or of slavery in Africa, or the establishment of equality of the sexes in Mohammedan countries. It needs no argument to show that the derangement of the general structure of conventionalities in any of these cases would be very considerable. In order to effect such an innovation a very far-reaching alteration of men's habits of thought would be involved also at other points of the scheme than the one immediately in question. The aversion to any such innovation amounts to a shrinking from an essentially alien scheme of life.

The revulsion felt by good people at any proposed departure from the accepted methods of life is a familiar fact of everyday experience. It is not unusual to hear those persons who dispense salutary advice and admonition to the community express themselves forcibly upon the far-reaching pernicious effects which the community would suffer from such relatively slight changes as the disestablishment of the Anglican Church, an increased facility of divorce, adoption of female suffrage, prohibition of the manufacture and sale of intoxicating beverages, abolition or restriction of inheritance, etc. Any one of these innovations would, we are told, "shake the social structure to its base," "reduce society to chaos," "subvert the foundations of morality," "make life intolerable," "confound the order of nature," etc. These various locutions are, no doubt, of the nature of hyperbole; but, at the same time, like all overstatement, they are evidence of a lively sense of the gravity of the consequences which they are intended to describe. The effect of these and like innovations in deranging the accepted scheme of life is felt to be of much graver consequence than the simple alteration of an isolated item in a series of contrivances for the convenience of men in society. What is true in so obvious a degree of innovations of first-rate importance is true in a less degree of changes of a smaller immediate importance. The aversion to change is in large part an aversion to the bother of making the readjustment which any given change will necessitate; and this solidarity of the system of institutions of any given culture or of any given people strengthens the instinctive resistance offered to any change in men's habits of thought, even in matters which, taken by themselves, are of minor importance.

A consequence of this increased reluctance, due to the solidarity of human institutions, is that any innovation calls for a greater expenditure of nervous energy in making the necessary readjustment than would otherwise be the case. It is not only that a change in established habits of thought is distasteful. The process of readjustment of the accepted theory of life involves a degree of mental effort—a more or less protracted and laborious effort to find and to keep one's bearings under the altered circumstances. This process requires a certain expenditure of energy, and so presumes, for its successful accomplishment, some surplus of energy beyond that absorbed in the daily struggle for subsistence. Consequently it follows that progress is hindered by underfeeding and excessive physical hardship, no less effectually than by such a luxurious life as will shut out discontent by cutting off the occasion for it. The abjectly poor, and all those persons whose energies are entirely absorbed by the struggle for daily sustenance, are conservative because they cannot afford the effort of taking thought for the day after to-morrow; just as the highly prosperous are conservative because they have small occasion to be discontented with the situation as it stands to-day.

From this proposition it follows that the institution of a leisure class acts to make the lower classes conservative by withdrawing from them as much as it may of the means of sustenance, and so reducing their consumption, and consequently their available energy, to such a point as to make them incapable of the effort required for the learning and adoption of new habits of thought. The accumulation of wealth at the upper end of the pecuniary scale implies privation at the lower end of the scale. It is a commonplace that, wherever it occurs, a considerable degree of privation among the body of the people is a serious obstacle to any innovation.

This direct inhibitory effect of the unequal distribution of wealth is seconded by an indirect effect tending to the same result. As has already been seen, the imperative example set by the upper class in fixing the canons of reputability fosters the practice of conspicuous consumption. The prevalence of conspicuous consumption as one of the main elements in the standard of decency among all classes is of course not traceable wholly to the example of the wealthy leisure class, but the practice and the insistence on it are no doubt strengthened by the example of the leisure class. The requirements of decency in this matter are very considerable and very imperative; so that even among classes whose pecuniary position is sufficiently strong to admit a consumption of goods considerably in excess of the subsistence minimum, the disposable surplus left over after the more imperative physical needs are satisfied is not infrequently diverted to the purpose of a conspicuous decency, rather than to added physical comfort and fulness of life. Moreover, such surplus energy as is available is also likely to be expended in the acquisition of goods for conspicuous consumption or conspicuous hoarding. The result is that the requirements of pecuniary reputability tend (1) to leave but a scanty subsistence minimum available for other than conspicuous consumption, and (2) to absorb any surplus energy which may be available after the bare physical necessities of life have been provided for. The outcome of the whole is a strengthening of the general conservative attitude of the community. The institution of a leisure class hinders cultural development immediately (1) by the inertia proper to the class itself, (2) through its prescriptive example of conspicuous waste and of conservatism, and (3) indirectly through that system of unequal distribution of wealth and sustenance on which the institution itself rests.

To this is to be added that the leisure class has also a material interest in leaving things as they are. Under the circumstances prevailing at any given time this class is in a privileged position, and any departure from the existing order may be expected to work to the detriment of the class rather than the reverse. The attitude of the class, simply as influenced by its class interest, should therefore be to let well-enough alone. This interested motive comes in to supplement the strong instinctive bias of the class, and so to render it even more consistently conservative than it otherwise would be.

All this, of course, has nothing to say in the way of eulogy or deprecation of the office of the leisure class as an exponent and vehicle of conservatism or reversion in social structure. The inhibition which it exercises may be salutary or the reverse. Whether it is the one or the other in any given case is a question of casuistry rather than of general theory. There may be truth in the view (as a question of policy) so often expressed by the spokesmen of the conservative element, that without some such substantial and consistent resistance to innovation as is offered by the conservative well-to-do classes, social innovation and experiment would hurry the community into untenable and intolerable situations; the only possible result of which would be discontent and disastrous reaction. All this, however, is beside the present argument.

But apart from all deprecation, and aside from all question as to the indispensability of some such check on headlong innovation, the leisure class, in the nature of things, consistently acts to retard that adjustment to the environment which is called social advance or development. The characteristic attitude of the class may be summed up in the maxim: "Whatever is, is right"; whereas the law of natural selection, as applied to human institutions, gives the axiom: "Whatever is, is wrong." Not that the institutions of to-day are wholly wrong for the purposes of the life of to-day, but they are, always and in the nature of things, wrong to some extent. They are the result of a more or less inadequate adjustment of the methods of living to a situation which prevailed at some point in the past development; and they are therefore wrong by something more than the interval which separates the present situation from that of the past. "Right" and "wrong" are of course here used without conveying any reflection as to what ought or ought not to be. They are applied simply from the (morally colourless) evolutionary standpoint and are intended to designate compatibility or incompatibility with the effective evolutionary process. The institution of a leisure class, by force of class interest and instinct, and by precept and prescriptive example, makes for the perpetuation of the existing maladjustment of institutions, and even favours a reversion to a somewhat more archaic scheme of life; a scheme which would be still farther out of adjustment with the exigencies of life under the existing situation even than the accredited, obsolescent scheme that has come down from the immediate past.

But after all has been said on the head of conservation of the good old ways, it remains true that institutions change and develop. There is a cumulative growth of customs and habits of thought; a selective adaptation of conventions and methods of life. Something is to be said of the office of the leisure class in guiding this growth as well as in retarding it; but little can be said here of its relation to institutional growth except as it touches the institutions that are primarily and immediately of an economic character. These institutions—the economic structure—may be roughly distinguished into two classes or categories, according as they serve one or the other of two divergent purposes of economic life.

To adapt the classical terminology, they are institutions of acquisition or of production; or to revert to terms already employed in a different connection in earlier chapters, they are pecuniary or industrial institutions; or in still other terms, they are institutions serving either the invidious or the non-invidious economic interest. The former category have to do with "business," the latter with industry, taking the latter word in the mechanical sense. The latter class are not often recognised as institutions, in great part because they do not immediately concern the ruling class, and are, therefore, seldom the subject of legislation or of deliberate convention. When they do receive attention they are commonly approached from the pecuniary or business side; that being the side or phase of economic life that chiefly occupies men's deliberations in our time, especially the deliberations of the upper classes. These classes have little else than a business interest in things economic, and on them at the same time it is chiefly incumbent to deliberate upon the community's affairs.

The relation of the leisure (that is, propertied non-industrial) class to the economic process is a pecuniary relation—a relation of acquisition, not of production; of exploitation, not of serviceability. Indirectly their economic office may, of course, be of the utmost importance to the economic life process; and it is by no means here intended to depreciate the economic function of the propertied class or of the captains of industry. The purpose is simply to point out what is the nature of the relation of these classes to the industrial process and to economic institutions. Their office is of a parasitic character, and their interest is to divert what substance they may to their own use, and to retain whatever is under their hand. The conventions of the business world have grown up under the selective surveillance of this principle of predation or parasitism. They are conventions of ownership; derivatives, more or less remote, of the ancient predatory culture. But these pecuniary institutions do not entirely fit the situation of to-day, for they have grown up under a past situation differing somewhat from the present. Even for effectiveness in the pecuniary way, therefore, they are not as apt as might be. The changed industrial life requires changed methods of acquisition; and the pecuniary classes have some interest in so adapting the pecuniary institutions as to give them the best effect for acquisition of private gain that is compatible with the continuance of the industrial process out of which this gain arises. Hence there is a more or less consistent trend in the leisure-class guidance of institutional growth, answering to the pecuniary ends which shape leisure-class economic life.

The effect of the pecuniary interest and the pecuniary habit of mind upon the growth of institutions is seen in those enactments and conventions that make for security of property, enforcement of contracts, facility of pecuniary transactions, vested interests. Of such bearing are changes affecting bankruptcy and receiverships, limited liability, banking and currency, coalitions of labourers or employers, trusts and pools. The community's institutional furniture of this kind is of immediate consequence only to the propertied classes, and in proportion as they are propertied; that is to say, in proportion as they are to be ranked with the leisure class. But indirectly these conventions of business life are of the gravest consequence for the industrial process and for the life of the community. And in guiding the institutional growth in this respect, the pecuniary classes, therefore, serve a purpose of the most serious importance to the community, not only in the conservation of the accepted social scheme, but also in shaping the industrial process proper.

The immediate end of this pecuniary instituional structure and of its amelioration is the greater facility of peaceable and orderly exploitation; but its remoter effects far outrun this immediate object. Not only does the more facile conduct of business permit industry and extra-industrial life to go on with less perturbation; but the resulting elimination of disturbances and complications calling for an exercise of astute discrimination in everyday affairs acts to make the pecuniary class itself superfluous. As fast as pecuniary transactions are reduced to routine, the captain of industry can be dispensed with. This consummation, it is needless to say, lies yet in the indefinite future. The ameliorations wrought in favour of the pecuniary interest in modern institutions tend, in another field, to substitute the "soulless" joint-stock corporation for the captain, and so they make also for the dispensability of the great leisure-class function of ownership. Indirectly, therefore, the bent given to the growth of economic institutions by the leisure-class influence is of very considerable industrial consequence.

. . . . . .

The institution of a leisure class has an effect not only upon social structure but also upon the individual character of the members of society. So soon as a given proclivity or a given point of view has won acceptance as an authoritative standard or norm of life it will react upon the character of the members of the society which has accepted it as a norm. It will to some extent shape their habits of thought and will exercise a selective surveillance over the development of men's aptiudes and inclinations. This effect is wrought partly by a coercive, educational adaptation of the habits of all individuals, partly by a selective elimination of the unfit individuals and lines of descent. Such human material as does not lend itself to the methods of life imposed by the accepted scheme suffers more or less elimination as well as repression. The principles of pecuniary emulation and of industrial exemption have in this way been erected into canons of life, and have become coercive factors of some importance in the situation to which men have to adapt themselves.

These two broad principles of conspicuous waste and industrial exemption affect the cultural development both by guiding men's habits of thought, and so controlling the growth of institutions, and by selectively conserving certain traits of human nature that conduce to facility of life under the leisure-class scheme, and so controlling the effective temper of the community. The proximate tendency of the institution of a leisure class in shaping human character runs in the direction of spiritual survival and reversion. Its effect upon the temper of a community is of the nature of an arrested spiritual development.

. . . . . .

The constituency of the leisure class is kept up by a continual selective process, whereby the individuals and lines of descent that are eminently fitted for an aggressive pecuniary competition are withdrawn from the lower classes. In order to reach the upper levels the aspirant must have, not only a fair average complement of the pecuniary aptitudes, but he must have these gifts in such an eminent degree as to overcome very material difficulties that stand in the way of his ascent. Barring accidents, the *nouveaux arrivés* are a picked body.

This process of selective admission has, of course, always been going on; ever since the fashion of pecuniary emulation set in,—which is much the same as saying, ever since the institution of a leisure class was first installed. But the precise ground of selection has not always been the same, and the selective process has therefore not always given the same results. In the early barbarian, or predatory stage proper, the test of fitness was prowess, in the naïve sense of the word. To gain entrance to the class, the candidate must be gifted with clannishness, massiveness, ferocity, unscrupulousness, and tenacity of purpose. These were the qualities that counted toward the accumulation and continued tenure of wealth. The economic basis of the leisure class, then as later, was the possession of wealth; but the methods of accumulating wealth, and the gifts required for holding it, have changed in some degree since the early days of the predatory culture. In consequence of the selective process the dominant traits of the early barbarian leisure class were bold aggression, an alert sense of status, and a free resort to fraud. The members of the class held their place by tenure of prowess. In the later barbarian culture society attained settled methods of acquisition and possession under the quasi-peaceable régime of status. Simple aggression and unrestrained violence in great measure gave place to shrewd practise and chicanery, as the best approved method of accumulating wealth. A different range of aptitudes and propensities would then be conserved in the leisure class. Masterful aggression, and the coorelative massiveness, together with a ruthlessly consistent sense of status, would still count among the most splendid traits of the class. These have remained in our traditions as the typical "aristocratic virtues." But with these were associated an increasing complement of the less obtrusive pecuniary virtues; such as providence, prudence, and chicane. As time has gone on, and the modern peaceable stage of pecuniary culture has been approached, the last-named range of aptitudes and habits has gained in relative effectiveness for pecuniary ends, and they have counted for relatively more in the selective process under which admission is gained and place is held in the leisure class.

The ground of selection has changed, until the aptitudes which now qualify for admission to the class are the pecuniary aptitudes only. What remains of the predatory barbarian traits is the tenacity of purpose or consistency of aim which distinguished the successful predatory barbarian from the peaceable savage whom he supplanted. But this trait can not be said characteristically to distinguish the pecuniarily successful upper-class man from the rank and file of the industrial classes. The training and the selection to which the latter are exposed in modern industrial life give a similarly decisive weight to this trait. Tenacity of purpose may rather be said to distinguish both these classes from two others: the shiftless ne'er-do-well and the lower-class delinquent. In point of natural endowment the pecuniary man compares with the delinquent in much the same way as the industrial man compares with the good-natured shiftless dependent. The ideal pecuniary man is like the ideal delinquent in his unscrupulous conversion of goods and persons to his own ends, and in a callous disregard of the feelings and wishes of others and of the remoter effects of his actions; but he is unlike him in possessing a keener sense of status, and in working more consistenly and far-sightedly to a remoter end. The kinship of the two types of temperament is further shown in a proclivity to "sport" and gambling, and a relish of aimless emulation. The ideal pecuniary man also shows a curious kinship with the delinquent in one of the concomitant variations of the predatory human nature. The delinquent is very commonly of a superstitious habit of mind; he is a great believer in luck, spells, divination and destiny, and in omens and shamanistic ceremony. Where circumstances are favourable, this proclivity is apt to express itself in a certain servile devotional fervour and a punctilious attention to devout observances; it may perhaps be better characterised as devoutness than as religion. At this point the temperament of the delinquent has more in common with the pecuniary and leisure classes than with the industrial man or with the class of shiftless dependents.

Life in a modern industrial community, or in other words life under the pecuniary culture, acts by a process of selection to develop and conserve a certain range of aptitudes and propensities. The present tendency of this selective process is not simply a reversion to a given, immutable ethnic type. It tends rather to a modification of human nature differing in some respects from any of the types or variants transmitted out of the past. The objective point of the evolution is not a single one. The temperament which the evolution acts to establish as normal differs from any one of the archaic variants of human nature in its greater stability of aim—greater singleness of purpose and greater persistence in effort. So far as concerns economic theory, the objective point of the selective process is on the whole single to this extent; although there are minor tendencies of considerable importance diverging from this line of development. But apart from this general trend the line of development is not single. As concerns economic theory, the development in other respects runs on two divergent lines. So far as regards the selective conservation of capacities or aptitudes in individuals, these two lines may be called the pecuniary and the industrial. As regards the conservation of propensities, spiritual attitude, or animus, the two may be called the invidious or self-regarding and the non-invidious or economical. As regards the intellectual or cognitive bent of the two directions of growth, the former may be characterised as the personal standpoint, of conation, qualitative relation, status, or worth; the latter as the impersonal standpoint, of sequence, quantitative relation, mechanical efficiency, or use.

The pecuniary employments call into action chiefly the former of these two ranges of aptitudes and propensities, and act selectively to conserve them in the population. The industrial employments, on the other hand, chiefly exercise the latter range, and act to conserve them. An exhaustive psychological analysis will show that each of these two ranges of aptitudes and propensities is but the multiform expression of a given temperamental bent. By force of the unity or singleness of the individual, the aptitudes, animus, and interests comprised in the first-named range belong together as expressions of a given variant of human nature. The like is true of the latter range. The two may be conceived as alternative directions of human life, in such a way that a given individual inclines more or less consistently to the one or the other. The tendency of the pecuniary life is, in a general way, to conserve the barbarian temperament, but with the substitution of fraud and prudence, or administrative ability, in place of that predilection for physical damage that characterises the early barbarian. This substitution of chicane in place of devastation takes place only in an uncertain degree. Within the pecuniary employments the selective action runs pretty consistently in this direction, but the discipline of pecuniary life, outside the competition for gain, does not work consistently to the same effect. The discipline of modern life in the consumption of time and goods does not act unequivocally to eliminate the aristocratic virtues or to foster the bourgeois virtues. The conventional scheme of decent living calls for a considerable exercise of the earlier barbarian traits. . . .

From what has been said, it appears that the leisure-class life and the leisure-class scheme of life should further the conservation of the barbarian temperament; chiefly of the quasi-peaceable, or bourgeois, variant, but also in some measure of the predatory variant. In the absence of disturbing factors, therefore, it should be possible to trace a difference of temperament between the classes of society. The aristocratic and the bourgeois virtues—that is to say the destructive and pecuniary traits—should be found chiefly among the upper classes, and the industrial virtues—that is to say the peaceable traits—chiefly among the classes given to mechanical industry.

In a general and uncertain way this holds true, but the test is not so readily applied nor so conclusive as might be wished. There are several assignable reasons for its partial failure. All classes are in a measure engaged in the pecuniary struggle, and in all classes the possession of the pecuniary traits counts towards the success and survival of the individual. Wherever the pecuniary culture prevails, the selective process by which men's habits of thought are shaped, and by which the survival of rival lines of descent is decided, proceeds proximately on the basis of fitness for acquisition. Consequently, if it were not for the fact that pecuniary efficiency is on the whole incompatible with industrial efficiency, the selective action of all occupations would tend to the unmitigated dominance of the pecuniary temperament. The result would be the installation of what has been known as the "economic man," as the normal and definitive type of human nature. But the "economic man," whose only interest is the self-regarding one and whose only human trait is prudence, is useless for the purposes of modern industry.

The modern industry requires an impersonal, non-invidious interest in the work in hand. Without this the elaborate processes of industry would be impossible, and would, indeed, never have been conceived. This interest in work differentiates the workman from the criminal on the one hand, and from the captain of industry on the other. Since work must be done in order to the continued life of the community, there results a qualified selection favouring the spiritual aptitude for work, within a certain range of occupations. This much, however, is to be conceded, that even within the industrial occupations the selective elimination of the pecuniary traits is an uncertain process, and that there is consequently an appreciable survival of the barbarian temperament even within these occupations. On this account there is at present no broad distinction in this respect between the leisure-class character and the character of the common run of the population.

The whole question as to a class distinction in respect of spiritual make-up is also obscured by the presence, in all classes of society, of acquired habits of life that closely simulate inherited traits and at the same time act to develop in the entire body of the population the traits which they simulate. These acquired habits, or assumed traits of character, are not commonly of an aristocratic cast. The prescriptive position of the leisure class as the exemplar of reputability has imposed many features of the leisure-class theory of life upon the lower classes; with the result that there goes on, always and throughout society, a more or less persistent cultivation of these aristocratic traits. On this ground also these traits have a better chance of survival among the body of the people than would be the case if it were not for the precept and example of the leisure class. As one channel, and an important one, through which this transfusion of aristocratic views of life, and consequently more or less archaic traits of character, goes on, may be mentioned the class of domestic servants. These have their notions of what is good and beautiful shaped by contact with the master class and carry the preconceptions so acquired back among their low-born equals, and so disseminate the higher ideals abroad through the community without the loss of time which this dissemeination might otherwise suffer. The saying, "Like master, like man," has a greater significance than is commonly appreciated for the rapid popular acceptance of many elements of upper-class culture.

There is also a further range of facts that go to lessen class differences as regards the survival of the pecuniary virtues. The pecuniary struggle produces an underfed class, of large proportions. This underfeeding consists in a deficiency of the necessaries of life or of the necessaries of a decent expenditure. In either case the result is a closely enforced struggle for the means with which to meet the daily needs; whether it be the physical or the higher needs. The strain of self-assertion against odds takes up the whole energy of the individual; he bends his efforts to compass his own invidious ends alone, and becomes continually more narrowly self-seeking. The industrial traits in this way tend to obsolescence through disuse. Indirectly, therefore, by imposing a scheme of pecuniary decency and by withdrawing as much as may be of the means of life from the lower classes, the institution of a leisure class acts to conserve the pecuniary traits in the body of the population. The result is an assimilation of the lower classes to the type of human nature that belongs primarily to the upper classes only.

It appears, therefore, that there is no wide difference in temperament between the upper and the lower classes; but it appears also that the absence of such a difference is in good part due to the prescriptive example of the leisure class and to the popular acceptance of those broad principles of conspicuous waste and pecuniary emulation on which the institution of a leisure class rests. The institution acts to lower the industrial efficiency of the community and retard the adaptation of human nature to the exigencies of modern industrial life. It affects the prevalent or effective human nature in a conservative direction, (1) by direct transmission of archaic traits, through inheritance within the class and wherever the leisure-class blood is transfused outside the class, and (2) by conserving and fortifying the traditions of the archaic régime, and so making the chances of survival of barbarian traits greater also outside the range of transfusion of leisure-class blood. . . .

JOHN DEWEY

"The Influence of Darwinism on Philosophy" 1909

Selection from *The Public and Its Problems* 1927

The name of John Dewey (1859–1952) is appropriately remembered in relation to so many ideas and movements that his role in the history of American thought is less easily indicated in a sourcebook of this kind than is the role of perhaps any other thinker represented within these two covers. Dewey did creative work in philosophy and psychology as early as the mid-1880s, rose to national prominence in the Progressive Era as a theorist of educational and political reform, and went on during the 1920s and 1930s to publish almost a dozen influential books that renewed his standing as the preeminent liberal intellectual in the United States. In his ninetieth year he coauthored a treatise on epistemology. The first of the two selections is ostensibly about Darwin, but this essay of 1909 actually gives voice to a vision of the whole of Western intellectual history since ancient times. This history is significant to Dewey as the setting in which human beings have come into possession of the scientific method, which he defines as a willingness to focus on changing particulars of experience instead of attending to the fixed essences and final causes that he associates with nonscientific thought. Darwin, seen in this perspective, takes up where Galileo left off and extends the method of science to plants and animals, thus opening up even the life of our own species as a field for experimental inquiry and hence for social engineering: Scientific method can now become "a method of moral and political diagnosis and prognosis." Dewey was firmly convinced that the advancement of science in human affairs was compatible with democracy and that science itself was, indeed, an expression of democracy. The second selection, taken from *The Public and Its Problems* (1927), formulates the political ideal of democracy in terms of a community of inquiry. Dewey's prose was oblique, but he managed to convey an earnest and almost messianic faith in the powers of human intelligence. His contemporary, Justice Oliver Wendell Holmes, Jr., caught well this quality when he observed that Dewey spoke as God would have spoken "had He been inarticulate but keenly desirous to tell you how it was." For a very effective, brief overview of Dewey's thought and career, see the introduction to David Sidorsky, ed., *John Dewey: The Essential Writings* (New York, 1977). The extent to which Dewey departed from his "pragmatic" forebears, Peirce and William James, is emphasized in a provocative and valuable book by R. W. Sleeper, *The Necessity of Pragmatism: John Dewey's Conception of Philosophy* (New Haven, 1986). Dewey's perpetuation in a secular context of the sensibility of liberal Protestantism is traced in Bruce Kuklick, *Churchmen and Philosophers: From Jonathan Edwards to John Dewey* (New Haven, 1985). Dewey's contributions as a theorist of liberalism are helpfully clarified in James T. Kloppenberg, *Uncertain Victory: Social Democracy and Progressivism in European and American Thought, 1870–1920* (New York, 1986).

"The Influence of Darwinism on Philosophy" 1909

That the publication of the *Origin of Species* marked an epoch in the development of the natural sciences is well known to the layman. That the combination of the very words origin and species embodied an intellectual revolt and introduced a new intellectual temper is easily overlooked by the expert. The conceptions that had reigned in the philosophy of nature and knowledge for two thousand years, the conceptions that had become the familiar furniture of the mind, rested on the assumption of the superiority of the fixed and final; they rested upon treating change and origin as signs of defect and unreality. In laying hands upon the sacred ark of absolute permanency, in treating the forms that had been regarded as types of fixity and perfection as originating and passing away, the *Origin of Species* introduced a mode of thinking that in the end was bound to transform the logic of knowledge, and hence the treatment of morals, politics, and religion.

No wonder, then, that the publication of Darwin's book, a half century ago, precipitated a crisis. The true nature of the controversy is easily concealed from us, however, by the theological clamor that attended it. The vivid and popular features of the anti-Darwinian row tended to leave the impression that the issue was between science on the one side and theology on the other. Such was not the case—the issue lay primarily within science itself, as Darwin himself early recognized. The theological outcry he discounted from the start, hardly noticing it save as it bore upon the "feelings of his female relatives." But for two decades before final publication he contemplated the possibility of being put down by his scientific peers as a fool or as crazy; and he set, as the measure of his success, the degree in which he should affect three men of science: Lyell in geology, Hooker in botany, and Huxley in zoology.

Religious considerations lent fervor to the controversy, but they did not provoke it. Intellectually, religious emotions are not creative but conservative. They attach themselves readily to the current view of the world and consecrate it. They steep and dye intellectual fabrics in the seething vat of emotions; they do not form their warp and woof. There is not, I think, an instance of any large idea about the world being independently generated by religion. Although the ideas that rose up like armed men against Darwinism owed their intensity to religious associations, their origin and meaning are to be sought in science and philosophy, not in religion.

Few words in our language foreshorten intellectual history as much as does the word species. The Greeks, in initiating the intellectual life of Europe, were impressed by characteristic traits of the life of plants and animals; so impressed indeed that they made these traits the key to defining nature and to explaining mind and society. And

Source: The Influence of Darwin on Philosophy and Other Essays in Contemporary Thought, John Dewey (New York: Holt, 1910), 1–19.

truly, life is so wonderful that a seemingly successful reading of its mystery might well lead men to believe that the key to the secrets of heaven and earth was in their hands. The Greek rendering of this mystery, the Greek formulation of the aim and standard of knowledge, was in the course of time embodied in the word species, and it controlled philosophy for two thousand years. To understand the intellectual face-about expressed in the phrase *Origin of Species,* we must, then, understand the long dominant idea against which it is a protest.

Consider how men were impressed by the facts of life. Their eyes fell upon certain things slight in bulk, and frail in structure. To every appearance, these perceived things were inert and passive. Suddenly, under certain circumstances, these things—henceforth known as seeds or eggs or germs—begin to change, to change rapidly in size, form, and qualities. Rapid and extensive changes occur, however, in many things—as when wood is touched by fire. But the changes in the living thing are orderly; they are cumulative; they tend constantly in one direction; they do not, like other changes, destroy or consume, or pass fruitless into wandering flux; they realize and fulfill. Each successive stage, no matter how unlike its predecessor, preserves its net effect and also prepares the way for a fuller activity on the part of its successor. In living beings, changes do not happen as they seem to happen elsewhere, any which way; the earlier changes are regulated in view of later results. This progressive organization does not cease till there is achieved a true final term, *τελὸς*, a completed, perfected end. This final form exercises in turn a plenitude of functions, not the least noteworthy of which is production of germs like those from which it took its own origin, germs capable of the same cycle of self-fulfilling activity.

But the whole miraculous tale is not yet told. The same drama is enacted to the same destiny in countless myriads of individuals so sundered in time, so severed in space, that they have no opportunity for mutual consultation and no means of interaction. As an old writer quaintly said, "things of the same kind go through the same formalities"—celebrate, as it were, the same ceremonial rites.

This formal activity which operates throughout a series of changes and holds them to a single course; which subordinates their aimless flux to its own perfect manifestation; which, leaping the boundaries of space and time, keeps individuals distant in space and remote in time to a uniform type of structure and function: this principle seemed to give insight into the very nature of reality itself. To it Aristotle gave the name, *εἶδος*. This terms the scholastics translated as *species*.

The force of this term was deepened by its application to everything in the universe that observes order in flux and manifests constancy through change. From the casual drift of daily weather, through the uneven recurrence of seasons and unequal return of seed time and harvest, up to the majestic sweep of the heavens—the image of eternity in time—and from this to the unchanging pure and contemplative intelligence beyond nature lies one unbroken fulfillment of ends. Nature as a whole is a progressive realization of purpose strictly comparable to the realization of purpose in any single plant or animal.

The conception of *εἶδος*, species, a fixed form and final cause, was the central principle of knowledge as well as of nature. Upon it rested the logic of science. Change as change is mere flux and lapse; it insults intelligence. Genuinely to know is to grasp a permanent end that realizes itself through changes, holding them thereby within the metes and bounds of fixed truth. Completely to know is to relate all special forms to their one single end and good: pure contemplative intelligence. Since, however, the scene of nature which directly confronts us is in change, nature as directly and practically experienced does not satisfy the conditions of knowledge. Human experience is in flux, and hence the instrumentalities of sense-perception and of inference based upon observation are condemned in advance. Science is compelled to aim at realities lying behind and beyond the processes of nature, and to carry on its search for these realities by means of rational forms transcending ordinary modes of perception and inference.

There are, indeed, but two alternative courses. We must either find the appropriate objects and organs of knowledge in the mutual interactions of changing things; or else, to escape the infection of change, we *must* seek them in some transcendent and supernal region. The human mind, deliberately as it were, exhausted the logic of the changeless, the final, and the transcendent, before it essayed adventure on the pathless wastes of generation and transformation. We dispose all too easily of the efforts of the schoolmen to interpret nature and mind in terms of real essences, hidden forms, and occult faculties, forgetful of the seriousness and dignity of ideas that lay behind. We dispose of them by laughing at the famous gentleman who accounted for the fact that opium put people to sleep on the ground it had a dormitive faculty. But the doctrine, held in our day, that knowledge of the plant that yields the poppy consists in referring the peculiarities of an individual to a type, to a universal form, a doctrine so firmly established that any other method of knowing was conceived to be unphilosophical and unscientific, is a survival of precisely the same logic. This identity of conception in the scholastic and anti-Darwinian theory may well suggest greater sympathy for what has become familiar as well as greater humility regarding the further unfamiliarities that history has in store.

Darwin was not, of course, the first to question the classic philosophy of nature and of knowledge. The beginnings of the revolution are in the physical science of the sixteenth and seventeenth centuries. When Galileo said: "It is my opinion that the earth is very noble and admirable by reason of so many and so different alterations and generations which are incessantly made therein," he expressed the changed temper that was coming over the world; the transfer of interest from the permanent to the changing. When Descartes said: "The nature of physical things is much more easily conceived when they are beheld coming gradually into existence, then when they are only considered as produced at once in a finished and perfect state," the modern world became self-conscious of the logic that was henceforth to control it, the logic of which Darwin's *Origin of Species* is the latest scientific achievement. Without the methods of Copernicus, Kepler, Galileo, and their successors in astronomy, physics, and chemistry, Darwin would have been helpless in the organic sciences. But prior to Darwin the impact of the new scientific method upon life, mind, and politics had been arrested, because between these ideal or moral interests and the inorganic world intervened the kingdom of plants and animals. The gates of the garden of life were barred to the new ideas; and only through this garden was there access to mind and politics. The influence of Darwin upon philosophy resides in his having conquered the phenomena of life for the principle of transition, and thereby freed the new logic for application to mind and morals and life. When he said of species what Galileo had said of the earth, *e pur se muove*, he emancipated, once for all, genetic and experimental ideas as an organon of asking questions and looking for explanations.

The exact bearings upon philosophy of the new logical outlook are, of course, as yet, uncertain and inchoate. We live in the twilight of intellectual transition. One must add the rashness of the prophet to the stubbornness of the partizan to venture a systematic exposition of the influence upon philosophy of the Darwinian method. At best, we can but inquire as to its general bearing—the effect upon mental temper and complexion, upon that body of half-conscious, half-instinctive intellectual aversions and preferences which determine, after all, our more deliberate intellectual enterprises. In this vague inquiry there happens to exist as a kind of touchstone a problem of long historic currency that has also been much discussed in Darwinian literature. I refer to the old problem of design versus chance, mind versus matter, as the causal explanation, first or final, of things.

As we have already seen, the classic notion of species carried with it the idea of purpose. In all living forms, a specific type is present directing the earlier stages of growth to the realization of its own perfection. Since this purposive regulative principle is not visible to the senses, it follows that it must be an ideal or rational force. Since, however, the perfect form is gradually approximated through the sensible changes, it also follows that in and through a sensible realm a rational ideal force is working out its own ultimate manifestation. These inferences were extended to nature: (*a*) She does nothing in vain; but all for an ulterior purpose. (*b*) Within natural sensible events there is therefore contained a spiritual causal force, which as spiritual escapes perception, but is apprehended by an enlightened reason. (*c*) The manifestation of this principle brings about a subordination of matter and sense to its own realization, and this ultimate fulfillment is the goal of nature and of man. The design argument thus operated in two directions. Purposefulness accounted for the intelligibility of nature and the possibility of science, while the absolute or cosmic character of this purposefulness gave sanction and worth to the moral and religious endeavors of man. Science was underpinned and morals authorized by one and the same principle, and their mutual agreement was eternally guaranteed.

This philosophy remained, in spite of sceptical and polemic outbursts, the official and regnant philosophy of Europe for over two thousand years. The expulsion of fixed first and final causes from astronomy, physics, and chemistry had indeed given the doctrine something of a shock. But, on the other hand, increased acquaintance with the details of plant and animal life operated as a counter-balance and perhaps even strengthened the argument from design. The marvelous adaptations of organisms to their environment, of organs to the organism, of unlike parts of a complex organ—like the eye—to the organ itself; the foreshadowing by lower forms of the higher; the preparation in earlier stages of growth for organs that only later had their functioning—these things were increasingly recognized with the progress of botany, zoology, paleontology, and embryology. Together, they added such prestige to the design argument that by the late eighteenth century it was, as approved by the sciences of organic life, the central point of theistic and idealistic philosophy.

The Darwinian principle of natural selection cut straight under this philosophy. If all organic adaptations are due simply to constant variation and the elimination of those variations which are harmful in the struggle for existence that is brought about by excessive reproduction, there is no call for a prior intelligent causal force to plan and preordain them. Hostile critics charged Darwin with materialism and with making chance the cause of the universe.

Some naturalists, like Asa Gray, favored the Darwinian principle and attempted to reconcile it with design. Gray held to what may be called design on the installment plan. If we conceive the "stream of variations" to be itself intended, we may suppose that each successive variation was designed from the first to be selected. In that case, variation, struggle, and selection simply define the mechanism of "secondary causes" through which the "first cause" acts; and the doctrine of design is none the worse off because we know more of its *modus operandi*.

Darwin could not accept this mediating proposal. He admits or rather he asserts that it is "impossible to conceive this immense and wonderful universe including man with his capacity of looking far backwards and far into futurity as the result of blind chance or necessity." But nevertheless he holds that since variations are in useless as well as useful directions, and since the latter are sifted out simply by the stress of the conditions of struggle for existence, the design argument as applied to living beings is unjustifiable; and its lack of support there deprives it of scientific value as applied to nature in general. If the variations of the pigeon, which under artificial selection give the pouter pigeon, are not preordained for the sake of the breeder, by what logic do we argue that variations resulting in natural species are pre-designed?

So much for some of the more obvious facts of the discussion of design versus chance, as causal principles of nature and of life as a whole. We brought up this discussion, you recall, as a crucial instance. What does our touchstone indicate as to the bearing of Darwinian ideas upon philosophy? In the first place, the new logic outlaws, flanks, dismisses—what you will—one type of problems and substitutes for it another type. Philosophy forswears inquiry after absolute origins and absolute finalities in order to explore specific values and the specific conditions that generate them.

Darwin concluded that the impossibility of assigning the world to chance as a whole and to design in its parts indicated the insolubility of the question. Two radically different reasons, however, may be given as to why a problem is insoluble. One reason is that the problem is too high for intelligence; the other is that the question in its very asking makes assumptions that render the question meaningless. The latter alternative is unerringly pointed to in the celebrated case of design versus chance. Once admit that the sole verifiable or fruitful object of knowledge is the particular set of changes that generate the object of study together with the consequences that then flow from it, and no intelligible question can be asked about what, by assumption, lies outside. To assert—as is often asserted—that specific values of particular truths, social bonds and forms of beauty, if they can be shown to be generated by concretely knowable conditions, are meaningless and in vain; to assert that they are justified only when they and their particular causes and effects have all at once been gathered up into some inclusive first cause and some exhaustive final goal, is intellectual atavism. Such argumentation is reversion to the logic that explained the extinction of fire by water through the formal essence of aqueousness and the quenching of thirst by water through the final cause of aqueousness. Whether used in the case of the special event or that of life as a whole, such logic only abstracts some aspect of the existing course of events in order to reduplicate it as a petrified eternal principle by which to explain the very changes of which it is the formalization.

When Henry Sidgwick casually remarked in a letter that as he grew older his interest in what or who made the world was altered into interest in what kind of a world it is anyway, his voicing of a common experience of our own day illustrates also the nature of that intellectual transformation effected by the Darwinian logic. Interest shifts from the wholesale essence back of special changes to the question of how special changes serve and defeat concrete purposes; shifts from an intelligence that shaped things once for all to the particular intelligences which things are even now shaping; shifts from an ultimate goal of good to the direct increments of justice and happiness that intelligent administration of existent conditions may beget and that present carelessness or stupidity will destroy or forego.

In the second place, the classic type of logic inevitably set philosophy upon proving that life *must* have certain qualities and values—no matter how experience presents the matter—because of some remote cause and eventual goal. The duty of wholesale justification inevitably accompanies all thinking that makes the meaning of special occurrences depend upon something that once and for all lies behind them. The habit of derogating from present meanings and uses prevents our looking the facts of experience in the face; it prevents serious acknowledgment of the evils they present and serious concern with the goods they promise but do not as yet fulfill. It turns thought to the business of finding a wholesale transcendent remedy for the one and guarantee for the other. One is reminded of the way many moralists and theologians greeted Herbert Spencer's recognition of an unknowable energy from which welled up the phenomenal physical processes without and the conscious operations within. Merely because Spencer labeled his unknowable energy "God," this faded piece of metaphysical goods was greeted as an important and grateful concession to the reality of the spiritual realm. Were it not for the deep hold of the habit of seeking justification for ideal values in the remote and transcendent, surely this reference of them to an unknowable absolute would be despised in comparison with the demonstrations of experience that knowable energies are daily generating about us precious values.

The displacing of this wholesale type of philosophy will doubtless not arrive by sheer logical disproof, but rather by growing recognition of its futility. Were it a thousand times true that opium produces sleep because of its dormitive energy, yet the inducing of sleep in the tired, and the recovery to waking life of the poisoned, would not be thereby one least step forwarded. And were it a thousand times dialectically demonstrated that life as a whole is regulated by a transcendent principle to a final inclusive goal, none the less truth and error, health and disease, good and evil, hope and fear in the concrete, would remain just what and where they now are. To improve our education, to ameliorate our manners, to advance our politics, we must have recourse to specific conditions of generation.

Finally, the new logic introduces responsibility into the intellectual life. To idealize and rationalize the universe at large is after all a confession of inability to master the courses of things that specifically concern us. As long as mankind suffered from this impotency, it naturally shifted a burden of responsibility that it could not carry over to the more competent shoulders of the transcendent cause. But if insight into specific conditions of value and into specific consequences of ideas is possible, philosophy must in time become a method of locating and interpreting the more serious of the conflicts that occur in life, and a method of projecting ways for dealing with them: a method of moral and political diagnosis and prognosis.

The claim to formulate *a priori* the legislative constitution of the universe is by its nature a claim that may lead to elaborate dialectic developments. But it is also one that removes these very conclusions from subjection to experimental test, for, by definition, these results make no differences in the detailed course of events. But a philosophy that humbles its pretensions to the work of projecting hypotheses for the education and conduct of mind, individual and social, is thereby subjected to test by the way in which the ideas it propounds work out in practice. In having modesty forced upon it, philosophy also acquires responsibility.

Doubtless I seem to have violated the implied promise of my earlier remarks and to have turned both prophet and partizan. But in anticipating the direction of the transformations in philosophy to be wrought by the Darwinian genetic and experimental logic, I do not profess to speak for any save those who yield themselves consciously or unconsciously to this logic. No one can fairly deny that at present there are two effects of the Darwinian mode of thinking. On the one hand, there are making many sincere and vital efforts to revise our traditional philosophic conceptions in accordance with its demands. On the other hand, there is as definitely a recrudescence of absolutistic philosophies; an assertion of a type of philosophic knowing distinct from that of the sciences, one which opens to us another kind of reality from that to which the sciences give access; an appeal through experience to something that essentially goes beyond experience. This reaction affects popular creeds and religious movements as well as technical philosophies. The very conquest of the biological sciences by the new ideas has led many to proclaim an explicit and rigid separation of philosophy from science.

Old ideas give way slowly; for they are more than abstract logical forms and categories. They are habits, predispositions, deeply engrained attitudes of aversion and preference. Moreover, the conviction persists—though history shows it to be a hallucination—that all the questions that the human mind has asked are questions that can be answered in terms of the alternatives that the questions themselves present. But in fact intellectual progress usually occurs through sheer abandonment of questions together with both of the alternatives they assume—an abandonment that results from their decreasing vitality and a change of urgent interest. We do not solve them: we get over them. Old questions are solved by disappearing, evaporating, while new questions corresponding to the changed attitude of endeavor and preference take their place. Doubtless the greatest dissolvent in contemporary thought of old questions, the greatest precipitant of new methods, new intentions, new problems, is the one effected by the scientific revolution that found its climax in the *Origin of Species*.

Selection from *The Public and Its Problems* 1927

. . . . . .

Regarded as an idea, democracy is not an alternative to other principles of associated life. It is the idea of community life itself. It is an ideal in the only intelligible sense of an ideal: namely, the tendency and movement of some thing which exists carried to its final limit, viewed as completed, perfected. Since things do not attain such fulfillment but are in actuality distracted and interfered with, democracy in this sense is not a fact and never will be. But neither in this sense is there or has there ever been anything which is a community in its full measure, a community unalloyed by alien elements. The idea or ideal of a community presents, however, actual phases of associated life as they are freed from restrictive and disturbing elements, and are contemplated as having attained their limit of development. Wherever there is conjoint activity whose consequences are appreciated as good by all singular persons who take part in it, and where the realization of the good is such as to effect an energetic desire and effort to sustain it in being just because it is a good shared by all, there is in so far a community. The clear consciousness of a communal life, in all its implications, constitutes the idea of democracy.

Only when we start from a community as a fact, grasp the fact in thought so as to clarify and enhance its constituent elements, can we reach an idea of democracy which is not utopian. The conceptions and shibboleths which are traditionally associated with the idea of democracy take on a veridical and directive meaning only when they are construed as marks and traits of an association which realizes the defining characteristics of a community. Fraternity, liberty and equality isolated from communal life are hopeless abstractions. Their separate assertion leads to mushy sentimentalism or else to extravagant and fanatical violence which in the end defeats its own aims. Equality then becomes a creed of mechanical identity which is false to facts and impossible of realization. Effort to attain it is divisive of the vital bonds which hold men together; as far as it puts forth issue, the outcome is a mediocrity in which good is common only in the sense of being average and vulgar. Liberty is then thought of as independence of social ties, and ends in dissolution and anarchy. It is more difficult to sever the idea of brotherhood from that of a community, and hence it is either practically ignored in the movements which identify democracy with Individualism, or else it is a sentimentally appended tag. In its just connection with communal experience, fraternity is another name for the consciously appreciated goods which accrue

Source: John Dewey, *The Later Works, 1925–1953*. Vol. 2, *1925–1927, Essays, Reviews, Miscellaney;* and *The Public and Its Problems*, ed. Jo Ann Boydston, with an Introduction by James Gouinlock, 328–32, 347–50.

from an association in which all share, and which give direction to the conduct of each. Liberty is that secure release and fulfillment of personal potentialities which take place only in rich and manifold association with others: the power to be an individualized self making a distinctive contribution and enjoying in its own way the fruits of association. Equality denotes the unhampered share which each individual member of the community has in the consequences of associated action. It is equitable because it is measured only by need and capacity to utilize, not by extraneous factors which deprive one in order that another may take and have. A baby in the family is equal with others, not because of some antecedent and structural quality which is the same as that of others, but in so far as his needs for care and development are attended to without being sacrificed to the superior strength, possessions and matured abilities of others. Equality does not signify that kind of mathematical or physical equivalence in virtue of which any one element may be substituted for another. It denotes effective regard for whatever is distinctive and unique in each, irrespective of physical and psychological inequalities. It is not a natural possession but is a fruit of the community when its action is directed by its character as a community.

Associated or joint activity is a condition of the creation of a community. But association itself is physical and organic, while communal life is moral, that is emotionally, intellectually, consciously sustained. Human beings combine in behavior as directly and unconsciously as do atoms, stellar masses and cells; as directly and unknowingly as they divide and repel. They do so in virtue of their own structure, as man and woman unite, as the baby seeks the breast and the breast is there to supply its need. They do so from external circumstances, pressure from without, as atoms combine or separate in presence of an electric charge, or as sheep huddle together from the cold. Associated activity needs no explanation; things are made that way. But no amount of aggregated collective action of itself constitutes a community. For beings who observe and think, and whose ideas are absorbed by impulses and become sentiments and interests, "we" is an inevitable as "I." But "we" and "our" exist only when the consequences of combined action are perceived and become an object of desire and effort, just as "I" and "mine" appear on the scene only when a distinctive share in mutual action is consciously asserted or claimed. Human associations may be ever so organic in origin and firm in operation, but they develop into societies in a human sense only as their consequences, being known, are esteemed and sought for. Even if "society" were as much an organism as some writers have held, it would not on that account be society. Interactions, transactions, occur *de facto* and the results of interdependence follow. But participation in activities and sharing in results are additive concerns. They demand *communication* as a prerequisite.

Combined activity happens among human beings; but when nothing else happens it passes as inevitably into some other mode of interconnected activity as does the interplay of iron and the oxygen of water. What takes place is wholly describable in terms of energy, or, as we say in the case of human interactions, of force. Only when there exist *signs* or *symbols* of activities and of their outcome can the flux be viewed as from without, be arrested for consideration and esteem, and be regulated. Lightning strikes and rives a tree or rock, and the resulting fragments take up and continue the process of interaction, and so on and on. But when phases of the process are represented by signs, a new medium is interposed. As symbols are related to one another, the important relations of a course of events are recorded and are preserved as meanings. Recollection and foresight are possible; the new medium facilitates calculation, planning, and a new kind of action which intervenes in what happens to direct its course in the interest of what is foreseen and desired.

Symbols in turn depend upon and promote communication. The results of conjoint experience are considered and transmitted. Events cannot be passed from one to another, but meanings may be shared by means of signs. Wants and impulses are then attached to common meanings. They are thereby transformed into desires and purposes, which, since they implicate a common or mutually understood meaning, present new ties, converting a conjoint activity into a community of interest and endeavor. Thus there is generated what, metaphorically, may be termed a general will and social consciousness: desire and choice on the part of individuals in behalf of activities that, by means of symbols, are communicable and shared by all concerned. A community thus presents an order of energies transmuted into one of meanings which are appreciated and mutually referred by each to every other on the part of those engaged in combined action. "Force" is not eliminated but is transformed in use and direction by ideas and sentiments made possible by means of symbols.

The work of conversion of the physical and organic phase of associated behavior into a community of action saturated and regulated by mutual interest in shared meanings, consequences which are translated into ideas and desired objects by means of symbols, does not occur all at once nor completely. At any given time, it sets a problem rather than marks a settled achievement. We are born organic beings associated with others, but we are not born members of a community. The young have to be brought within the traditions, outlook and interests which characterize a community by means of education: by unremitting instruction and by learning in connection with the phenomena of overt association. Everything which is distinctively human is learned, not native, even though it could not be learned without native structures which mark man off from other animals. To learn in a human way and to human effect is not just to acquire added skill through refinement of original capacities.

To learn to be human is to develop through the give-and-take of communication an effective sense of being an individually distinctive member of a community; one who understands and appreciates its beliefs, desires and methods, and who contributes to a further conversion of organic powers into human resources and values. But this translation is never finished. The old Adam, the unregenerate element in human nature, persists. It shows itself wherever the method obtains of attaining results by use of force instead of by the method of communication and enlightenment. It manifests itself more subtly, pervasively and effectually when knowledge and the instrumentalities of skill which are the product of communal life are employed in the service of wants and impulses which have not themselves been modified by reference to a shared interest. To the doctrine of "natural" economy which held that commercial exchange would bring about such an interdependence that harmony would automatically result, Rousseau gave an adequate answer in advance. He pointed out that interdependence provides just the situation which makes it possible and worth while for the stronger and abler to exploit others for their own ends, to keep others in a state of subjection where they can be utilized as animated tools. The remedy he suggested, a return to a condition of independence based on isolation, was hardly seriously meant. But its desperateness is evidence of the urgency of the problem. Its negative character was equivalent to surrender of any hope of solution. By contrast it indicates the nature of the only possible solution: the perfecting of the means and ways of communication of meanings so that genuinely shared interest in the consequences of interdependent activities may inform desire and effort and thereby direct action.

. . . . . .

A glance at the situation shows that the physical and external means of collecting information in regard to what is happening in the world have far outrun the intellectual phase of inquiry and organization of its results. Telegraph, telephone, and now the radio, cheap and quick mails, the printing press, capable of swift reduplication of material at low cost, have attained a remarkable development. But when we ask what sort of material is recorded and how it is organized, when we ask about the intellectual form in which the material is presented, the tale to be told is very different. "News" signifies something which has just happened, and which is new just because it deviates from the old and regular. But its *meaning* depends upon relation to what it imports, to what its social consequences are. This import cannot be determined unless the new is placed in relation to the old, to what has happened and been integrated into the course of events. Without coördination and consecutiveness, events are not events, but mere occurrences, intrusions; an event implies that out of which a happening proceeds. Hence even if we discount the influence of private interests in procuring suppression, secrecy and misrepresentation, we have here an explanation of the triviality and "sensational" quality of so much of what passes as news. The catastrophic, namely, crime, accident, family rows, personal clashes and conflicts, are the most obvious forms of breaches of continuity; they supply the element of shock which is the strictest meaning of sensation; they are the *new* par excellence, even though only the date of the newspaper could inform us whether they happened last year or this, so completely are they isolated from their connections.

So accustomed are we to this method of collecting, recording and presenting social changes, that it may well sound ridiculous to say that a genuine social science would manifest its reality in the daily press, while learned books and articles supply and polish tools of inquiry. But the inquiry which alone can furnish knowledge as a precondition of public judgments must be contemporary and quotidian. Even if social sciences as a specialized apparatus of inquiry were more advanced than they are, they would be comparatively impotent in the office of directing opinion on matters of concern to the public as long as they are remote from application in the daily and unremitting assembly and interpretation of "news." On the other hand, the tools of social inquiry will be clumsy as long as they are forged in places and under conditions remote from contemporary events.

What has been said about the formation of ideas and judgments concerning the public apply as well to the distribution of the knowledge which makes it an effective possession of the members of the public. Any separation between the two sides of the problem is artificial. The discussion of propaganda and propagandism would alone, however, demand a volume, and could be written only by one much more experienced than the present writer. Propaganda can accordingly only be mentioned, with the remark that the present situation is one unprecedented in history. The political forms of democracy and quasi-democratic habits of thought on social matters have compelled a certain amount of public discussion and at least the simulation of general consultation in arriving at political decisions. Representative government must at least seem to be founded on public interests as they are revealed to public belief. The days are past when government can be carried on without any pretense of ascertaining the wishes of the governed. In theory, their assent must be secured. Under the older forms, there was no need to muddy the sources of opinion on political matters. No current of energy flowed from them. To-day the judgments popularly formed on political matters are so important, in spite of all factors to the contrary, that there is an enormous premium upon all methods which affect their formation.

The smoothest road to control of political conduct is by control of opinion. As long as interests of pecuniary profit are powerful, and a public has not located and identified itself, those who have this interest will have an unresisted motive for tampering with the springs of political action in all that affects them. Just as in the conduct of industry and exchange generally the technological factor is obscured, deflected and defeated by "business," so specifically in the management of publicity. The gathering and sale of subject-matter having a public import is part of the existing pecuniary system. Just as industry conducted by engineers on a factual technological basis would be a very different thing from what it actually is, so the assembling and reporting of news would be a very different thing if the genuine interests of reporters were permitted to work freely.

One aspect of the matter concerns particularly the side of dissemination. It is often said, and with a great appearance of truth, that the freeing and perfecting of inquiry would not have any especial effect. For, it is argued, the mass of the reading public is not interested in learning and assimilating the results of accurate investigation. Unless these are read, they cannot seriously affect the thought and action of members of the public; they remain in secluded library alcoves, and are studied and understood only by a few intellectuals. The objection is well taken save as the potency of art is taken into account. A technical high-brow presentation would appeal only to those technically high-brow; it would not be news to the masses. Presentation is fundamentally important, and presentation is a question of art. A newspaper which was only a daily edition of a quarterly journal of sociology or political science would undoubtedly possess a limited circulation and a narrow influence. Even at that, however, the mere existence and accessibility of such material would have some regulative effect. But we can look much further than that. The material would have such an enormous and widespread human bearing that its bare existence would be an irresistible invitation to a presentation of it which would have a direct popular appeal. The freeing of the artist in literary presentation, in other words, is as much a precondition of the desirable creation of adequate opinion on public matters as is the freeing of social inquiry. Men's conscious life of opinion and judgment often proceeds on a superficial and trivial plane. But their lives reach a deeper level. The function of art has always been to break through the crust of conventionalized and routine consciousness. Common things, a flower, a gleam of moonlight, the song of a bird, not things rare and remote, are means with which the deeper levels of life are touched so that they spring up as desire and thought. This process is art. Poetry, the drama, the novel, are proofs that the problem of presentation is not insoluble. Artists have always been the real purveyors of news, for it is not the outward happening in itself which is new, but the kindling by it of emotion, perception and appreciation.

We have but touched lightly and in passing upon the conditions which must be fulfilled if the Great Society is to become a Great Community; a society in which the ever-expanding and intricately ramifying consequences of associated activities shall be known in the full sense of that word, so that an organized, articulate Public comes into being. The highest and most difficult kind of inquiry and a subtle, delicate, vivid and responsive art of communication must take possession of the physical machinery of transmission and circulation and breathe life into it. When the machine age has thus perfected its machinery it will be a means of life and not its despotic master. Democracy will come into its own, for democracy is a name for a life of free and enriching communion. It had its seer in Walt Whitman. It will have its consummation when free social inquiry is indissolubly wedded to the art of full and moving communication.

JANE ADDAMS

"The Subjective Necessity of Social Settlements" 1892

Jane Addams (1860–1935) was one of the most influential and indefatigable social reformers in all American history. Although based in Chicago at Hull-House—the settlement house she created to serve the needs of a poor, largely immigrant neighborhood—she helped to lead a host of national movements, including the 1912 presidential campaign of Theodore Roosevelt. Addams was the founding president of the Woman's International League for Peace and Freedom and in 1931 shared the Nobel Peace Prize. Addams wrote widely on the theory and practice of social reform and international reconciliation. In the selection that follows, she scrutinizes in a social and religious context the motives of men and women who, like herself, had devoted themselves to the improvement of society. "The Subjective Necessity of Social Settlements" was first delivered as an address to a conference of social workers in 1892, but it gained fame as a classic statement of reform commitment after 1910 when it appeared in Addam's most widely appreciated book, *Twenty Years at Hull-House*. For Addams's life and work, see Alan Davis, *An American Heroine: The Life and Legend of Jane Addams* (New York, 1973). For an interpretation of Addams as the primordial example of the American intellectual as a critic of society, see Christopher Lasch, *The New Radicalism in America 1889–1963: The Emergence of the Intellectual as a Social Type* (New York, 1965), 3–37.

. . . . . .

This paper is an attempt to analyze the motives which underlie a movement based, not only upon conviction, but upon genuine emotion, wherever educated young people are seeking an outlet for that sentiment of universal brotherhood, which the best spirit of our times is forcing from an emotion into a motive. These young people accomplish little toward the solution of this social problem, and bear the brunt of being cultivated into unnourished, oversensitive lives. They have been shut off from the common labor by which they live which is a great source of moral and physical health. They feel a fatal want of harmony between their theory and their lives, a lack of coördination between thought and action. I think it is hard for us to realize how seriously many of them are taking to the notion of human brotherhood, how eagerly they long to give tangible expression to the democratic ideal. These young men and women, longing to socialize their democracy, are animated by certain hopes which may be thus loosely formulated; that if in a democratic country nothing can be permanently achieved save through the masses of the people, it will be impossible to establish a higher political life than the people themselves crave; that it is difficult to see how the notion of a higher civic life can be fostered save through common intercourse; that the blessings which we associate with a life of refinement and cultivation can be made universal and must be made universal if they are to be permanent; that the good we secure for ourselves is precarious and uncertain, is floating in mid-air, until it is secured for all of us and incorporated into our common life. It is easier to state these hopes than to formulate the line of motives, which I believe to constitute the trend of the subjective pressure toward the Settlement. There is something primordial about these motives, but I am perhaps overbold in designating them as a great desire to share the race life. We all bear traces of the starvation struggle which for so long made up the life of the race. Our very organism holds memories and glimpses of that long life of our ancestors which still goes on among so many of our contemporaries. Nothing so deadens the sympathies and shrivels the power of enjoyment as the persistent keeping away from the great opportunities for helpfulness and a continual ignoring of the starvation struggle which makes up the life of at least half the race. To shut one's self away from that half of the race life is to shut one's self away from the most vital part of it; it is to live out but half the humanity to which we have been born heir and to use but half our faculties. We have all had longings for a fuller life which should include the use of these faculties. These longings are the physical complement of the "Intimations of Immortality," on which no ode has yet been written. To portray these would be the work of a poet, and it is hazardous for any but a poet to attempt it.

You may remember the forlorn feeling which occasionally seizes you when you arrive early in the morning a stranger in a great city: the stream of laboring people goes past you as you gaze through the plate-glass window of your hotel; you see hard workingmen lifting great burdens; you hear the driving and jostling of huge carts and your heart sinks with a sudden sense of futility. The door opens behind you and you turn to the man who brings you in your breakfast with a quick sense of human fellowship. You find yourself praying that you may never lose your hold on it all. A more poetic prayer would be that the great mother breasts of our common humanity, with its labor and suffering and its homely comforts, may never be withheld from you. You

Source: Twenty Years at Hull-House, Jane Addams (New York: Macmillan, 1910), 91–100.

turn helplessly to the waiter and feel that it would be almost grotesque to claim from him the sympathy you crave because civilization has placed you apart, but you resent your position with a sudden sense of snobbery. Literature is full of portrayals of these glimpses: they come to shipwrecked men on rafts; they overcome the differences of an incongruous multitude when in the presence of a great danger or when moved by a common enthusiasm. They are not, however, confined to such moments, and if we were in the habit of telling them to each other, the recital would be as long as the tales of children are, when they sit down on the green grass and confide to each other how many times they have remembered that they lived once before. If these childish tales are the stirring of inherited impressions, just so surely is the other the striving of inherited powers.

"It is true that there is nothing after disease, indigence and a sense of guilt, so fatal to health and to life itself as the want of a proper outlet for active faculties." I have seen young girls suffer and grow sensibly lowered in vitality in the first years after they leave school. In our attempt then to give a girl pleasure and freedom from care we succeed, for the most part, in making her pitifully miserable. She finds "life" so different from what she expected it to be. She is besotted with innocent little ambitions, and does not understand this apparent waste of herself, this elaborate preparation, if no work is provided for her. There is a heritage of noble obligation which young people accept and long to perpetuate. The desire for action, the wish to right wrong and alleviate suffering haunts them daily. Society smiles at it indulgently instead of making it of value to itself. The wrong to them begins even farther back, when we restrain the first childish desires for "doing good" and tell them that they must wait until they are older and better fitted. We intimate that social obligation begins at a fixed date, forgetting that it begins with birth itself. We treat them as children who, with strong-growing limbs, are allowed to use their legs but not their arms, or whose legs are daily carefully exercised that after a while their arms may be put to high use. We do this in spite of the protest of the best educators, Locke and Pestalozzi. We are fortunate in the meantime if their unused members do not weaken and disappear. They do sometimes. There are a few girls who, by the time they are "educated," forget their old childish desires to help the world and to play with poor little girls "who haven't play things." Parents are often inconsistent: they deliberately expose their daughters to knowledge of the distress in the world; they send them to hear missionary addresses on famines in India and China; they accompany them to lectures on the suffering in Siberia; they agitate together over the forgotten region of East London. In addition to this, from babyhood the altruistic tendencies of these daughters are persistently cultivated. They are taught to be self-forgetting and self-sacrificing, to consider the good of the whole before the good of the ego. But when all this information and culture show results, when the daughter comes back from college and begins to recognize her social claim to the "submerged tenth," and to evince a disposition to fulfill it, the family claim is strenuously asserted; she is told that she is unjustified, ill-advised in her efforts. If she persists, the family too often are injured and unhappy unless the efforts are called missionary and the religious zeal of the family carry them over their sense of abuse. When this zeal does not exist, the result is perplexing. It is a curious violation of what we would fain believe a fundamental law—that the final return of the deed is upon the head of the doer. The deed is that of exclusiveness and caution, but the return, instead of falling upon the head of the exclusive and cautious, falls upon a young head full of generous and unselfish plans. The girl loses something vital out of her life to which she is entitled. She is restricted and unhappy; her elders, meanwhile, are unconscious of the situation and we have all the elements of a tragedy.

We have in America a fast-growing number of cultivated young people who have no recognized outlet for their active faculties. They hear constantly of the great social maladjustment, but no way is provided for them to change it, and their uselessness hangs about them heavily. Huxley declares that the sense of usefulness is the severest shock which the human system can sustain, and that if persistently sustained, it results in atrophy of function. These young people have had advantages of college, of European travel, and of economic study, but they are sustaining this shock of inaction. They have pet phrases, and they tell you that the things that make us all alike are stronger than the things that make us different. They say that all men are united by needs and sympathies far more permanent and radical than anything that temporarily divides them and sets them in opposition to each other. If they affect art, they say that the decay in artistic expression is due to the decay in ethics, that art when shut away from the human interests and from the great mass of humanity is self-destructive. They tell their elders with all the bitterness of youth that if they expect success from them in business or politics or in whatever lines their ambition for them has run, they must let them consult all of humanity; that they must let them find out what the people want and how they want it. It is only the stronger young people, however, who formulate this. Many of them dissipate their energies in so-called enjoyment. Others not content with that, go on studying and go back to college for their second degrees; not that they are especially fond of study, but because they want something definite to do, and their powers have been trained in the direction of mental accumulation. Many are buried beneath this mental accumulation which lowered vitality and discontent. Walter Besant says they have had the vision that Peter had when he saw the great sheet let down from heaven, wherein was neither clean nor unclean. He calls it the sense of humanity. It is not philanthropy nor benevolence, but a thing fuller and wider than either of these.

This young life, so sincere in its emotion and good phrase and yet so undirected, seems to me as pitiful as the other great mass of destitute lives. One is supplementary to the other, and some method of communication can surely be devised. Mr. Barnett, who urged the first Settlement—Toynbee Hall, in East London—recognized this need of outlet for the young men of Oxford and Cambridge, and hoped that the Settlement would supply the communication. It is easy to see why the Settlement movement originated in England, where the years of education are more constrained and definite than they are here, where class distinctions are more rigid. The necessity of it was greater there, but we are fast feeling the pressure of the need and meeting the necessity for Settlements in America. Our young people feel nervously the need of putting theory into action, and respond quickly to the Settlement form of activity.

Other motives which I believe make toward the Settlement are the result of a certain renaissance going forward in Christianity. The impulse to share the lives of the poor, the desire to make social service, irrespective of propaganda, express the spirit of Christ, is as old as Christianity itself. We have no proof from the records themselves that the early Roman Christians, who strained their simple art to the point of grotesqueness in their eagerness to record a "good news" on the walls of the catacombs, considered this good news a religion. Jesus had no set of truths labeled Religious. On the contrary, his doctrine was that all truth is one, that the appropriation of it is freedom. His teaching had no dogma to mark it off from truth and action in general. He himself called it a revelation—a life. These early Roman Christians received the Gospel message, a command to love all men, with a certain joyous simplicity. The image of the Good Shepherd is blithe and gay beyond the gentlest shepherd of Greek mythology; the hart no longer pants, but rushes to the water brooks. The Christians looked for the continuous revelation, but believed what Jesus said, that this revelation, to be retained and made manifest, must be put into terms of action; that action is the only medium man has for receiving and appropriating truth; that the doctrine must be known through the will.

That Christianity has to be revealed and embodied in the line of social progress is a corollary to the simple proposition that man's action is found in his social relationships in the way in which he connects with his fellows; that his motives for action are the zeal and affection with which he regards his fellows. By this simple process was created a deep enthusiasm for humanity, which regarded man as at once the organ and the object of revelation; and by this process came about the wonderful fellowship, the true democracy of the early Church, that so captivates the imagination. The early Christians were pre-eminently nonresistant. They believed in love as a cosmic force. There was no inconoclasm during the minor peace of the Church. They did not yet denounce nor tear down temples, nor preach the end of the world. They grew to a mighty number but it never occurred to them, either in their weakness or in their strength, to regard other men for an instant as their foes or as aliens. The spectacle of the Christians loving all men was the most astounding Rome had ever seen. They were eager to sacrifice themselves for the weak, for children, and for the aged; they identified themselves with slaves and did not avoid the plague; they longed to share the common lot that they might receive the constant revelation. It was a new treasure which the early Christians added to the sum of all treasures, a joy hitherto unknown in the world—the joy of finding the Christ which lieth in each man, but which no man can unfold save in fellowship. A happiness ranging from the heroic to the pastoral enveloped them. They were to possess a revelation as long as life had new meaning to unfold, new action to propose.

I believe that there is a distinct turning among many young men and women toward this simple acceptance of Christ's message. They resent the assumption that Christianity is a set of ideas which belong to the religious consciousness, whatever that may be. They insist that it cannot be proclaimed and instituted apart from the social life of the community and that it must seek a simple and natural expression in the social organism itself. The Settlement movement is only one manifestation of that wider humanitarian movement which throughout Christendom, put pre-eminently in England, is endeavoring to embody itself, not in a sect, but in society itself.

I believe that this turning, this renaissance of the early Christian humanitarianism, is going on in America, in Chicago, if you please, without leaders who write or philosophize, without much speaking, but with a bent to express in social service and in terms of action the spirit of Christ. Certain it is that spiritual force is found in the Settlement movement, and it is also true that this force must be evoked and must be called into play before the success of any Settlement is assured. There must be the overmastering belief that all that is noblest in life is common to men as men, in order to accentuate the likenesses and ignore the differences which are found among the people whom the Settlement constantly brings into juxtaposition. It may be true, as the Positivists insist, that the very religious fervor of man can be turned into love for his race, and his desire for a future life into content to live in the echo of his deeds;

Paul's formula of seeking for the Christ which lieth in each man and founding our likenesses on him, seems a simpler formula to many of us.

In a thousand voices singing the Hallelujah Chorus in Handel's "Messiah," it is possible to distinguish the leading voices, but the differences of training and cultivation between them and the voices of the chorus, are lost in the unity of purpose and in the fact that they are all human voices lifted by a high motive. This is a weak illustration of what a Settlement attempts to do. It aims, in a measure, to develop whatever of social life its neighborhood may afford, to focus and give form to that life, to bring to bear upon it the results of cultivation and training; but it receives in exchange for the music of isolated voices the volume and strength of the chorus. It is quite impossible for me to say in what proportion or degree the subjective necessity which led to the opening of Hull-House combined the three trends: first, the desire to interpret democracy in social terms; secondly, the impulse beating at the very source of our lives, urging us to aid in the race progress; and, thirdly, the Christian movement toward humanitarianism. It is difficult to analyze a living thing; the analysis is at best imperfect. Many more motives may blend with the three trends; possibly the desire for a new form of social success due to the nicety of imagination, which refuses worldly pleasures unmixed with the joys of self-sacrifice; possibly a love of approbation, so vast that it is not content with the treble clapping of delicate hands, but wishes also to hear the brass notes from toughened palms, may mingle with these.

The Settlement, then, is an experimental effort to aid in the solution of the social and industrial problems which are engendered by the modern conditions of life in a great city. It insists that these problems are not confined to any one portion of a city. It is an attempt to relieve, at the same time, the overaccumulation at one end of society and the destitution at the other; but it assumes that this overaccumulation and destitution is most sorely felt in the things that pertain to social and educational privileges. From its very nature it can stand for no political or social propaganda. It must, in a sense, give the warm welcome of an inn to all such propaganda, if perchance one of them be found an angel. The one thing to be dreaded in the Settlement is that it lose its flexibility, its power of quick adaptation, its readiness to change its methods as its environment may demand. It must be open to conviction and must have a deep and abiding sense of tolerance. It must be hospitable and ready for experiment. It should demand from its residents a scientific patience in the accumulation of facts and the steady holding of their sympathies as one of the best instruments for that accumulation. It must be grounded in a philosophy whose foundation is on the solidarity of the human race, a philosophy which will not waver when the race happens to be represented by a drunken woman or an idiot boy. Its residents must be emptied of all conceit of opinion and all self-assertion, and ready to arouse and interpret the public opinion of their neighborhood. They must be content to live quietly side by side with their neighbors, until they grow into a sense of relationship and mutual interests. Their neighbors are held apart by differences of race and language which the residents can more easily overcome. They are bound to see the needs of their neighborhood as a whole, to furnish data for legislation, and to use their influence to secure it. In short, residents are pledged to devote themselves to the duties of good citizenship and to the arousing of the social energies which too largely lie dormant in every neighborhood given over to industrialism. They are bound to regard the entire life of their city as organic, to make an effort to unify it, and to protest against its overdifferentiation.

It is always easy to make all philosophy point one particular moral and all history adorn one particular tale; but I may be forgiven the reminder that the best speculative philosophy sets forth the solidarity of the human race; that the highest moralists have taught that without the advance and improvement of the whole, no man can hope for any lasting improvement in his own moral or material individual condition; and that the subjective necessity for Social Settlements is therefore identical with that necessity, which urges us on toward social and individual salvation.

OLIVER WENDELL HOLMES, JR.

"Natural Law"
1918

Oliver Wendell Holmes, Jr., (1841–1935) did more than any other American thinker to develop and popularize the insight that law is a living, changing part of culture, responsive to the shifting circumstances with which societies must cope. He argued along these lines as early as 1881, when he published his greatest work, *The Common Law,* but Holmes achieved broader influence during the Progressive Era and the 1920s while serving as a justice of the U.S. Supreme Court. Although Holmes was aloof from the reform movements of this era, his refusal to defend the vested interests of his upper-class milieu endeared him to younger, liberal intellectuals, who tended to exaggerate his "progressive" tendencies. For a study of Holmes's thought that emphasizes his place in the liberal tradition, see Morton G. White, *Social Thought in America: The Revolt Against Formalism* (New York, 2nd ed., 1957). For a more comprehensive analysis that emphasizes Holmes's aristocratic biases and his unwillingness to make commitments, see Yosal Rogat, "The Judge as Spectator," *University of Chicago Law Review* 31 (Winter 1964), 213–56. "Natural Law," published in 1919, expresses the historicist bent of Holmes's jurisprudence and displays the aphoristic style in which he dealt with theoretical issues.

It is not enough for the knight of romance that you agree that his lady is a very nice girl—if you do not admit that she is the best that God ever made or will make, you must fight. There is in all men a demand for the superlative, so much so that the poor devil who has no other way of reaching it attains it by getting drunk. It seems to me that this demand is at the bottom of the philosopher's effort to prove that truth is absolute and of the jurist's search for criteria of universal validity which he collects under the head of natural law.

I used to say, when I was young, that truth was the majority vote of that nation that could lick all others. Certainly we may expect that the received opinion about the present war will depend a good deal upon which side wins (I hope with all my soul it will be mine), and I think that the statement was correct in so far as it implied that our test of truth is a reference to either a present or an imagined future majority in favor of our view. If, as I have suggested elsewhere, the truth may be defined as the system of my (intellectual) limitations, what gives it objectivity is the fact that I find my fellow man to a greater or less extent (never wholly) subject to the same *Can't Helps.* If I think that I am sitting at a table I find that the other persons present agree with me; so if I say that the sum of the angles of a triangle is equal to two right angles. If I am in a minority of one they send for a doctor or lock me up; and I am so far able to transcend the to me convincing testimony of my senses or my reason as to recognize that if I am alone probably something is wrong with my works.

Certitude is not the test of certainty. We have been cock-sure of many things that were not so. If I may quote myself again, property, friendship, and truth have a common root in time. One can not be wrenched from the rocky crevices into which one has grown for many years without feeling that one is attacked in one's life. What we most love and revere generally is determined by early associations. I love granite rocks and barberry bushes, no doubt because with them were my earliest joys that reach back through the past eternity of my life. But while one's experience thus makes certain preferences dogmatic for oneself, recognition of how they came to be so leaves one able to see that others, poor souls, may be equally dogmatic about something else. And this again means scepticism. Not that one's belief or love does not remain. Not that we would not fight and die for it if important—we all, whether we know it or not—are fighting to make the kind of a world that we should like—but that we have learned to recognize that others will fight and die to make a different world, with equal sincerity or belief. Deep-seated preferences can not be argued about—you can not argue a man into liking a glass of beer—and therefore, when differences are sufficiently far reaching we try to kill the other man rather than let him have his way. But that is perfectly consistent with admitting that, so far as appears, his grounds are just as good as ours.

The jurists who believe in natural law seem to me to be in that naïve state of mind that accepts what has been familiar and accepted by them and their neighbors as something that must be accepted by all men everywhere. No doubt it is true that, so far as we can see ahead, some arrangements and the rudiments of familiar institutions seem to be necessary elements in any society that may spring from our own and that would seem to us to be civilized—some form of permanent association between the sexes—some residue of property individually owned—some mode of binding oneself

Source: Collected Legal Papers, Oliver Wendell Holmes, Jr., 310–16.

to specified future conduct—at the bottom of all, some protection for the person. But without speculating whether a group is imaginable in which all but the last of these might disappear and the last be subject to qualifications that most of us would abhor, the question remains as to the *Ought* of natural law.

It is true that beliefs and wishes have a transcendental basis in the sense that their foundation is arbitrary. You can not help entertaining and feeling them, and there is an end of it. As an arbitrary fact people wish to live, and we say with various degrees of certainty that they can do so only on certain conditions. To do it they must eat and drink. That necessity is absolute. It is a necessity of less degree but practically general that they should live in society. If they live in society, so far as we can see, there are further conditions. Reason working on experience does tell us, no doubt, that if our wish to live continues, we can do it only on those terms. But that seems to me the whole of the matter. I see no *a priori* duty to live with others and in that way, but simply a statement of what I must do if I wish to remain alive. If I do live with others they tell me that I must do and abstain from doing various things or they will put the screws on to me. I believe that they will, and being of the same mind as to their conduct I not only accept the rules but come in time to accept them with sympathy and emotional affirmation and begin to talk about duties and rights. But for legal purposes a right is only the hypostasis of a prophecy—the imagination of a substance supporting the fact that the public force will be brought to bear upon those who do things said to contravene it—just as we talk of the force of gravitation accounting for the conduct of bodies in space. One phrase adds no more than the other to what we know without it. No doubt behind these legal rights is the fighting will of the subject to maintain them, and the spread of his emotions to the general rules by which they are maintained; but that does not seem to me the same thing as the supposed *a priori* discernment of a duty or the assertion of a preëxisting right. A dog will fight for his bone.

The most fundamental of the supposed preëxisting rights—the right to life—is sacrificed without a scruple not only in war, but whenever the interest of society, that is, of the predominant power in the community, is thought to demand it. Whether that interest is the interest of mankind in the long run no one can tell, and as, in any event, to those who do not think with Kant and Hegel it is only an interest, the sanctity disappears. I remember a very tenderhearted judge being of opinion that closing a hatch to stop a fire and the destruction of a cargo was justified even if it was known that doing so would stifle a man below. It is idle to illustrate further, because to those who agree with me I am uttering commonplaces and to those who disagree I am ignoring the necessary foundations of thought. The *a priori* men generally call the dissentients superficial. But I do agree with them in believing that one's attitude on these matters is closely connected with one's general attitude toward the universe. Proximately, as has been suggested, it is determined largely by early associations and temperament, coupled with the desire to have an absolute guide. Men to a great extent believe what they want to—although I see in that no basis for a philosophy that tells us what we should want to want.

Now when we come to our attitude toward the universe I do not see any rational ground for demanding the superlative—for being dissatisfied unless we are assured that our truth is cosmic truth, if there is such a thing—that the ultimates of a little creature on this earth are the last word of the unimaginable whole. If a man sees no reason for believing that significance, consciousness and ideals are more than marks of the finite, that does not justify what has been familiar in French sceptics: getting upon a pedestal and professing to look with haughty scorn upon a world in ruins. The real conclusion is that the part can not swallow the whole—that our categories are not, or may not be, adequate to formulate what we cannot know. If we believe that we come out of the universe, not it out of us, we must admit that we do not know what we are talking about when we speak of brute matter. We do know that a certain complex of energies can wag its tail and another can make syllogisms. These are among the powers of the unknown, and if, as may be, it has still greater powers that we can not understand, as Fabre in his studies of instinct would have us believe, studies that gave Bergson one of the strongest strands for his philosophy and enabled Maeterlinck to make us fancy for a moment that we heard a clang from behind phenomena—if this be true, why should we not be content? Why should we employ the energy that is furnished to us by the cosmos to defy it and shake our fist at the sky? It seems to me silly.

That the universe has in it more than we understand, that the private soldiers have not been told the plan of the campaign, or even that there is one, rather than some vaster unthinkable to which every predicate is an impertinence, has no bearing upon our conduct. We still shall fight—all of us because we want to live, some, at least, because we want to realize our spontaneity and prove our powers, for the joy of it, and we may leave to the unknown the supposed final valuation of that which in any event has value to us. It is enough for us that the universe has produced us and has within it, as less than it, all that we believe and love. If we think of our existence not as that of a little god outside, but as that of a ganglion within, we have the infinite behind us. It gives us our only but our adequate significance. A grain of sand has the same, but what competent person supposes that he understands a grain of sand? That is as much beyond our grasp as man. If our imagination is strong enough to accept the vision of ourselves as parts inseverable from the rest, and to extend our final interest beyond the boundary of our skins, it justifies the sacrifice even of our lives for ends outside of ourselves. The motive, to be sure, is the common wants and ideals that we find in man. Philosophy does not furnish motives, but it shows men that they are not fools for doing what they already want to do. It opens to the forlorn hopes on which we throw ourselves away, the vista of the farthest stretch of human thought, the chords of a harmony that breathes from the unknown.

RANDOLPH BOURNE

"Trans-National America"
1916

"The War and the Intellectuals"
1917

In "Trans-National America" (1916), Randolph Bourne (1886–1918) condemned the Anglo-conformist ideology often associated with the figure of the melting pot and called instead for the dynamic mixing and mingling of diverse peoples in the interests of new cultural combinations. Bourne was the most influential of the handful of intellectuals who opposed the nativism dominant among Americans of Protestant, Anglo-Saxon stock during the era of World War I. The ideal of cosmopolitanism to which Bourne gave voice was destined during the next several decades to serve as a rallying point for immigrant intellectuals as well as for antiprovincial WASPS like Bourne himself. This function of the cosmopolitan ideal is addressed in David A. Hollinger, "Ethnic Diversity, Cosmopolitanism, and the Emergence of the American Liberal Intelligentsia," in Hollinger's *In the American Province: Studies in the History and Historiography of Ideas* (Bloomington, Ind., 1985), 56–73. Bourne is also remembered for his vindication, during World War I, of the vocation of the intellectual as an independent critic of prevailing authorities. Nowhere did he uphold this vocation more adamantly and idealistically than in "The War and the Intellectuals" (1917), the second Bourne essay herein. The brief but brilliant career of this legendary American critic is sketched in Carl Resek's introduction to Randolph S. Bourne, *War and the Intellectuals: Collected Essays, 1915–1919* (New York, 1964), vii–xv. A more extensive account can be found in Edward Abrahams, *The Lyrical Left: Randolph Bourne, Alfred Steiglitz, and the Origins of Cultural Radicalism in America* (Charlottesville, Va., 1986).

"Trans-National America" 1916

No reverberatory effect of the great war has caused American public opinion more solicitude than the failure of the "melting-pot." The discovery of diverse nationalistic feelings among our great alien population has come to most people as an intense shock. It has brought out the unpleasant inconsistencies of our traditional beliefs. We have had to watch hard-hearted old Brahmins virtuously indignant at the spectacle of the immigrant refusing to be melted, while they jeer at patriots like Mary Antin who write about "our forefathers." We have had to listen to publicists who express themselves as stunned by the evidence of vigorous nationalistic and cultural movements in this country among Germans, Scandinavians, Bohemians, and Poles, while in the same breath they insist that the alien shall be forcibly assimilated to that Anglo-Saxon tradition which they unquestioningly label "American."

As the unpleasant truth has come upon us that assimilation in this country was proceeding on lines very different from those we had marked out for it, we found ourselves inclined to blame those who were thwarting our prophecies. The truth became culpable. We blamed the war, we blamed the Germans. And then we discovered with a moral shock that these movements had been making great headway before the war even began. We found that the tendency, reprehensible and paradoxical as it might be, has been for the national clusters of immigrants, as they became more and more firmly established and more and more prosperous, to cultivate more and more assiduously the literatures and cultural traditions of their homelands. Assimilation, in other words, instead of washing out the memories of Europe, made them more and more intensely real. Just as these clusters became more and more objectively American, did they become more and more German or Scandinavian or Bohemian or Polish.

To face the fact that our aliens are already strong enough to take a share in the direction of their own destiny, and that the strong cultural movements represented by the foreign press, schools, and colonies are a challenge to our facile attempts, is not, however, to admit the failure of Americanization. It is not to fear the failure of democracy. It is rather to urge us to an investigation of what Americanism may rightly mean. It is to ask ourselves whether our ideal has been broad or narrow—whether perhaps the time has not come to assert a higher ideal than the "melting-pot." Surely we cannot be certain of our spiritual democracy when, claiming to melt the nations within us to a comprehension of our free and democratic institutions, we fly into panic at the first sign of their own will and tendency. We act as if we wanted Americanization to take place only on our own terms, and not by the consent of the governed. All our elaborate machinery of settlement and school and union, of social and political naturalization, however, will move with friction just in so far as it neglects to take into account this strong and virile insistence that America shall be what the immigrant will

Source: Atlantic Monthly, 118 (July 1916), 86–97.

have a hand in making it, and not what a ruling class, descendant of those British stocks which were the first permanent immigrants, decide that America shall be made. This is the condition which confronts us, and which demands a clear and general readjustment of our attitude and our ideal.

Mary Antin is right when she looks upon our foreign-born as the people who missed the Mayflower and came over on the first boat they could find. But she forgets that when they did come it was not upon other Mayflowers, but upon a "Maiblume," a "Fleur de Mai," a "Fior di Maggio," a "Majblomst." These people were not mere arrivals from the same family, to be welcomed as understood and long-loved, but strangers to the neighborhood, with whom a long process of settling down had to take place. For they brought with them their national and racial characters, and each new national quota had to wear slowly away the contempt with which its mere alienness got itself greeted. Each had to make its way slowly from the lowest strata of unskilled labor up to a level where it satisfied the accredited norms of social success.

We are all foreign-born or the descendants of foreign-born, and if distinctions are to be made between us they should rightly be on some other ground than indigenousness. The early colonists came over with motives no less colonial than the later. They did not come to be assimilated in an American melting-pot. They did not come to adopt the culture of the American Indian. They had not the smallest intention of "giving themselves without reservation" to the new country. They came to get freedom to live as they wanted to. They came to escape from the stifling air and chaos of the old world; they came to make their fortune in a new land. They invented no new social framework. Rather they brought over bodily the old ways to which they had been accustomed. Tightly concentrated on a hostile frontier, they were conservative beyond belief. Their pioneer daring was reserved for the objective conquest of material resources. In their folkways, in their social and political institutions, they were, like every colonial people, slavishly imitative of the mother-country. So that, in spite of the "Revolution," our whole legal and political system remained more English than the English, petrified and unchanging, while in England law developed to meet the needs of the changing times.

It is just this English-American conservatism that has been our chief obstacle to social advance. We have needed the new peoples—the order of the German and Scandinavian, the turbulence of the Slav and Hun—to save us from our own stagnation. I do not mean that the illiterate Slav is now the equal of the New Englander of pure descent. He is raw material to be educated, not into a New Englander, but into a socialized American. . . . Let us cease to think of ideals like democracy as magical qualities inherent in certain peoples. Let us speak, not of inferior races, but of inferior civilizations. We are all to educate and to be educated. These peoples in America are in a common enterprise. It is not what we are now that concerns us, but what this plastic next generation may become in the light of a new cosmopolitan ideal.

We are not dealing with static factors, but with fluid and dynamic generations. To contrast the older and the newer immigrants and see the one class as democratically motivated by love of liberty, and the other by mere money-getting, is not to illuminate the future. To think of earlier nationalities as culturally assimilated to America, while we picture the later as a sodden and resistive mass, makes only for bitterness and misunderstanding. There may be a difference between these earlier and these later stocks, but it lies neither in motive for coming nor in strength of cultural allegiance to the homeland. The truth is that no more tenacious cultural allegiance to the mother country has been shown by any alien nation than by the ruling class of Anglo-Saxon descendants in these American States. English snobberies, English religion, English literary styles, English literary reverences and canons, English ethics, English superiorities, have been the cultural food that we have drunk in from our mothers' breasts. The distinctively American spirit—pioneer, as distinguished from the reminiscently English—that appears in Whitman and Emerson and James, has had to exist on sufferance alongside of this other cult, unconsciously belittled by our cultural makers of opinion. No country has perhaps had so great indigenous genius which had so little influence on the country's traditions and expressions. The unpopular and dreaded German-American of the present day is a beginning amateur in comparison with those foolish Anglophiles of Boston and New York and Philadelphia whose reversion to cultural type sees uncritically in England's cause the cause of Civilization, and, under the guise of ethical independence of thought, carries along European traditions which are no more "American" than the German categories themselves. . . .

The non-English American can scarcely be blamed if he sometimes thinks of the Anglo-Saxon predominance in America as little more than a predominance of priority. The Anglo-Saxon was merely the first immigrant, the first to found a colony. He has never really ceased to be the descendant of immigrants, nor has he ever succeeded in transforming that colony into a real nation, with a tenacious, richly woven fabric of native culture. Colonials from the other nations have come and settled down beside him. They found no definite native culture which should startle them out of their colonialism, and consequently they looked back to their mother-country, as the earlier Anglo-Saxon immigrant was looking back to his. What has been offered the newcomer has been the chance to learn English, to become a citizen, to salute the flag. And those elements of our ruling classes who are responsible for the public schools, the settlements, all the organizations for amelioration in the cities, have every reason to be proud of the care and labor which they have devoted to absorbing the immigrant. His opportunities the immigrant has taken to gladly, with almost a pathetic eagerness to make his way in the new land without friction or disturbance. The common language has made not only for the necessary communication, but for all the amenities of life.

If freedom means the right to do pretty much as one pleases, so long as one does not interfere with others, the immigrant has found freedom, and the ruling element has been singularly liberal in its treatment of the invading hordes. But if freedom means a democratic coöperation in determining the ideals and purposes and industrial and social institutions of a country, then the immigrant has not been free, and the Anglo-Saxon element is guilty of just what every dominant race is guilty of in every European country: the imposition of its own culture upon the minority peoples. The fact that this imposition has been so mild and, indeed, semi-conscious does not alter its quality. And the war has brought out just the degree to which that purpose of "Americanizing," that is, "Anglo-Saxonizing," the immigrant has failed.

For the Anglo-Saxon now in his bitterness to turn upon the other peoples, talk about their "arrogance," scold them for not being melted in a pot which never existed, is to betray the unconscious purpose which lay at the bottom of his heart. It betrays too the possession of a racial jealousy similar to that of which he is now accusing the so-called "hyphenates." Let the Anglo-Saxon be proud enough of the heroic toil and heroic sacrifices which moulded the nation. But let him ask himself, if he had had to depend on the English descendants, where he would have been living to-day. To those of us who see in the exploitation of unskilled labor the strident red *leit-motif* of our civilization, the settling of the country presents a great social drama as the waves of immigration broke over it.

Let the Anglo-Saxon ask himself where he would have been if these races had not come? Let those who feel the inferiority of the non-Anglo-Saxon immigrant contemplate that region of the States which has remained the most distinctively American," the South. Let him ask himself whether he would really like to see the foreign hordes Americanized into such an Americanization. Let him ask himself how superior this native civilization is to the great "alien" states of Wisconsin and Minnesota, where Scandinavians, Poles, and Germans have self-consciously labored to preserve their traditional culture, while being outwardly and satisfactorily American. Let him ask himself how much more wisdom, intelligence, industry and social leadership has come out of these alien states than out of all the truly American ones. The South, in fact, while this vast Northern development has gone on, still remains an English colony, stagnant and complacent, having progressed culturally scarcely beyond the early Victorian era. It is culturally sterile because it has had no advantage of cross-fertilization like the Northern states. What has happened in states such as Wisconsin and Minnesota is that strong foreign cultures have struck root in a new and fertile soil. America has meant liberation, and German and Scandinavian political ideas and social energies have expanded to a new potency. The process has not been at all the fancied "assimilation" of the Scandinavian or Teuton. Rather has it been a process of their assimilation of us—I speak as an Anglo-Saxon. The foreign cultures have not been melted down or run together, made into some homogeneous Americanism, but have remained distinct but coöperating to the greater glory and benefit, not only of themselves but of all the native "Americanism" around them.

What we emphatically do not want is that these distinctive qualities should be washed out into a tasteless, colorless fluid of uniformity. Already we have far too much of this insipidity,—masses of people who are cultural half-breeds, neither assimilated Anglo-Saxons nor nationals of another culture. Each national colony in this country seems to retain in its foreign press, its vernacular literature, its schools, its intellectual and patriotic leaders, a central cultural nucleus. From this nucleus the colony extends out by imperceptible gradations to a fringe where national characteristics are all but lost. Our cities are filled with these half-breeds who retain their foreign names but have lost the foreign savor. This does not mean that they have actually been changed into New Englanders or Middle Westerners. It does not mean that they have been really Americanized. It means that, letting slip from them whatever native culture they had, they have substituted for it only the most rudimentary American—the American culture of the cheap newspaper, the "movies," the popular song, the ubiquitous automobile. The unthinking who survey this class call them assimilated, Americanized. The great American public school has done its work. With these people our institutions are safe. We may thrill with dread at the aggressive hyphenate, but this tame flabbiness is accepted as Americanization. The same moulders of opinion whose ideal is to melt the different races into Anglo-Saxon gold hail this poor product as the satisfying result of their alchemy.

Yet a truer cultural sense would have told us that it is not the self-conscious cultural nuclei that sap at our American life, but these fringes. It is not the Jew who sticks proudly to the faith of his fathers and boasts of that venerable culture of his who is dangerous to America, but the Jew who has lost the Jewish fire and become a mere elementary, grasping animal. It is not the Bohemian who supports the Bohemian schools in Chicago whose influence is sinister, but the Bohemian who has made money and has got into ward politics. Just so surely as we tend to disintegrate these nuclei of nationalistic culture do we tend to create hordes of men and women without a spiritual country, cultural outlaws, without taste, without standards but those of the mob. We sentence them to live on the most rudimentary planes of American life. The influences at the centre of the nuclei are centripetal. They make for the intelligence and the social values which mean an enhancement of life. And just because the foreign-born retains this expressiveness is he likely to be a better citizen of the American community. The influences at the fringe, however, are centrifugal, anarchical. They make for detached fragments of peoples. Those who came to find liberty achieve only license. They become the flotsam and jetsam of American life, the downward undertow of our civilization with its leering cheapness and falseness of taste and spiritual outlook, the absence of mind and sincere feeling which we see in our slovenly towns, our vapid moving pictures, our popular novels, and in the vacuous faces of the crowds on the city street. This is the cultural wreckage of our time, and it is from the fringes of the Anglo-Saxon as well as the other stocks that it falls. America has as yet no impelling integrating force. It makes too easily for this detritus of cultures. In our loose, free country, no constraining national purpose, no tenacious folk-tradition and folk-style hold the people to a line.

The war has shown us that not in any magical formula will this purpose be found. No intense nationalism of the European plan can be ours. But do we not begin to see a new and more adventurous ideal? Do we not see how the national colonies in America, deriving power from the deep cultural heart of Europe and yet living here in mutual toleration, freed from the age-long tangles of races, creeds, and dynasties, may work out a federated ideal? America is transplanted Europe, but a Europe that has not been disintegrated and scattered in the transplanting as in some Dispersion. Its colonies live here inextricably mingled, yet not homogeneous. They merge but they do not fuse.

America is a unique sociological fabric, and it bespeaks poverty of imagination not to be thrilled at the incalculable potentialities of so novel a union of men. To seek no other goal than the weary old nationalism,—belligerent, exclusive, inbreeding, the poison of which we are witnessing now in Europe,—is to make patriotism a hollow sham, and to declare that, in spite of our boastings, America must ever be a follower and not a leader of nations.

If we come to find this point of view plausible, we shall have to give up the search for our native "American" culture. With the exception of the South and that New England which, like the Red Indian, seems to be passing into solemn oblivion, there is no distinctively American culture. It is apparently our lot rather to be a federation of cultures. This we have been for half a century, and the war has made it ever more evident that this is what we are destined to remain. This will not mean, however, that there are not expressions of indigenous genius that could not have sprung from any other soil. Music, poetry, philosophy, have been singularly fertile and new. Strangely enough, American genius has flared forth just in those directions which are least understanded of the people. If the American note is bigness, action, the objective as contrasted with the reflective life, where is the epic expression of this spirit? Our drama and our fiction, the peculiar fields for the expression of action and objectivity, are somehow exactly the fields of the spirit which remain poor and mediocre. American materialism is in some way inhibited from getting into impressive artistic form its own energy with which it bursts. Nor is it any better in architecture, the least romantic and subjective of all the arts. We are inarticulate of the very values which we profess to idealize. But in the finer forms—music, verse, the essay, philosophy—the American genius puts forth work equal to any of its contemporaries. Just in so far as our American genius has expressed the pioneer spirit, the adventurous, forward-looking drive of a colonial empire, is it representative of that whole America of the many races and peoples, and not of any partial or traditional enthusiasm. And only as that pioneer note is sounded can we really speak of the American culture. As long as we thought of Americanism in terms of the "melting-pot," our American cultural tradition lay in the past. It was something to which the new Americans were to be moulded. In the light of our changing ideal of Americanism, we must perpetrate the paradox that our American cultural tradition lies in the future. It will be what we all together make out of this incomparable opportunity of attacking the future with a new key.

Whatever American nationalism turns out to be, it is certain to become something utterly different from the nationalisms of twentieth-century Europe. This wave of reactionary enthusiasm to play the orthodox nationalistic game which is passing over the country is scarcely vital enough to last. We cannot swagger and thrill to the same national self-feeling. We must give new edges to our pride. We must be content to avoid the unnumbered woes that national patriotism has brought in Europe, and that fiercely heightened pride and self-consciousness. Alluring as this is, we must allow our imaginations to transcend this scarcely veiled belligerency. We can be serenely too proud to fight if our pride embraces the creative forces of civilization which armed contest nullifies. We can be too proud to fight if our code of honor transcends that of the schoolboy on the playground surrounded by his jeering mates. Our honor must be positive and creative, and not the mere jealous and negative protectiveness against metaphysical violations of our technical rights. When the doctrine is put forth that in one American flows the mystic blood of all our country's sacred honor, freedom, and prosperity, so that an injury to him is to be the signal for turning our whole nation into that clan-feud of horror and reprisal which would be war, then we find ourselves back among the musty schoolmen of the Middle Ages, and not in any pragmatic and realistic America of the twentieth century.

We should hold our gaze to what America has done, not what mediaeval codes of dueling she has failed to observe. We have transplanted European modernity to our soil, without the spirit that inflames it and turns all its energy into mutual destruction. Out of these foreign peoples there has somehow been squeezed the poison. An America, "hyphenated" to bitterness, is somehow non-explosive. For, even if we all hark back in sympathy to a European nation, even if the war has set every one vibrating to some emotional string twanged on the other side of the Atlantic, the effect has been one of almost dramatic harmlessness.

. . . . . .

The failure of the melting-pot, far from closing the great American democratic experiment, means that it has only just begun. Whatever American nationalism turns out to be, we see already that it will have a color richer and more exciting than our ideal has hitherto encompassed. In a world which has dreamed of internationalism, we find that we have all unawares been building up the first international nation. The voices which have cried for a tight and jealous nationalism of the European pattern are failing. From that ideal, however valiantly and disinterestedly it has been set for us, time and tendency have moved us further and further away. What we have achieved has been rather a cosmopolitan federation of national colonies, of foreign cultures, from whom the sting of devastating competition has been removed. America is already the world-federation in miniature, the continent where for the first time in history has been achieved that miracle of hope, the peaceful living side by side, with character substantially preserved, of the most heterogeneous peoples under the sun. Nowhere else has such contiguity been anything but the breeder of misery. Here, notwithstanding our tragic failures of adjustment, the outlines are already too clear not to give us a new vision and a new orientation of the American mind in the world.

It is for the American of the younger generation to accept this cosmopolitanism, and carry it along with self-conscious and fruitful purpose. In his colleges, he is already getting, with the study of modern history and politics, the modern literatures, economic geography, the privilege of a cosmopolitan outlook such as the people of no other nation of to-day in Europe can possibly secure. If he is still a colonial, he is no longer the colonial of one partial culture, but of many. He is a colonial of the world. Colonialism has grown into cosmopolitanism, and his mother-land is no one nation, but all who have anything life-enhancing to offer to the spirit. That vague sympathy which the France of ten years ago was feeling for the world—a sympathy which was drowned in the terrible reality of war—may be the modern American's, and that in a positive and aggressive sense. If the American is parochial, it is in sheer wantonness or cowardice. His provincialism is the measure of his fear of bogies or the defect of his imagination.

Indeed, it is not uncommon for the eager Anglo-Saxon who goes to a vivid American university to-day to find his true friends not among his own race but among the acclimatized German or Austrian, the acclimatized Jew, the acclimatized Scandinavian or Italian. In them he finds the cosmopolitan note. In these youths, foreign-born or the children of foreign-born parents, he is likely to find many of his old inbred morbid problems washed away. These friends are oblivious to the repressions of that tight little society in which he so provincially grew up. He has a pleasurable sense of liberation from the stale and familiar attitudes of those whose ingrowing culture has scarcely created anything vital for his America of to-day. He breathes a larger air. In his new enthusiasms for continental literature, for unplumbed Russian depths, for French clarity of thought, for Teuton philosophies of power, he feels himself citizen of a larger world. He may be absurdly superficial, his outward-reaching wonder may ignore all the stiller and homelier virtues of his Anglo-Saxon home, but he has at least found the clue to that international mind which will be essential to all men and women of good-will if they are ever to save this Western world of ours from suicide. His new friends have gone through a similar evolution. America has burned most of the baser metal also from them. Meeting now with this common American background, all of them may yet retain that distinctiveness of their native cultures and their national spiritual slants. They are more valuable and interesting to each other for being different, yet that difference could not be creative were it not for this new cosmopolitan outlook which America has given them and which they all equally possess.

A college where such a spirit is possible even to the smallest degree, has within itself already the seeds of this international intellectual world of the future. It suggests that the contribution of America will be an intellectual internationalism which goes far beyond the mere exchange of scientific ideas and discoveries and the cold recording of facts. It will be an intellectual sympathy which is not satisfied until it has got at the heart of the different cultural expressions, and felt as they feel. It may have immense preferences, but it will make understanding and not indignation its end. Such a sympathy will unite and not divide.

Against the thinly disguised panic which calls itself "patriotism" and the thinly disguised militarism which calls itself "preparedness" the cosmopolitan ideal is set. This does not mean that those who hold it are for a policy of drift. They, too, long passionately for an integrated and disciplined America. But they do not want one which is integrated only for domestic economic exploitation of the workers or for predatory economic imperialism among the weaker peoples. They do not want one that is integrated by coercion or militarism, or for the truculent assertion of a mediaeval code of honor and of doubtful rights. They believe that the most effective integration will be one which coördinates the diverse elements and turns them consciously toward working out together the place of America in the world-situation. They demand for integration a genuine integrity, a wholeness and soundness of enthusiasm and purpose which can only come when no national colony within our America feels that it is being discriminated against or that its cultural case is being prejudged. This strength of coöperation, this feeling that all who are here may have a hand in the destiny of America, will make for a finer spirit of integration than any narrow "Americanism" or forced chauvinism.

In this effort we may have to accept some form of that dual citizenship which meets with so much articulate horror among us. Dual citizenship we may have to recognize as the rudimentary form of that international citizenship to which, if our words mean anything, we aspire. We have assumed unquestioningly that mere participation in the political life of the United States must cut the new citizen off from all sympathy with his old allegiance. Anything but a bodily transfer of devotion from one sovereignty to another has been viewed as a sort of moral treason against the Republic. We have insisted that the immigrant whom we welcomed escaping from the very exclusive nationalism of his European home shall forthwith adopt a nationalism just as exclusive, just as narrow, and even less legitimate because it is founded on no warm traditions of his own. Yet a nation like France is said to permit a formal and legal dual citizenship even at the present time. Though a citizen of hers may pretend to cast off his allegiance in favor of some other sovereignty, he is still subject to her laws when he returns. Once a citizen, always a citizen, no matter how many new citizenships he may embrace. And such a dual citizenship seems to us sound and right. For it recognizes that, although the Frenchman may accept the formal institutional framework of his new country and indeed become intensely loyal to it, yet his Frenchness he will never lose. What makes up the fabric of his soul will always be of this Frenchness, so that unless he becomes utterly degenerate he will always to some degree dwell still in his native environment.

Indeed, does not the cultivated American who goes to Europe practice a dual citizenship, which, if not formal, is no less real? The American who lives abroad may be the least expatriate of men. If he falls in love with French ways and French thinking and French democracy and seeks to saturate himself with the new spirit, he is guilty of at least a dual spiritual citizenship. He may be still American, yet he feels himself through sympathy also a Frenchman. And he finds that this expansion involves no shameful conflict within him, no surrender of his native attitude. He has rather for the first time caught a glimpse of the cosmopolitan spirit. And after wandering about through many races and civilizations he may return to America to find them all here living vividly and crudely, seeking the same adjustment that he made. He sees the new peoples here with a new vision. They are no longer masses of aliens, waiting to be "assimilated," waiting to be melted down into the indistinguishable dough of Anglo-Saxonism. They are rather threads of living and potent cultures, blindly striving to weave themselves into a novel international nation, the first the world has seen. In an Austria-Hungary or a Prussia the stronger of these cultures would be moving almost instinctively to subjugate the weaker. But in America those wills-to-power are turned in a different direction into learning how to live together.

Along with dual citizenship we shall have to accept, I think, that free and mobile passage of the immigrant between America and his native land again which now arouses so much prejudice among us. We shall have to accept the immigrant's return for the same reason that we consider justified our own flitting about the earth. To stigmatize the alien who works in America for a few years and returns to his own land, only perhaps to seek American fortune again, is to think in narrow nationalistic terms. It is to ignore the cosmopolitan significance of this migration. It is to ignore the fact that the returning immigrant is often a missionary to an inferior civilization.

This migratory habit has been especially common with the unskilled laborers who have been pouring into the United States in the last dozen years from every country in southeastern Europe. Many of them return to spend their earnings in their own country or to serve their country in war. But they return with an entirely new critical outlook, and a sense of the superiority of American organization to the primitive living around them. This continued passage to and fro has already raised the material standard of living in many regions of these backward countries. For these regions are thus endowed with exactly what they need, the capital for the exploitation of their natural resources, and the spirit of enterprise. America is thus educating these laggard peoples from the very bottom of society up, awaking vast masses to a new-born hope for the future. In the migratory Greek, therefore, we have not the parasitic alien, the doubtful American asset, but a symbol of that cosmopolitan interchange which is coming, in spite of all war and national exclusiveness.

Only America, by reason of the unique liberty of opportunity and traditional isolation for which she seems to stand, can lead in this cosmopolitan enterprise. Only the American—and in this category I include the migratory alien who has lived with us and caught the pioneer spirit and a sense of new social vistas—has the chance to become that citizen of the world. America is coming to be, not a nationality but a trans-nationality, a weaving back and forth, with the other lands, of many threads of all sizes and colors. Any movement which attempts to thwart this weaving, or to dye the fabric any one color, or disentangle the threads of the strands, is false to this cosmopolitan vision. I do not mean that we shall necessarily glut ourselves with the raw product of humanity. It would be folly to absorb the nations faster than we could weave them. We have no duty either to admit or reject. It is purely a question of expediency. What concerns us is the fact that the strands are here. We must have a policy and an ideal for an actual situation. Our question is, What shall we do with our

America? How are you likely to get the more creative America—by confining our imaginations to the ideal of the melting-pot, or broadening them to some such cosmopolitan conception as I have been vaguely sketching?

The war has shown America to be unable, though isolated geographically and politically from a European world-situation, to remain aloof and irresponsible. She is a wandering star in a sky dominated by two colossal constellations of states. Can she not work out some position of her own, some life of being in, yet not quite of, this seething and embroiled European world? This is her only hope and promise. A trans-nationality of all the nations, it is spiritually impossible for her to pass into the orbit of any one. It will be folly to hurry herself into a premature and sentimental nationalism, or to emulate Europe and play fast and loose with the forces that drag into war. No Americanization will fulfill this vision which does not recognize the uniqueness of this trans-nationalism of ours. The Anglo-Saxon attempt to fuse will only create enmity and distrust. The crusade against "hyphenates" will only inflame the partial patriotism of trans-nationals, and cause them to assert their European traditions in strident and unwholesome ways. But the attempt to weave a wholly novel international nation out of our chaotic America will liberate and harmonize the creative power of all these peoples and give them the new spiritual citizenship, as so many individuals have already been given, of a world.

Is it a wild hope that the undertow of opposition to metaphysics in international relations, opposition to militarism, is less a cowardly provincialism than a groping for this higher cosmopolitan ideal? One can understand the irritated restlessness with which our proud pro-British colonists contemplate a heroic conflict across the seas in which they have no part. It was inevitable that our necessary inaction should evolve in their minds into the bogey of national shame and dishonor. But let us be careful about accepting their sensitiveness as final arbiter. Let us look at our reluctance rather as the first crude beginnings of assertion on the part of certain strands in our nationality that they have a right to a voice in the construction of the American ideal. Let us face realistically the America we have around us. Let us work with the forces that are at work. Let us make something of this trans-national spirit instead of outlawing it. Already we are living this cosmopolitan America. What we need is everywhere a vivid consciousness of the new ideal. Deliberate headway must be made against the survivals of the melting-pot ideal for the promise of American life.

We cannot Americanize America worthily by sentimentalizing and moralizing history. When the best schools are expressly renouncing the questionable duty of teaching patriotism by means of history, it is not the time to force shibboleth upon the immigrant. This form of Americanization has been heard because it appealed to the vestiges of our old sentimentalized and moralized patriotism. This has so far held the field as the expression of the new American's new devotion. The inflections of other voices have been drowned. They must be heard. We must see if the lesson of the war has not been for hundreds of these later Americans a vivid realization of their trans-nationality, a new consciousness of what America meant to them as a citizenship in the world. It is the vague historic idealisms which have provided the fuel for the European flame. Our American ideal can make no progress until we do away with this romantic gilding of the past.

All our idealisms must be those of future social goals in which all can participate, the good life of personality lived in the environment of the Beloved Community. No mere doubtful triumphs of the past, which redound to the glory of only one of our trans-nationalities, can satisfy us. It must be a future America, on which all can unite, which pulls us irresistibly toward it, as we understand each other more warmly.

To make real this striving amid dangers and apathies is work for a younger *intelligentsia* of America. Here is an enterprise of integration into which we can all pour ourselves, of a spiritual welding which should make us, if the final menace ever came, not weaker, but infinitely strong.

"The War and the Intellectuals"
1917

To those of us who still retain an irreconcilable animus against war, it has been a bitter experience to see the unanimity with which the American intellectuals have thrown their support to the use of war-technique in the crisis in which America found herself. Socialists, college professors, publicists, new-republicans, practitioners of literature have vied with each other in confirming with their intellectual faith the collapse of neutrality and the riveting of the war-mind on a hundred million more of the world's people. And the intellectuals are not content with confirming our belligerent gesture. They are now complacently asserting that it was they who effectively willed it, against the hesitation and dim perceptions of the American democratic masses. A war made deliberately by the intellectuals! A calm moral verdict, arrived at after a penetrating study of inexorable facts! Sluggish masses, too remote from the world-conflict to be stirred, too lacking in intellect to perceive their danger! An alert intellectual class, saving the people in spite of themselves, biding their time with Fabian strategy until the nation could be moved into war without serious resistance! An intellectual class, gently guiding a nation through sheer force of ideas into what the other nations entered only through predatory craft or popular hysteria or militarist madness! A war free from any taint of self-seeking, a war that will secure the triumph of democracy and internationalize the world! This is the picture which the more self-conscious intellectuals have formed of themselves, and which they are slowly impressing upon a population which is being led no man knows whither by an indubitably intellectualized President. And they are right, in that the war certainly did not spring from either the ideals or the prejudices, from the national ambitions or hysterias, of the American people, however acquiescent the masses prove to be, and however clearly the intellectuals prove their putative intuition.

Those intellectuals who have felt themselves totally out of sympathy with this drag toward war will seek some explanation for this joyful leadership. They will want to understand this willingness of the American intellect to open the sluices and flood us with the sewage of the war spirit. We cannot forget the virtuous horror and stupefaction which filled our college professors when they read the famous manifesto of their ninety-three German colleagues in defence of their war. To the American academic mind of 1914 defence of war was inconceivable. From Bernhardi it recoiled as from a blasphemy, little dreaming that two years later would find it creating its own cleanly reasons for imposing military service on the country and for talking of the rough rude currents of health and regeneration that war would send through the American body politic. They would have thought anyone mad who talked of shipping American men by the hundreds of thousands—conscripts—to die on the fields of France. Such a spiritual change seems catastrophic when we shoot our minds back to those

Source: Seven Arts, 2 (June 1917), 133–46.

days when neutrality was a proud thing. But the intellectual progress has been so gradual that the country retains little sense of the irony. The war sentiment, begun so gradually but so perseveringly by the preparedness advocates who came from the ranks of big business, caught hold of one after another of the intellectual groups. With the aid of Roosevelt, the murmurs became a monotonous chant, and finally a chorus so mighty that to be out of it was at first to be disreputable and finally almost obscene. And slowly a strident rant was worked up against Germany which compared very creditably with the German fulminations against the greedy power of England. The nerve of the war-feeling centred, of course, in the richer and older classes of the Atlantic seaboard, and was keenest where there were French or English business and particularly social connections. The sentiment then spread over the country as a class-phenomenon, touching everywhere those upper-class elements in each section who identified themselves with this Eastern ruling group. It must never be forgotten that in every community it was the least liberal and least democratic elements among whom the preparedness and later the war sentiment was found. The farmers were apathetic, the small business men and workingmen are still apathetic towards the war. The election was a vote of confidence of these latter classes in a President who would keep the faith of neutrality. The intellectuals, in other words, have identified themselves with the least democratic forces in American life. They have assumed the leadership for war of those very classes whom the American democracy has been immemorially fighting. Only in a world where irony was dead could an intellectual class enter war at the head of such illiberal cohorts in the avowed cause of world-liberalism and world-democracy. No one is left to point out the undemocratic nature of this war-liberalism. In a time of faith, skepticism is the most intolerable of all insults.

Our intellectual class might have been occupied, during the last two years of war, in studying and clarifying the ideals and aspirations of the American democracy, in discovering a true Americanism which would not have been merely nebulous but might have federated the different ethnic groups and traditions. They might have spent the time in endeavoring to clear the public mind of the cant of war, to get rid of old mystical notions that clog our thinking. We might have used the time for a great wave of education, for setting our house in spiritual order. We could at least have set the problem before ourselves. If our intellectuals were going to lead the administration, they might conceivably have tried to find some way of securing peace by making neutrality effective. They might have turned their intellectual energy not to the problem of jockeying the nation into war, but to the problem of using our vast neutral power to attain democratic ends for the rest of the world and ourselves without the use of the malevolent technique of war. They might have failed. The point is that they scarcely tried. The time was spent not in clarification and education, but in a mulling over of nebulous ideals of democracy and liberalism and civilization which had never meant anything fruitful to those ruling classes who now so glibly used them, and in giving free rein to the elementary instinct of self-defence. The whole era has been spiritually wasted. The outstanding feature has been not its Americanism but its intense colonialism. The offence of our intellectuals was not so much that they were colonial—for what could we expect of a nation composed of so many national elements?—but that it was so one-sidedly and partisanly colonial. The official, reputable expression of the intellectual class has been that of the English colonial. Certain portions of it have been even more loyalist than the King, more British even than Australia. Other colonial attitudes have been vulgar. The colonialism of the other American stocks was denied a hearing from the start. America might have been made a meeting-ground for the different national attitudes. An intellectual class, cultural colonists of the different European nations, might have threshed out the issues here as they could not be threshed out in Europe. Instead of this, the English colonials in university and press took command at the start, and we became an intellectual Hungary where thought was subject to an effective process of Magyarization. The reputable opinion of the American intellectuals became more and more either what could be read pleasantly in London, or what was written in an earnest effort to put Englishmen straight on their war-aims and war-technique. This Magyarization of thought produced as a counter-reaction a peculiarly offensive and inept German apologetic, and the two partisans divided the field between them. The great masses, the other ethnic groups, were inarticulate. American public opinion was almost as little prepared for war in 1917 as it was in 1914.

The sterile results of such an intellectual policy are inevitable. During the war the American intellectual class has produced almost nothing in the way of original and illuminating interpretation. Veblen's "Imperial Germany"; Patten's "Culture and War," and addresses; Dewey's "German Philosophy and Politics"; a chapter or two in Weyl's "American Foreign Policies";—is there much else of creative value in the intellectual repercussion of the war? It is true that the shock of war put the American intellectual to an unusual strain. He had to sit idle and think as spectator not as actor. There was no government to which he could docilely and loyally tender his mind as did the Oxford professors to justify England in her own eyes. The American's training was such as to make the fact of war almost incredible. Both in his reading of history and in his lack of economic perspective he was badly prepared for it. He had to explain to himself something which was too colossal for the modern mind, which outran any language or terms which we had to interpret it in. He had to expand his sympathies to the breaking-point, while pulling the past and present into some sort of interpretative order. The intellectuals in the fighting countries had only to rationalize and justify what their country was already doing. Their task was easy. A neutral, however, had really to search out the truth. Perhaps perspective was too much to ask of any mind. Certainly the older colonials among our college professors let their prejudices at once dictate their thought. They have been comfortable ever since. The war has taught them nothing and will teach them nothing. And they have had the satisfaction, under the rigor of events, of seeing prejudice submerge the intellects of their younger colleagues. And they have lived to see almost their entire class, pacifists and democrats too, join them as apologists for the "gigantic irrelevance" of war.

We have had to watch, therefore, in this country the same process which so shocked us abroad,—the coalescence of the intellectual classes in support of the military programme. In this country, indeed, the socialist intellectuals did not even have the grace of their German brothers and wait for the declaration of war before they broke for cover. And when they declared for war they showed how thin was the intellectual veneer of their socialism. For they called us in terms that might have emanated from any bourgeois journal to defend democracy and civilization, just as if it was not exactly against those very bourgeois democracies and capitalist civilizations that socialists had been fighting for decades. But so subtle is the spiritual chemistry of the "inside" that all this intellectual cohesion—herd-instinct become herd-intellect—which seemed abroad so hysterical and so servile, comes to us here in highly rational terms. We go to war to save the world from subjugation! But the German intellectuals went to war to save their culture from barbarization! And the French went to war to save their beautiful France! And the English to save international honor! And Russia, most altruistic and self-sacrificing of all, to save a small State from destruction! Whence is our miraculous intuition of our moral spotlessness? Whence our confidence that history will not unravel huge economic and imperialist forces upon which our rationalizations float like bubbles? The Jew often marvels that his race alone should have been chosen as the true people of the cosmic God. Are not our intellectuals equally fatuous when they tell us that our war of all wars is stainless and thrillingly achieving for good?

An intellectual class that was wholly rational would have called insistently for peace and not for war. For months the crying need has been for a negotiated peace, in order to avoid the ruin of a deadlock. Would not the same amount of resolute statesmanship thrown into intervention have secured a peace that would have been a subjugation for neither side? Was the terrific bargaining power of a great neutral ever really used? Our war followed, as all wars follow, a monstrous failure of diplomacy. Shamefacedness should now be our intellectuals' attitude, because the American play for peace was made so little more than a polite play. The intellectuals have still to explain why, willing as they now are to use force to continue the war to absolute exhaustion, they were not willing to use force to coerce the world to a speedy peace.

Their forward vision is no more convincing than their past rationality. We go to war now to internationalize the world! But surely their League to Enforce Peace is only a palpable apocalyptic myth, like the syndicalists' myth of the "general strike." It is not a rational programme so much as a glowing symbol for the purpose of focusing belief, of setting enthusiasm on fire for international order. As far as it does this it has pragmatic value, but as far as it provides a certain radiant mirage of idealism for this war and for a world-order founded on mutual fear, it is dangerous and obnoxious. Idealism should be kept for what is ideal. It is depressing to think that the prospect of a world so strong that none dare challenge it should be the immediate ideal of the American intellectual. If the League is only a makeshift, a coalition into which we enter to restore order, then it is only a description of existing fact, and the idea should be treated as such. But if it is an actually prospective outcome of the settlement, the keystone of American policy, it is neither realizable nor desirable. For the programme of such a League contains no provision for dynamic national growth or for international economic justice. In a world which requires recognition of economic internationalism far more than of political internationalism, an idea is reactionary which proposes to petrify and federate the nations as political and economic units. Such a scheme for international order is a dubious justification for American policy. And if American policy had been sincere in its belief that our participation would achieve international beatitude, would we not have made our entrance into the war conditional upon a solemn general agreement to respect in the final settlement these principles of international order? Could we have afforded, if our war was to end war by the establishment of a league of honor, to risk the defeat of our vision and our betrayal in the settlement? Yet we are in the war, and no such solemn agreement was made, nor has it even been suggested.

The case of the intellectuals seems, therefore, only very speciously rational. They could have used their energy to force a just peace or at least to devise other means than war for carrying through American policy. They could have used their intellectual energy to ensure that our participation in the war meant the international order which they wish. Intellect was not so used. It was used to lead an apathetic nation into an irresponsible war, without guarantees from those belligerents whose cause we were saving. The American intellectual, therefore, has been rational neither in his hindsight nor his foresight. To explain him we must look beneath the intellectual reasons to the emotional disposition. It is not so much what they thought as how they felt that explains our intellectual class. Allowing for colonial sympathy, there was still the personal shock in a world-war which outraged all our preconceived notions of the way the world was tending. It reduced to rubbish most of the humanitarian internationalism and democratic nationalism which had been the emotional thread of our intellectuals' life. We had suddenly to make a new orientation. There were mental conflicts. Our latent colonialism strove with our longing for American unity. Our desire for peace strove with our desire for national responsibility in the world. That first lofty and remote and not altogether unsound feeling of our spiritual isolation from the conflict could not last. There was the itch to be in the great experience which the rest of the world was having. Numbers of intelligent people who had never been stirred by the horrors of capitalistic peace at home were shaken out of their slumber by the horrors of war in Belgium. Never having felt responsibility for labor wars and oppressed masses and excluded races at home, they had a large fund of idle emotional capital to invest in the oppressed nationalities and ravaged villages of Europe. Hearts that had felt only ugly contempt for democratic strivings at home beat in tune with the struggle for freedom abroad. All this was natural, but it tended to over-emphasize our responsibility. And it threw our thinking out of gear. The task of making our own country detailedly fit for peace was abandoned in favor of a feverish concern for the management of the war, advice to the fighting governments on all matters, military, social and political, and a gradual working up of the conviction that we were ordained as a nation to lead all erring brothers towards the light of liberty and democracy. The failure of the American intellectual class to erect a creative attitude toward the war can be explained by these sterile mental conflicts which the shock to our ideals sent raging through us.

Mental conflicts end either in a new and higher synthesis or adjustment, or else in a reversion to more primitive ideas which have been outgrown but to which we drop when jolted out of our attained position. The war caused in America a recrudescence of nebulous ideals which a younger generation was fast outgrowing because it had passed the wistful stage and was discovering concrete ways of getting them incarnated in actual institutions. The shock of the war threw us back from this pragmatic work into an emotional bath of these old ideals. There was even a somewhat rarefied rivival of our primitive Yankee boastfulness, the reversion of senility to that republican childhood when we expected the whole world to copy our republican institutions. We amusingly ignored the fact that it was just that Imperial German regime, to whom we are to teach the art of self-government, which our own Federal structure, with its executive irresponsible in foreign policy and with its absence of parliamentary control, most resembles. And we are missing the exquisite irony of the unaffected homage paid by the American democratic intellectuals to the last and most detested of Britain's tory premiers as the representative of a "liberal" ally, as well as the irony of the selection of the best hated of America's bourbon "old guard" as the missionary of American democracy to Russia.

The intellectual state that could produce such things is one where reversion has taken place to more primitive ways of thinking. Simple syllogisms are substituted for analysis, things are known by their labels, our heart's desire dictates what we shall see. The American intellectual class, having failed to make the higher syntheses, regresses to ideas that can issue in quick, simplified action. Thought becomes any easy rationalization of what is actually going on or what is to happen inevitably tomorrow. It is true that certain groups did rationalize their colonialism and attach the doctrine of the inviolability of British seapower to the doctrine of a League of Peace. But this agile resolution of the mental conflict did not become a higher synthesis, to be creatively developed. It gradually merged into a justification for our going to war. It petrified into a dogma to be propagated. Criticism flagged and emotional propaganda began. Most of the socialists, the college professors and the practitioners of literature, however, have not even reached this high-water mark of synthesis. Their mental conflicts have been resolved much more simply. War in the interests of democracy! This was almost the sum of their philosophy. The primitive idea to which they regressed became almost insensibly translated into a craving for action, irresponsibility, the end of anxious and torturing attempts to reconcile peace-ideals with the drag of the world towards Hell. An end to the pain of trying to adjust the facts to what they ought to be! Let us consecrate the facts as ideal! Let us join the greased slide towards war! The momentum increased. Hesitations, ironies, consciences, considerations,—all were drowned in the elemental blare of doing something aggressive, colossal. The new-found Sabbath "peacefulness of being at war"! The thankfulness with which so many intellectuals lay down and floated with the current betrays the hesitation and suspense through which they had been. The American university is a brisk and happy place these days. Simple, unquestioning action has superseded the knots of thought. The thinker dances with reality.

With how many of the acceptors of war has it been mostly a dread of intellectual suspense? It is a mistake to suppose that intellectuality necessarily makes for suspended judgments. The intellect craves certitude. It takes effort to keep it supple and pliable. In a time of danger and disaster we jump desperately for some dogma to cling to. The time comes, if we try to hold out, when our nerves are sick with fatigue, and we seize in a great healing wave of release some doctrine that can be immediately translated into action. Neutrality meant suspense, and so it became the object of loathing to frayed nerves. The vital myth of the League of Peace provides a dogma to jump to. With war the world becomes motor again and speculation is brushed aside like cobwebs. The blessed emotion of self-defense intervenes too, which focused millions in Europe. A few keep up a critical pose after war is begun, but since they usually advise action which is in one-to-one correspondence with what the mass is already doing, their criticism is little more than a rationalization of the common emotional drive.

The results of war on the intellectual class are already apparent. Their thought becomes little more than a description and justification of what is going on. They turn upon any rash one who continues idly to speculate. Once the war is on, the conviction spreads that individual thought is helpless, that the only way one can count is as a cog in the great wheel. There is no good holding back. We are told to dry our unnoticed and ineffective tears and plunge into the great work. Not only is everyone forced into line, but the new certitude becomes idealized. It is a noble realism which opposes itself to futile obstruction and the cowardly refusal to face facts. This realistic boast is so loud and sonorous that one wonders whether realism is always a stern and intelligent grappling with realities. May it not be sometimes a mere surrender to the actual, an abdication of the ideal through a sheer fatigue from intellectual suspense? The pacifist is roundly scolded for refusing to face the facts, and for retiring into his own world of sentimental desire. But is the realist, who refuses to challenge or criticise facts, entitled to any more credit than that which comes from following the line of least resistance? The realist thinks he at least can control events by linking himself to the forces that are moving. Perhaps he can. But if it is a question of controlling war, it is difficult to see how the child on the back of a mad elephant is to be any more effective in stopping the beast than is the child who tries to stop him from the ground. The ex-humanitarian, turned realist, sneers at the snobbish neutrality, colossal conceit, crooked thinking, dazed sensibilities, of those who are still unable to find any balm of consolation for this war. We manufacture consolations here in America while there are probably not a dozen men fighting in Europe who did not long ago give up every reason for their being there except that nobody knew how to get them away.

But the intellectuals whom the crisis has crystallized into an acceptance of war have put themselves into a terrifyingly strategic position. It is only on the craft, in the stream, they say, that one has any chance of controlling the current forces for liberal purposes. If we obstruct, we surrender all power for influence. If we responsibly approve, we then retain our power for guiding. We will be listened to as responsible thinkers, while those who obstructed the coming of war have committed intellectual suicide and shall be cast into outer darkness. Criticism by the ruling powers will only be accepted from those intellectuals who are in sympathy with the general tendency of the war. Well, it is true that they may guide, but if their stream leads to disaster and the frustration of national life, is their guiding any more than a preference whether they shall go over the right-hand or the left-hand side of the precipice? Meanwhile, however, there is comfort on board. Be with us, they call, or be negligible, irrelevant. Dissenters are already excommunicated. Irreconcilable radicals, wringing their hands among the debris, become the most despicable and impotent of men. There seems no choice for the intellectual but to join the mass of acceptance. But again the terrible dilemma arises,—either support what is going on, in which case you count for nothing because you are swallowed in the mass and great incalculable forces bear you on; or remain aloof, passively resistant, in which case you count for nothing because you are outside the machinery of reality.

Is there no place left, then, for the intellectual who cannot yet crystallize, who does not dread suspense, and is not yet drugged with fatigue? The American intellectuals, in their preoccupation with reality, seem to have forgotten that the real enemy is War rather than imperial Germany. There is work to be done to prevent this war of ours from passing into popular mythology as a holy crusade. What shall we do with leaders who tell us that we go to war in moral spotlessness, or who make "democracy" synonymous with a republican form of government? There is work to be done in still shouting that all the revolutionary by-products will not justify the war, or make war anything else than the most noxious complex of all the evils that afflict men. There must be some to find no consolation whatever, and some to sneer at those who buy the cheap emotion of sacrifice. There must be some irreconcilables left who will not even accept the war with walrus tears. There must be some to call unceasingly for peace, and some to insist that the terms of settlement shall be not only liberal but democratic. There must be some intellectuals who are not willing to use the old discredited counters again and to support a peace which would leave all the old inflammable materials of armament lying about the world. There must still be opposition to any contemplated "liberal" world-order founded on military coalitions. The "irreconcilable" need not be disloyal. He need not even be "impossibilist." His apathy towards war should take the form of a heightened energy and enthusiasm for the education, the art, the interpretation that make for life in the midst of the world of death. The intellectual who retains his animus against war will push out more boldly than ever to make his case solid against it. The old ideals crumble; new ideals must be forged. His mind will continue to roam widely and ceaselessly. The thing he will fear most is premature crystallization. If the American intellectual class rivets itself to a "liberal" philosophy that perpetuates the old errors, there will then be need for "democrats" whose task will be to divide, confuse, disturb, keep the intellectual waters constantly in motion to prevent any such ice from ever forming.

MARGARET MEAD

Selection from *Coming of Age in Samoa*
1928

The most obvious function performed by social scientists in modern America has been a cognitive one: the advancement of knowledge about society. Another, more subtle function has been a moral one: the articulation and criticism of standards for conduct. The role of the public moralist had long been performed by the clergy and by men and women of letters, but in the twentieth century this role increasingly came to be filled by psychologists, anthropologists, sociologists, and other practitioners of social science. The anthropologist Margaret Mead (1901–78) was perhaps the most influential single example of "the social scientist as public moralist." Mead wrote thirty-four books on a multitude of topics, many of which were only remotely anthropological. She was a formidable presence in American intellectual life for half a century, beginning with her *Coming of Age in Samoa* (1928), from which the selection that follows is taken. Mead's study of adolescent girls in Samoa was offered frankly as a means of fostering a critical perspective on the growing-up experiences of young people in Mead's own society. In our excerpt she sums up the lessons she wishes readers to derive from her study. Mead was an inveterate enemy of American middle-class provincialism and invited her readers to develop a diverse culture in which individuals could choose between a great variety of ways of life. Although she expressed much sympathy for the homogeneous, easygoing culture she attributed to the people of Samoa, she defended the heterogeneous, complex culture of modern America and sought to foster the knowledge and attitudes that would better equip Americans to take advantage of their opportunities. A readable, popular biography is Jane Howard, *Margaret Mead: A Life* (New York, 1984). The quality of Mead's fieldwork as an anthropologist has been a matter of dispute, especially in recent years. For a brief, judicious commentary on this controversy see the remarks of James Clifford in the *Times Literary Supplement* May 13, 1983, 475–76.

For many chapters we have followed the lives of Samoan girls, watched them change from babies to baby tenders, learn to make the oven and weave fine mats, forsake the life of the gang to become more active members of the household, defer marriage through as many years of casual love-making as possible, finally marry and settle down to rearing children who will repeat the same cycle. As far as our material permitted, an experiment has been conducted to discover what the process of development was like in a society very different from our own. Because the length of human life and the complexity of our society did not permit us to make our experiment here, to choose a group of baby girls and bring them to maturity under conditions created for the experiment, it was necessary to go instead to another country where history had set the stage for us. There we found girl children passing through the same process of physical development through which our girls go, cutting their first teeth and losing them, cutting their second teeth, growing tall and ungainly, reaching puberty with their first menstruation, gradually reaching physical maturity, and becoming ready to produce the next generation. It was possible to say: Here are the proper conditions for an experiment; the developing girl is a constant factor in America and in Samoa; the civilisation of America and the civilisation of Samoa are different. In the course of development, the process of growth by which the girl baby becomes a grown woman, are the sudden and conspicuous bodily changes which take place at puberty accompanied by a development which is spasmodic, emotionally charged, and accompanied by an awakened religious sense, a flowering of idealism, a great desire for assertion of self against authority—or not? Is adolescence a period of mental and emotional distress for the growing girl as inevitably as teething is a period of misery for the small baby? Can we think of adolescence as a time in the life history of every girl child which carries with it symptoms of conflict and stress as surely as it implies a change in the girl's body?

Following the Samoan girls through every aspect of their lives we have tried to answer this question, and we found throughout that we had to answer it in the negative. The adolescent girl in Samoa differed from her sister who had not reached puberty in one chief respect, that in the older girl certain bodily changes were present which were absent in the younger girl. There were no other great differences to set off the group passing through adolescence from the group which would become adolescent in two years or the group which had become adolescent two years before.

And if one girl past puberty is undersized while her cousin is tall and able to do heavier work, there will be a difference between them, due to their different physical endowment, which will be far greater than that which is due to puberty. The tall, husky girl will be isolated from her companions, forced to do longer, more adult tasks, rendered shy by a change of clothing, while her cousin, slower to attain her growth, will still be treated as a child and will have to solve only the slightly fewer problems of childhood. The precedent of educators here who recommend special tactics in the treatment of adolescent girls translated into Samoan terms would read: Tall girls are different from short girls of the same age, we must adopt a different method of educating them.

But when we have answered the question we set out to answer we have not finished with the problem. A further question presents itself. If it is proved that adoles-

Source: Coming of Age in Samoa, Margaret Mead, 195–206, 234–35, 244–48.

cence is not necessarily a specially difficult period in a girl's life—and proved it is if we can find any society in which that is so—then what accounts for the presence of storm and stress in American adolescents? First, we may say quite simply, that there must be something in the two civilisations to account for the difference. If the same process takes a different form in two different environments, we cannot make any explanations in terms of the process, for that is the same in both cases. But the social environment is very different and it is to it that we must look for an explanation. What is there in Samoa which is absent in America, what is there in America which is absent in Samoa, which will account for this difference?

Such a question has enormous implications and any attempt to answer it will be subject to many possibilities of error. But if we narrow our question to the way in which aspects of Samoan life which irremediably affect the life of the adolescent girl differ from the forces which influence our growing girls, it is possible to try to answer it.

The background of these differences is a broad one, with two important components; one is due to characteristics which are Samoan, the other to characteristics which are primitive.

The Samoan background which makes growing up so easy, so simple a matter, is the general casualness of the whole society. For Samoa is a place where no one plays for very high stakes, no one pays very heavy prices, no one suffers for his convictions or fights to the death for special ends. Disagreements between parent and child are settled by the child's moving across the street, between a man and his village by the man's removal to the next village, between a husband and his wife's seducer by a few fine mats. Neither poverty nor great disasters threaten the people to make them hold their lives dearly and tremble for continued existence. No implacable gods, swift to anger and strong to punish, disturb the even tenor of their days. Wars and cannibalism are long since passed away and now the greatest cause for tears, short of death itself, is a journey of a relative to another island. No one is hurried along in life or punished harshly for slowness of development. Instead the gifted, the precocious, are held back, until the slowest among them have caught the pace. And in personal relations, caring is as slight. Love and hate, jealousy and revenge, sorrow and bereavement, are all matters of weeks. From the first months of its life, when the child is handed carelessly from one woman's hands to another's, the lesson is learned of not caring for one person greatly, not setting high hopes on any one relationship.

And just as we may feel that the Occident penalises those unfortunates who are born into Western civilisation with a taste for meditation and a complete distaste for activity, so we may say that Samoa is kind to those who have learned the lesson of not caring, and hard upon those few individuals who have failed to learn it. Lola and Mala and little Siva, Lola's sister, all were girls with a capacity for emotion greater than their fellows. And Lola and Mala, passionately desiring affection and too violently venting upon the community their disappointment over their lack of it, were both delinquent, unhappy misfits in a society which gave all the rewards to those who took defeat lightly and turned to some other goal with a smile.

In this casual attitude towards life, in this avoidance of conflict, of poignant situations, Samoa contrasts strongly not only with America but also with most primitive civilisations. And however much we may deplore such an attitude and feel that important personalities and great art are not born in so shallow a society, we must recognise that here is a strong factor in the painless development from childhood to womanhood.

For where no one feels very strongly, the adolescent will not be tortured by poignant situations. There are no such disastrous choices as those which confronted young people who felt that the service of God demanded forswearing the world forever, as in the Middle Ages, or cutting off one's finger as a religious offering, as among the Plains Indians. So, high up in our list of explanations we must place the lack of deep feeling which the Samoans have conventionalised until it is the very framework of all their attitudes toward life.

And next there is the most striking way in which all isolated primitive civilisation and many modern ones differ from our own, in the number of choices which are permitted to each individual. Our children grow up to find a world of choices dazzling their unaccustomed eyes. In religion they may be Catholics, Protestants, Christian Scientists, Spiritualists, Agnostics, Atheists, or even pay no attention at all to religion. This is an unthinkable situation in any primitive society not exposed to foreign influence. There is one set of gods, one accepted religious practice, and if a man does not believe, his only recourse is to believe less than his fellows; he may scoff but there is no new faith to which he may turn. Present-day Manu'a approximates this condition; all are Christians of the same sect. There is no conflict in matters of belief although there is a difference in practice between Church-members and non-Church-members. And it was remarked that in the case of several of the growing girls the need for choice between these two practices may some day produce a conflict. But at present the Church makes too slight a bid for young unmarried members to force the adolescent to make any decision.

Similarly, our children are faced with half a dozen standards of morality: a double sex standard for men and women, a single standard for men and women, and groups which advocate that the single standard should be freedom while others argue that the single standard should be absolute monogamy. Trial marriage, companionate marriage, contract marriage—all these possible solutions of a social impasse are paraded before the growing children while the actual conditions in their own communities and the moving pictures and magazines inform them of mass violations of every code, violations which march under no banners of social reform.

The Samoan child faces no such dilemma. Sex is a natural, pleasurable thing; the freedom with which it may be indulged in is limited by just one consideration, social status. Chiefs' daughters and chiefs' wives should indulge in no extra-marital experiments. Responsible adults, heads of households and mothers of families should have too many important matters on hand to leave them much time for casual amorous adventures. Every one in the community agrees about the matter, the only dissenters are the missionaries who dissent so vainly that their protests are unimportant. But as soon as a sufficient sentiment gathers about the missionary attitude with its European standard of sex behaviour, the need for choice, the forerunner of conflict, will enter into Samoan society.

Our young people are faced by a series of different groups which believe different things and advocate different practices, and to each of which some trusted friend or relative may belong. So a girl's father may be a Presbyterian, an imperialist, a vegetarian, a teetotaler, with a strong literary preference for Edmund Burke, a believer in the open shop and a high tariff, who believes that woman's place is in the home, that young girls should wear corsets, not roll their stockings, not smoke, nor go riding with young men in the evening. But her mother's father may be a Low Episcopalian, a believer in high living, a strong advocate of States' Rights and the Monroe Doctrine, who reads Rabelais, likes to go to musical shows and horse races. Her aunt is an agnostic, an ardent advocate of woman's rights, an internationalist who rests all her hopes on Esperanto, is devoted to Bernard Shaw, and spends her spare time in campaigns of anti-vivisection. Her elder brother, whom she admires exceedingly, has just spent two years at Oxford. He is an Anglo-Catholic, an enthusiast concerning all things mediaeval, writes mystical poetry, reads Chesterton, and means to devote his life to seeking for the lost secret of mediaeval stained glass. Her mother's younger brother is an engineer, a strict materialist, who never recovered from reading Haeckel in his youth; he scorns art, believes that science will save the world, scoffs at everything that was said and thought before the nineteenth century, and ruins his health by experiments in the scientific elimination of sleep. Her mother is of a quietistic frame of mind, very much interested in Indian philosophy, a pacifist, a strict non-participator in life, who in spite of her daughter's devotion to her will not make any move to enlist her enthusiasms. And this may be within the girl's own household. Add to it the groups represented, defended, advocated by her friends, her teachers, and the books which she reads by accident, and the list of possible enthusiasms, of suggested allegiances, incompatible with one another, becomes appalling.

The Samoan girl's choices are far otherwise. Her father is a member of the Church and so is her uncle. Her father lives in a village where there is good fishing, her uncle in a village where there are plenty of cocoanut crabs. Her father is a good fisherman and in his house there is plenty to eat; her uncle is a talking chief and his frequent presents of bark cloth provide excellent dance dresses. Her paternal grandmother, who lives with her uncle, can teach her many secrets of healing; her maternal grandmother, who lives with her mother, is an expert weaver of fans. The boys in her uncle's village are admitted younger into the *Aumaga* and are not much fun when they come to call; but there are three boys in her own village whom she likes very much. And her great dilemma is whether to live with her father or her uncle, a frank, straightforward problem which introduces no ethical perplexities, no question of impersonal logic. Nor will her choice be taken as a personal matter, as the American girl's allegiance to the views of one relative might be interpreted by her other relatives. The Samoans will be sure she chose one residence rather than the other for perfectly good reasons, the food was better, she had a lover in one village, or she had quarrelled with a lover in the other village. In each case she was making concrete choices within one recognised pattern of behaviour. She was never called upon to make choices involving an actual rejection of the standards of her social group, such as the daughter of Puritan parents, who permits indiscriminate caresses, must make in our society.

And not only are our developing children faced by a series of groups advocating different and mutually exclusive standards, but a more perplexing problem presents itself to them. Because our civilisation is woven of so many diverse strands, the ideas which any one group accepts will be found to contain numerous contradictions. So if the girl has given her allegiance whole-heartedly to some one group and has accepted in good faith their asseverations that they alone are right and all other philosophies of life are Antichrist and anathema, her troubles are still not over. While the less thoughtful receives her worst blows in the discovery that what father thinks is good, grandfather thinks is bad, and that things which are permitted at home are banned at school, the more thoughtful child has subtler difficulties in store for her. If she has philosophically accepted the fact that there are several standards among which she must choose, she may still preserve a childlike faith in the coherence of her chosen philosophy.

Beyond the immediate choice which was so puzzling and hard to make, which perhaps involved hurting her parents or alienating her friends, she expects peace. But she has not reckoned with the fact that each of the philosophies with which she is confronted is itself but the half-ripened fruit of compromise. If she accept Christianity, she is immediately confused between the Gospel teachings concerning peace and the value of human life and the Church's whole-hearted acceptance of war. The compromise made seventeen centuries ago between the Roman philosophy of war and domination, and the early Church doctrine of peace and humility, is still present to confuse the modern child. If she accepts the philosophic premises upon which the Declaration of Independence of the United States was founded, she finds herself faced with the necessity of reconciling the belief in the equality of man and our institutional pledges of equality and opportunity with our treatment of the Negro and the Oriental. The diversity of standards in present-day society is so striking that the dullest, the most incurious, cannot fail to notice it. And this diversity is so old, so embodied in semi-solutions, in those compromises between different philosophies which we call Christianity, or democracy, or humanitariansim, that it baffles the most intelligent, the most curious, the most analytical.

So for the explanation of the lack of poignancy in the choices of growing girls in Samoa, we must look to the temperament of the Samoan civilisation which discounts strong feeling. But for the explanation of the lack of conflict we must look principally to the difference between a simple, homogenous primitive civilisation, a civilisation which changes so slowly that to each generation it appears static, and a motley, diverse, heterogeneous modern civilisation.

. . . . . .

We have been comparing point for point, our civilisation and the simpler civilisation of Samoa, in order to illuminate our own methods of education. If now we turn from the Samoan picture and take away only the main lesson which we learned there, that adolescence is not necessarily a time of stress and strain, but that cultural conditions make it so, can we draw any conclusions which might bear fruit in the training of our adolescents?

At first blush the answer seems simple enough. If adolescents are only plunged into difficulties and distress because of conditions in their social environment, then by all means let us so modify that environment as to reduce this stress and eliminate this strain and anguish of adjustment. But, unfortunately, the conditions which vex our adolescents are the flesh and bone of our society, no more subject to straightforward manipulation upon our part than is the language which we speak. We can alter a syllable here, a construction there; but the great and far-reaching changes in linguistic structure (as in all parts of culture) are the work of time, a work in which each individual plays an unconscious and inconsiderable part. The principal causes of our adolescents' difficulty are the presence of conflicting standards and the belief that every individual should make his or her own choices, coupled with a feeling that choice is an important matter. Given these cultural attitudes, adolescence, regarded now not as a period of physiological change, for we know that physiological puberty need not produce conflict, but as the beginning of mental and emotional maturity, is bound to be filled with conflicts and difficulties. A society which is clamouring for choice, which is filled with many articulate groups, each urging its own brand of salvation, its own variety of economic philosophy, will give each new generation no peace until all have chosen or gone under, unable to bear the conditions of choice. The stress is in our civilisation, not in the physical changes through which our children pass, but it is none the less real nor the less inevitable in twentieth-century America.

. . . . . .

Granting that society presents too many problems to her adolescents, demands too many momentous decisions on a few months' notice, what is to be done about it? One panacea suggested would be to postpone at least some of the decisions, keep the child economically dependent, or segregate her from all contact with the other sex, present her with only one set of religious ideas until she is older, more poised, better able to deal critically with the problems which will confront her. In a less articulate fashion, such an idea is back of various schemes for the prolongation of youth, through raising the working age, raising the school age, shielding school children from a knowledge of controversies like evolution versus fundamentalism, or any knowledge of sex hygiene or birth control. Even if such measures, specially initiated and legislatively enforced, could accomplish the end which they seek and postpone the period of choice, it is doubtful whether such a development would be desirable. It is unfair that very young children should be the battleground for conflicting standards, that their development should be hampered by propagandist attempts to enlist and condition them too young. It is probably equally unfair to culturally defer the decisions too late. Loss of one's fundamental religious faith is more of a wrench at thirty than at fifteen simply in terms of the number of years of acceptance which have accompanied the belief. A sudden knowledge of hitherto unsuspected aspects of sex, or a shattering of all the old conventions concerning sex behaviour, is more difficult just in terms of the strength of the old attitudes. Furthermore, in practical terms, such schemes would be as they are now, merely local, one state legislating against evolution, another against birth control, or one religious group segregating its unmarried girls. And these special local movements would simply unfit groups of young people for competing happily with children who had been permitted to make their choices earlier. Such an educational scheme, in addition to being almost impossible of execution, would be a step backward and would only beg the question.

Instead, we must turn all of our educational efforts to training our children for the choices which will confront them. Education, in the home even more than at school, instead of being a special pleading for one régime, a desperate attempt to form one particular habit of mind which will withstand all outside influences, must be a preparation for those very influences. Such an education must give far more attention to mental and physical hygiene than it has given hitherto. The child who is to choose wisely must be healthy in mind and body, handicapped in no preventable fashion. And even more importantly, this child of the future must have an open mind. The home must cease to plead an ethical cause or a religious belief with smiles or frowns, caresses or threats. The children must be taught how to think, not what to think. And because old errors die slowly, they must be taught tolerance, just as to-day they are taught intolerance. They must be taught that many ways are open to them, no one sanctioned above its alternative, and that upon them and upon them alone lies the burden of choice. Unhampered by prejudices, unvexed by too early conditioning to any one standard, they must come clear-eyed to the choices which lie before them.

For it must be realised by any student of civilisation that we pay heavily for our heterogeneous, rapidly changing civilisation; we pay in high proportions of crime and delinquency, we pay in the conflicts of youth, we pay in an ever-increasing number of neuroses, we pay in the lack of a coherent tradition without which the development of art is sadly handicapped. In such a list of prices, we must count our gains carefully, not to be discouraged. And chief among our gains must be reckoned this possibility of choice, the recognition of many possible ways of life, where other civilisations have recognised only one. Where other civilisations give a satisfactory outlet to only one temperamental type, be he mystic or soldier, business man or artist, a civilisation in which there are many standards offers a possibility of satisfactory adjustment to individuals of many different temperamental types, of diverse gifts and varying interests.

At the present time we live in a period of transition. We have many standards but we still believe that only one standard can be the right one. We present to our children the picture of a battle-field where each group is fully armoured in a conviction of the righteousness of its cause. And each of these groups make forays among the next generation. But it is unthinkable that a final recognition of the great number of ways in which man, during the course of history and at the present time, is solving the problems of life, should not bring with it in turn the downfall of our belief in a single standard. And when no one group claims ethical sanction for its customs, and each group welcomes to its midst only those who are temperamentally fitted for membership, then we shall have realised the high point of individual choice and universal toleration which a heterogeneous culture and a heterogeneous culture alone can attain. Samoa knows but one way of life and teaches it to her children. Will we, who have the knowledge of many ways, leave our children free to choose among them?

EDMUND WILSON

"An Appeal to Progressives"

1931

The economic depression of the 1930s led many liberals who had been "betting on capitalism," as Edmund Wilson (1895–1972) puts it, to consider radical alternatives. Perhaps the means of production should, indeed, be taken out of private hands and assigned to a government acting in the public interest. Although nothing of the sort was to actually happen, the argument for a socialist alternative to capitalism was a prominent theme in the discourse of the 1930s. As Wilson made the argument in the following *New Republic* article of 1931, even the program of communism might have something to offer Americans, especially if it could be "taken away" from the Communist party and developed in the context of American democracy. The story of the attraction of American intellectuals to communism is best told in Daniel Aaron, *Writers on the Left* (New York, 1961). For Wilson, the making of arguments for socialistic alternatives to capitalism was but one episode in an exceedingly diversified literary career. Wilson wrote major books on symbolist literature, the history of socialism, and the literature of the American Civil War in addition to dozens of volumes of poems, plays, fiction, and criticism. The best single introduction to his life and thought is Lewis Dabney's "Introduction" in Dabney, ed., *The Portable Edmund Wilson* (New York, 1983), xi–xlv.

. . . . . .

. . . American optimism has taken a serious beating; the national morale is weak. The energy and the faith for a fresh start seem now not to be forthcoming: a dreadful apathy, unsureness and discouragement is felt to have fallen upon us. It is as if we were afraid to go on with what we were doing before or as if we had no longer the heart for it. I want to suggest that the present depression may be nothing less than one of the turning-points in our history, our first real crisis since the Civil War. The Americans at the present time seem to be experiencing not merely an economic breakdown but a distinct psychological change. From the time of the Civil War on, all our enthusiasm and creative energy went into the development of our tremendous resources. This development had two aspects: one was the exploration of the continent and the engineering feats involved in reclaiming it; the other the amassing of gigantic fortunes. Today the discoveries have all been made: we no longer look toward the West, as the Europeans once looked to America, as to a world of untold treasures and wonders—and the excitement of mastering new seacoasts, new rivers, forests, prairies and mountains seems now completely spent. This was already true at the time of the European War (when, incidentally, we were running into a business depression), but the war gave us a new objective—new discoveries, the discovery of Europe; new heroic stunts of engineering, the transportation of our army to France. Since the end of the war, however, we have, as a people, had nothing to carry us along except the momentum of money-making. We have been trying still to find in it the exhilaration of the money-making of our earlier period, which had been largely the exhilaration of the wildness and size of the continent—the breaking it in to the harness of the railroads, the stumbling upon sudden riches. But during these last years our hope and our faith have all been put behind the speed of mass production, behind stupendous campaigns of advertising, behind cyclones of salesmanship. Our buoyancy had been becoming hysterical. And the reaction from an hysterical exhilaration is a slump into despondency and inertia. What we have lost is, it may be, not merely our way in the economic labyrinth but our conviction of the value of what we were doing. Money-making and the kind of advantages which a money-making society provides for money to buy are not enough to satisfy humanity—neither is a system like ours in which everyone is out for himself and devil take the hindmost, with no common purpose and little common culture to give life stability and sense. Our idolization of our aviators—our extravagant excitement over Lindbergh and our romantic admiration (now beginning to cool off) for Byrd—has been like a last desperate burst of American idealism, a last impulse to dissociate our national soul from a precipitate progress that was taking us from automobiles and radios straight through electric refrigerators to Tom Thumb golf-courses.

The old American ideal and legend of the poor boy who gets to be a millionaire, which gradually came to take the place of the poor boy who got to be President, has today lost almost all its glamor. Not only do people not hope to be Hoover—they do not even hope so often as they did to be Carnegie or Henry Ford. The romance of the legend of the poor boy was the romance of the old democratic chance, of the career open to the talents—but the realities of a millionaire society have turned out to be the

Source: The Shores of Light, Edmund Wilson, 524–33.

monstrosities of capitalism: the children of the successful poor boy get lazy and sick on their father's money, and the poor boys who afterwards arrive on the scene discover that—with the crippling of the grain market, the elimination of the factory worker by the development of the machine and the decimation of the white-collar class, even though sometimes apparently well on their way to getting in on the big money themselves, by enormous business mergers—the career is no longer open to the extent that had originally been hoped. What began as the libertarian adventure of eighteenth-century middle-class democracy seems to have ended in the cul de sac of an antiquated economic system. And capitalist-minded as the Americans have now become, they seem to feel they are in a cul de sac. It is as if they did not dare to go on. In spite of the fundamental absurdity of so much of what we have lately been doing, we are considerably better educated and more intelligent than we once were, and since the war we have been closer to Europe. The Buicks and Cadillacs, the bad gin and Scotch, the radio concerts interrupted by advertising talks, the golf and bridge of the suburban household, which the bond salesman can get for his money, can hardly compensate him for daily work of a kind in which it is utterly impossible to imagine a normal human being taking satisfaction or pride—and the bond salesman is the type of the whole urban office class. The brokers and bankers who are shooting themselves and jumping out of windows have been disheartened by the precariousness of their profession—but would they be killing themselves if they loved it? Who today, in fact, in the United States, can really love our meaningless life, where the manufacturer raises the workers' wages only in order to create a demand for the gadgets which for better or worse he happens to have an interest in selling them, while agriculture goes hang, and science and art are left to be exploited by the commercial laboratories, the market for commercial art illustration and the New York publishers' racket, or to be fed in a haphazard way by a dole from the fortunes of rich men who have been conscience-stricken or simply overpowered at finding themselves at the end of their careers with enough money on their hands to buy out an old-fashioned empire?

We liberals have professed not to love it, yet we have tried to believe in it, none the less. In a country where money changes hands so often and social position fluctuates so easily, where the minds of the working class have seemed largely to have been absorbed into the psychology of the middle class, we have been unable to believe in the Marxist doctrine that capitalism must eventually give rise to class warfare, and we have perhaps never taken sufficiently seriously Karl Marx's prediction that for many years to come the stupid automatic acquisitive instinct of humanity would still be so far ahead of its capacity for intelligent and disinterested behavior that the system of private enterprise would never even be able to run itself with foresight enough to avoid a wreck. It used to be pointed out that in America our support of this system was indestructible, since the stock market made it possible for anybody who had been able to save a little money to become a capitalist himself, with interests presumably identical with those of J. P. Morgan and Charlie Schwab. But can we expect that to be true in the future?—and even if people persist in aspiring to be stock-market capitalists, should they be encouraged in this or even left to their luck? Should they not rather be shown that their interests are incompatible with capitalism itself?

Yet the truth is that we liberals and progressives have been betting on capitalism—and that most of our heroes and allies: heterodox professors like Dewey and Beard, survivors of the old republican tradition like Woodrow Wilson and Justice Holmes, able and well-educated labor organizers like the officers of the Amalgamated, intelligent journalists like Lippmann and Chase, though all sincere and outspoken democrats, have been betting on capitalism, too. And now, in the abyss of starvation and bankruptcy into which the country has fallen, with no sign of any political leadership which will be able to pull us out, our liberalism seems to have little to offer beyond a discreet recommendation of public ownership of water power and certain other public utilities, a cordial feeling that labor ought to organize in a non-social-revolutionary way and a protest, invariably ineffective, against a few of the more obviously atrocious of the jailings, beatings-up and murders with which the industrialists have been trying to keep the working class docile.

Doesn't this program today seem rather inadequate? We liberals have always insisted on the desirability of a planned society—the phrase "social control" has been our blessed Mesopotamian word. If this means anything, does it not mean socialism? And should we not do well to make this plain? It may be said that at the present time it is utopian in America to talk about socialism; but with the kind of administrations that the country has lately been getting, do not all our progressive proposals, however reasonable or modest, seem utopian? Is it not obvious . . . that a government like our present one is incapable of acting in good faith in even the simple matter of preserving the water power which is supposed to be operated for the general benefit from being exploited by private profiteers? Our society has finally produced in its specialized professional politicians one of the most useless and obnoxious groups which has perhaps ever disgraced human history—a group that seems unique among governing classes in having managed to be corrupt, uncultivated and incompetent all at once. We know that we are not even able to depend on them today to protect us against the frankly disreputable race of blackmailers, thieves and assassins who dominate our municipal life. We know that we cannot even complain that the racketeers are breaking the laws which are supposed to be guaranteed by the government, because the government differs little from the racketeers. How can we expect them, then, to check the relatively respectable scoundrels who merely rob us of the public utilities by more or less legalistic means?

Yet, as I say, it may be true that, with the present breakdown, we have come to the end of something, and that we are ready to start on a different tack. If we look back through the depressions of the last fifty years, we see that through every one of them there always remained something for which the Americans could still legitimately feel ambition or enthusiasm, something to challenge the national spirit and appeal to the national imagination. After 1885, there were still the West and the consolidation of the railroads; after the prolonged depression of the nineties, the final consolidation of great industries such as United States Steel as well as the crusade led by Theodore Roosevelt against these great corporations in the interests of the dangerously increasing number of those who were being injured by the process of consolidation, and the robustious Rooseveltian imperialism; after the slump of the early years of the European War, our entrance into the war; and after the slump that followed the war, the period of the glorification of the automobile and the airplane. Today the further consolidation of the big business units is ruining more people even than in Roosevelt's time, and there is no sign of a Roosevelt or a Wilson to revive our political vision and to persuade the people who are out of luck that something is about to be done for them. It may be that the whole money-making and -spending psychology has definitely played itself out, and that the Americans would be willing, for the first time now, to put their traditional idealism and their genius for organization behind a radical social experiment. The future is as blank in the United States today as the situation is desperate: the President seems so inhibited by dread of encouraging subversive forces and by faith in the capacity of the capitalist system to right itself and survive that it is impossible for him to act, and when he tries so, he is deadlocked by Congress; nor have the industrialists or the financiers come forward with any constructive proposal. But this very blindness of the outlook may mean that we are looking in the wrong direction and that help may be coming from some other quarter. In the meantime, one gets the impression that the people who don't deal in ideas are doing more thinking at the present time than the professional ideologues.

The minds of the general public have, furthermore, been more affected by the example of Soviet Russia than is easily grasped by anyone who has been in the habit of assuming that it is only the radical or liberal who understands what Russia is up to, and that the ordinary American citizen is bound to be stupidly prejudiced against the Soviet system. During the NEP period in Russia, the capitalist powers were relieved to feel that the Russians had been forced to recognize the impracticability of Communism and were quietly returning to laissez faire. But with the inauguration of the Five-Year Plan to eliminate capitalist business in Russia, the aspect of things changed. The apparent success of the plan has had its effect on all classes in all the rest of the world—on the Americans, surely, not least. In the course of this winter of our capitalist quandary, the Soviets have been emerging from the back pages of the New York newspapers and are now given much and prominent space—even to interviews with Stalin's mother; and behind what one reads on the subject in even the reactionary papers, one feels as much admiration as resentment. After all, the great Communist project is distinguished by almost all the features that Americans have been taught to glorify—the extreme of efficiency and economy combined with the ideal of a herculean program—like a Liberty Loan drive—to be put over by concerted action to the tune of impassioned boosting. The Russians, furthermore, on their own side, have been studying American methods: they have imported a thousand American engineers and put them at the head of enormous enterprises with practically a free hand, and one would not be at all surprised to hear that Mr. Edward L. Bernays had been in Moscow at the time of the recent trial. We have already, in spite of the Treasury regulation, been doing a good deal of trading with Russia, and an important New York bank was at one time on the point of advancing to the Soviets [a] loan. . . .

The Communists in the United States assume that, by their very nature, neither our government nor our business is capable of learning anything from or of associating itself with the Soviets. They believe that a war against Russia is inevitable. They believe, moreover, that they themselves constitute a trained compact minority which, at the moment when American capitalism shall have finally broken down completely and been left helpless in its ignorance and anarchic selfishness, will be able to step in and man the works. To liberals, this idea has always sounded absurd, but who will say that it is entirely fantastic today when the machine is so badly in need of repairs, and one can see no political group in any position of power that has either a sensible plan or even good intentions? I believe that if the American radicals and progressives who repudiate the Marxist dogma and the strategy of the Communist Party still hope to accomplish anything valuable, they must take Communism away from the Communists, and take it without ambiguities, asserting that their ultimate goal is the ownership by the government of the means of production. If we want to prove the Communists wrong, if we want to demonstrate that the virtue has not gone out of American democracy, if we want to confute the Marxist cynicism implied by "economic laws" the catastrophic outcome of which is, after all, predicted only on an assumption of the incurable swinishness and inertia of human nature—if we seriously want to do this, as American opposition must not be afraid to dynamite the old conceptions and shibboleths and to substitute new ones as shocking as necessary. Who knows but they may seem less shocking to the ordinary suffering public than to us shibboleth-experts ourselves? When Joe Dos Passos proposed last summer that what was really needed in the United States was a publicity expert like Ivy Lee to familiarize the public with the idea of Communism and induce people at least to remain neutral toward Communist agitation instead of clapping all the Communists in jail, the suggestion, to some, sounded comic. Yet Dos Passos at once had a letter from a publicity man in San Francisco, who said that the same idea had recently occurred to him and that he would like nothing better than a chance to carry it out. There are some signs that the liberals are having ideas as well as the publicity men: Stuart Chase has said lately that the past year may represent "the end of an epoch" and has offered a set of suggestions for rescuing the economic structure, and John Dewey has just proposed to Senator Norris that he lead a new political party. The extreme illiberalism of the post-Wilsonian period has had the effect of discouraging liberals. We have gone on complaining and recommending, but with a vigor that has tended to diminish in proportion as we came to be conscious that people were not listening to us. Who knows but, if we spoke out now with confidence and boldness, we might find our public at last?

Part Three

To Formulate the Modern

Introduction

The charge to America to define "the modern" had been articulated by Walt Whitman well before the turn of the twentieth century, but not until the middle of the twentieth century did the conscious effort to act on this charge become a preoccupation of American thinkers and writers. By then, America was no longer an intellectual upstart watched by a sometimes bemused and avuncular Europe; on the contrary, the business of constituting "modern life" belonged as comfortably to Americans as to anyone. This transition was based not only on the maturation of intellectual subcultures within the United States, it was based also—and dramatically—on the migration to America of European intellectuals fleeing Nazism. Hence a symbol for the transition in America's role in modern intellectual life is the émigré philosopher Rudolf Carnap, with whose statement of logical positivism Part Three begins.

Carnap also represents the extremity of the influence of science in the formulation of general philosophical and cultural issues. For him, ideas that could not be subjected to scientific tests were not only untrue, but were without any meaning whatsoever. This strict approach to truth and meaning was one way to be "modern." To some contemporaries, however, it was quite behind the times. Even myths have genuine meaning for us, many literary intellectuals insisted. A truly "modern" view must throw over lingering ninteenth-century conceptions of truth and falsity, they argued, and accept instead a more ambiguous sense of poetic and even religious "truth." This antiscientific reaction reached an extreme in the writings of the most famous American theologian of the twentieth century, Reinhold Niebuhr, whose effort to defend Protestant Christianity as both meaningful and true follows Carnap in these pages.

Yet preoccupation with the notion of "modernity" was perhaps the most intense in discussions of literature, the arts, and social scientific perspectives on human affairs. Lionel Trilling's lengthy commentary on "modern" literature as an element of an undergraduate education represents here this preoccupation's literary dimension. Trilling addresses the ideas and texts that have come to be the most consistently associated with the term "modernism." The social scientific side of the search for a viable "modern" civilization is represented by brief, highly diverse selections from B. F. Skinner, a psychologist, and two sociologists, Daniel Bell, and C. Wright Mills. Skinner urges that we get beyond premodern notions of human freedom, whereas Bell ponders the possibility that Western Civilization may be passing into a distinctly nonideological age. Mills seeks to vindicate both the political involvement associated with ideologies and the traditional intellectual and moral values that Skinner believes to have outlived their utility.

The vision of a modern society projected by the preacher and civil rights leader Martin Luther King, Jr., entailed racial equality. King neutralized criticisms of the civil rights movement by arguing that these criticisms—especially as brought by King's fellow religionists—were grounded in anachronistic assumptions about race, politics, and religion. King spoke within an ideology of the type Bell thought to be on the decline and affirmed a notion of freedom criticized by Skinner.

Nothing more vividly illustrates the diversity and contention of the effort to formulate the "modern," however, than the contrast between Carnap's logical positivism and the ideas set forth by the historian Thomas S. Kuhn and the philosopher Richard Rorty in the last two selections of Part Three. Kuhn emphasizes the contingency of human knowledge—however scientific—and the inevitable dependence of this knowledge on particular historical social conditions that Carnap and his allies regarded as impediments to science. Rorty's historicism is more radical and sweeping than Kuhn's and is focused here on the issue of the foundations of political morality. There are no such foundations any more for morals than for science, insists Rorty, who uses the term "postmodernist" very loosely to represent one way of formulating the "modern": The pragmatic effort to develop and revise one's inherited tradition without claiming for that tradition a transcendent basis in nature, reason, or divine will.

Recommendations for Further Reading

Daniel J. Singal, ed., "Modernist Culture in America," Special Issue of *American Quarterly,* 39 (1987), 3–173; Malcolm Bradbury and Alan McFarlane, *Modernism* (London, 1976); Hugh Kenner, *A Homemade World: The American Modernist Writers* (New York, 1975); Richard Bernstein, *The Restructuring of Political and Social Theory* (New York, 1976); Christopher Brookeman, *American Culture and Society Since the 1930s* (London, 1984); Richard Pells, *Radical Visions and American Dreams: Culture and Social Thought in the Depression Years* (New York, 1973); Warren I. Susman, *Culture as History: The Transformation of American Society in the Twentieth Century* (New York, 1984); Daniel Joseph Singal, *The War Within: From Victorian to Modernist Thought in the South, 1919–1945* (Chapel Hill, 1982); Terry A. Cooney, *The Rise of the New York Intellectuals: Partisan Review and Its Circle, 1934–1945* (Madison, Wis., 1986); H. Stuart Hughes, *The Sea Change: The Migration of Social Thought, 1930–1965* (New York, 1975); Richard King, *The Party of Eros: Radical Social Thought and the Realm of Freedom* (New York, 1972); Serge Guilbaut, *How New York Stole the Idea of Modern Art: Abstract Expressionism, Freedom, and the Cold War,* trans. Arthur Goldhammer (Chicago, 1983); James Sloan Allen, *The Romance of Commerce and Culture: Capitalism, Modernism, and the Chicago-Aspen Crusade for Cultural Reform* (Chicago, 1983).

RUDOLF CARNAP

"The Rejection of Metaphysics" 1935

A suspicion of nonscientific modes of thought intensified during the second quarter of the twentieth century, especially among academic intellectuals concerned with the advancement of the social sciences. The most rigorous expression of this suspicion was logical positivism, a movement inspired and led by philosophers who emigrated to the United States from Central Europe. Prominent among these émigrés was Rudolf Carnap (1891–1970), from whose *Philosophy and Logical Syntax* (1935) the following selection is taken. Carnap presents an account of scientific verification, and insists that unless a statement has the potential to be tested in this way, the statement is meaningless. On this view, only the propositions of mathematics and the empricial sciences can be said to have any sense to them. Statements in other fields may perform an "expressive function," Carnap explains. Hence Carnap's standard for "meaningful" discourse is much stricter than the standard defended or taken for granted by many other, scientifically oriented philosophers, including Dewey. The selection from the theologian Reinhold Niebuhr, that follows this one, affords a yet sharper contrast to Carnap. For a lucid, accessible history of logical positivism, see Laurence D. Smith, *Behaviorism and Logical Positivism: A Reassessment of the Alliance* (Stanford, Ca., 1986), 27–65. For Carnap himself and his interaction with other philosophers of his generation, see Paul A. Schilpp, ed., *The Philosophy of Rudolf Carnap* (La Salle, Ill., 1963).

The problems of philosophy as usually dealt with are of very different kinds. From the point of view which I am here taking we may distinguish mainly three kinds of problems and doctrines in traditional philosophy. For the sake of simplicity we shall call these parts *Metaphysics, Psychology,* and *Logic*. Or, rather, there are not three distinct regions, but three sorts of components which in most theses and questions are combined: a metaphysical, a psychological, and a logical component.

The considerations that follow belong to the third region: we are here carrying out *Logical Analysis*. The function of logical analysis is to analyse all knowledge, all assertions of science and of everyday life, in order to make clear the sense of each such assertion and the connections between them. One of the principal tasks of the logical analysis of a given proposition is to find out the method of verification for that proposition. The question is: What reasons can there be to assert this proposition; or: How can we become certain as to its truth or falsehood? This question is called by the philosophers the epistemological question; epistemology or the philosophical theory of knowledge is nothing other than a special part of logical analysis, usually combined with some psychological questions concerning the process of knowing.

What, then, is the method of verification of a proposition? Here we have to distinguish between two kinds of verification: direct and indirect. If the question is about a proposition which asserts something about a present perception, e.g. "Now I see a red square on a blue ground," then the proposition can be tested directly by my present perception. If at present I do see a red square on a blue ground, the proposition is directly verified by this seeing; if I do not see that, it is disproved. To be sure, there are still some serious problems in connection with direct verification. We will however not touch on them here, but give our attention to the question of *indirect* verification, which is more important for our purposes. A proposition P which is not directly verifiable can only be verified by direct verification of propositions deduced from P together with other already verified propositions.

Let us take the proposition P_1: "This key is made of iron." There are many ways of verifying this proposition; e.g.: I place the key near a magnet; then I perceive that the key is attracted. Here the deduction is made in this way:

Premises:

P_1: "This key is made of iron"; the proposition to be examined.

P_2: "If an iron thing is placed near a magnet, it is attracted"; this is a physical law, already verified.

P_3: "This object—a bar—is a magnet;" proposition already verified.

P_4: "The key is placed near the bar"; this is now directly verified by our observation.

From these four premises we can deduce the conclusion:

P_5: "The key will now be attracted by the bar."

This proposition is a prediction which can be examined by observation. If we look, we either observe the attraction or we do not. In the first case we have found a positive instance, an instance of verification of the proposition P_1 under consideration; in the second case we have a negative instance, an instance of disproof of P_1.

Source: Philosophy and Logical Syntax, Rudolf Carnap (London: Kegan Paul, 1935), 9–38.

In the first case the examination of the proposition P_1 is not finished. We may repeat the examination by means of a magnet, i.e. we may deduce other propositions similar to P_5 by the help of the same or similar premises as before. After that, or instead of that, we may make an examination by electrical tests, or by mechanical, chemical, or optical tests, etc. If in these further investigations all instances turn out to be positive, the certainty of the proposition P_1 gradually grows. We may soon some to a degree of certainty sufficient for all practical purposes, but *absolute* certainty we can never attain. The number of instances deducible from P_1 by the help of other propositions already verified or directly verifiable is *infinite*. Therefore there is always a possibility of finding in the future a negative instance, however small its probability may be. Thus the proposition P_1 *can never be completely verified*. For this reason it is called an *hypothesis*.

So far we have considered an individual proposition concerning one single thing. If we take a general proposition concerning all things or events at whatever time and place, a so-called natural *law,* it is still clearer that the number of examinable instances is infinite and so the proposition is an hypothesis.

Every assertion P in the wide field of science has this character, that it either asserts something about present perceptions or other experiences, and therefore is verifiable by them, or that propositions about future perceptions are deducible from P together with some other already verified propositions. If a scientist should venture to make an assertion from which no perceptive propositions could be deduced, what should we say to that? Suppose, e.g., he asserts that there is not only a gravitational field having an effect on bodies according to the known laws of gravitation, but also a *levitational field,* and on being asked what sort of effect this levitational field has, according to his theory, he answers that there is no observable effect; in other words, he confesses his inability to give rules according to which we could deduce perceptive propositions from his assertion. In that case our reply is: your assertion is no assertion at all; it does not speak about anything; it is nothing but a series of empty words; it is simply without sense.

It is true that he may have images and even feelings connected with his words. This fact may be of psychological importance; logically it is irrevelant. What gives theoretical meaning to a proposition is not the attendant images and thoughts, but the possibilty of deducing from it perceptive propositions, in other words, the possibility of verification. To give sense to a proposition the presence of images is not sufficient; it is not even necessary. We have no actual image of the electro-magnetic field, nor even, I should say, of the gravitational field. Nevertheless the proposition which physicists assert about these fields have a perfect sense, because perceptive propositions are deducible from them. I by no means object to the proposition just mentioned about a levitational field that we do not know how to imagine or conceive such a field. My only objection to that proposition is that we are not told how to verify it.

What we have been doing so far is *logical analysis*. Now we are going to apply these considerations not to propositions of physics as before, but to propositions of *metaphysics*. Thus our investigation belongs to *logic*, to the third of the three parts of philosophy spoken about before, but the *objects* of this investigation belong to the first part.

I will call *metaphysical* all those propositions which claim to represent knowledge about something which is over or beyond all experience, e.g. about the real Essence of things, about Things in themselves, the Absolute, and such like. I do not include in metaphysics those theories—sometimes called metaphysical—whose object is to arrange the most general propositions of the various regions of scientific knowledge in a well-ordered system; such theories belong actually to the field of empirical science, not of philosophy, however daring they may be. The sort of propositions I wish to denote as metaphysical may most easily be made clear by some examples: "The Essence and Principle of the world is Water," said Thales; "Fire," said Heraclitus; "the Infinite," said Anaximander; "Number," said Pythagoras. "All things are nothing but shadows of eternal ideas which themselves are in a spaceless and timeless sphere," is a doctrine of Plato. From the Monists we learn: "There is only one principle on which all that is, is founded"; but the Dualists tell us: "There are two principles." The Materialists say: "All that is, is in its essence material," but the Spiritualists say: "All that is, is spiritual." To metaphysics (in our sense of the word) belong the principal doctrines of Spinoza, Schelling, Hegel, and—to give at least one name of the present time—Bergson.

Now let us examine this kind of proposition from the point of view of *verifiability*. It is easy to realise that such propositions are not verifiable. From the proposition: "The Principle of the world is Water" we are not able to deduce any proposition asserting any preceptions or feelings or experiences whatever which may be expected for the future. Therefore the proposition, "The Principle of the world is Water," asserts nothing at all. It is perfectly analogous to the proposition in the fictive example above about the levitational field and therefore it has no more sense than that proposition. The Water-Metaphysician—as we may call him—has no doubt many images connected with his doctrine; but they cannot give sense to the proposition, any more than they could in the case of the levitational field. Metaphysicians cannot avoid making their propositions non-verifiable, because if they made them verifiable, the decision about the truth or falsehood of their doctrines would depend upon experience and therefore belong to the region of empirical science. This consequence they wish to avoid, because they pretend to teach knowledge which is of a higher level than that of empirical science. Thus they are compelled to cut all connection between their propositions and experience; and precisely by this procedure they deprive them of any sense.

So far I have considered only examples of such propositions as are usually called metaphysical. The judgment I have passed on these propositions, namely, that they have no empirical sense, may perhaps appear not very astonishing, and even trivial. But it it to be feared that the reader will experience somewhat more difficulty in agreement when I now proceed to apply that judgment also to philosophical doctrines of the type which is usually called epistemological. I prefer to call them also metaphysical because of their similarity, in the point under consideration, to the propositions usually so called. What I have in mind are the doctrines of Realism, Idealism, Solipsism, Positivism and the like, taken in their traditional form as asserting or denying the Reality of something. The Realist asserts the Reality of the external world, the Idealist denies it. The Realist—usually at least—asserts also the Reality of other minds, the Solipsist—an especially radical Idealist—denies it, and asserts that only his own mind or consciousness is real. Have these assertions sense?

Perhaps it may be said that assertions about the reality or unreality of something occur also in empirical science, where they are examined in an empirical way, and that therefore they have sense. This is quite true. But we have to distinguish between two concepts of reality, one occurring in empirical propositions and the other occuring in the philosophical propositions just mentioned. When a zoologist asserts the reality of kangaroos, his assertion means that there are things of a certain sort which can be found and perceived at certain times and places; in other words that there are objects of a certain sort which are elements of the space-time-system of the physical world. This assertion is of course verifiable; by empirical investigation every zoologist arrives at a positive verification, independent of whether he is a Realist or an Idealist. Between the Realist and the Idealist there is full agreement as to the question of the reality of things of such and such sort, i.e. of the possibility of locating elements of such and such sort in the system of the physical world. The disagreement begins only when the question about the Reality of the physical world as a whole is raised. But this question has no sense, because the reality of anything is nothing else than the possibility of its being placed in a certain system, in this case, in the space-time-system of the physical world, and such a question has sense only if it concerns the system itself.

The same result is obtained by applying the criterion explained before: the possibility of deducing perceptive propositions. While from the assertion of the reality or the existence of kangaroos we *can* deduce perceptive propositions, from the assertion of the Reality of the physical world this is not possible; neither is it possible from the opposite assertion of the Unreality of the physical world. Therefore both assertions have no empirical content—no sense at all. It is to be emphasized that this criticism of having no sense applies equally to the assertion of Unreality. Sometimes the views of the *Vienna Circle* have been mistaken for a denial of the Reality of the physical world, but we make no such denial. It is true that we reject the thesis of the Reality of the physical world; but we do not reject it as false, but as having no sense, and its Idealistic *anti*-thesis is subject to exactly the same rejection. We neither assert nor deny these theses, we reject the whole question.

All the considerations which apply to the question of the Reality of the physical world apply also to the other philosophical questions of Reality, e.g. the Reality of other minds, the Reality of the given, the Reality of universals, the Reality of qualities, the Reality of relations, the Reality of numbers, etc. If any philosophical thesis answering any of these questions positively or negatively is added to the system of scientific hypotheses, this system will not in the least become more effective; we shall not be able to make any further prediction as to future experiences. Thus all these philosophical theses are deprived of empirical content, of theoretical sense; they are pseudo-theses.

If I am right in this assertion, the philosophical problems of Reality—as distinguished from the empirical problems of reality—have the same logical character as the problems (or rather, pseudo-problems) of transcendental metaphysics earlier referred to. For this reason I call those problems of Reality not epistemological problems—as they usually are called—but metaphysical.

. . . . . .

One division of philosophy, which by some philosophers is considered the most important, has not been mentioned at all so far, namely, the philosophy of values, with its main branch, moral philosophy or *Ethics*. The word "Ethics" is used in two different senses. Sometimes a certain empirical investigation is called "Ethics," viz. psychological and sociological investigations about the actions of human beings, especially regarding the origin of these actions from feelings and volitions and their effects upon other people. Ethics in this sense is an empirical, scientific investigation; it belongs to empirical science rather than to philosophy. Fundamentally different from this is ethics in the second sense, as the philosophy of moral values or moral norms, which one can designate normative ethics. This is not an investigation of facts, but a pretended investigation of what is good and what is evil, what it is right to do and what it is wrong to do. Thus the purpose of this philosophical, or normative, ethics is to state norms for human action or judgments about moral values.

It is easy to see that it is merely a difference of formulation, whether we state a norm or a value judgment. A norm or rule has an imperative form, for instance: "Do not kill!" The corresponding value judgment would be: "Killing is evil." This difference of formulation has become practically very important, especially for the development of philosophical thinking. The rule, "Do not kill," has grammatically the imperative form and will therefore not be regarded as an assertion. But the value statement, "Killing is evil," although, like the rule, it is merely an expression of a certain wish, has the grammatical form of an assertive proposition. Most philosophers have been deceived by this form into thinking that a value statement is really an assertive proposition, and must be either true or false. Therefore they give reasons for their own value statements and try to disprove those of their opponents. But actually a value statement is nothing else than a command in a misleading grammatical form. It may have effects upon the actions of men, and these effects may either be in accordance with our wishes or not; but it is neither true nor false. It does not assert anything and can neither be proved nor disproved.

This is revealed as soon as we apply to such statements our method of logical analysis. From the statement "Killing is evil" we cannot deduce any proposition about future experiences. Thus this statement is not verifiable and has no theoretical sense, and the same thing is true of all other value statements.

Perhaps somebody will contend in opposition that the following proposition is deducible: "If a person kills anybody he will have feelings of remorse." But this proposition is in no way deducible from the proposition "Killing is evil." It is deducible only from psychological propositions about the character and the emotional reactions of the person. These propositions are indeed verifiable and not without sense. They belong to psychology, not to philosophy; to psychological ethics (if one wishes to use this word), not to philosophical or normative ethics. The propositions of normative ethics, whether they have the form of rules or the form of value statements, have no theoretical sense, are not scientific propositions (taking the word scientific to mean any assertive proposition).

To avoid misunderstanding it must be said that we do not at all deny the possibility and importance of a scientific investigation of value statements as well as of acts of valuation. Both of these are acts of individuals and are, like all other kinds of acts, possible objects of empirical investigation. Historians, psychologists, and sociologists may give analyses and causal explanations of them, and such historical and psychological propositions about acts of valuation and about value statements are indeed meaningful scientific propositions which belong to ethics in the first sense of this word. But the value statements themselves are here only objects of investigation; they are not propositions in these theories, and have, here as elsewhere, no theoretical sense. Therefore we assign them to the realm of metaphysics.

Now we have analysed the propositions of metaphysics in a wide sense of this word, including not only transcendental metaphysics, but also the problems of philosophical Reality and lastly normative ethics. Perhaps many will agree that the propositions of all these kinds of metaphysics are not verifiable, i.e. that their truth cannot be examined by experience. And perhaps many will even grant that for this reason they have not the character of scientific propositions. But when I say that they are without sense, assent will probably seem more difficult. Someone may object: these propositions in the metaphysical books obviously have an effect upon the reader, and sometimes a very strong effect; therefore they certainly *express* something. That is quite true, they *do* express something, but nevertheless they have no sense, no theoretical content.

We have here to distinghish two function of language, which we may call the expressive function and the representative function. Almost all the conscious and unconscious movements of a person, including his linguistic utterances, express something of his feelings, his present mood, his temporary or permanent dispositions to reaction, and the like. Therefore we may take almost all his movements and words as symptoms from which we can infer something about his feelings or his character. That is the expressive function of movements and words. But besides that, a certain portion of linguistic utterences (e.g. "this book is black"), as distinguished from other linguistic utterances and movements, has a second function: these utterances represent a certain state of affairs; they tell us that something is so and so; they assert something, they predicate something, they judge something.

In special cases, this asserted state may be the same as that which is inferred from a certain expressive utterance; but even in such cases we must sharply distinguish between the assertion and the expression. If, for instance, somebody is laughing, we may take this as a symptom of his merry mood; if on the other hand he tells us without laughing: "Now I am merry," we can learn from his words the same thing which we inferred in the first case from his laughing. Nevertheless, there is a fundamental difference between the laughter and the words: "I am merry now." This linguistic utterance *asserts* the merry mood, and therefore it is either true or false. The laughter does not assert the merry mood but *expresses* it. It is neither true nor false, because it does not assert anything, although it may be either genuine or deceptive.

Now many linguistic utterances are analogous to laughing in that they have only an expressive function, no representative function. Examples of this are cries like "Oh, Oh" or, on a higher level, lyrical verses. The aim of a lyrical poem in which occur the words "sunshine" and "clouds," is not to inform us of certain meteorological facts, but to express certain feelings of the poet and to excite similar feelings in us. A lyrical poem has no assertional sense, no theoretical sense, it does not contain knowledge.

The meaning of our anti-metaphysical thesis may now be more clearly explained. This thesis asserts that metaphysical propositions—like lyrical verses—have only an expressive function, but no representative function. Metaphysical propositions are neither true nor false, because they assert nothing, they contain neither knowledge nor error, they lie completely outside the field of knowledge, of theory, outside the discussion of truth or falsehoods. But they are, like laughing, lyrics, and music, expressive. They express not so much temporary feelings as permanent emotional or volitional dispositions. Thus, for instance, a Metaphysical system of Monism may be an expression of an even and harmonious mode of life, a Dualistic system may be an expression of the emotional state of someone who takes life as an eternal struggle; an ethical system of Rigorism may be expressive of a strong sense of duty or perhaps of a desire to rule severely. Realism is often a symptom of the type of constitution called by psychologists extraverted, which is characterized by easily forming connections with men and things; Idealism, of an opposite constitution, the so-called introverted type, which has a tendency to withdraw from the unfriendly world and to live within its own thoughts and fancies.

Thus we find a great similarity between metaphysics and lyrics. But there is one decisive difference between them. Both have no representative function, no theoretical content. A metaphysical proposition, however—as distinguished from a lyrical verse—*seems* to have some, and by this not only is the reader deceived, but the metaphysician himself. He believes that in his metaphysical treatise he has asserted something, and is led by this into argument and polemics against the propositions of some other metaphysican. A poet, however, does not assert that the verses of another are wrong or erroneous; he usually contents himself with calling them bad.

The non-theoretical character of metaphysics would not be in itself a defect; all arts have this non-theoretical character without thereby losing their high value for personal as well as for social life. The danger lies in the *deceptive* character of metaphysics; it gives the illusion of knowledge without actually giving any knowledge. This is the reason why we reject it.

When we have eliminated metaphysical problems and doctrines from the region of knowledge or theory, there remain still two kinds of philosophical questions: psychological and logical. Now we shall eliminate the psychological questions also, not from the region of knowledge, but from philosophy. Then, finally, philosophy will be reduced to logic alone (in a wide sense of this word).

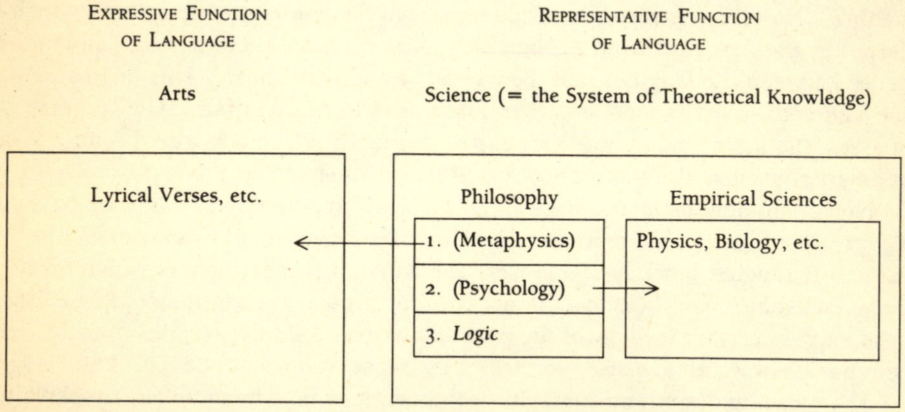

Psychological questions and propositions are certainly not without sense. From such propositions we can deduce other propositions about future experiences and by their help we can verify the psychological propositions. But the propositions of psychology belong to the region of empirical science in just the same way as do the propositions of chemistry, biology, history and the like. The character of psychology is by no means more philosophical than that of the other sciences mentioned. When we look at the historical development of the sciences we see that philosophy has been the mother of them all. One science after another has been detached from philosophy and has become an independent science. Only in our time has the umbilical cord between psychology and philosophy been cut. Many philosophers have not yet realized quite clearly that psychology is no longer an embryo, but an independent organism, and that psychological questions have to be left to empirical research.

Of course we have no objection to connecting psychological and logical investigations, any more than to connecting investigations of any scientific kind. We reject only the confusion of the two kinds of questions. We demand that they should be clearly distinguished even where in practice they are combined. The confusion sometimes consists in dealing with a logical question as if it were a psychological one. This mistake—called Psychologism—leads to the opinion that logic is a science concerning thinking, that is, either concerning the actual operation of thinking or the rules according to which thinking should proceed. But as a matter of fact the investigation of operations of thinking as they really occur is a task for psychology and has nothing to do with logic.

. . . . . .

The only proper task of *Philosophy* is *Logical Analysis.* And how the principal question to be answered here will be: "*What is logical analysis?*" In our considerations so far we have already practised logical analysis: we have tried to determine the character of physical hypotheses, of metaphysical propositions (or rather, pseudo-propositions), of psychological propositions. And now we have to apply logical analysis to logical analysis itself; we have to determine the character of the propositions of logic, of those propositions which are the results of logical analysis.

The opinion that metaphysical propositions have no sense because they do not concern any facts, has already been expressed by *Hume.* He writes in the last chapter of his "Enquiry Concerning Human Understanding" (published in the year 1748) as follows: "It seems to me, that the only objects of the abstract sciences or of demonstration, are quantity and number. . . . All other enquiries of men regard only matter of fact and existence; and these are evidently incapable of demonstration. . . . When we run over libraries, persuaded of these principles, what havoc must we make? If we take in our hand any volume, of divinity or school metaphysics, for instance; let us ask, Does it contain any abstract reasoning concerning quantity or number? No. Does it contain any experimental reasoning concerning matter of fact and existence? No. Commit it then to the flames: for it can contain nothing but sophistry and illusion." We agree with this view of Hume, which says—translated into our terminology—that only the propositions of mathematics and empirical science have sense, and that all other propositions are without sense.

But now it may perhaps be objected: "How about your own propositions? In consequence of your view your own writings, including this book, would be without sense, for they are neither mathematical nor empirical, that is, verifiable by experience." What answer can be given to this objection? What is the character of my propositions and in general of the propositions of logical analysis? This question is decisive for the consistency of the view which has been explained here.

An answer to the objection is given by Wittgenstein in his book *Tractatus Logico-*

Philosophicus. This author has developed most radically the view that the propositions of metaphysics are shown by logical analysis to be without sense. How does he reply to the criticism that in that case his own propositions are also without sense? He replies by agreeing with it. He writes: "The result of philosophy is not a number of 'philosophical propositions,' but to make propositions clear" (p. 77). "My propositions are elucidatory in this way: he who understands me finally recognizes them as senseless, when he has climbed out through them, on them, over them. (He must so to speak throw away the ladder, after he has climbed up on it.) He must surmount these propositions; then he sees the world rightly. Whereof one cannot speak, thereof one must be silent" (p. 189).

I, as well as my friends in the Vienna Circle, owe much to Wittgenstein, especially as to the analysis of metaphysics. But on the point just mentioned I cannot agree with him. In the first place he seems to me to be inconsistent in what he does. He tells us that one cannot state philosophical propositions and that whereof one cannot speak, thereof one must be silent; and then instead of keeping silent, he writes a whole philosophical book. Secondly, I do not agree with his statement that all his propositions are quite as much without sense as metaphysical propositions are. My opinion is that a great number of his propositions (unfortunately not all of them) have in fact sense; and that the same is true for all propositions of logical analysis. . . .

REINHOLD NIEBUHR

"The Truth in Myths"
1937

Reinhold Niebuhr (1892–1971) was for several decades the nation's most quoted and respected critic of modern thought's drift away from explicitly Christian foundations. Niebuhr owed much of his influence to the skill with which he—a Protestant preacher and seminary professor—brought the perspectives of liberal theology to bear on the political, social, and cultural issues of the middle third of the twentieth century. An effective polemicist against pacificism, communism, and other utopian projects under attack in the 1940s and 1950s, Niebuhr won a large following among secular intellectuals ("atheists for Niebuhr," such men and women were sometimes called). Although Niebuhr was sometimes associated in the public mind with the neo-orthodox movement led by the Swiss theologian, Karl Barth, his most vital engagements were decidedly more worldly and contemporary than Barth's. Niebuhr took his theoretical bearings instead from the liberal tradition in German theology, especially as represented by the émigré, Paul Tillich. From this tradition Niebuhr derived the notion of "mythic truths," which he then developed as a basis for justifying what he took to be the essential claims of Christianity. Nowhere did Niebuhr make a more cogent argument on behalf of this crucial notion than in the essay of 1937 reprinted herein. Niebuhr's thought and career is the subject of an excellent study by Richard Wightman Fox, *Reinhold Niebuhr: A Biography* (New York, 1986).

In the lexicon of the average modern, particularly in America, a myth is a piece of fiction, usually inherited from the childhood of the race. The scientific outlook of our mature culture has supposedly invalidated the truth value of these primitive stories in which gods and devils, nymphs and satyrs, fairies and witches are portrayed in actions and attitudes which partly transcend and partly conform to human limitations. They are regarded as the opulent fruits of an infantile imagination which are bound to wither under the sober discipline of a developed intelligence. Science has displaced mythology. A careful observation of the detailed phenomena of life and history yields more credible explanations of life's mysteries than these fanciful accounts of the origin of life or the genesis of evil or these fantastic pictures of the universe. When we have the conception of evolution we do not need the story of creation, and when we see man's slow ascent toward the ideal we have no place for a mythical "fall" to account for the origin of evil in the world. The reign of law revealed by science invalidates the miracles which abound in all religions; and the insight into, and power over, his own future given to the modern man through his intelligence frees him of the need to seek salvation in the myths of religion. Such are the convictions which belong to the unquestioned certainties of the modern man.

Since mythical elements are irrevocably enshrined in the canons of all religions it has become the fashion of modern religion to defend itself against the criticisms of science by laborious reinterpretations of is central affirmations with the purpose of sloughing off the mythical elements, apologizing for them as inevitable concepts of infantile cultures, and extracting the perennially valid truths from these husks of the past. Unfortunately the protagonists of modern religion usually fail to placate the devotees of the scientific method by these diligent but not too dignified laborers. They are met by the contemptuous suggestion that they have been merely insinuating new meanings into ancient phrases, and that they have gained nothing for their pains but what might have been secured more simply by a scientific analysis of the known facts of life and existence. If science has the final word and authority about life, as many of those theologians who have been most anxious to adjust religion to the scientific world-view have assumed, this suggestion is plausible enough. Indeed some of the supposedly abiding truths which have been distilled from ancient myths by this process of reinterpretation have lost their religious essence so completely, have been flattened and deflated to such a degree in the process of adaptation, that the charge of the empiricists and naturalists seem perfectly justified.

The modern protagonists of religion made the mistake of retreating too far and too quickly when the exigencies of the cultural situation demanded a retreat. Their error was to disavow permanent myth with primitive myth. Religion had no right to insist on the scientific accuracy of its mythical heritage. From this position a retreat was necessary. That part of mythology which is derived from prescientific thought, which does not understand the causal relations in the natural and historical world, must naturally be sacrificed in a scientific age. But there is a permanent as well as a primitive myth in every great mythical heritage. This deals with aspects of reality which are suprascientific rather than prescientific. Modernistic religion has been so thin on the whole because it did not understand this distinction and thus sacrificed what is abiding with what is primitive in religious myth.

What are the aspects of reality which can be stated only in mythical terms?

The most obvious aspect of reality which can not be comprehended in terms of scientific concepts is the aspect of value. It is true that the value of things for a particular individual can always be stated in terms of aesthetic myths. The aesthetic myth (such as "Hail to thee, blithe Spirit! Bird thou never wert," in Shelley's ode "To a Skylark") makes no claim about the ultimate value of a thing in a total scheme of purpose. It merely asserts value in terms of the moods and purposes of an individual in a given instance. The purely aesthetic and nonreligious myth is therefore skeptical about values in the ultimate sense. "Poetry," declares Santayana, "is religion which is no longer believed."

The aesthetic myth becomes transmuted into a religious myth when it seeks to comprehend facts and occurrences in terms of their organic relation to the whole conceived in teleological terms. For only if things are related to each other organically in a total meaningful existence can it be claimed that they have value. Religion, to transpose Santayana's phrase, is poetry which is believed. Religion seeks mythically to grasp life in its unity and wholeness. This unity and wholeness can never be expressed in terms of complete rationality; for reason only observes and deduces. What it observes is concrete reality in its multifarious forms. Its deductions are based upon the sequences which it observes in nature and history. But these sequences reveal nothing of the eternal unity in all organic growth.

For this reason scientific descriptions of reality always tend to a mechanistic interpretation of it. The facts of organic growth can be comprehended and described only by mythically transferring the inner unity of the human consciousness (where unity is directly experienced and apprehended) to the external world. A certain amount of primitive myth is always involved in this process (its analogy to animism of primitive mythology is apparent). But is it also permanent myth in the sense that it is permanently valid, since reality is actually organic and not mechanical in its processes.

A full analysis of the organic aspect of life reveals another quality of existence which can not be comprehended in terms of rationality and which might be defined as the dimension of depth in existence. If the relatedness of things to each other is more than mechanical, the source of their unity lies beyond, behind, and above the observable phenomena. "The world of things as they are," to quote Professor William P. Montague, "is not self-explanatory; it bears the earmarks, if not of a manufactured product, at least of a thing which has been derived from something other than itself." Not only the secret of its unity but of its growth (the emergence of novelty) lies beyond itself. Sciences may carefully observe certain processes of life and history and describe how or under what concatenation of circumstances certain forms, biological or social, were transmuted into other forms. But it can only describe these processes after the fact, and it is forced to treat each new emergent as following necessarily from the forces which immediately preceded it. It is, therefore, constantly tempted to commit the logical fallacy of *post hoc; ergo propter hoc*. It is, in short, compelled to deny the idea of creation.

The idea of creation is a typical mythical idea. It relates the source of life to observable life in terms which defy rationality. The primitive myth speaks of God making man out of clay, and breathing the breath of life into him. But the idea of creation remains mythical even when the primitive myth is discarded. If the myth is completely rationalized the creator becomes the first cause. Insofar as he is merely a cause, among many causes, creation is denied and every new fact in history is explained in terms of previous facts. Insofar as he is a uniquely first cause the limits of logic in dealing with the problem of causation in history are recognized but the recognition is left in negative form. Thus when religion refuses to yield the idea of creation to the idea of evolution it is following an instinct for the truth. When, as has been frequently the case in modern religion, it apologetically declares that nothing but a difference in terminology is involved ("Some call it evolution and others call it God") it is erroneously yielding to the prejudices of a scientific age.

The myth of creation not only expresses dynamic and organic qualities in reality which can not be stated in rational terms, but paradoxical qualities which elude the canons of logic. The dimension of depth in life contains such a paradox. All life and existence in its concrete forms suggests not only sources but possibilities beyond itself. These possibilities must be implied in the source or they would not be true possibilities. God is, in other words, both the ultimate ground of reality and its ultimate goal. "Religion," to quote Professor Montague in a revealing phrase, " . . . is the acceptance of the momentous possibility—that what is highest in spirit is also deepest in nature, that the ideal and the real are at least to some extent identified, not merely evanescently in our own lives but in the universe itself."

The myth of creation, in which God is neither identified with the historical world nor separated from it, offers the basis upon which all theologies are built in which God is conceived as both the ground and the ultimate fulfillment of a meaningful world, as both the creator and the judge of historical existence. This paradox is really the only ground of an effective ethic because it alone harmonizes ethical and metaphysical interests, and gives us a picture of a world which is really a universe, but not so unqualifiedly a meaningful world as to obscure the fact of evil and the possibility of a dynamic ethics. Every dynamic ethics depends upon the dimension of depth in life and upon a description of this dimension, which neither equates the metrical and mechanistic aspect of concrete existence with meaning and value, nor completely separates the world of value and ideals from the facts of concrete existence.

Efforts to describe the unity and meaningfulness of the world and existence in purely rational terms must ultimately choose between a metaphysics which inclines to monistic idealism (and may finally degenerate into a dualism) or a science which inclines to a mechanistic monism. Most of the modern efforts to arrive at a unified picture of life and reality have been under the direct influence of science rather than metaphysics. When science disavows both myth and metaphysics it has only two alternatives, in its attempt to construct a total world picture. It may picture the world and life as a mechanism, held together by the mechanical processes which it believes to have discovered by its observations. But there is only superficial unity and no meaningfulness in such a world. There is no place in it for the kind of vital and organic unity which the self experiences in its own self-consciousness. The logical ultimate of such a world-view is found in behavioristic psychology which denies the unity of consciousness as a reality. But such an ultimate is self-destructive because it invalidates the truth value of everything discovered by the conscious self about the world in which it lives. It is furthermore destructive of human vitality because it is impossible to live with zest if no purposes can be found worthy of our striving. A purely mechanical world is bereft of purpose and meaningfulness.

The other alternative (more generally followed) is to introduce mythical and transcendent elements covertly (usually unconsciously) into the supposedly scientific accounts of life and history. Our modern culture has maintained its spiritual life by such a covert myth, the idea of progress. It is possible to speak of progress in interpreting the endless changes of life only if some measuring rod of value can be found with which to gauge the process. But the rod must not be a part of the process. It must transcend it. The rod taken by modern culture has usually been some ethical ideal, inherited from religion. The confidence that the processes of nature support and contribute to the victory of this ethical ideal is really a rationalized version of the Christian myth of salvation. Unfortunately it is more optimistic and really less credible than the Christian myth. It derives its credulous optimism from the fact that it sacrificed the primary myth of creation prematurely and thus identifies the processes of history too uncritically with the transcendent ideal implied in these processes. It is only through the myth of creation that it is possible to assert both the meaningfulness of life and the fact of evil. To say that God created the world is to assert its meaningfulness; and to distinguish between the creator and his creation is to make a place for the reality of evil in the inevitable relativities of time and history.

Philosophy, before modern science made the futile effort to give a unified account of the world without metaphysical presuppositions, usually sought to comprehend the unity of life and the meaningfulness of existence by viewing all things from the perspective of the unity of human consciousness and bringing all forms of life under the categories of human reason. The world was declared meaningful because it is rational. While it is not exact to identify philosophical idealism with the method of philosophy as such and to equate naturalism with the method of science, such a distinction is roughly correct. Philosophy from Plato to Hegel was predominantly idealistic in interpreting reality in terms of rationality. The confidence that external reality conforms to the categories of human consciousness is itself a rationalized form of religious faith. It is true of course that men have partially validated this confidence by bringing the external world under the control of their practical purposes by acting upon their faith. But they would have been unable to do this if they had not initiated their efforts on the assumption that the structure of life is relevant to the forms of mind. Bertrand Russell is right, therefore, when he declares that philosophies which ascribe meaning and value to external reality are rationalized mythologies. He may be less correct in suggesting that the ascription of meaning to the world is always unwarranted.

The real difficulty with idealistic philosophies is that they are rationalized myths which lost their virtue in the process of rationalization. Idealistic philosophy is unable to do justice to either the heights or depths of life. It is unable to do justice to its heights because for it the transcendent source and goal of the meaning of life is still within the limits of human rationality. Thus the God of philosophical idealism is always less than a living creator. He is also less than the holy and perfect God of religious faith, though Plato overcomes this difficulty by frankly turning to myth and declaring "that the good is not essence but soars even beyond essence in dignity and power." The potentialities of life are in other words greater than can be comprehended in terms of the "essences" which are always the constructs of the human mind.

The God of philosophical idealism is always something more as well as something less than the living creator (the source) and the holy God (the goal) of existence. He is the totality of existence. Therefore idealism cannot deal adequately with the problem of evil. By rationalizing reality it brings it into a premature harmony; for a rational universe has no place for the incoherence of evil. It discovers therefore that partial evil is universal good and lames the energy of moral effort. The real fact is that mystery of both good and evil in human life and in the world cannot be completely comprehended or stated in perfectly rational terms. Every sensitive human spirit is conscious of belonging to an order of reality which embodies values beyond his achievements; but he is also conscious of incarnating forces of evil which mysteriously defy this order.

When philosophy deals with the problem of evil it either denies the reality of evil by lifting all processes of history into the category of the rational and the divine; or it reacts from this monism and optimism, and culminates in an extreme dualism in which the entire concrete, physical, and historical world are either relegated to meaninglessness or equated with evil. This dualism is prompted on the one hand by the failure of monism to do justice to the dimension of depth in life (that is, to the contrast between real and the ideal) and on the other hand to the basic difficulties of a rationalistic ontology. The totality of existence is first comprehended in rational categories; but since the facts of existence do not conform to these categories, those which are not rational are relegated to a lower order of existence. Finally this lower order of existence is pronounced either evil or illusory.

This entire history is symbolized in the trend of thought from Aristotle to Plotinus. In Aristotle the material world produces a hierarchy of existence in which the pure being of God is the apex. In Plotinus the pure being of God is the only real being; it prompts emanations of mind, soul, and body, each with a lower order of existence than the former. The logical culmination of such rationalized religions is to be found significantly in Buddhism in which the only reality is an eternal existence which has been freed of all the characteristics of historic and corporeal life and therefore of every conceivable content.

Neither the vital thrust of life, nor its organic unities nor its disharmonies nor its highest possibilities can be expressed in terms of logic and rational consistency. The dynamic and creative energy of life can be described but not comprehended by reason. The unities of life are organic, and reason can only logically assemble after analytically dividing, thus reducing the organic to a mechanical unity. The disharmonies of life are paradoxically related to its harmonies, as mechanism is paradoxically related to the world of meaning and purpose and every rational scheme of coherence fails to do justice to the tragic realities of evil and to its paradoxical relation with the good.

The dimension of depth in existence has thus far been dealt with only as if it were a fact in the world external to man. But it is really man, with his capacity of transcending the world and transcending himself, who comprehends this depth in existence, and feels it within himself. Man is a creature of both necessity and freedom. He is inserted in the mechanisms of nature and bound by them. Yet he also gains freedom over them by his capacity to envisage purposes and ideals more inclusive than those to which he is driven by nature's impulses. For him the problem of evil is therefore also a problem of sin. His freedom endows him with responsiblity and his responsibility spells guilt. The impulse of nature is not evil in the beast because it has no alternatives. But every human action is a choice between alternatives. An external description of the act may prove that a particular action was inevitable because a dominant impulse or set of forces actuated it. But an internal description of an act of choice can never escape a comparison between the act and a higher possibility. It is for this reason that religion, which has a grasp of this dimension of depth, deals with the fact of sin, while science, with its external descriptions, always inclines to deny the reality of sin and the fact of human responsibility.

In spite of the fact that the responsibiity of freedom enters into every moral act, purely moralistic descriptions of human sin are as erroneous as purely deterministic and external descriptions of human conduct. The relation of man to freedom and to mechanism is paradoxical. His conscious self is never in complete control of the mechanisms of impulse with which nature has endowed him. Yet it is in sufficient control not only to check these impulses in the interest of a more inclusive purpose but to interfere with the harmony of natural impulses, and to transmute the harmless impulses of nature into demonic lusts and imperialistic purposes. It is, in other words, the nature of human sin that it arises at the juncture of nature and spirit and is as much the corruption of nature by spirit as the corruption of spirit by nature.

All this is darkly expressed in the myth of the fall in Christian theology, much more adequately than in rational explanations of human evil. In explanations which achieve full rational coherence, evil is either attributed to the ultimate source of being (as in various forms of monism), in which case the reality of evil is really denied; or it is attributed to the world of matter, nature and historical concretion (as in various forms of dualism) in which case the fall is equated with creation (in gnosticism for instance), and impulses of nature are regarded as the source of evil while the direction of mind is regarded as the source of all good. Modern liberalism, with its confidence in increasing virtue through increasing control of reason over impulse, is a particularly naïve version of this kind of dualism, though liberalism rests upon a metaphysical foundation of naturalistic monism.

Against these rationalistic versions the myth of the fall expresses these ideas: that an element of human perversity is always involved in human sin since a degree of freedom enters into every human action; that nevertheless sin is inevitable since all men are inserted into the paradoxical relation of freedom and mechanism and cannot escape the possibility of destroying the harmony of nature without achieving the ultimate harmony of spirit; and, finally, that this inevitability is not to be attributed merely to the fact of nature, finiteness, and the world of concrete mechanism and physical impulse. The fact that the fall came after creation, and is not synonymous or contemporaneous with it, in the Jewish-Christian myth, has always saved Christian orthodoxy from falling into dualistic heresies, no matter how strongly tempted it has been in various periods of Christian history. Modern theology has been scornful of the doctrine of original sin (a corollary of the myth of the fall in Christian orthodoxy), because in its moralism and optimism it imagined the possibility of escape from the paradoxical human situation of finiteness and freedom. Orthodoxy, leaning upon mythical insights, has been truer to the facts of the total human situation upon this point.

The real situation is that man's very self-consciousness and capacity for self-transcendence is not only the prerequisite of his morality but the fateful and inevitable cause of his sin. It is because man can transcend nature and himself that he is able to conceive of himself as the center of all life and the clue to the meaning of existence. It is this monstrous pretension of his egoism, the root of all imperialism and human cruelty, which is the very essence of sin. To recognize all this is not to accept the story of the fall as history. The modern dialectical theology of Germany calls it *Urgeschichte,* and that is perhaps as good a term as any. Whenever orthodoxy insists upon the literal truth of such myths it makes a bad historical science out of true religious insights. It fails to distinguish between what is primitive and what is permanent, what is prescientific and what is supra-scientific in great myths.

The religious myths of salvation spring from the same necessity as the myths of creation and the fall. The modern man thinks himself emancipated from the need of religious assurances of salvation. They seem to him theological and unreal. The only redemption in which he believes is moral redemption, the actual conquest of evil by the good. But he can regard the problem of salvation as so simple only because he has equated evil and sin with ignorance. Once the element of perversity in evil is recognized, salvation in the full sense is possible only if the will is changed (conversion), and if the guilt of the past is pardoned. In all genuine religious experiences of salvation there is a sense of new moral power and an assurance of pardon. This is in other words a transaction between a transcendent God, who is not bound by the iron laws of necessity in history, and a transcendent self, which also stands above these laws both in the evil that it has committed and in the moral will by which it overcomes its previous perversity. If sin is not merely imperfection and weakness but an act of the will, reconciliation is possible only through an act of the will of the Divine; and this can be revealed only if divine forgiveness achieves some form and symbol in history (the Incarnation).

The absurdity of theologies which try to define the two natures of Christ and to distinguish between the temporal and the eternal in the mythical God-man, prove how impossible it is to bring essential myth into the categories of rationality. A completely rationalized myth loses its virtue because it ceases to point to the realm of transcendence beyond history, or, pointing to it, fails to express the organic and paradoxical relationship between the conditioned and the unconditioned. That is why, as Clutton-Brock observed, religion is forced to tell many little lies in the interest of a great truth, while science inclines to tell many little truths in the interest of a great lie. The great truth in the interest of which many little lies are told is that life and history have meaning and that the source and the fulfillment of that meaning lie beyond history. The great lie in the interest of which science tells many little truths is that spatio-temporal realities are self-contained and self-explanatory and that a scientific description of sequences is an adequate analysis of causes.

It has been previously suggested that the myths of art are related to those of religion. It could be claimed, in further elaboration of this thesis, that great art is bound to be religious; for great art is more than the objectivization of a particular sentiment or sense of meaning. It is a symbolization of the universal in the particular, to use Goethe's definition of great art. Its analyses of particular situations or its objectivizations of particular sentiments contain suggestions of the total human situation. But the very quality in them which points to the universal or the transcendent makes them something more and less than a scientific description of the facts.

A portrait is mythical as compared with the scientific exactitude of a photograph. Though a wise photographer will try to catch the permanent and significant rather than the passing mood of his subject he is always limited by the physical facts. The artist, on the other hand, falsifies some of the physical details in order to arrive at a symbolic expression of the total character of his subject, this total character being a transcendent fact which is never completely embodied in any given moment of the subject's existence. A really great portrait goes beyond this and not only symbolizes the transcendent personality of the subject, but contains suggestions of a universal human mood. The artistic license of the artist belongs in the same category as the artistic license of religion. In both cases it is subject to abuses. The artist may falsify reality and produce a caricature of his subject rather than a true portrait; and religious myths may falsify the facts of history and experience. But at their best, both artist and prophet reveal the heights and depths of human experience by picturing the surface with something more and less than scientific exactness.

Critics of Greek literature are agreed that Euripides' *Electra* is inferior to the *Choephori* of Aeschylus and the *Electra* of Sophocles, all three dramas dealing with the same theme, the vengeance of Orestes upon his mother. But the prejudices of modern culture have made it difficult to give the reason for this inferiority as simply as it might be given. Euripides is the secularist among the three great dramatists. Under his pen the great myths are naturalized and secularized so that human actions and attitudes become the inevitable causes and consequences of succeeding and preceding actions. He thus dissipates the power of Greek tragedy; for at its best it fills us with a sense of the beauty and terror of life by suggesting that human destinies are woven by forces vaster than human wills. Greek drama at its best lies close to its source, Dionysiac religion. Like all great art, it shares with religion the intention and the power to illumine the facts of life and the course of history by pointing to sources of meaning which lie beyond the facts we see and the history we experience.

The ultimate problem of myth is always the problem of God. Myths may begin by picturing good and evil spirits and by personalizing the forces of wind and water, of sun and moon and the starry heavens. Since every natural phenomenon can be explained in terms of a preceding one the myth becomes useless when science discovers the chain of causation. But meanwhile mythical knowledge has been driven from the effort to seek the transcendent cause behind each phenomenon to the search after the ultimate source of the meaning of all existence.

The approach to the transcendent source of meaning confronts us with a problem which seems practically insoluble. If the meaningfulness of life points to a source beyond itself, how is it possible to say anything about that transcendence, and how can anything that may be said be verified as true? "The vision into the Absolute," declares Professor Morris Cohen, "is either into a fathomless depth in which no distinctions are visible or into a fulness of being that exceeds our human comprehension." Mysticism has usually insisted on the distinctionless aspect of the transcendent. By seeking the absolute through a progressive elimination of temporal distinctions it finally arrived at the knowledge of God; but the God it found was emptiness and void. It could say nothing about him but that he negated the reality of significance of temporal existence. The final logic of this method is consistently expressed in Buddhism in which the ultimate is a distinctionless reality which serves only to destroy the meaning of temporal existence. Something of the same logic is to be found in all mystic asceticism. Thus the search after meaning becomes self-devouring. An ultimate source of meaning is found about which nothing can be said except that it destroys the meaning of mundane existence.

Philosophical idealism has searched for the transcendent in terms of its "fulness of being"; but being jealous of the fullness which "exceeds our comprehension" it defined the ultimate in terms of totality and rationality. By defining the transcendent in terms of totality it obscured the fact that temporal existence reveals not only glimpses of meaning but suggestions of chaos which defy meaning and order. By defining the transcendent in terms of rationality it destroyed its transcendence; for human reason is a part and product of the temporal process, and a rational picture of the transcendent obscures the very qualities of transcendence and ultrarationality. Since, however, reason has its own transcendent perspective over the natural processes and even a degree of transcendence over its own processes (therefore a rational appreciation of the limits of rationality), the efforts of philosophical idealism to comprehend the meaning of existence are never without a measure of truth or without some suggestion of its own limitations.

The effort of modern naturalism to comprehend the meaning of existence by denying the reality or validity of any transcendence behind and beyond the temporal process, usually leads, as we have seen, to an unconscious ascription of transcendence to the processes of nature and therefore to an introduction of ethical meaning into the process. In ethical naturalism an ethical meaning is given to the historic process even more immediately and unqualifiedly than in philosophical idealism. Modern naturalism is thus an even more uncritical rationalism than philosophical idealism. Its fruits are invariably either despair in a meaningless world or sentimentality in a world too simply meaningful. Modern culture is torn by conflict between the two attitudes.

The inadequacy of purely rational approaches invariably forces a return to a purer mythical approach in which the transcendent is defined and ceases to be mere emptiness, but is defined in terms which insist that it is more (and therefore less) than mere totality. But the problem of religion is how it may define God without resorting to a dogmatic acceptance of whatever mythical definition a particular historic tradition has entrusted to a certain portion of the religious community. The modern reaction against naturalism and rationalism expressed in Barthianism fails, significantly, to escape dogmatism. It is superior to the older dogmatisms of orthodox religion in that it does not insist on the scientific and rational validity of the mythical details of its tradition. The fall and the resurrection are not conceived as historical in its theology. But the total truth of the biblical myth is asserted dogmatically with no effort to validate Christianity in experience against competition with other religions.

How is it possible to escape this dogmatism? It is possible only if it be realized that though human knowledge and experience always point to a source of meaning in life which transcends knowledge and experience, there are nevertheless suggestions of the character of this transcendence in experience. Great myths have actually been born out of profound experience and are constantly subject to verification by experience. It may be simplest to illustrate this point in terms of a specific religious doctrine, the Christian doctrine that God is love and that love is the highest moral ideal.

The ideal of love is not a caprice of mythology. It is not true because the cross has revealed it. The cross justifies itself to human faith because it symbolizes an ideal which establishes points of relevance with the deepest experiences and insights of human life.

The ideal of love can be validated as the ultimate moral ideal because it stands in a verifiable transcendent relation to all rational idealism. It is both the fulfillment and the abyss of the rational ideal of justice. Justice is the highest rational moral ideal because reason must seek to deal with human relations and moral conduct in terms of the ascertainable causes and consequences of action. A good act must be rewarded and an evil one punished. The interests of my neighbor must be guarded; but my own interests deserve protection as well. Yet all rational justice constantly sinks to something less than justice. Remedial justice fails to "do justice" to the causes which prompted an evil act because it is ignorant of the operations of mind and conscience in that secret place where actions are compounded. If reason should grow imaginative ("Love is justice grown imaginative," declares Santayana), and make shrewd guesses about the source of evil actions, it will result in a fairer justice. But if it should become so sensitive as to recognize that the evil in the other has its source in the self or the self's society it will destroy every form of remedial justice. "Let him who is without sin cast the first stone." Thus love is both the fulfillment and the denial of remedial and punitive justice.

Love is related to distributive justice in the same manner. It is "right" that I protect my own interests as well as those of my neighbor. But an imaginative regard for the interests of my neighbor will be concerned for his needs even if they are in competition with mine. Such an imaginative concern for the neighbor's interests transcends all ordinary conceptions of equity and enjoins actions of generosity which no society can ever enjoin or regularize. But this same tendency toward the fulfillment of justice in love leads to the negation of justice by love. The neighbor's interests are avowed rather than my own and no effort is made to protect myself against the neighbor ("resist not evil"). Thus morality is fed by a realm of transcendent possibilities in which the canons of the good, established in ordinary experience, are both fulfilled and negated. That is why Jesus could symbolize the mercy of God through the impartiality of nature in which the sun shines on the evil and the good and rain falls upon the just and the unjust. The impartiality of nature is something less than human justice—and a symbol of something more, the mercy of God.

The cross in Christian faith is the myth of the truth of the ideal of love. The Christ of Christian faith is both human and divine. His actions represent both human possibilities and the limits of human possibilities. But the possibilities which transcend the human are relevant to human experience and every moral experience suggests these ultimate possibilities. Therefore parental affection is a symbol of the love of God. ("If ye then being evil, know how to give good gifts unto your children, how much more will your heavenly Father give good gifts to them that ask him.")

The transcendent source of the meaning of life is thus in such relation to all temporal process that a profound insight into any process or reality yields a glimpse of the reality which is beyond it. This reality can be revealed and expressed only in mythical terms. These mythical terms are the most adequate symbols of reality because the reality which we experience constantly suggests a center and source of reality, which not only transcends immediate experience, but also finally transcends the rational forms and categories by which we seek to apprehend and describe it.

B. F. SKINNER

Selection from *Beyond Freedom and Dignity*
1971

B. F. Skinner (1904–) has insisted that the survival of our culture depends on the development of a technology of behavior. We must be willing to plan what human beings do, Skinner has argued, and we must not flinch at the idea of subjecting human beings to control. In the selection from *Beyond Freedom and Dignity* (New York, 1971) that follows, Skinner defends this social vision against complaints to the effect that so "scientific" a view of human beings serves to diminish their humanity. Skinner developed his ideas in the course of a long and distinguished career as an experimental psychologist, working with laboratory animals as well as with human subjects. Although Skinner speaks here as an essayist and public moralist, his ideas were also set forth in a best-selling utopian novel, *Walden Two* (1948). Skinner himself continues to dominate what is written about his career and thought. He is the author of three autobiographical volumes, *Particulars of My Life* (New York, 1976), *The Shaping of a Behaviorist* (New York, 1979), and *A Matter of Consequences* (New York, 1983).

Almost all living things act to free themselves from harmful contacts. A kind of freedom is achieved by the relatively simple forms of behavior called reflexes. A person sneezes and frees his respiratory passages from irritating substances. He vomits and frees his stomach from indigestible or poisonous food. He pulls back his hand and frees it from a sharp or hot object. More elaborate forms of behavior have similar effects. When confined, people struggle ("in rage") and break free. When in danger they flee from or attack its source. Behavior of this kind presumably evolved because of its survival value; it is as much a part of what we call the human genetic endowment as breathing, sweating, or digesting food. And through conditioning similiar behavior may be acquired with respect to novel objects which could have played no role in evolution. These are no doubt minor instances of the struggle to be free, but they are significant. We do not attribute them to any love of freedom; they are simply forms of behavior which have proved useful in reducing various threats to the individual and hence to the species in the course of evolution.

A much more important role is played by behavior which weakens harmful stimuli in another way. It is not acquired in the form of conditioned reflexes, but as the product of a different process called operant conditioning. When a bit of behavior is followed by a certain kind of consequence, it is more likely to occur again, and a consequence having this effect is called a reinforcer. Food, for example, is a reinforcer to a hungry organism; anything the organism does that is followed by the receipt of food is more likely to be done again whenever the organism is hungry. Some stimuli are called negative reinforcers; any response which reduces the intensity of such a stimulus—or ends it—is more likely to be emitted when the stimulus recurs. Thus, if a person escapes from a hot sun when he moves under cover, he is more likely to move under cover when the sun is again hot. The reduction in temperature reinforces the behavior it is "contingent upon"—that is, the behavior it follows. Operant conditioning also occurs when a person simply avoids a hot sun—when, roughly speaking, he escapes from the *threat* of a hot sun.

Negative reinforcers are called aversive in the sense that they are the things organisms "turn away from." The term suggests a spatial separation—moving or running away from something—but the essential relation is temporal. In a standard apparatus used to study the process in the laboratory, an arbitrary response simply weakens an aversive stimulus or brings it to an end. A great deal of physical technology is the result of this kind of struggle for freedom. Over the centuries, in erratic ways, men have constructed a world in which they are relatively free of many kinds of threatening or harmful stimuli—extremes of temperature, sources of infection, hard labor, danger, and even those minor aversive stimuli called discomfort.

Escape and avoidance play a much more important role in the struggle for freedom when the aversive conditions are generated by other people. Other people can be aversive without, so to speak, trying: they can be rude, dangerous, contagious, or annoying, and one escapes from them or avoids them accordingly. They may also be "intentionally" aversive—that is, they may treat other people aversively because of what follows. Thus, a slave driver induces a slave to work by whipping him when he stops; by resuming work the slave escapes from the whipping (and incidentally reinforces the slave driver's behavior in using the whip). A parent nags a child until the child performs a task; by performing the task the child escapes nagging (and reinforces the parent's behavior). The blackmailer threatens exposure unless the victim pays; by paying, the victim escapes from the threat (and reinforces the practice). A teacher threatens corporal punishment or failure until his students pay attention; by paying attention the students escape from the threat of punishment (and reinforce the teacher for threatening it). In one form or another intentional aversive control is the pattern of most social coordination—in ethics, religion, government, economics, education, psychotherapy, and family life.

A person escapes from or avoids aversive treatment by behaving in ways which reinforce those who treated him aversively until he did so, but he may escape in other ways. For example, he may simply move out of range. A person may escape from slavery, emigrate or defect from a government, desert from an army, become an apostate from a religion, play truant, leave home, or drop out of a culture as a hobo, hermit, or hippie. Such behavior is as much a product of the aversive conditions as the behavior the conditions were designed to evoke. The latter can be guaranteed only by sharpening the contingencies or by using stronger aversive stimuli.

Another anomalous mode of escape is to attack those who arrange aversive conditions and weaken or destroy their power. We may attack those who crowd us or annoy us, as we attack the weeds in our garden, but again the struggle for freedom is mainly directed toward intentional controllers—toward those who treat others aversively in order to induce them to behave in particular ways. Thus, a child may stand up to his parents, a citizen may overthrow a government, a communicant may reform a religion, a student may attack a teacher or vandalize a school, and a dropout may work to destroy a culture.

It is possible that man's genetic endowment supports this kind of struggle for freedom: when treated aversively people tend to act aggressively or to be reinforced by signs of having worked aggressive damage. Both tendencies should have had evolutionary advantages, and they can easily be demonstrated. If two organisms which have been coexisting peacefully receive painful shocks, they immediately exhibit characteristic patterns of aggression toward each other. The aggressive behavior is not necessarily directed toward the actual source of stimulation; it may be "displaced" toward any convenient person or object. Vandalism and riots are often forms of undirected or misdirected aggression. An organism which has received a painful shock will also, if possible, act to gain access to another organism toward which it can act aggressively. The extent to which human aggression exemplifies innate tendencies is not clear, and many of the ways in which people attack and thus weaken or destroy the power of intentional controllers are quite obviously learned.

What we may call the "literature of freedom" has been designed to induce people to escape from or attack those who act to control them aversively. The content of the literature is the philosophy of freedom, but philosophies are among those inner causes which need to be scrutinized. We say that a person behaves in a given way because he possesses a philosophy, but we infer the philosophy from the behavior and therefore cannot use it in any satisfactory way as an explanation, at least until it is in turn explained. The literature of freedom, on the other hand, has a simple objective status. It consists of books, pamphlets, manifestoes, speeches, and other verbal products, designed to induce people to act to free themselves from various kinds of intentional control. It does not impart a philosophy of freedom; it induces people to act.

The literature often emphasizes the aversive conditions under which people live, perhaps by contrasting them with conditions in a freer world. It thus makes the conditions more aversive, "increasing the misery" of those it is trying to rescue. It also identifies those from whom one is to escape or those whose power is to be weakened through attack. Characteristic villains of the literature are tyrants, priests, generals, capitalists, martinet teachers, and domineering parents.

The literature also prescribes modes of action. It has not been much concerned with escape, possibly because advice has not been needed; instead, it has emphasized how controlling power may be weakened or destroyed. Tyrants are to be overthrown, ostracized, or assassinated. The legitimacy of a government is to be questioned. The ability of a religious agency to mediate supernatural sanctions is to be challenged. Strikes and boycotts are to be organized to weaken the economic power which supports aversive practices. The argument is strengthened by exhorting people to act, describing likely results, reviewing successful instances on the model of the advertising testimonial, and so on.

The would-be controllers do not, of course, remain inactive. Governments make escape impossible by banning travel or severely punishing or incarcerating defectors. They keep weapons and other sources of power out of the hands of revolutionaries. They destroy the written literature of freedom and imprison or kill those who carry it orally. If the struggle for freedom is to succeed, it must then be intensified.

The importance of the literature of freedom can scarcely be questioned. Without help or guidance people submit to aversive conditions in the most surprising way. This is true even when the aversive conditions are part of the natural environment. Darwin observed, for example, that the Fuegians seemed to make no effort to protect themselves from the cold; they wore only scant clothing and made little use of it against the weather. And one of the most striking things about the struggle for freedom from intentional control is how often it has been lacking. Many people have submitted to the most obvious religious, governmental, and economic controls for centuries, striking for freedom only sporadically, if at all. The literature of freedom has made an essential contribution to the elimination of many aversive practices in government, religion, education, family life, and the production of goods.

The contributions of the literature of freedom, however, are not usually described in these terms. Some traditional theories could conceivably be said to define freedom as the absence of aversive control, but the emphasis has been on how that condition *feels*. Other traditional theories could conceivably be said to define freedom as a person's condition when he is behaving under nonaversive control, but the emphasis has been upon a state of mind associated with doing what one wants. According to John Stuart Mill, "Liberty consists in doing what one desires." The literature of freedom has been important in changing practice (it has changed practices whenever it has had any effect whatsoever), but it has nevertheless defined its task as the changing of states of mind and feelings. Freedom is a "possession." A person escapes from or destroys the power of a controller in order to feel free, and once he feels free and can do what he desires, no further action is recommended and none is prescribed by the literature of freedom, except perhaps external vigilance lest control be resumed.

The feeling of freedom becomes an unreliable guide to action as soon as would-be controllers turn to nonaversive measures, as they are likely to do to avoid the problems raised when the controllee escapes or attacks. Nonaversive measures are not as conspicuous as aversive and are likely to be acquired more slowly, but they have obvious advantages which promote their use. Productive labor, for example, was once the result of punishment: the slave worked to avoid the consequences of not working. Wages exemplify a different principle; a person is paid when he behaves in a given way so that he will continue to behave in that way. Although it has long been recognized that rewards have useful effects, wage systems have evolved slowly. In the nineteenth century it was believed that an industrial society required a hungry labor force; wages would be effective only if the hungry worker could exchange them for food. By making labor less aversive—for instance, by shortening hours and improving conditions—it has been possible to get men to work for lesser rewards. Until recently teaching was almost entirely aversive: the student studied to escape the consequences of not studying, but nonaversive techniques are gradually being discovered and used. The skillful parent learns to reward a child for good behavior rather than punish him for bad. Religious agencies move from the threat of hellfire to an emphasis on God's love, and governments turn from aversive sanctions to various kinds of inducements, as we shall note again shortly. What the layman calls a reward is a "positive reinforcer," the effects of which have been exhaustively studied in the experimental analysis of operant behavior. The effects are not as easily recognized as those of aversive contingencies because they tend to be deferred, and applications have therefore been delayed, but techniques as powerful as the older aversive techniques are now available.

A problem arises for the defender of freedom when the behavior generated by positive reinforcement has deferred aversive consequences. This is particularly likely to be the case when the process is used in intentional control, where the gain to the controller usually means a loss to the controllee. What are called conditioned positive reinforcers can often be used with deferred aversive results. Money is an example. It is reinforcing only after it has been exchanged for reinforcing things, but it can be used as a reinforcer when exchange is impossible. A counterfeit bill, a bad check, a stopped check, or an unkept promise are conditioned reinforcers, although aversive consequences are usually quickly discovered. The archetypal pattern is the gold brick. Countercontrol quickly follows: we escape from or attack those who misuse conditioned reinforcers in this way. But the misuse of many social reinforcers often goes unnoticed. Personal attention, approval, and affection are usually reinforcing only if there has been some connection with already effective reinforcers, but they can be used when a connection is lacking. The simulated approval and affection with which parents and teachers are often urged to solve behavior problems are counterfeit. So are flattery, backslapping, and many other ways of "winning friends."

Genuine reinforcers can be used in ways which have aversive consequences. A government may prevent defection by making life more interesting—by providing bread and circuses and by encouraging sports, gambling, the use of alcohol and other drugs, and various kinds of sexual behavior, where the effect is to keep people within reach of aversive sanctions. The Goncourt brothers noted the rise of pornography in the France of their day: "Pornographic literature," they wrote, "serves a Bas-Empire . . . one tames a people as one tames lions, by masturbation."

Genuine positive reinforcement can also be misused because the sheer quantity of reinforcers is not proportional to the effect on behavior. Reinforcement is usually only intermittent, and the schedule of reinforcement is more important than the amount received. Certain schedules generate a great deal of behavior in return for very little reinforcement, and the possibility has naturally not been overlooked by would-be controllers. Two examples of schedules which are easily used to the disadvantage of those reinforced may be noted.

In the incentive system known as piece-work pay, the worker is paid a given amount for each unit of work performed. The system seems to guarantee a balance between the goods produced and the money received. The schedule is attractive to management, which can calculate labor costs in advance, and also to the worker, who can control the amount he earns. This so-called "fixed-ratio" schedule of reinforcement can, however, be used to generate a great deal of behavior for very little return. It induces the worker to work fast, and the ratio can then be "stretched"—that is, more work can be demanded for each unit of pay without running the risk that the worker will stop working. His ultimate condition—hard work with very little pay—may be acutely aversive.

A related schedule, called variable-ratio, is at the heart of all gambling systems. A gambling enterprise pays people for giving it money—that is, it pays them when they make bets. But it pays on a kind of schedule which sustains betting even though, in the long run, the amount paid is less than the amount wagered. At first the mean ratio may be favorable to the bettor; he "wins." But the ratio can be stretched in such a way that he continues to play even when he begins to lose. The stretching may be accidental (an early run of good luck which grows steadily worse may create a dedicated gambler), or the ratio may be deliberately stretched by someone who controls the odds. In the long run the "utility" is negative: the gambler loses all.

It is difficult to deal effectively with deferred aversive consequences because they do not occur at a time when escape or attack is feasible—when, for example, the controller can be identified or is within reach. But the immediate reinforcement is positive and goes unchallenged. The problem to be solved by those who are concerned with freedom is to create immediate aversive consequences. A classical problem concerns "self-control." A person eats too much and gets sick but survives to eat too much again. Delicious food or the behavior evoked by it must be made sufficiently aversive so that a person will "escape from it" by not eating it. (It might be thought that he can escape from it only before eating it, but the Romans escaped afterward through the use of a vomitorium.) Current aversive stimuli may be conditioned. Something of the sort is done when eating too much is called wrong, gluttonous, or sinful. Other kinds of behavior to be suppressed may be declared illegal and punished accordingly. The more deferred the aversive consequences the greater the problem. It has taken a great deal of "engineering" to bring the ultimate consequences of smoking cigarettes to bear on the behavior. A fascinating hobby, a sport, a love affair, or a large salary may compete with activities which would be more reinforcing in the long run, but the run is too long to make countercontrol possible. That is why countercontrol is exerted, if at all, only by those who suffer aversive consequences but are not subject to positive reinforcement. Laws are passed against gambling, unions oppose piece-work pay, and no one is allowed to pay young children to work for them or to pay anyone for engaging in immoral behavior, but these measures may be strongly opposed by those whom they are designed to protect. The gambler objects to antigambling laws and the alcoholic to any kind of prohibition; and a child or prostitute may be willing to work for what is offered.

The literature of freedom has never come to grips with techniques of control which do not generate escape or counterattack because it has dealt with the problem in terms of states of mind and feelings. In his book *Sovereignty,* Bertrand de Jouvenel quotes two important figures in that literature. According to Leibnitz, "Liberty consists in the power to do what one wants to do," and according to Voltaire, "When I can do what I want to do, there is my liberty for me." But both writers add a concluding phrase: Leibnitz, " . . . or in the power to want what can be got," and Voltaire, more candidly, " . . . but I can't help wanting what I do want." Jouvenel relegates these comments to a footnote, saying that the power to want is a matter of "interior liberty" (the freedom of the inner man!) which falls outside the "gambit of freedom."

A person wants something if he acts to get it when the occasion arises. A person who says "I want something to eat" will presumably eat when something becomes available. If he says "I want to get warm," he will presumably move into a warm place when he can. These acts have been reinforced in the past by whatever was wanted. What a person *feels* when he feels himself wanting something depends upon the circumstances. Food is reinforcing only in a state of deprivation, and a person who wants something to eat may feel parts of that state—for example, hunger pangs. A person who wants to get warm presumably feels cold. Conditions associated with a high probability of responding may also be felt, together with aspects of the present occasion which are similar to those of past occasions upon which behavior has been reinforced. Wanting is not, however, a feeling, nor is a feeling the reason a person acts to get what he wants. Certain contingencies have raised the probability of behavior and at the same time have created conditions which may be felt. Freedom is a matter of contingencies of reinforcement, not of the feelings the contingencies generate. The distinction is particularly important when the contingencies do not generate escape or counterattack.

The uncertainty which surrounds the countercontrol of nonaversive measures is easily exemplified. In the 1930's it seemed necessary to cut agricultural production. The Agricultural Adjustment Act authorized the Secretary of Agriculture to make "rental or benefit payments" to farmers who agreed to produce less—to pay the farmers, in fact, what they would have made on the food they agreed not to produce. It would have been unconstitutional to *compel* them to reduce production, but the government argued that it was merely inviting them to do so. But the Supreme Court recognized that positive inducement can be as irresistible as aversive measures when it ruled that "the power to confer or withhold unlimited benefit is the power to coerce or destroy." The decision was later reversed, however, when the Court ruled that "to hold that motive or temptation is equivalent to coercion is to plunge the law into endless difficulties." We are considering some of these difficulties.

The same issue arises when a government runs a lottery in order to raise revenue to reduce taxes. The government takes the same amount of money from its citizens in both cases, though not necessarily from the same citizens. By running a lottery it avoids certain unwanted consequences: people escape from heavy taxation by moving away or they counterattack by throwing a government which imposes new taxes out of office. A lottery, taking advantage of a stretched variable-ratio schedule of reinforcement, has neither of these effects. The only opposition comes from those who in general oppose gambling enterprises and who are themselves seldom gamblers.

A third example is the practice of inviting prisoners to volunteer for possibly dangerous experiments—for example, on new drugs—in return for better living conditions or shortened sentences. Everyone would protest if the prisoners were forced to participate, but are they really free when positively reinforced, particularly when the condition to be improved or the sentence to be shortened has been imposed by the state?

The issue often arises in more subtle forms. It has been argued, for example, that uncontrolled contraceptive services and abortion do not "confer unrestricted freedom to reproduce or not to reproduce because they cost time and money." Impoverished members of society should be given compensation if they are to have a truly "free choice." If the just compensation exactly offsets the time and money needed to practice birth control, then people will indeed be free of the control exerted by the loss of time and money, but whether or not they then have children will still depend upon other conditions which have not been specified. If a nation generously reinforces the practices of contraception and abortion, to what extent are its citizens free to have or not to have children?

Uncertainty about positive control is evident in two remarks which often appear in the literature of freedom. It is said that even though behavior is completely determined, it is better that a man "feel free" or "believe that he is free." If this means that it is better to be controlled in ways which have no aversive consequences, we may agree, but if it means that it is better to be controlled in ways against which no one revolts, it fails to take account of the possibility of deferred aversive consequences. A second comment seems more appropriate: "It is better to be a conscious slave than a happy one." The word "slave" clarifies the nature of the ultimate consequences being considered: they are exploitative and hence aversive. What the slave is to be conscious of is his misery; and a system of slavery so well designed that it does not breed revolt is the real threat. The literature of freedom has been designed to make men "conscious" of aversive control, but in its choice of methods it has failed to rescue the happy slave.

One of the great figures in the literature of freedom, Jean-Jacques Rousseau, did not fear the power of positive reinforcement. In his remarkable book *Émile* he gave the following advice to teachers:

> Let [the child] believe that he is always in control, though it is always you [the teacher] who really controls. There is no subjugation so perfect as that which keeps the appearance of freedom, for in that way one captures volition itself. The poor baby, knowing nothing, able to do nothing, having learned nothing, is he not at your mercy? Can you not arrange everything in the world which surrounds him? Can you not influence him as you wish? His work, his play, his pleasures, his pains, are not all these in your hands and without his knowing? Doubtless he ought to do only what he wants; but he ought to want to do only what you want him to do; he

> ought not to take a step which you have not foreseen; he ought not to open his mouth without your knowing what he will say.

Rousseau could take this line because he had unlimited faith in the benevolence of teachers, who would use their absolute control for the good of their students. But . . . benevolence is no guarantee against the misuse of power, and very few figures in the history of the struggle for freedom have shown Rousseau's lack of concern. On the contrary, they have taken the extreme position that all control is wrong. In so doing they exemplify a behavioral process called generalization. Many instances of control are aversive, in either their nature or their consequences, and hence all instances are to be avoided. The Puritans carried the generalization a step further by arguing that most positive reinforcement was wrong, whether or not it was intentionally arranged, just because it occasionally got people into trouble.

The literature of freedom has encouraged escape from or attack upon all controllers. It has done so by making any indication of control aversive. Those who manipulate human behavior are said to be evil men, necessarily bent on exploitation. Control is clearly the opposite of freedom, and if freedom is good, control must be bad. What is overlooked is control which does not have aversive consequences at any time. Many social practices essential to the welfare of the species involve the control of one person by another, and no one can suppress them who has any concern for human achievements. . . . [I]n order to maintain the position that all control is wrong, it has been necessary to disguise or conceal the nature of useful practices, to prefer weak practices just because they can be disguised or concealed, and—a most extraordinary result indeed!—to perpetuate punitive measures.

The problem is to free men, not from control, but from certain kinds of control, and it can be solved only if our analysis takes all consequences into account. How people feel about control, before or after the literature of freedom has worked on their feelings, does not lead to useful distinctions.

Were it not for the unwarranted generalization that all control is wrong, we should deal with the social environment as simply as we deal with the nonsocial. Although technology has freed men from certain aversive features of the environment, it has not freed them from the environment. We accept the fact that we depend upon the world around us, and we simply change the nature of the dependency. In the same way, to make the social environment as free as possible of aversive stimuli we do not need to destroy that environment or escape from it; we need to redesign it.

. . . . . .

Man's struggle for freedom is not due to a will to be free, but to certain behavioral processes characteristic of the human organism, the chief effect of which is the avoidance of or escape from so-called "aversive" features of the environment. Physical and biological technologies have been mainly concerned with natural aversive stimuli; the struggle for freedom is concerned with stimuli intentionally arranged by other people. The literature of freedom has identified the other people and has proposed ways of escaping from them or weakening or destroying their power. It has been successful in reducing the aversive stimuli used in intentional control, but it has made the mistake of defining freedom in terms of states of mind or feelings, and it has therefore not been able to deal effectively with techniques of control which do not breed escape or revolt but nevertheless have aversive consequences. It has been forced to brand all control as wrong and to misrepresent many of the advantages to be gained from a social environment. It is unprepared for the next step, which is not to free men from control but to analyze and change the kinds of control to which they are exposed.

DANIEL BELL

"The End of Ideology in the West"
1960

In the wake of the violent excesses associated with Hitler and Stalin—two bona fide ideologues—political ideologies came under sharp suspicion during the 1950s. The sociologist Daniel Bell (1919–) was among a host of American intellectuals who gave voice to this suspicion, who believed that the problems of industrial society defied the solutions offered by the traditional Right and Left, and who placed their political hopes on a nondoctrinaire pluralistic consensus of enlightened democratic capitalists. Although the catch phrase for this anti-ideological impulse was contributed by Bell's book, *The End of Ideology: On the Exhaustion of Political Ideas in the Fifties* (New York, 1960), Bell's actual formulation of this impulse was ambivalent. He was troubled by the widespread turning away from systematic political argument that accompanied the rejection of the "terrible simplifiers," the ideologues. The animated discussion stimulated by Bell is represented in the anthology, *The End of Ideology Debate* (New York, 1968), edited by Chaim I. Waxman. Bell's thought and career during the years leading up to the "end of ideology debate" is the subject of an excellent historical study: Howard Brick, *Daniel Bell and the Decline of Intellectual Radicalism: Social Theory and Political Reconciliation in the 1940s* (Madison, Wis., 1986).

Men commit the error of not knowing when to limit their hopes.
—Machiavelli

There have been few periods in history when man felt his world to be durable, suspended surely, as in Christian allegory, between chaos and heaven. In an Egyptian papyrus of more than four thousand years ago, one finds: " . . . impudence is rife . . . the country is spinning round and round like a potter's wheel . . . the masses are like timid sheep without a shepherd . . . one who yesterday was indigent is now wealthy and the sometime rich overwhelm him with adulation." The Hellenistic period as described by Gilbert Murray was one of a "failure of nerve"; there was "the rise of pessimism, a loss of self-confidence, of hope in this life and of faith in normal human effort." And the old scoundrel Talleyrand claimed that only those who lived before 1789 could have tasted life in all its sweetness.

This age, too, can add appropriate citations—made all the more wry and bitter by the long period of bright hope that preceded it—for the two decades between 1930 and 1950 have an intensity peculiar in written history: world-wide economic depression and sharp class struggles; the rise of fascism and racial imperialism in a country that had stood at an advanced stage of human culture; the tragic self-immolation of a revolutionary generation that had proclaimed the finer ideals of man; destructive war of a breadth and scale hitherto unknown; the bureaucratized murder of millions in concentration camps and death chambers.

For the radical intellectual who had articulated the revolutionary impulses of the past century and a half, all this has meant an end to chiliastic hopes, to millenarianism, to apocalyptic thinking—and to ideology. For ideology, which once was a road to action, has come to be a dead end.

Whatever its origins among the French *philosophes,* ideology as a way of translating ideas into action was given its sharpest phrasing by the left Hegelians, by Feuerbach and by Marx. For them, the function of philosophy was to be critical, to rid the present of the past. ("The tradition of all the dead generations weighs like a nightmare on the brain of the living," wrote Marx.) Feuerbach, the most radical of all the left Hegelians, called himself Luther II. Man would be free, he said, if we could demythologize religion. The history of all thought was a history of progressive disenchantment, and if finally, in Christianity, God had been transformed from a parochial deity to a universal abstraction, the function of criticism—using the radical tool of alienation, or self-estrangement—was to replace theology by anthropology, to substitute Man for God. Philosophy was to be directed at life, man was to be liberated from the "specter of abstractions" and extricated from the bind of the supernatural. Religion was capable only of creating "false consciousness." Philosophy would reveal "true consciousness." And by placing Man, rather than God, at the center of consciousness, Feuerbach sought to bring the "infinite into the finite."

If Feuerbach "descended into the world," Marx sought to transform it. And where Feuerbach proclaimed anthropology, Marx, reclaiming a root insight of Hegel, emphasized History and historical contexts. The world was not generic Man, but men; and

Source: The End of Ideology: On the Exhaustion of Political Ideas in the Fifties, Daniel Bell, 393–402 (Collier Edition, 1961).

of men, classes of men. Men differed because of their class position. And truths were class truths. All truths, thus, were masks, or partial truths, but the real truth was the revolutionary truth. And this real truth was rational.

Thus a dynamic was introduced into the analysis of ideology, and into the creation of a new ideology. By demythologizing religion, one recovered (from God and sin) the potential in man. By the unfolding of history, rationality was revealed. In the struggle of classes, true consciousness, rather than false consciousness, could be achieved. But if truth lay in action, one must act. The left Hegelians, said Marx, were only *littérateurs.* (For them a magazine was "practice.") For Marx, the only real action was in politics. But action, revolutionary action as Marx conceived it, was not mere social change. It was, in its way, the resumption of all the old millenarian, chiliastic ideas of the Anabaptists. It was, in its new vision, a new ideology.

Ideology is the conversion of ideas into social levers. Without irony, Max Lerner once entitled a book "Ideas Are Weapons." This is the language of ideology. It is more. It is the commitment to the consequences of ideas. When Vissarion Belinsky, the father of Russian criticism, first read Hegel and became convinced of the philosophical correctness of the formula "what is, is what ought to be," he became a supporter of the Russian autocracy. But when it was shown to him that Hegel's thought contained the contrary tendency, that dialectically the "is" evolves into a different form, he became a revolutionary overnight. "Belinsky's conversion," comments Rufus W. Mathewson, Jr., "illustrates an attitude toward ideas which is both passionate and myopic, which responds to them on the basis of their immediate relevances alone, and inevitably reduces them to tools."

What gives ideology its force is its passion. Abstract philosophical inquiry has always sought to eliminate passion, and the person, to rationalize all ideas. For the ideologue, truth arises in action, and meaning is given to experience by the "transforming moment." He comes alive not in contemplation, but in "the deed." One might say, in fact, that the most important, latent, function of ideology is to tap emotion. Other than religion (and war and nationalism), there have been few forms of channelizing emotional energy. Religion symbolized, drained away, dispersed emotional energy from the world onto the litany, the liturgy, the sacraments, the edifices, the arts. Ideology fuses these energies and channels them into politics.

But religion, at its most effective, was more. It was a way for people to cope with the problem of death. The fear of death—forceful and inevitable—and more, the fear of violent death, shatters the glittering, imposing, momentary dream of man's power. The fear of death, as Hobbes pointed out, is the source of conscience; the effort to avoid violent death is the source of law. When it was possible to believe, really believe, in heaven and hell, then some of the fear of death could be tempered or controlled; without such belief, there is only the total annihilation of the self.

It may well be that with the decline in religious *faith* in the last century and more, this fear of death as total annihilation, unconsciously expressed, has probably increased. One may hypothesize, in fact, that here is a cause of the breakthrough of the irrational, which is such a marked feature of the changed moral temper of our time. Fanaticism, violence, and cruelty are not, of course, unique in human history. But there was a time when such frenzies and mass emotions could be displaced, symbolized, drained away, and dispersed through religious devotion and practice. Now there is only this life, and the assertion of self becomes possible—for some even necessary—in the domination over others. One can challenge death by emphasizing the omnipotence of a movement (as in the "inevitable" victory of communism), or overcome death (as did the "immortality" of Captain Ahab) by bending others to one's will. Both paths are taken, but politics, because it can institutionalize power, in the way that religion once did, becomes the ready avenue for domination. The modern effort to transform the world chiefly or solely through politics (as contrasted with the religious transformation of the self) has meant that all other institutional ways of mobilizing emotional energy would necessarily atrophy. In effect, sect and church became party and social movement.

A social movement can rouse people when it can do three things: simplify ideas, establish a claim to truth, and, in the union of the two, demand a commitment to action. Thus, not only does ideology transform ideas, it transforms people as well. The nineteenth-century ideologies, by emphasizing inevitability and by infusing passion into their followers, could compete with religion. By identifying inevitability with progress, they linked up with the positive values of science. But more important, these ideologies were linked, too, with the rising class of intellectuals, which was seeking to assert a place in society.

The differences between the intellectual and the scholar, without being invidious, are important to understand. The scholar has a bounded field of knowledge, a tradition, and seeks to find his place in it, adding to the accumulated, tested knowledge of the past as to a mosaic. The scholar, qua scholar, is less involved with his "self." The intellectual begins with *his* experience, *his* individual perceptions of the world, *his* privileges and deprivations, and judges the world by these sensibilities. Since his own status is of high value, his judgments of the society reflect the treatment accorded him. In a business civilization, the intellectual felt that the wrong values were being honored, and rejected the society. Thus there was a "built-in" compulsion for the free-floating intellectual to become political. The ideologies, therefore, which emerged from the nineteenth century had the force of the intellectuals behind them. They embarked upon what William James called "the faith ladder," which in its vision of the future cannot distinguish possibilities from probabilities, and converts the latter into certainties.

Today, these ideologies are exhausted. The events behind this important sociological change are complex and varied. Such calamities as the Moscow Trials, the Nazi-Soviet pact, the concentration camps, the suppression of the Hungarian workers, form one chain; such social changes as the modification of capitalism, the rise of the Welfare State, another. In philosophy, one can trace the decline of simplistic, rationalistic beliefs and the emergence of new stoic-theological images of man, e.g. Freud, Tillich, Jaspers, etc. This is not to say that such ideologies as communism in France and Italy do not have a political weight, or a driving momentum from other sources. But out of all this history, one simple fact emerges: for the radical intelligentsia, the old ideologies have lost their "truth" and their power to persuade.

Few serious minds believe any longer that one can set down "blueprints" and through "social engineering" bring about a new utopia of social harmony. At the same time, the older "counter-beliefs" have lost their intellectual force as well. Few "classic" liberals insist that the State should play no role in the economy, and few serious conservatives, at least in England and on the Continent, believe that the Welfare State is "the road to serfdom." In the Western world, therefore, there is today a rough consensus among intellectuals on political issues: the acceptance of a Welfare State; the desirability of decentralized power; a system of mixed economy and of political pluralism. In that sense, too, the ideological age has ended.

And yet, the extraordinary fact is that while the old nineteenth-century ideologies and intellectual debates have become exhausted, the rising states of Asia and Africa are fashioning new ideologies with a different appeal for their own people. These are the ideologies of industrialization, modernization, Pan-Arabism, color, and nationalism. In the distinctive difference between the two kinds of ideologies lies the great political and social problems of the second half of the twentieth century. The ideologies of the nineteenth century were universalistic, humanistic, and fashioned by intellectuals. The mass ideologies of Asia and Africa are parochial, instrumental, and created by political leaders. The driving forces of the old ideologies were social equality and, in the largest sense, freedom. The impulsions of the new ideologies are economic development and national power.

And in this appeal, Russia and China have become models. The fascination these countries exert is no longer the old idea of the free society, but the new one of economic growth. And if this involves the wholesale coercion of the population and the rise of new elites to drive the people, the new repressions are justified on the ground that without such coercions economic advance cannot take place rapidly enough. And even for some of the liberals of the West, "economic development" has become a new ideology that washes away the memory of old disillusionments.

It is hard to quarrel with an appeal for rapid economic growth and modernization, and few can dispute the goal, as few could ever dispute an appeal for equality and freedom. But in this powerful surge—and its swiftness is amazing—any movement that instates such goals risks the sacrifice of the present generation for a future that may see only a new exploitation by a new elite. For the newly risen countries, the debate is not over the merits of communism—the content of that doctrine has long been forgotten by friends and foes alike. The question is an older one: whether new societies can grow by building democratic institutions and allowing people to make choices—and sacrifices—voluntarily, or whether the new elites, heady with power, will impose totalitarian means to transform their countries. Certainly in these traditional and old colonial societies where the masses are apathetic and easily manipulated, the answer lies with the intellectual classes and their conceptions of the future.

Thus one finds, at the end of the fifties, a disconcerting caesura. In the West, among the intellectuals, the old passions are spent. The new generation, with no meaningful memory of these old debates, and no secure tradition to build upon, finds itself seeking new purposes within a framework of political society that has rejected, intellectually speaking, the old apocalyptic and chiliastic visions. In the search for a "cause," there is a deep, desperate, almost pathetic anger. The theme runs through a remarkable book, *Convictions,* by a dozen of the sharpest young Left Wing intellectuals in Britain. They cannot define the content of the "cause" they seek, but the yearning is clear. In the U.S. too there is a restless search for a new intellectual radicalism. Richard Chase, in his thoughtful assessment of American society, *The Democratic Vista,* insists that the greatness of nineteenth-century America for the rest of the world consisted in its radical vision of man (such a vision as Whitman's), and calls for a new radical criticism today. But the problem is that the old politico-economic radicalism (pre-occupied with such matters as the socialization of industry) has lost its meaning, while the stultifying aspects of contemporary culture (e.g., television) cannot be redressed in political terms. At the same time, American culture has almost completely accepted the avant-garde, particularly in art, and the older academic styles have been driven out completely. The irony, further, for those who seek "causes" is that the workers, whose grievances were once the driving energy for social change, are more satisfied with the society than the intellectuals. The workers have not achieved utopia, but their expectations were less than those of the intellectuals, and the gains correspondingly larger.

The young intellectual is unhappy because the "middle way" is for the middle-aged, not for him; it is without passion and is deadening. Ideology, which by its nature is an all-or-none affair, and temperamentally the thing he wants, is intellectually devitalized, and few issues can be formulated any more, intellectually, in ideological terms. The emotional energies—and needs—exist, and the question of how one mobilizes these energies is a difficult one. Politics offers little excitement. Some of the younger intellectuals have found an outlet in science or university pursuits, but often at the expense of narrowing their talent into mere technique; others have sought self-expression in the arts, but in the wasteland the lack of content has meant, too, the lack of the necessary tension that creates new forms and styles.

Whether the intellectuals in the West can find passions outside of politics is moot. Unfortunately, social reform does not have any unifying appeal, nor does it give a younger generation the outlet for "self-expression" and "self-definition" that it wants. The trajectory of enthusiasm has curved East, where, in the new ecstasies for economic utopia, the "future" is all that counts.

The end of ideology is not—should not be—the end of utopia as well. If anything, one can begin anew the discussion of utopia only by being aware of the trap of ideology. The point is that ideologists are "terrible simplifiers." Ideology makes it unnecessary for people to confront individual issues on their individual merits. One simply turns to the ideological vending machine, and out comes the prepared formulae. And when these beliefs are suffused by apocalyptic fervor, ideas become weapons, and with dreadful results.

There is now, more than ever, some need for utopia, in the sense that men need—as they have always needed—some vision of their potential, some manner of fusing passion with intelligence. Yet the ladder to the City of Heaven can no longer be a "faith ladder," but an empirical one: a utopia has to specify *where* one wants to go, *how* to get there, the costs of the enterprise, and some realization of, and justification for the determination of *who* is to pay.

The end of ideology closes the book, intellectually speaking, on an era, the one of easy "left" formulae for social change. But to close the book is not to turn one's back upon it. This is all the more important now when a "new Left," with few memories of the past, is emerging. This "new Left" has passion and energy, but little definition of the future. Its outriders exult that it is "on the move." But where it is going, what it means by Socialism, how to guard against bureaucratization, what one means by democratic planning or workers' control—any of the questions that require hard thought, are only answered by bravura phrases.

It is in attitudes towards Cuba and the new States in Africa that the meaning of intellectual maturity, and of the end of ideology, will be tested. For among the "new Left," there is an alarming readiness to create a *tabula rasa,* to accept the word "Revolution" as an absolution for outrages, to justify the suppression of civil rights and opposition—in short, to erase the lessons of the last forty years with an emotional alacrity that is astounding. The fact that many of these emerging social movements are justified in their demands for freedom, for the right to control their own political and economic destinies, does not mean they have a right to a blank check for everything they choose to do in the name of their emancipation. Nor does the fact that such movements take power in the name of freedom guarantee that they will not turn out to be as imperialist, as grandeur-concerned (in the name of Pan-Africanism or some other ideology), as demanding their turn on the stage of History, as the States they have displaced.

If the end of ideology has any meaning, it is to ask for the end of rhetoric, and rhetoricians, of "revolution" of the day when the young French anarchist Vaillant tossed a bomb into the Chamber of Deputies, and the literary critic Laurent Tailhade declared in his defense: "What do a few human lives matter; it was a *beau geste*." (A *beau geste* that ended, one might say, in a mirthless jest: two years later, Tailhade lost an eye when a bomb was thrown into a restaurant.) Today, in Cuba, as George Sherman, reporting for the *London Observer* summed it up: "The Revolution is law today although nobody has said clearly what that law is. You are expected to be simply for or against it and judge and be judged accordingly. Hatred and intolerance are wiping out whatever middle ground may have existed."

The problems which confront us at home and in the world are resistant to the old terms of ideological debate between"left" and "right," and if "ideology" by now, and with good reason, is an irretrievably fallen word, it is not necessary that "utopia" suffer the same fate. But it will if those who now call loudest for new utopias begin to justify degrading *means* in the name of some Utopian or revolutionary *end,* and forget the simple lessons that if the old debates are meaningless, some old verities are not—the verities of free speech, free press, the right of opposition and of free inquiry.

And if the intellectual history of the past hundred years has any meaning—and lesson—it is to reassert Jefferson's wisdom (aimed at removing the dead hand of the past, but which can serve as a warning against the heavy hand of the future as well), that "the present belongs to the living." This is the wisdom that revolutionists, old and new, who are sensitive to the fate of their fellow men, rediscover in every generation. "I will never believe," says a protagonist in a poignant dialogue written by the gallant Polish philosopher Leszek Kolakowski, "that the moral and intellectual life of mankind follows the law of economics, that is by saving today we can have more tomorrow; that we should use lives now so that truth will triumph or that we should profit by crime to pave the way for nobility."

And these words, written during the Polish "thaw," when the intellectuals had asserted, from their experience with the "future," the claims of humanism, echo the protest of the Russian writer Alexander Herzen, who, in a dialogue a hundred years ago, reproached an earlier revolutionist who would sacrifice the present mankind for a promised tomorrow: "Do you truly wish to condemn all human beings alive today to the sad role of caryatids . . . supporting a floor for others some day to dance on? . . . This alone should serve as a warning to people: an end that is infinitely remote is not an end, but, if you like, a trap; an end must be nearer—it ought to be, at the very least, the labourer's wage or pleasure in the work done. Each age, each generation, each life has its own fullness. . . ."

C. WRIGHT MILLS

Selection from *The Sociological Imagination*
1959

C. Wright Mills (1916–62) agreed with his Columbia colleague Daniel Bell that the inherited ideological traditions were running out of steam, but Mills developed a less hopeful analysis of the prospects of democratic political culture. Mills invoked the figure of "The Cheerful Robot," and sometimes doubted that industrial society had the political capability to prevent the degeneration of human beings into robots, cheerful or gloomy. His fellow social scientists, it seemed to Mills, were facilitating the consolidation of a technocratic social and economic order in which fundamental political issues were never formulated. In a book of 1959, *The Sociological Imagination,* from which our selection is a chapter, Mills called on social scientists and on intellectuals generally to confront the contradictions of modern society and to vindicate once again the values of reason and freedom that were proving to be elusive. Information about Mills's life and career is available in Irving Louis Horowitz, *C. Wright Mills: An American Utopian* (New York, 1983). The most cogent critical introduction to Mills is Jim Miller, "Democracy and the Intellectual: C. Wright Mills Reconsidered," *Salmagundi,* 70–71 (1986), 82–101.

The climax of the social scientist's concern with history is the idea he comes to hold of the epoch in which he lives. The climax of his concern with biography is the idea he comes to hold of man's basic nature, and of the limits it may set to the transformation of man by the course of history.

All classic social scientists have been concerned with the salient characteristics of their time—and the problem of how history is being made within it; with "the nature of human nature"—and the variety of individuals that come to prevail within their periods. Marx and Sombart and Weber, Comte and Spencer, Durkheim and Veblen, Mannheim, Schumpeter, and Michels—each in his own way has confronted these problems. In our immediate times, however, many social scientists have not. Yet it is precisely now, in the second half of the twentieth century, that these concerns become urgent as issues, persistent as troubles, and vital for the cultural orientation of our human studies.

Nowadays men everywhere seek to know where they stand, where they may be going, and what—if anything—they can do about the present as history and the future as responsibility. Such questions as these no one can answer once and for all. Every period provides its own answers. But just now, for us, there is a difficulty. We are now at the ending of an epoch, and we have got to work out our own answers.

We are at the ending of what is called The Modern Age. Just as Antiquity was followed by several centuries of Oriental ascendancy, which Westerners provincially call The Dark Ages, so now The Modern Age is being succeeded by a post-modern period. Perhaps we may call it: The Fourth Epoch.

The ending of one epoch and the beginning of another is, to be sure, a matter of definition. But definitions, like everything social, are historically specific. And now our basic definitions of society and of self are being overtaken by new realities. I do not mean merely that never before within the limits of a single generation have men been so fully exposed at so fast a rate to such earthquakes of change. I do not mean merely that we feel we are in an epochal kind of transition, and that we struggle to grasp the outline of the new epoch we suppose ourselves to be entering. I mean that when we try to orient ourselves—if we do try—we find that too many of our old expectations and images are, after all, tied down historically: that too many of our standard categories of thought and of feeling as often disorient us as help to explain what is happening around us; that too many of our explanations are derived from the great historical transition from the Medieval to the Modern Age; and that when they are generalized for use today, they become unwieldy, irrelevant, not convincing. I also mean that our major orientations—liberalism and socialism—have virtually collapsed as adequate explanations of the world and of ourselves.

These two ideologies came out of The Enlightenment, and they have had in common many assumptions and values. In both, increased rationality is held to be the prime condition of increased freedom. The liberating notion of progress by reason, the faith in science as a unmixed good, the demand for popular education and the faith in its political meaning for democracy—all these ideals of The Enlightenment have rested upon the happy assumption of the inherent relation of reason and freedom. Those thinkers who have done the most to shape our ways of thinking have proceeded under

Source: The Sociological Imagination, C. Wright Mills, 165–76. Footnotes omitted.

this assumption. It lies under every movement and nuance of the work of Freud: To be free, the individual must become more rationally aware; therapy is an aid to giving reason its chance to work freely in the course of an individual's life. The same assumption underpins the main line of marxist work: Men, caught in the irrational anarchy of production, must become rationally aware of their position in society; they must become "class conscious"—the marxian meaning of which is a rationalistic as any term set forth by Bentham.

Liberalism has been concerned with freedom and reason as supreme facts about the individual; marxism, as supreme facts about man's role in the political making of history. The liberals and the radicals of The Modern Period have generally been men who believed in the rational making of history and of his own biography by the free individual.

But what has been happening in the world makes evident, I believe, why the ideas of freedom and of reason now so often seem so ambiguous in both the new capitalist and the communist societies of our time: why marxism has so often become a dreary rhetoric of bureaucratic defense and abuse; and liberalism, a trivial and irrelevant way of masking social reality. The major developments of our time, I believe, can be correctly understood neither in terms of the liberal nor the marxian interpretation of politics and culture. These ways of thought arose as guidelines to reflection about types of society which do not now exist. John Stuart Mill never examined the kinds of political economy now arising in the capitalist world. Karl Marx never analyzed the kinds of society now arising in the communist bloc. And neither of them ever thought through the problems of the so-called underdeveloped countries in which seven out of ten men are trying to exist today. Now we confront new kinds of social structure which, in terms of "modern" ideals, resist analysis in the liberal and in the socialist terms we have inherited.

The ideological mark of The Fourth Epoch—that which sets it off from The Modern Age—is that the ideas of freedom and of reason have become moot; that increased rationality may not be assumed to make for increased freedom.

The role of reason in human affairs and the idea of the free individual as the seat of reason are the most important themes inherited by twentieth-century social scientists from the philosophers of the Enlightenment. If they are to remain the key values in terms of which troubles are specified and issues focused, then the ideals of reason and of freedom must now be re-stated as problems in more precise and solvable ways than have been available to earlier thinkers and investigators. For in our time these two values, reason and freedom, are in obvious yet subtle peril.

The underlying trends are well known. Great and rational organizations—in brief, bureaucracies—have indeed increased, but the substantive reason of the individual at large has not. Caught in the limited milieux of their everyday lives, ordinary men often cannot reason about the great structures—rational and irrational—of which their milieux are subordinate parts. Accordingly, they often carry out series of apparently rational actions without any ideas of the ends they serve, and there is the increasing suspicion that those at the top as well—like Tolstoy's generals—only pretend they know. The growth of such organizations, within an increasing division of labor, sets up more and more spheres of life, work, and leisure, in which reasoning is difficult or impossible. The soldier, for example, "carries out an entire series of functionally rational actions accurately without having any idea as to the ultimate end of this action" or the function of each act within the whole. Even men of technically supreme intelligence may efficiently perform their assigned work and yet not know that it is to result in the first atom bomb.

Science, it turns out, is not a technological Second Coming. That its techniques and its rationality are given a central place in a society does not mean that men live reasonably and without myth, fraud, and superstition. Universal education may lead to technological idiocy and nationalist provinciality—rather than to the informed and independent intelligence. The Mass distribution of historic culture may not lift the level of cultural sensibility, but rather, merely banalize it—and compete mightily with the chance for creative innovation. A high level of bureaucratic rationality and of technology does not mean a high level of either individual or social intelligence. From the first you cannot infer the second. For social, technological, or bureaucratic rationality is not merely a grand summation of the individual will and capacity to reason. The very chance to acquire that will and that capacity seems in fact often to be decreased by it. Rationally organized social arrangements are not necessarily a means of increased freedom—for the individual or for the society. In fact, often they are a means of tyranny and manipulation, a means of expropriating the very chance to reason, the very capacity to act as a free man.

Only from a few commanding positions or—as the case may be—merely vantage points, in the rationalized structure is it readily possible to understand the structural forces at work in the whole which thus affect each limited part of which ordinary men are aware.

The forces that shape these milieux do not originate within them, nor are they controllable by those sunk in them. Moreover, these milieux are themselves increasingly rationalized. Families as well as factories, leisure as well as work, neighborhoods as well as states—they, too, tend to become parts of a functionally rational totality—or they are subject to uncontrolled and irrational forces.

The increasing rationalization of society, the contradiction between such rationality and reason, the collapse of the assumed coincidence of reason and freedom—these developments lie back of the rise into view of the man who is "with" rationality but without reason, who is increasingly self-rationalized and also increasingly uneasy. It is in terms of this type of man that the contemporary problem of freedom is best stated. Yet such trends and suspicions are often not formulated as problems, and they are certainly not widely acknowledged as issues or felt as a set of troubles. Indeed, it is the fact of its unrecognized character, its lack of formulation, that is the most important feature of the contemporary problem of freedom and reason.

From the individual's standpoint, much that happens seems the result of manipulation, of management, of blind drift; authority is often not explicit; those with power often feel no need to make it explicit and to justify it. That is one reason why ordinary men, when they are in trouble or when they sense that they are up against issues, cannot get clear targets for thought and for action; they cannot determine what it is that imperils the values they vaguely discern as theirs.

Given these effects of the ascendant trend of rationalization, the individual "does the best he can." He gears his aspirations and his work to the situation he is in, and from which he can find no way out. In due course, he does not seek a way out: he adapts. That part of his life which is left over from work, he uses to play, to consume, "to have fun." Yet this sphere of consumption is also being rationalized. Alienated from production, from work, he is also alienated from consumption, from genuine leisure. This adaptation of the individual and its effects upon his milieux and self results not only in the loss of his chance, and in due course, of his capacity and will to reason; it also affects his chances and his capacity to act as a free man. Indeed, neither the value of freedom nor of reason, it would seem, are known to him.

Such adapted men are not necessarily unintelligent, even after they have lived and worked and played in such circumstances for quite some time. Karl Mannheim has made the point in a clear way by speaking of "self rationalization," which refers to the way in which an individual, caught in the limited segments of great, rational organizations, comes systematically to regulate his impulses and his aspirations, his manner of life and his ways of thought, in rather strict accordance with "the rules and regulations of the organization." The rational organization is thus an alienating organization: the guiding principles of conduct and reflection, and in due course of emotion as well, are not seated in the individual conscience of the Reformation man, or in the independent reason of the Cartesian man. The guiding principles, in fact, are alien to and in contradiction with all that has been historically understood as individuality. It is not too much to say that in the extreme development the chance to reason of most men is destroyed, as rationality increases and its locus, its control, is moved from the individual to the big-scale organization. There is then rationality without reason. Such rationality is not commensurate with freedom but the destroyer of it.

It is no wonder that the ideal of individuality has become moot: in our time, what is at issue is the very nature of man, the image we have of his limits and possibilities as man. History is not yet done with its exploration of the limits and meanings of "human nature." We do not know how profound man's psychological transformation from the Modern Age to the contemporary epoch may be. But we must now raise the question in an ultimate form: Among contemporary men will there come to prevail, or even to flourish, what may be called The Cheerful Robot?

We know of course that man can be turned into a robot, by chemical and psychiatric means, by steady coercion and by controlled environment; but also by random pressures and unplanned sequences of circumstances. But can he be made to want to become a cheerful and willing robot? Can he be happy in this condition, and what are the qualities and the meanings of such happiness? It will no longer do merely to assume, as a metaphysic of human nature, that down deep in man-as-man there is an urge for freedom and a will to reason. Now we must ask: What in man's nature, what in the human condition today, what in each of the varieties of social structure makes for the ascendancy of the cheerful robot? And what stands against it?

The advent of the alienated man and all the themes which lie behind his advent now affect the whole of our serious intellectual life and cause our immediate intellectual malaise. It is a major theme of the human condition in the contemporary epoch and of all studies worthy of the name. I know of no idea, no theme, no problem, that is so deep in the classic tradition—and so much involved in the possible default of contemporary social science.

It is what Karl Marx so brilliantly discerned in his earlier essays on "alienation"; it is the chief concern of Georg Simmel in his justly famous essay on "The Metropolis"; Graham Wallas was aware of it in his work on The Great Society. It lies behind Fromm's conception of the "automaton." The fear that such a type of man will become ascendant underlies many of the more recent uses of such classic sociological conceptions as "status and contract," "community and society." It is the hard meaning of such notions as Riesman's "other-directed" and Whyte's "social ethic." And of course, most popularly, the triumph—if it may be called that—of such a man is the key meaning of George Orwell's *1984*.

On the positive side—a rather wistful side nowadays—the larger meanings of Freud's "id," Marx's "Freiheit," George Mead's "I," Karen Horney's "spontaneity," lie in the use of such conceptions against the triumph of the alienated man. They are trying to find some center in man-as-man which would enable them to believe that in the end he cannot be made into, that he cannot finally become, such an alien creature—alien to nature, to society, to self. The cry for "community" is an attempt, a mistaken one I believe, to assert the conditions that would eliminate the probability of such a man, and it is because many humanist thinkers have come to believe that many psychiatrists by their practice produce such alienated and self-rationalized men that they reject these adaptive endeavors. Back of all this—and much more of traditional and current worrying and thinking among serious and sensible students of man—there lies the simple and decisive fact that the alienated man is the antithesis of the Western image of the free man. The society in which this man, this cheerful robot, flourishes is the antithesis of the free society—or in the literal and plain meaning of the word, of a democratic society. The advent of this man points to freedom as trouble, as issue, and—let us hope—as problem for social scientists. Put as a trouble of the individual—of the terms and values of which he is uneasily unaware—it is the trouble called "alienation." As an issue for publics—to the terms and values of which they are mainly indifferent—it is no less than the issue of democratic society, as fact and as aspiration.

It is just because this issue and this trouble are not now widely recognized, and so do not in fact exist as explicit troubles and issues, that the uneasiness and the indifference that betoken them are so deep and so wide in meaning and in effect. That is a major part of the problem of freedom today, seen in its political context, and it is a major part of the intellectual challenge which the formulation of the problem of freedom offers to contemporary social scientists.

It is not merely paradoxical to say that the values of freedom and reason are back of the absence of troubles, back of the uneasy feeling of malaise and alienation. In a similar manner, the issue to which modern threats to freedom and reason most typically lead is, above all, the absence of explicit issues—to apathy rather than to issues explicitly defined as such.

The issues and troubles have not been clarified because the chief capacities and qualities of man required to clarify them are the very freedom and reason that are threatened and dwindling. Neither the troubles nor the issues have been seriously formulated as the problems of the kinds of social science I have been criticizing. . . . The promise of classic social science, in considerable part, is that they will be.

The troubles and issues raised up by the crises of reason and freedom cannot of course be formulated as one grand problem, but neither can they be confronted, much less solved, by handling each of them microscopically as a series of small-scale issues, or of troubles confined to a scatter of milieux. They are structural problems, and to state them requires that we work in the classic terms of human biography and of epochal history. Only in such terms can the connections of structure and milieux that effect these values today be traced and casual analysis be conducted. The crisis of individuality and the crisis of history-making; the role of reason in the free individual life and in the making of history—in the re-statement and clarification of these problems lies the promise of the social sciences.

The moral and the intellectual promise of social science is that freedom and reason will remain cherished values, that they will be used seriously and consistently and imaginatively in the formulation of problems. But this is also the political promise of what is loosely called Western culture. Within the social sciences, political crises and intellectual crises of our time coincide: serious work in either sphere is also work in the other. The political traditions of classic liberalism and of classic socialism together exhaust our major political traditions. The collapse of these traditions as ideologies has had to do with the decline of free individuality and the decline of reason in human affairs. Any contemporary political re-statement of liberal and socialist goals must include as central the idea of a society in which all men would become men of substantive reason, whose independent reasoning would have structural consequences for their societies, its history, and thus for their own life fates.

The interest of the social scientist in social structure is not due to any view that the future is structurally determined. We study the structural limits of human decision in an attempt to find points of effective intervention, in order to know what can and what must be structurally changed if the role of explicit decision in history making is to be enlarged. Our interest in history is not owing to any view that the future is inevitable, that the future is bounded by the past. That men have lived in certain kinds of society in the past does not set exact or absolute limits to the kinds of society they may create in the future. We study history to discern the alternatives within which human reason and human freedom can now make history. We study historical social structures, in brief, in order to find within them the ways in which they are and can be controlled. For only in this way can we come to know the limits and the meaning of human freedom.

Freedom is not merely the chance to do as one pleases; neither is it merely the opportunity to choose between set alternatives. Freedom is, first of all, the chance to formulate the available choices, to argue over them—and then, the opportunity to choose. That is why freedom cannot exist without an enlarged role of human reason in human affairs. Within an individual's biography and within a society's history, the social task of reason is to formulate choices, to enlarge the scope of human decisions in the making of history. The future of human affairs is not merely some set of variables to be predicted. The future is what is to be decided—within the limits, to be sure, of historical possibility. But this possibility is not fixed; in our time the limits seem very broad indeed.

Beyond this, the problem of freedom is the problem of how decisions about the future of human affairs are to be made and who is to make them. Organizationally, it is the problem of a just machinery of decision. Morally, it is the problem of political responsibility. Intellectually, it is the problem of what are now the possible futures of human affairs. But the larger aspects of the problem of freedom today concern not only the nature of history and the structural chance for explicit decisions to make a difference in its course; they concern also the nature of man and the fact that the value of freedom cannot be based upon "man's basic nature." The ultimate problem of freedom is the problem of the cheerful robot, and it arises in this form today because today it has become evident to us that *all* men do *not* naturally *want* to be free; that all men are not willing or not able, as the case may be, to exert themselves to acquire the reason that freedom requires.

Under what conditions do men come to *want* to be free and capable of acting freely? Under what conditions are they willing and able to bear the burdens freedom does impose and to see these less as burdens than as gladly undertaken self-transformations? And on the negative side: Can men be made to want to become *cheerful* robots?

In our time, must we not face the possibility that the human mind as a social fact might be deteriorating in quality and cultural level, and yet not many would notice it because of the overwhelming accumulation of technological gadgets? Is not that one meaning of rationality without reason? Of human alienation? Of the absence of any free role for reason in human affairs? The accumulation of gadgets hides these meanings: Those who use these devices do not understand them; those who invent them do not understand much else. That is why we may *not*, without great ambiguity, use technological abundance as the index of human quality and cultural progress.

To formulate any problem requires that we state the values involved and the threat to those values. for it is the felt threat to cherished values—such as those of freedom and reason—that is the necessary moral substance of all significant problems of social inquiry, and as well of all public issues and private troubles.

The values involved in the cultural problem of individuality are conveniently embodied in all that is suggested by the ideal of The Renaissance Man. The threat to that ideal is the ascendancy among us of The Cheerful Robot.

The values involved in the political problem of history making are embodied in the Promethean ideal of its human making. The threat to that ideal is twofold: On the one hand, history making may well go by default, men may continue to abdicate its wilful making, and so merely drift. On the other hand, history may indeed be made—but by narrow elite circles without effective responsibility to those who must try to survive the consequences of their decisions and of their defaults.

I do not know the answer to the question of political irresponsibility in our time or to the cultural and political question of The Cheerful Robot. But is it not clear that no answers will be found unless these problems are at least confronted? Is it not obvious, that the ones to confront them, above all others, are the social scientists of the rich societies? That many of them do not now do so is surely the greatest human default being committed by privileged men in our times.

MARTIN LUTHER KING, JR.

"Letter from the Birmingham Jail" 1963

When the civil rights leader Martin Luther King, Jr., (1929–68) was jailed in Birmingham, Alabama, along with twenty-four hundred other antisegregationist demonstrators, a group of local white clergy published an attack on King. The black preacher from Atlanta had broken laws prohibiting blacks from using certain public accommodations and had otherwise promoted "unwise and untimely" demonstrations, according to their statement. King responded from his jail cell. His "Letter from the Birmingham Jail" began as a local document of a local dispute, but when published in *The Christian Century* on June 12, 1963, it quickly became the central text in the nationwide discussion of the theory of civil disobedience. King began his letter with a detailed account of Birmingham city politics and of the process by which the Southern Christian Leadership Conference—of which King was president—had become involved in the struggle to desegregate Birmingham. The selection below begins at the point in the letter when King turns to the issue of just versus unjust laws. Although King's distinctly religious and strictly nonviolent approach was not to the tastes of everyone concerned with civil rights, the argument made in the letter won wide acclaim. The following year, King was awarded the Nobel Peace Prize. For a comprehensive biography of King, see David J. Garrow, *Bearing the Cross: Martin Luther King, Jr., and the Southern Christian Leadership Conference* (New York, 1987).

. . . . . .

You express a great deal of anxiety over our willingness to break laws. This is certainly a legitimate concern. Since we so diligently urge people to obey the Supreme Court's decision of 1954 outlawing segregation in the public schools, at first glance it may seem rather paradoxical for us consciously to break laws. One may well ask, "How can you advocate breaking some laws and obeying others?" The answer lies in the fact that there are two types of laws: just and unjust. I agree with St. Augustine that "an unjust law is no law at all."

Now what is the difference between the two? How does one determine whether a law is just or unjust? A just law is a man-made code that squares with the moral law or the law of God. An unjust law is a code that is out of harmony with the moral law. To put it in the terms of St. Thomas Aquinas, an unjust law is a human law that is not rooted in eternal law and natural law. Any law that uplifts human personality is just. Any law that degrades human personality is unjust. All segretation statutes are unjust because segregation distorts the soul and damages the personality. It gives the segregator a false sense of superiority and the segregated a false sense of inferiority. Segregation, to use the terminology of the Jewish philosopher Martin Buber, substitutes an "I-it" relationship for an "I-thou" relationship and ends up relegating persons to the status of things. Hence segregation is not only politically, economically and sociologically unsound, it is sinful. Paul Tillich has said that sin is separation. Is not segregation an existential expression of man's tragic separation, his awful estrangement, his terrible sinfulness? Thus it is that I can urge men to disobey segregation ordinances, for such ordinances are morally wrong.

Let us consider some of the ways in which a law can be unjust. A law is unjust, for example, if the majority group compels a minority group to obey the statute but does not make it binding on itself. By the same token a law in all probability is just if the majority is itself willing to obey it. Also, a law is unjust if it is inflicted on a minority that, as a result of being denied the right to vote, had no part in enacting or devising the law. Who can say that the legislature of Alabama which set up that state's segregation laws was democratically elected? Throughout Alabama all sorts of devious methods are used to prevent Negroes from becoming registered voters, and there are some counties in which, even though Negroes constitute a majority of the population, not a single Negro is registered. Can any law enacted under such circumstances be considered democratically structured?

Sometimes a law is just on its face and unjust in its application. For instance, I have been arrested on a charge of parading without a permit. Now there is nothing wrong in having an ordinance which requires a permit for a parade. But such an ordinance becomes unjust when it is used to maintain segregation and to deny citizens the First-amendment privilege of peaceful assembly and protest.

I hope you are able to see the distincton I am trying to point out. In no sense do I advocate evading the law, as would the rabid segregationist. That would lead to anarchy. One who breaks an unjust law must do so *openly, lovingly,* and with a willingness to accept the penalty. I submit that an individual who breaks a law that conscience

Source: Christian Century, 80 June 12, 1963, 769–75.

tells him is unjust and who willingly accepts the penalty of imprisonment in order to arouse the conscience of the community over its injustice is in reality expressing the highest respect for law.

Of course, there is nothing new about this kind of civil disobedience. It was evidenced sublimely in the refusal of Shadrach, Meshach and Abednego to obey the laws of Nebuchadnezzar, on the ground that a higher moral law was at stake. It was practiced superbly by the early Christians who were willing to face hungry lions rather than submit to certain unjust laws of the Roman empire. To a degree, academic freedom is a reality today because Socrates practiced civil disobedience. We should never forget that everything Adolf Hitler did in Germany was "legal" and everything the Hungarian freedom fighters did in Hungary was "illegal." It was "illegal" to aid and comfort a Jew in Hitler's Germany. Even so, I am sure that had I lived in Germany at the time I would have aided and comforted my Jewish brothers. If today I lived in a communist country where certain principles dear to the Christian faith are suppressed, I would openly advocate disobeying that country's antireligious laws.

I must make two honest confessions to you, my Christian and Jewish brothers. First, I must confess that over the past few years I have been gravely disappointed with the white moderate. I have almost reached the regrettable conclusion that the Negro's great stumbling block in his stride toward freedom is not the White Citizen's Counciler or the Klu Klux Klanner but the white moderate who is more devoted to "order" than to justice; who prefers a negative peace which is the absence of tension to a positive peace which is the presence of justice; who constantly says "I agree with you in the goal you seek, but I cannot agree with your methods"; who paternalistically believes he can set the timetable for another man's freedom; who lives by a mythical concept of time and who constantly advises the Negro to wait for a "more convenient season." Shallow understanding from people of good will is more frustrating than absolute misunderstanding from people of ill will. Lukewarm acceptance is much more bewildering than outright rejection.

I had hoped that the white moderate would understand that law and order exist for the purpose of extablishing justice and that when they fail in this purpose they block social progress. I had hoped that the white moderate would understand that the present tension in the south is a necessary phase of the transition from an obnoxious negative peace, in which the Negro passively accepted his unjust plight, to a substantive and positive peace, in which all men will respect the dignity and worth of human personality. Actually, we who engage in nonviolent direct action are not the creators of tension. We merely bring to the surface the hidden tension that is already alive. We bring it out in the open where it can be seen and dealt with. Like a boil that can never be cured so long as it is covered up but must be opened with all its pus-flowing ugliness to the natural medicines of air and light, injustice must be exposed, with all the tension its exposure creates, to the light of human conscience and the air of national opinion before it can be cured.

In your statement you assert that our actions, even though peaceful, must be condemned because they precipitate violence. But is this a logical assertion? Isn't this like condemning a robbed man because his possession of money precipitated an act of robbery? Isn't this like condemning Socrates because his unswerving commitment to truth and his philosophical inquiries precipitated the act by the misguided populace in which they made him drink hemlock? Isn't this like condemning Jesus because his unique God-consciousness and never-ceasing devotion to God's will precipitated the evil act of crucifixion? We must come to see that, as the federal courts have consistently affirmed, it is wrong to urge an individual to cease his efforts to gain his basic constitutional rights because the quest may precipitate violence. Society must protect the robbed and punish the robber.

I had also hoped that the white moderate would reject the myth concerning time in relation to the struggle for freedom. I have just received a letter from a white brother in Texas. He writes: "All Christians know that the colored poeple will receive equal rights eventually, but it is possible that you are in too great a religious hurry. It has taken Christianity almost 2,000 years to accomplish what it has. The teachings of Christ take time to come to earth." Such an attitude stems from a tragic misconception of time, from the strangely irrational notion that there is something in the very flow of time that will inevitably cure all ills. Actually, time itself is neutral; it can be used either destructively or constructively. More and more I feel that the people of ill will have used time much more effectively than have the people of good will. We will have to repent in this generation not merely for the hateful words and actions of the bad people but for the appalling silence of the good people. Human progress never rolls in on wheels of inevitability; it comes through the tireless efforts of men willing to be coworkers with God, and without this hard work time itself becomes an ally of the forces of social stagnation. We must use time creatively, in the knowledge that the time is always ripe to do right. Now is the time to make real the promise of democracy and transform our pending national elegy into a creative psalm of brotherthood. Now is the time to lift our national policy from the quicksand of racial injustice to the solid rock of human dignity.

You speak of our activity in Birmingham as extreme. At first I was rather disappointed that fellow clergymen would see my nonviolent efforts as those of an extremist. I began thinking about the fact that I stand in the middle of two opposing forces in the Negro community. One is a force of complacency made up of Negroes who, as a result of long years of oppression, are so completely drained of self-respect and a sense of "somebodiness" that they have adjusted to segregation, and of a few middle class Negroes who, because of a degree of academic and economic security and because in some ways they profit by segregation, have unconsciously become insensitive to the problems of the masses. The other force is one of bitterness and hatred, and it comes perilously close to advocating violence. It is expressed in the various black nationalist groups that are springing up across the nation, the largest and best-known being Elijah Muhammad's Muslim movement. Nourished by the Negro's frustration over the continued existence of racial discrimination, this movement is made up of people who have lost faith in America, who have absolutely repudiated Christianity, and who have concluded that the white man is an incorrigible "devil."

I have tried to stand between these two forces, saying that we need emulate neither the "do-nothingism" of the complacent nor the hatred of the black nationalist. For there is the more excellent way of love and nonviolent protest. I am grateful to God that, through the influence of the Negro church, the way of nonviolence became an integral part of our struggle.

If this philosophy had not emerged, by now many streets of the south would, I am convinced, be flowing with blood. And I am further convinced that if our white brothers dismiss as "rabble-rousers" and "outside agitators" those of us who employ nonviolent direct action and if they refuse to support our nonviolent efforts, millions of Negroes will, out of frustration and despair, seek solace and security in black nationalist ideologies—a development that would inevitably lead to a frightening racial nightmare.

Oppressed people cannot remain oppressed forever. The yearning for freedom eventually manifests itself, and that is what has happened to the American Negro. Something within has reminded him of his birthright of freedom, and something without has reminded him that it can be gained. Consciously or unconsciously, he has been caught up by the *Zeitgeist,* and with his black brothers of Africa and his brown and yellow brothers of Asia, South America and the Caribbean, the U.S. Negro is moving with a sense of great urgency toward the promised land of racial justice. If one recognizes this vital urge that has engulfed the Negro community, he should readily understand why public demonstrations are taking place. The Negro has many pent-up resentments and latent frustrations, and he must release them. So let him march; let him make prayer pilgrimages to the city hall; let him go on freedom rides—and try to understand why he must do so. If his repressed emotions are not released in nonviolent ways, they will seek expression through violence; this is not a threat but a fact of history. I have not said to my people, "Get rid of your discontent." Rather, I have tried to say that this normal and healthy discontent can be channeled into the creative outlet of nonviolent direct action. And now this approach is being termed extremist.

But though I was initially disappointed at being categorized as an extremist, as I continued to think about the matter I gradually gained a measure of satisfaction from the label. Was not Jesus an extremist for love: "Love your enemies, bless them that curse you, do good to them that hate you, and pray for them which despitefully use you, and persecute you." Was not Amos an extremist for justice: "Let justice roll down like waters and righteousness like an everflowing stream." Was not Paul an extremist for the Christian gospel: "I bear in my body the marks of the Lord Jesus." Was not Martin Luther an extremist: "Here I stand; I can do no other so help me God." And John Bunyan: "I will stay in jail to the end of my days before I make a butchery of my conscience." And Abraham Lincoln: "This nation cannot survive half slave and half free." And Thomas Jefferson: "We hold these truths to be self-evident, that all men are created equal. . . . " So the question is not whether we will be extremists but what kind of extremists we will be. Will we be extremists for hate or for love? Will we be extremists for the preservation of injustice or for the extension of justice? Perhaps the south, the nation and the world are in dire need of creative extremists.

I had hoped that the white moderate would see this need. Perhaps I was too optimistic; perhaps I expected too much. I suppose I should have realized that few members of the oppressor race can understand the deep groans and passionate yearnings of the oppressed race, and still fewer have the vision to see that injustice must be rooted out by strong, persistent and determined action. I am thankful, however, that some of our white brothers have grasped the meaning of this social revolution and committed themselves to it. They are still all too few in quantity, but they are big in quality. Some—such as Ralph McGill, Lillian Smith, Harry Golden and James McBride-Dabbs—have written about our struggle in eloquent and prophetic terms. Others have marched with us down nameless streets of the south. They have languished in filthy, roach-infested jails, suffering the abuse and brutality of policemen who view them as "dirty nigger lovers." Unlike so many of their moderate brothers and sisters, they have recognized the urgency of the moment and sensed the need for powerful "action" antidotes to combat the disease of segregation.

Let me take note of my other major disappointment. Though there are some notable exceptions, I have also been disappointed with the white church and its leadership. I do not say this as one of those negative critics who can always find something wrong with the church. I say this as a minister of the gospel, who loves the church; who was nurtured in its bosom; who has been sustained by its spiritual blessings and who will remain true to it as long as the cord of life shall lengthen.

When I was suddenly catapulted into the leadership of the bus protest in Montgomery, Alabama, a few years ago I felt we would be supported by the white church. I felt that the white ministers, priests and rabbis of the South would be among our strongest allies. Instead, some have been outright opponents, refusing to understand the freedom movement and misrepresenting its leaders; all too many others have been more cautious than courageous and have remained silent and secure behind stained-glass windows.

In spite of my shattered dreams I came to Birmingham with the hope that the white religious leadership of this community would see the justice of our cause and with deep moral concern would serve as the channel through which our just grievances could reach the power structure. But again I have been disappointed.

I have heard numerous southern religious leaders admonish their worshipers to comply with a desegregation decision because it is the *law*, but I have longed to hear white ministers declare, "Follow this decree because integration is morally *right* and because the Negro is your brother." In the midst of blatant injustices inflicted upon the Negro I have watched white churchmen stand on the sideline and mouth pious irrelevancies and sanctimonious trivialities. In the midst of a mighty struggle to rid our nation of racial and economic injustice I have heard many ministers say, "Those are social issues with which the gospel has no real concern," and I have watched many churches commit themselves to a completely otherworldly religion which makes a strange, unbiblical distinction between body and soul, between the sacred and the secular.

We are moving toward the close of the 20th century with a religious community largely adjusted to the status quo—a taillight behind other community agencies rather than a headlight leading men to higher levels of justice.

I have traveled the length and breadth of Alabama, Mississippi and all the other southern states. On sweltering summer days and crisp autumn mornings I have looked at the south's beautiful churches with their lofty spires pointing heavenward, and at her impressive religious education buildings. Over and over I have found myself asking: "What kind of people worship here? Who is their God? Where were their voices when the lips of Governor Barnett dripped with words of interposition and nullification? Where were they when Governor Wallace gave a clarion call for defiance and hatred? Where were their voices of support when bruised and weary Negro men and women decided to rise from the dark dungeons of complacency to the bright hills of creative protest?"

Yes, these questions are still in my mind. In deep disappointment I have wept over the laxity of the church. But be assured that my tears have been tears of love. There can be no deep disappointment where there is not deep love. Yes, I love the church. How could I do otherwise? I am in the rather unique position of being the son, the grandson and the great-grandson of preachers. Yes, I see the church as the body of Christ. But, oh! How we have blemished and scarred that body through social neglect and through fear of being nonconformists.

There was a time when the church was very powerful—in the time when the early Christians rejoiced at being deemed worthy to suffer for what they believed. In those days the church was not merely a thermometer that recorded the ideas and principles of popular opinion; it was a thermostat that transformed the mores of society. Whenever the early Christians entered a town the power structure immediately sought to convict them for being "disturbers of the peace" and "outside agitators." But the Christians pressed on, in the conviction that they were "a colony of heaven," called to obey God rather than man. Small in number, they were big in commitment. By their effort and example they brought an end to such ancient evils as infanticide and gladiatorial contest.

Things are different now. So often the contemporary church is a weak, ineffectual voice with an uncertain sound. So often it is an archdefender of the status quo. Far from being disturbed by the presence of the church, the power structure of the average community is consoled by the church's silent—and often even vocal—sanction of things as they are.

But the judgment of God is upon the church as never before. If today's church does not recapture the sacrificial spirit of the early church, it will lose its authenticity, forfeit the loyalty of millions, and be dismissed as an irrelevant social club with no meaning for the 20th century. Every day I meet young people whose disappointment with the church has turned into outright disgust.

Perhaps I have once again been too optimistic. Is organized religion too inextricably bound to the status quo to save our nation and the world? Perhaps I must turn my faith to the inner spiritual church, the church within the church, as the true *ecclesia* and the hope of the world. But again I am thankful to God that some noble souls from the ranks of organized religion have broken loose from the paralyzing chains of conformity and joined us as active partners in the struggle for freedom. They have left their secure congregations and walked the streets of Albany, Georgia, with us. They have gone down the highways of the south on torturous rides for freedom. Yes, they have gone to jail with us. Some have been kicked out of their churches, have lost the support of their bishops and fellow ministers. But they have acted in the faith that right defeated is stronger than evil triumphant. Their witness has been the spiritual salt that has preserved the true meaning of the gospel in these troubled times. They have carved a tunnel of hope through the dark mountain of disappointment.

I hope the church as a whole will meet the challenge of this decisive hour. But even if the church does not come to the aid of justice, I have no despair about the future. I have no fear about the outcome of our struggle in Birmingham, even if our motives are at present misunderstood. We will reach the goal of freedom in Birmingham and all over the nation, because the goal of America is freedom. Abused and scorned though we may be, our destiny is tied up with America's destiny. Before the pilgrims landed at Plymouth we were here. Before the pen of Jefferson etched across the pages of history the mighty words of the Declaration of Independence, we were here. For more than two centuries our forebears labored in this country without wages; they made cotton king; they built the homes of their masters while suffering gross injustice and shameful humiliation—and yet out of a bottomless vitality they continued to thrive and develop. If the inexpressible cruelties of slavery could not stop us, the opposition we now face will surely fail. We will win our freedom because the sacred heritage of our nation and the eternal will of God are embodied in our echoing demands.

Before closing I feel impelled to mention one other point in your statement that has troubled me profoundly. You warmly commended the Birmingham police force for keeping "order" and "preventing violnce." I doubt that you would have so warmly commended the police force if you had seen its angry dogs sinking their teeth into six unarmed, nonviolent Negroes. I doubt that you would so quickly commend the policemen if you were to observe their ugly and inhuman treatment of Negroes here in the city jail; if you were to watch them push and curse old Negro women and young Negro girls; if you were to see them slap and kick old Negro men and young boys; if you were to observe them, as they did on two occasions, refuse to give us food because we wanted to sing our grace together. I cannot join you in your praise of the Birmingham police department.

It is true that the police have exercised discipline in handling the demonstrators. In this sense they have conducted themselves rather "nonviolently" in public. But for what purpose? To preserve the evil system of segregation. Over the past few years I have consistently preached that nonviolence demands that the means we use must be as pure as the ends we seek. I have tried to make clear that it is wrong to use immoral means to attain moral ends. But now I must affirm that it is just as wrong, or perhaps even more so, to use moral means to preserve immoral ends. Perhaps Mr. Connor and his policemen have been rather nonviolent in public, as was Chief Pritchett in Albany, Georgia, but they have used the moral means of nonviolence to maintain the immoral end of racial injustice. As T. S. Eliot has said, there is no greater treason than to do the right deed for the wrong reason.

I wish you had commended the Negro sit-inners and demonstrators of Birmingham for their sublime courage, their willingness to suffer and their amazing discipline in the midst of great provocation. One day the south will recognize its real heroes. They will be the James Merediths, with a noble sense of purpose facing jeering and hostile mobs and the agonizing loneliness that characterizes the life of the pioneer. They will be old, oppressed, battered Negro women, symbolized in a 72-year-old woman in Montgomery, Alabama, who rose up with a sense of dignity and with her people decided not to ride segregated buses, and who responded with ungrammatical profundity to one who inquired about her: "My feet is tired, but my soul is rested." They will be the young high school and college students, the young ministers of the gospel and a host of their elders courageously and nonviolently sitting in at lunch counters and willingly going to jail for conscience' sake. One day the South will know that when these disinherited children of God sat down at lunch counters they were in reality standing up for what is best in the American dream and for the most sacred values in our Judeo-Christian heritage, thereby bringing our nation back to those great wells of democracy which were dug deep by the founding fathers in their formulation of the Constitution and the Declaration of Independence.

Never before have I written so long a letter. I can assure you that it would have been much shorter if I had been writing from a comfortable desk, but what else can one do when he is alone for days in a narrow jail cell, other than write long letters, think long thoughts and pray long prayers?

If I have said anything in this letter that overstates the truth and indicates an unreasonable impatience, I beg you to forgive me. If I have said anything that *under*-states the truth and indicates my having a patience that allows me to settle for anything less than brotherhood, I beg God to forgive me.

I hope this letter finds you strong in the faith. I also hope that circumstances will soon make it possible for me to meet each of you, not as an integrationist or a civil rights leader but as a fellow clergyman and a Christian brother. Let us all hope that the dark clouds of racial prejudice will soon pass away and the deep fog of misunderstanding will be lifted from our fear-drenched communities and in some not too distant tomorrow the radiant stars of love and brotherhood will shine over our great nation with all their scintillating beauty.

LIONEL TRILLING

"On the Teaching of Modern Literature"
1961

Modernism is often identified as the twentieth-century's most commanding movement in literature and the arts. Not everyone who has so identified modernism has agreed upon just what defines it, but most celebrants of this multitudinous movement have at least emphasized its self-consciousness, its determination to face the worst as well as the best in the human prospect, and its penchant for aesthetic and moral complexity. The literary critic Lionel Trilling (1905–75) was among the most probing and influential commentators on modernist literature during the midcentury decades, when the prestige of this distinctive body of writing was at its height. In the essay of 1961 reprinted herein, Trilling reacts to many of the classics of modernism in the specific personal, moral, and professional context of college teaching. Although he expresses his admiration, and even his awe, for the great modernists, he betrays also a dual ambivalence: Is the impact of this literature on students altogether healthy? And is this literature trivialized when one is obliged to address it at the level of a midterm essay? Trilling's career is ably analyzed in William Chace, *Lionel Trilling: Criticism and Politics* (Stanford, Ca., 1980). The special standing accorded to modernist literature by Trilling and his contemporaries is addressed in David A. Hollinger, "The Canon and Its Keepers," in Hollinger's *In the American Province: Studies in the History and Historiography of Ideas* (Bloomington, Ind., 1985), 74–91.

I propose to consider here a particular theme of modern literature which appears so frequently and with so much authority that it may be said to constitute one of the shaping and controlling ideas of our epoch. I can identify it by calling it the disenchantment of our culture with culture itself—it seems to me that the characteristic element of modern literature, or at least of the most highly developed modern literature, is the bitter line of hostility to civilization which runs through it. It happens that my present awareness of this theme is involved in a personal experience, and I am impelled to speak of it not abstractly but with the husks of the experience clinging untidily to it. I shall go so far in doing this as to describe the actual circumstances in which the experience took place. These circumstances are pedagogic—they consist of some problems in teaching modern literature to undergraduates and my attempt to solve these problems. I know that pedagogy is a depressing subject to all persons of sensibility, and yet I shall not apologize for touching upon it because the emphasis upon the teaching of literature and especially of modern literature is in itself one of the most salient and significant manifestations of the culture of our time. Indeed, if, having in mind Matthew Arnold's lecture, "On the Modern Element in Literature," we are on the hunt for *the* modern element in modern literature, we might want to find it in the susceptibility of modern literature to being made into an academic subject.

For some years I have taught the course in modern literature in Columbia College. I did not undertake it without misgiving and I have never taught it with an undivided mind. My doubts do not refer to the value of the literature itself, only to the educational propriety of its being studied in college. These doubts persist even though I wholly understand that the relation of our collegiate education to modernity is no longer an open question. The unargued assumption of most curriculums is that the real subject of all study is the modern world; that the justification of all study is its immediate and presumably practical relevance to modernity; that the true purpose of all study is to lead the young person to be at home in, and in control of, the modern world. There is really no way of quarreling with the assumption or with what follows upon it, the instituting of courses of which the substance is chiefly contemporary or at least makes ultimate reference to what is contemporary.

It might be asked why anyone should *want* to quarrel with the assumption. To that question I can return only a defensive, eccentric, self-depreciatory answer. It is this: that to some of us who teach and who think of our students as the creators of the intellectual life of the future, there comes a kind of despair. It does not come because our students fail to respond to ideas, rather because they respond to ideas with a happy vagueness, a delighted glibness, a joyous sense of power in the use of received or receivable generalizations, a grateful wonder at how easy it is to formulate and judge, at how little resistance language offers to their intentions. When that despair strikes us, we are tempted to give up the usual and accredited ways of evaluating education, and instead of prizing responsiveness and aptitude, to set store by some sign of personal character in our students, some token of individual will. We think of this as taking the form of resistance and imperviousness, of personal density or gravity, of some power of supposing that ideas are real, a power which will lead a young man to say what Goethe thought was the modern thing to say, "But is this really true—is it true for *me?*" And to say this not in the facile way, not following the progressive edu-

Source: Beyond Culture, Lionel Trilling, 3–27. Copyright © 1961 by Lionel Trilling. Reprinted by permission of Harcourt Brace Jovanovich, Inc. Footnotes omitted.

cational prescription to "think for yourself," which means to think in the progressive pieties rather than in the conservative pieties (if any of the latter do still exist), but to say it from his sense of himself as a person rather than as a bundle of attitudes and responses which are all alert to please the teacher and the progressive community.

We can't do anything about the quality of personal being of our students, but we are led to think about the cultural analogue of a personal character that is grave, dense, and resistant—we are led to think about the past. Perhaps the protagonist of Thomas Mann's story, "Disorder and Early Sorrow" comes to mind, that sad Professor Cornelius with his intense and ambivalent sense of history. For Professor Cornelius, who is a historian, the past is dead, is death itself, but for that very reason it is the source of order, value, piety, and even love. If we think about education in the dark light of the despair I have described, we wonder if perhaps there is not to be found in the past that quiet place at which a young man might stand for a few years, at least a little beyond the competing attitudes and generalizations of the present, at least a little beyond the contemporary problems which he is told he can master only by means of attitudes and generalizations, that quiet place in which he can be silent, in which he can *know* something—in what year the Parthenon was begun, the order of battle at Trafalgar, how Linear B was deciphered: almost anything at all that has nothing to do with the talkative and attitudinizing present, anything at all but variations on the accepted formulations about *anxiety,* and *urban society,* and *alienation,* and *Gemeinschaft* and *Gesellschaft,* all the matter of the academic disciplines which are founded upon the modern self-consciousness and the modern self-pity. The modern self-pity is certainly not without its justification; but, if the circumstances that engender it are ever to be overcome, we must sometimes wonder whether this work can be done by minds which are taught in youth to accept these sad conditions of ours as the only right objects of contemplation. And quite apart from any practical consequences, one thinks of the simple aesthetic personal pleasure of having to do with young minds, and maturing minds, which are free of cant, which are, to quote an old poet, "fierce, moody, patient, venturous, modest, shy."

This line of argument I have called eccentric and maybe it ought to be called obscurantist and reactionary. Whatever it is called, it is not likely to impress a Committee on the Curriculum. It was, I think, more or less the line of argument of my department in Columbia College, when, up to a few years ago, it would decide, whenever the question came up, not to carry its courses beyond the late nineteenth century. But our rationale could not stand against the representations which a group of students made to our Dean and which he communicated to us. The students wanted a course in modern literature—very likely, in the way of students, they said that it was a scandal that no such course was being offered in the College. There was no argument that could stand against this expressed desire: we could only capitulate and then with pretty good grace, muster the arguments that justified our doing so. Was not the twentieth century more than half over? Was it not nearly fifty years since Eliot wrote "Portrait of a Lady"? George Meredith had not died until 1909, and even the oldest among us had read one of his novels in a college course—many American universities had been quick to bring into their purview the literature of the later nineteenth century, and even the early twentieth century; there was a strong supporting tradition for our capitulation. Had not Yeats been Matthew Arnold's contemporary for twenty-three years?

Our resistance to the idea of the course had never been based on an adverse judgment of the literature itself. We are a department not only of English but of comparative literature, and if the whole of modern literature is surveyed, it could be said—and we were willing to say it—that no literature of the past surpassed the literature of our time in power and magnificence. Then too, it is a difficult literature, and it is difficult not merely as defenders of modern poetry say that all literature is difficult. We nowadays believe that Keats is a very difficult poet, but his earlier readers did not. We now see the depths and subtleties of Dickens, but his contemporary readers found him as simply available as a plate of oysters on the half shell. Modern literature, however, shows its difficulties at first blush; they are literal as well as doctrinal difficulties—if our students were to know their modern literary heritage, surely they needed all the help that a teacher can give?

These made cogent reasons for our decision to establish, at long last, the course in modern literature. They also made a ground for our display of a certain mean-spirited, last-ditch vindictiveness. I recall that we said something like, "Very well, if they want the modern, let them have it—let them have it, as Henry James says, full in the face. We shall give the course, but we shall give it on the highest level, and if they think, as students do, that the modern will naturally meet them in a genial way, let them have their gay and easy time with Yeats and Eliot, with Joyce and Proust and Kafka, with Lawrence, Mann, and Gide."

Eventually the course fell to me to give. I approached it with an uneasiness which has not diminshed with the passage of time—it has, I think, even increased. It arises, this uneasiness, from my personal relation with the works that form the substance of the course. Almost all of them have been involved with me for a long time—I invert the natural order not out of lack of modesty but taking the cue of W. H. Auden's remark that a real book reads us. I have been read by Eliot's poems and by *Ulysses* and by *Remembrance of Things Past* and by *The Castle* for a good many years now, since early youth. Some of these books at first rejected me; I bored them. But as I grew older and they knew me better, they came to have more sympathy with me and to understand my hidden meanings. Their nature is such that our relationship has been very intimate. No literature has ever been so shockingly personal as that of our time—it asks every question that is forbidden in polite society. It asks us if we are content with our marriages, with our family lives, with our professional lives, with our friends. It is all very well for me to describe my course in the College catalogue as "paying particular attention to the role of the writer as a critic of his culture"—this is sheer evasion: the questions asked by our literature are not about our culture but about ourselves. It asks us if we are content with ourselves, if we are saved or damned—more than with anything else, our literature is concerned with salvation. No literature has ever been so intensely spiritual as ours. I do not venture to call it actually religious, but certainly it has the special intensity of concern with the spiritual life which Hegel noted when he spoke of the great modern phenomenon of the secularization of spirituality.

I do not know how other teachers deal with this extravagant personal force of modern literature, but for me it makes difficulty. Nowadays the teaching of literature inclines to a considerable technicality, but when the teacher has said all that can be said about formal matters, about verse-patterns, metrics, prose conventions, irony, tension, etc., he must confront the necessity of bearing personal testimony. He must use whatever authority he may possess to say whether or not a work is true; and if not, why not; and if so, why so. He can do this only at considerable cost to his privacy.

How does one say that Lawrence is right in his great rage against the modern emotions, against the modern sense of life and ways of being, unless one speaks from the intimacies of one's own feelings, and one's own sense of life, and one's own wished-for way of being? How, except with the implication of personal judgment, does one say to students that Gide is perfectly accurate in his representation of the awful boredom and slow corruption of respectable life? Then probably one rushes in to say that this doesn't of itself justify homosexuality and the desertion of one's dying wife, certainly not. But then again, having paid one's *devoirs* to morality, how does one rescue from morality Gide's essential point about the supreme rights of the individual person, and without making it merely historical, academic?

My first response to the necessity of dealing with matters of this kind was resentment of the personal discomfort it caused me. These are subjects we usually deal with either quite unconsciously or in the privacy of our own conscious minds, and if we now and then disclose our thoughts about them, it is to friends of equal age and especial closeness. Or if we touch upon them publicly, we do so in the relative abstractness and anonymity of print. To stand up in one's own person and to speak of them in one's own voice to an audience which each year grows younger as one grows older—that is not easy, and probably it is not decent.

And then, leaving aside the personal considerations, or taking them merely as an indication of something wrong with the situation, can we not say that, when modern literature is brought into the classroom, the subject being taught is betrayed by the pedagogy of the subject? We have to ask ourselves whether in our day too much does not come within the purview of the academy. More and more, as the universities liberalize themselves, and turn their beneficent imperialistic gaze upon what is called Life Itself, the feeling grows among our educated classes that little can be experienced unless it is validated by some established intellectual discipline, with the result that experience loses much of its personal immediacy for us and becomes part of an accredited societal activity. This is not entirely true and I don't want to play the boring academic game of pretending that it *is* entirely true, that the university mind wilts and withers whatever it touches. I must believe and I do believe, that the university study of art is capable of confronting the power of a work of art fully and courageously. I even believe that it can discover and disclose power where it has not been felt before. But the university study of art achieves this end chiefly with works of art of an older period. Time has the effect of seeming to quiet the work of art, domesticating it and making it into a classic, which is often another way of saying that it is an object of merely habitual regard. University study of the right sort can reverse this process and restore to the old work its freshness and force—can, indeed, disclose unguessed-at power. But with the works of art of our own present age, university study tends to accelerate the process by which the radical and subversive work becomes the classic work, and university study does this in the degree that it is vivacious and responsive and what is called non-academic. In one of his poems Yeats mocks the literary scholars, "the bald heads forgetful of their sins," "the old, learned, respectable bald heads," who edit the poems of the fierce and passionate young men.

> Lord, what would they say
> Did their Catullus walk this way?

Yeats, of course, is thinking of his own future fate, and no doubt there is all the radical and comical discrepancy that he sees between the poet's passions and the scholars' close-eyed concentration on the text. Yet for my part, when I think of Catullus, I am moved to praise the tact of all those old heads, from Heinsius and Bentley to Munro and Postgate, who worked on Codex G and Codex O and drew conclusions from them about the lost Codex V—for doing only this and for not trying to realize and demonstrate the true intensity and the true quality and the true cultural meaning of Catullus's passion and managing to bring it somehow into eventual accord with their respectability and baldness. Nowadays we who deal with books in universities live in fear that the World, which we imagine to be a vital, palpitating, passionate, reality-loving World, will think of us as old, respectable, and bald, and we see to it that in our dealings with Yeats (to take him as the example) his wild cry of rage and sexuality is heard by our students and quite thoroughly understood by them as—what is it that we eventually call it?—*a significant expression of our culture*. The exasperation of Lawrence and the subversiveness of Gide, by the time we have dealt with them boldly and straightforwardly, are notable instances of the *alienation of modern man as exemplified by the artist*. "Compare Yeats, Gide, Lawrence, and Eliot in the use which they make of the theme of sexuality to criticize the deficiencies of modern culture. Support your statement by specific references to the work of each author. [Time: one hour.]" And the distressing thing about our examination questions is that they are not ridiculous, they make perfectly good sense—such good sense that the young person who answers them can never again know the force and terror of what has been communicated to him by the works he is being examined on.

Very likely it was with the thought of saving myself from the necessity of speaking personally and my students from having to betray the full harsh meaning of a great literature that I first taught my course in as *literary* a way as possible. A couple of decades ago the discovery was made that a literary work is a structure of words: this doesn't seem a surprising thing to have learned except for its polemical tendency, which is to urge us to minimize the amount of attention we give to the poet's social and personal will, to what he wants to happen outside the poem as a result of the poem; it urges us to fix our minds on what is going on inside the poem. For me this polemical tendency has been of the greatest usefulness, for it has corrected my inclination to pay attention chiefly to what the poet *wants*. For two or three years I directed my efforts toward dealing with the matter of the course chiefly as structures of words, in a formal way, with due attention paid to the literal difficulty which marked so many of the works. But it went against the grain. It went against my personal grain. It went against the grain of the classroom situation, for formal analysis is best carried on by question-and-answer, which needs small groups, and the registration for the course in modern literature in any college is sure to be large. And it went against the grain of the authors themselves—structures of words they may indeed have created, but these structures were not pyramids or triumphal arches, they were manifestly contrived to be not static and commemorative but mobile and aggressive, and one does not describe a quinquereme or a howitzer or a tank without estimating how much *damage* it can do.

Eventually I had to decide that there was only one way to give the course, which was to give it without strategies and without conscious caution. It was not honorable, either to the students or to the authors, to conceal or disguise my relation to the literature, my commitment to it, my fear of it, my ambivalence toward it. The literature had to be dealt with in the terms it announced for itself. As for the students, I have never given assent to the modern saw about "teaching students, not subjects"—I have always thought it right to teach subjects, believing that if one give his first loyalty to the subject, the student is best instructed. So I resolved to give the course with no considerations in mind except my own interests. And since my own interests lead me to see literary situations as cultural situations, and cultural situations as great elaborate fights about moral issues, and moral issues as having something to do with gratuitously chosen images of personal being, and images of personal being as having something to do with literary style, I felt free to begin with what for me was a first concern, the animus of the author, the objects of his will, the things he wants or wants to have happen.

My cultural and non-literary method led me to decide that I would begin the course with a statement of certain themes or issues that might especially engage our attention. I even went so far in non-literariness as to think that my purposes would best be served if I could contrive a "background" for the works we would read—I wanted to propose a history for the themes or issues that I hoped to discover. I did not intend that this history should be either very extensive or very precise. I wanted merely to encourage a *sense* of a history, some general intuition of a past, in students who, as it seems to me, have not been provided with any such thing by their education and who are on the whole glad to be without it. And because there is as yet no adequate general work of history of the culture of the last two hundred years, I asked myself what books of the age just preceding ours had most influenced our literature, or, since I was far less concerned with showing influence than with discerning a tendency, what older books might seem to fall into a line the direction of which pointed to our own literature and thus might serve as a prolegomenon to the course.

It was virtually inevitable that the first work that should have sprung to mind was Sir James Frazer's *The Golden Bough*, not, of course, the whole of it, but certain chapters, those that deal with Osiris, Attis, and Adonis. Anyone who thinks about modern literature in a systematic way takes for granted the great part played in it by myth, and especially by those examples of myth which tell about gods dying and being reborn—the imagination of death and rebirth, reiterated in the ancient world in innumerable variations that are yet always the same, captivated the literary mind at the very moment when, as all accounts of the modern age agree, the most massive and compelling of all the stories of resurrection had lost much of its hold upon the world.

Perhaps no book has had so decisive an effect upon modern literature as Frazer's. It was beautifully to my purpose that it had first been published ten years before the twentieth century began. Yet forty-three years later, in 1933, Frazer delivered a lecture, very eloquent, in which he bade the world be of good hope in the face of the threat to the human mind that was being offered by the Nazi power. He was still alive in 1941. Yet he had been born in 1854, three years before Matthew Arnold gave the lecture "On the Modern Element in Literature." Here, surely, was history, here was the past I wanted, beautifully connected with our present. Frazer was wholly a man of the nineteenth century, and the more so because the eighteenth century was so congenial to him—the lecture of 1933 in which he predicted the Nazi defeat had as its subject Condorcet's *Progress of the Human Mind;* when he took time from his anthropological studies to deal with literature, he prepared editions of Addison's essays and Cowper's letters. He had the old lost belief in the virtue and power of rationality. He loved and counted on order, decorum, and good sense. This great historian of the primitive imagination was in the dominant intellectual tradition of the

West which, since the days of the pre-Socratics, has condemned the ways of thought that we call primitive.

It can be said of Frazer that in his conscious intention he was a perfect representative of what Arnold meant when he spoke of a modern age. And perhaps nothing could make clearer how the conditions of life and literature have changed in a hundred years than to note the difference between the way in which Arnold defines the modern element in literature and the way in which we must define it.

Arnold used the word *modern* in a wholly honorific sense. So much so that he seems to dismiss all temporal idea from the word and makes it signify certain timeless intellectual and civic virtues—his lecture, indeed, was about the modern element in the ancient literatures. A society, he said, is a modern society when it maintains a condition of repose, confidence, free activity of the mind, and the tolerance of divergent views. A society is modern when it affords sufficient material well-being for the conveniences of life and the development of taste. And, finally, a society is modern when its members are intellectually mature, by which Arnold means that they are willing to judge by reason, to observe facts in a critical spirit, and to search for the law of things. By this definition Periclean Athens is for Arnold a modern age, Elizabethan England is not; Thucydides is a modern historian, Sir Walter Raleigh is not.

I shall not go into further details of Arnold's definition or description of the modern. I have said enough, I think, to suggest what Arnold was up to, what he wanted to see realized as the desideratum of his own society, what ideal he wanted the works of intellect and imagination of his own time to advance. And at what a distance his ideal of the modern puts him from our present sense of modernity, from our modern literature! To anyone conditioned by our modern literature, Arnold's ideal of order, convenience, decorum, and rationality might well seem to reduce itself to the small advantages and excessive limitations of the middle-class life of a few prosperous nations of the nineteenth century. Arnold's historic sense presented to his mind the long, bitter, bloody past of Europe, and he seized passionately upon the hope of true civilization at last achieved. But the historic sense of our literature has in mind a long excess of civilization to which may be ascribed the bitterness and bloodiness both of the past and of the present and of which the peaceful aspects are to be thought of as mainly contemptible—its order achieved at the cost of extravagant personal repression, either that of coercion or that of acquiescence; its repose otiose; its tolerance either flaccid or capricious; its material comfort corrupt and corrupting; its taste a manifestation either of timidity or of pride; its rationality attained only at the price of energy and passion.

For the understanding of this radical change of opinion nothing is more illuminating than to be aware of the doubleness of mind of the author of *The Golden Bough*. I have said that Frazer in his conscious mind and in his first intention exemplifies all that Arnold means by the modern. He often speaks quite harshly of the irrationality and the orgiastic excesses of the primitive religions he describes, and even Christianity comes under his criticism both because it stands in the way of rational thought and because it can draw men away from intelligent participation in the life of society. But Frazer had more than one intention, and he had an unconscious as well as a conscious mind. If he deplores the primitive imagination, he also does not fail to show it as wonderful and beautiful. It is the rare reader of *The Golden Bough* who finds the ancient beliefs and rituals wholly alien to him. It is to be expected that Frazer's adduction of the many pagan analogues to the Christian mythos will be thought by Christian readers to have an adverse effect on faith, it was undoubtedly Frazer's purpose that it should, yet many readers will feel that Frazer makes all faith and ritual indigenous to humanity, virtually biological; they feel, as De Quincey put it, that not to be at least a *little* superstitious is to lack generosity of mind. Scientific though his purpose was, Frazer had the effect of validating those old modes of experiencing the world which modern men, beginning with the Romantics, have sought to revive in order to escape from positivism and common sense.

The direction of the imagination upon great and mysterious objects of worship is not the only means men use to liberate themselves from the bondage of quotidian fact, and although Frazer can scarcely be held accountable for the ever-growing modern attraction to the extreme mental states—to rapture, ecstasy, and transcendence, which are achieved by drugs, trance, music and dance, orgy, and the derangement of personality—yet he did provide a bridge to the understanding and acceptance of these states, he proposed to us the idea that the desire for them and the use of them for heuristic purposes is a common and acceptable manifestation of human nature.

This one element of Frazer's masterpiece could scarcely fail to suggest the next of my prolegomenal works. It is worth remarking that its author was in his own way as great a classical scholar as Frazer himself—Nietzsche was Professor of Classical Philology at the University of Basel when, at the age of twenty-seven, he published his essay *The Birth of Tragedy.* After the appearance of this stunningly brilliant account of Greek civilization, of which Socrates is not the hero but the villain, what can possibly be left to us of that rational and ordered Greece, that modern, that eighteenth-century, Athens that Arnold so entirely relied on as the standard for juding all civilizations? Professor Kaufmann is right when he warns us against supposing that Nietzsche exalts Dionysus over Apollo and tells us that Nietzsche "emphasizes the Dionysiac only because he feels that the Apolonian genius of the Greeks cannot be fully understood apart from it." But no one reading Nietzsche's essay for the first time is likely to heed this warning. What will reach him before due caution intervenes, before he becomes aware of the portentous dialectic between Dionysus and Apollo, is the excitement of suddenly being liberated from Aristotle, the joy of finding himself acceding to the author's statement that "art rather than ethics constitutes the essential metaphysical activity of man," that tragedy has its source in the Dionysiac rapture, "whose closest analogy is furnished by physical intoxication," and that this rapture, in which "the individual forgets himself completely," was in itself no metaphysical state but an orgiastic display of lust and cruelty, "of sexual promiscuity overriding every form of tribal law." This sadic and masochistic frenzy, Nietzsche is at pains to insist, needs the taming hand of Apollo before it can become tragedy, but it is the primal stuff of the great art, and to the modern experience of tragedy this explanation seems far more pertinent than Aristotle's, with its eagerness to forget its origin in its achievement of a state of noble imperturbability.

Of supreme importance in itself, Nietzsche's essay had for me the added pedagogic advantage of allowing me to establish a historical line back to William Blake. Nothing is more characteristic of modern literature than its discovery and canonization of the primal, non-ethical energies, and the historical point could be made the better by remarking the correspondence of thought of two men of different nations and separated from each other by a good many decades, for Nietzsche's Dionysian orgy and Blake's Hell are much the same thing.

Whether or not Jospeh Conrad read either Blake or Nietzsche I do not know, but his *Heart of Darkness* follows in their line. This very great work has never lacked for the admiration it deserves, and it has been given a kind of canonical place in the legend of modern literature by Eliot's having it so clearly in mind when he wrote *The Waste Land* and his having taken from it the epigraph to "The Hollow Men." But no one, to my knowledge, has ever confronted in an explicit way its strange and terrible message of ambivalence toward the life of civilization. Consider that its protagonist, Kurtz, is a progressive and a liberal and that he is the highly respected representative of a society which would have us believe it is benign, although in fact it is vicious. Consider too that he is a practitioner of several arts, a painter, a writer, a musician, and into the bargain a political orator. He is at once the most idealistic and the most practically successful of all the agents of the Belgian exploitation of the Congo. Everybody knows the truth about him which Marlow discovers—that Kurtz's success is the result of a terrible ascendancy he has gained over the natives of his distant station, an ascendancy which is derived from his presumed magical or divine powers, that he has exercised his rule with an extreme of cruelty, that he has given himself to unnamable acts of lust. This is the world of the darker pages of *The Golden Bough*. It is one of the great points of Conrad's story that Marlow speaks of the primitive life of the jungle not as being noble or charming or even free but as being base and sordid—and for *that* reason compelling: he himself feels quite overtly its dreadful attraction. It is to this devilish baseness that Kurtz has yielded himself, and yet Marlow, although he does indeed treat him with hostile irony, does not find it possible to suppose that Kurtz is anything but a hero of the spirit. For me it is still ambiguous whether Kurtz's famous deathbed cry, "The horror! The horror! refers to the approach of death or to his experience of savage life. Whichever it is, to Marlow the fact that Kurtz could utter this cry at the point of death, while Marlow himself, when death threatens him, can know it only as a weary grayness, marks the difference between the ordinary man and a hero of the spirit. Is this not the essence of the modern belief about the nature of the artist, the man who goes down into that hell which is the historical beginning of the human soul, a beginning not outgrown but established in humanity as we know it now, preferring the reality of this hell to the bland lies of the civilization that has overlaid it?

This idea is proposed again in the somewhat less powerful but still very moving work with which I followed *Heart of Darkness,* Thomas Mann's *Death in Venice*. I wanted this story not so much for its account of an extravagantly Apollonian personality surrendering to forces that, in his Apollonian character, he thought shameful—although this was certainly to my purpose—but rather for Aschenbach's fevered dreams of the erotic past, and in particular that dream of the goat-orgy which Mann, being the kind of writer he is, having the kind of relation to Nietzsche he had, might well have written to serve as an illustration of what *The Birth of Tragedy* means by religious frenzy, the more so, of course, because Mann chooses that particular ogiastic ritual, the killing and eating of the goat, from which tragedy is traditionally said to have been derived.

A notable element of this story in which the birth of tragedy plays an important part is that the degradation and downfall of the protagonist is not represented as tragic in the usual sense of the word—that is, it is not represented as a great deplorable event. It is a commonplace of modern literary thought that the tragic mode is not available even to the gravest and noblest or our writers. I am not sure that this is the deprivation that some people think it to be and a mark of our spiritual inferiority. But if we ask why it has come about, one reason may be that we have learned to think our way back through tragedy to the primal stuff out of which tragedy arose. If we consider the primitive forbidden ways of conduct which traditionally in tragedy lead to punishment by death, we think of them as being the path to reality and truth, to an ultimate self-realization. We have always wondered if tragedy itself may not have been saying just this in a deeply hidden way, drawing us to think of the hero's sin and death as somehow conferring justification, even salvation of a sort—no doubt this is what Nietzsche had in mind when he said that "tragedy denies ethics." What tragedy once seemed to hint, our literature now is willing to say quite explicitly. If Mann's Aschenbach dies at the height of his intellectual and artistic powers, overcome by a passion that his ethical reason condemns, we do not take this to be a defeat, rather a kind of terrible rebirth: at his latter end the artist knows a reality that he had until now refused to admit to consciousness.

Thoughts like these suggested that another of Nietzsche's works, *The Genealogy of Morals,* might be in point. It proposes a view of society which is consonant with the belief that art and not ethics constitutues the essential metaphysical activity of man and with the validation and ratification of the primitive energies. Nietzsche's theory of the social order dismisses all ethical impluse from its origins—the basis of society is to be found in the rationalization of cruelty: as simple as that. Nietzsche has no ultimate Utopian intention in saying this, no hope of revising the essence of the social order, although he does believe that its pain can be mitigated. He represents cruelty as a social necessity, for only by its exercise could men ever have been induced to develop a continuity of will: nothing else than cruel pain could have created in mankind that memory of intention which makes society possible. The method of cynicism which Nietzsche pursued—let us be clear that it is a method and not an attitude—goes so far as to describe punishment in terms of the pleasure derived from the exercise of cruelty: "Compensation," he says, "consists in a legal warrant entitling one man to exercise his cruelty on another." There follows that most remarkable passage in which Nietzsche describes the process whereby the individual turns the cruelty of punishment against himself and creates the bad conscience and the consciousness of guilt which manifests itself as a pervasive anxiety. Nietzsche's complexity of mind is beyond all comparison, for in this book which is dedicated to the liberation of the conscience, Nietzsche makes his defense of the bad conscience as a decisive force in the interests of culture. It is much the same line of argument that he takes when, having attacked the Jewish morality and the priestly existence in the name of the health of the spirit, he reminds us that only by his sickness does man become interesting.

From *The Genealogy of Morals* to Freud's *Civilization and Its Discontents* is but a step, and some might think that, for pedagogic purposes, the step is so small as to make the second book supererogatory. But although Freud's view of society and culture has indeed a very close affinity to Nietzsche's, Freud does add certain considerations which are essential to our sense of the modern disposition.

For one thing, he puts to us the question of whether or not we want to *accept* civilization. It is not the first time that the paradox of civilization has been present to the mind of civilized people, the sense that civilization makes men behave worse and suffer more than does some less developed state of human existence. But hitherto all such ideas were formulated in a moralizing way—civilization was represented at being "corrupt," a divagation from a state of innocence. Freud had no illusions about a primitive innocence, he conceived no practicable alternative to civilization. In consequence, there was a unique force to the question he asked: whether we wished to accept civilization, with all its contradictions, with all its pains—pains, for "discontents" does not accurately describe what Freud has in mind. He had his own answer to the question—his tragic, or stoic, sense of life dictated it: we do well to accept it, although we also do well to cast a cold eye on the fate that makes it our better part to accept it. Like Nietzsche, Freud thought that life was justified by our heroic response to its challenge.

But the question Freud posed has not been set aside or closed up by the answer that he himself gave to it. His answer, like Nietzsche's, is essentially in the line of traditional humanism—we can see this in the sternness with which he charges women not to interfere with men in the discharge of their cultural duty, not to claim men for love and the family to the detriment of their free activity in the world. But just here lies the matter of Freud's question that the world more and more believes Freud himself did not answer. The pain that civilization inflicts is that of the instinctual renunciation that civilization demands, and it would seem that fewer and fewer people wish to say with Freud that the loss of instinctual gratification, emotional freedom, or love, is compensated for either by the security of civilizaed life or by the stern pleasures of the masculine moral character.

With Freud's essay I brought to a close my list of prolegomenal books for the first term of the course. I shall not do much more than mention the books with which I introduced the second term, but I should like to do at least that. I began with *Rameau's Nephew,* thinking that the peculiar moral authority which Diderot assigns to the envious, untalented, unregenerate protagonist was peculiarly relevant to the line taken by the ethical explorations of modern literature. Nothing is more characteristic of the literature of our time than the replacement of the hero by what has come to be called the anti-hero, in whose indifference to or hatred of ethical nobility there is presumed to lie a special authenticity. Diderot is quite overt about this—he himself in his public character is the deuteragonist, the "honest consciousness," as Hegel calls him, and he takes delight in the discomfiture of the decent, dull person he is by the Nephew's nihilistic mind.

It seemed to me too that there was a particular usefulness in the circumstance that this anti-hero should avow so openly his *envy,* which Tocqueville has called the ruling emotion of democracy, and that, although he envied anyone at all who had access to the creature-comforts and the social status which he lacked, what chiefly animated him was envy of men of genius. Ours is the first cultural epoch in which many men aspire to high achievement in the arts and, in their frustration, form a dispossessed class which cuts across the conventional class lines, making a proletariat of the spirit.

Although *Rameau's Nephew* was not published until fairly late in the century, it was known in manuscript by Goethe and Hegel; it suited the temper and won the admiration of Marx and Freud for reasons that are obvious. And there is ground for supposing that it was known to Dostoevski, whose *Notes from Underground* is a restatement of the essential idea of Diderot's dialogue in terms both more extreme and less genial. The Nephew is still on the defensive—he is naughtily telling secrets about the nature of man and society. But Dostoevski's underground man shouts aloud his envy and hatred and carries the ark of his self-hatred and alienation into a remorseless battle with what he calls "the good and the beautiful," mounting an attack upon every belief not merely of bourgeois society but of the whole humanist tradition. The inclusion of *Notes from Underground* among my prolegomenal books constituted something of a pedagogic risk, for if I wished to emphasize the subversive tendency of modern literature, here was a work which made all subsequent subversion seem like affirmation, so radical and so brilliant was its negation of our traditional pieties and its affirmation of our new pieties.

I hesitated in compunction before following *Notes from Underground* with Tolstoi's *Death of Ivan Ilyitch,* which so ruthlessly and with such dreadful force destroys the citadel of the commonplace life in which we all believe we can take refuge from ourselves and our fate. But I did assign it and then two of Pirandello's plays which, in the atmosphere of the sordidness of the commonplace life, undermine all certitudes of the commonplace, common-sense mind.

From time to time I have raised with myself the question of whether my choice of these prolegomenal works was not extravagant, quite excessively tendentious. I have never been able to believe that it is. And if these works do indeed serve to indicate in an accurate way the nature of modern literature, a teacher might find it worth asking how his students respond to the strong dose.

One response I have already described—the readiness of the students to engage in the process that we might call the socialization of the anti-social, or the acculturation of the anti-cultural, or the legitimization of the subversive. When the term-essays come in, it is plain to me that almost none of the students have been taken aback by what they have read: they have wholly contained the attack. The chief exceptions are the few who simply do not comprehend, although they may be awed by, the categories of our discourse. In their papers, like poor hunted creatures in a Kafka story, they take refuge first in misunderstood large phrases, then in bad grammar, then in general incoherence. After my pedagogical exasperation has run its course, I find that I am sometimes moved to give them a queer respect, as if they had stood up and said what in fact they don't have the wit to stand up and say: "Why do you harry us? Leave us alone. We are not Modern Man. We are the Old People. Ours is the Old Faith. We serve the little Old Gods, the gods of the copybook maxims, the small, dark, somewhat powerful deities of lawyers, doctors, engineers, accountants. With them is neither sensibility not *angst.* With them is no disgust—it is they, indeed, who make ready the way for 'the good and the beautiful' about which low-minded doubts have been raised in this course, that 'good and beautiful' which we do not possess and don't want to possess but which we know justifies our lives. Leave us alone and let us worship our gods in the way they approve, in peace and unawareness." Crass, but—to use that interesting modern word which we have learned from the curators of museums—authentic. The rest, the minds that give me the A papers and the B papers and even the C+ papers, move through the terrors and mysteries of modern literature like so many Parsifals, asking no questions at the behest of wonder and fear. Or like so many seminarists who have been sytematically instructed in the constitution of Hell and the ways to damnation. Or like so many *readers,* entertained by moral horror stories. I asked them to look into the Abyss, and, both dutifully and gladly, they have looked into the Abyss, and the Abyss has greeted them with the grave courtesy of all objects of serious study, saying: "Interesting, am I not? And *exciting,* if you consider how deep I am and what dread beasts lie at my bottom. Have it well in mind that a knowledge of me contributes materially to your being whole, or well-rounded, men."

In my distress over the outrage I have conspired to perpetrate upon a great literature, I wonder if perhaps I have not been reading these papers too literally. After all, a term-essay is not a diary of the soul, it is not an occasion for telling the truth. What my students might reveal of their true feelings to a younger teacher they will not reveal to me; they will give me what they conceive to be the proper response to the official version of terror I have given them. I bring to mind their faces, which are not necessarily the faces of the authors of these unperturbed papers, nor are they, not yet, the faces of fathers of families, or of theatergoers, or of buyers of modern paintings: not yet. I must think it possible that in ways and to a degree which they keep secret they have responded directly and personally to what they have read.

And if they have? And if they have, am I the more content?

What form would I want their response to take? It is a teacher's question that I am asking, not a critic's. We have decided in recent years to think of the critic and the teacher of literature as one and the same, and no doubt it is both possible and useful to do so. But there are some points at which the functions of the two do not coincide, or can be made to coincide only with great difficulty. Of criticism we have been told, by Arnold, that "it must be apt to study and praise elements that for fulness of spiritual perfection are wanted, even though they belong to a power which in the practical sphere may be maleficent." But teaching, or at least undergraduate teaching, is not given the same licensed mandate—cannot be given it because the teacher's audience, which stands before his very eyes, as the critic's audience does not, asks questions about "the practical sphere," as the critic's audience does not. For instance, on the very day that I write this, when I had said to my class all I could think of to say about *The Magic Mountain* and invited questions and comments, one student asked, "How would you generalize the idea of the educative value of illness, so that it would be applicable not only to a particular individual, Hans Castorp, but to young people at large?" It makes us smile, but it was asked in all seriousness, and it is serious in its substance, and it had to be answered seriously, in part by the reflection that this idea, like so many ideas encountered in the books of the course, had to be thought of as having reference only to the private life; that it touched the public life only in some indirect or tangential way; that it really ought to be encountered in solitude, even in secrecy, since to talk about it in public and in our academic setting was to seem to propose for it a public practicality and thus to distort its meaning. To this another student replied; he said that, despite the public ritual of the classroom, each student inevitably experienced the books in privacy and found their meaning in reference to his own life. True enough, but the teacher sees the several privacies coming together to make a group, and they propose—no doubt the more because they come together every Monday, Wednesday, and Friday at a particular hour—the idea of a community, that is to say, "the practical sphere."

This being so, the teacher cannot escape the awareness of certain circumstances which the critic, who writes for an ideal, uncircumstanced reader, has no need to take into account. The teacher considers, for example, the social situation of his students—they are not of patrician origin, they do not come from homes in which stubbornness, pride, and conscious habit prevail, nor are they born into a culture marked by these traits, a culture in which other interesting and valuable things compete with and resist ideas; they come, mostly, from "good homes" in which authority and valuation are weak or at least not very salient and bold, so that ideas have for them, at their present stage of development, a peculiar power and preciousness. And in this connection the teacher will have in mind the special prestige that our culture, in its upper reaches, gives to art, and to the ideas that art proposes—the agreement, ever growing in assertiveness, that art yields more truth than any other intellectual activity. In this culture what a shock it is to encounter Santayana's acerb skepticism about art, or Keat's remark, which the critics and scholars never take notice of, presumably because they suppose it to be an aberration, that poetry is "not so fine a thing as philosophy—For the same reason that an eagle is not so fine a thing as a truth." For many students no ideas that they will encounter in any college discipline will equal in force and sanction the ideas conveyed to them by modern literature.

The author of *The Magic Mountain* once said that all his work could be understood as an effort to free himself from the middle class, and this, of course, will serve to describe the chief intention of all modern literature. And the means of freedom which Mann prescribes (the characteristic irony notwithstanding) is the means of freedom which in effect all of modern literature prescribes. It is, in the words of Clavdia Chauchat, "*se perdre et même . . . se laisser dépérir,*" and thus to name the means is to make plain that the end is not merely freedom from the middle class but freedom from society itself. I venture to say that the idea of losing oneself up to the point of self-destruction, of surrendering oneself to experience without regard to self-interest or conventional morality, of escaping wholly from the societal bonds, is an "element" somewhere in the mind of every modern person who dares to think of what Arnold in his unaffected Victorian way called "the fulness of spiritual perfection. But the teacher who undertakes to present modern literature to his students may not allow that idea to remain in the *somewhere* of his mind; he must take it from the place where it exists habitual and unrealized and put it in the conscious forefront of his thought. And if he is committed to an admiration of modern literature, he must also be committed to this chief idea of modern literature. I press the logic of the situation not in order to question the legitimacy of the commitment, or even the propriety of expressing the commitment in the college classroom (although it does seem odd!), but to confront those of us who do teach modern literature with the striking actuality of our enterprise.

THOMAS S. KUHN

Selection from *The Structure of Scientific Revolutions* 1962

The extraordinary discussion surrounding *The Structure of Scientific Revolutions* is an indicator not only of the insight of its author, the historian of science, Thomas S. Kuhn (1922–), but also of the significance assigned by twentieth-century intellectuals to issues in the theoretical basis of science. This book of 1962 quickly became one of the most widely quoted and earnestly assessed academic works of the past generation. The best point of access to the controversy over Kuhn's work is Gary Gutting, ed., *Paradigms and Revolutions: Applications and Appraisals of Thomas Kuhn's Philosophy of Science* (Notre Dame, Ind., 1980). Much of the controversy centers around arguments made by Kuhn in our selection, the penultimate chapter of *Structure*. Here, Kuhn places the logical aspect of scientific "proof" in a larger, social, and psychological context. New theories become accepted as true by communities of scientists not because these theories satisfy some absolute criteria of validity, according to Kuhn, but rather because these new theories seem more capable than competing theories of satisfying certain, special needs of these communities. Nothing is more needed by such communities than a framework to guide future scientific work directed at explaining the particular problems upon which the community happens to have focused its immediate attention. When Kuhn speaks in these pages of competing "paradigms," he refers to these general theoretical frameworks that serve to guide specialized scientific work. When the relevant scientific community replaces an old paradigm with another, a "revolution" is constituted, as in several of the historical episodes to which Kuhn alludes: the intellectual innovations we associate with the names of Copernicus, Newton, and Darwin.

. . . . . .

What is the process by which a new candidate for paradigm replaces its predecessor? Any new interpretation of nature, whether a discovery or a theory, emerges first in the mind of one or a few individuals. It is they who first learn to see science and the world differently, and their ability to make the transition is facilitated by two circumstances that are not common to most other members of their profession. Invariably their attention has been intensely concentrated upon the crisis-provoking problems; usually, in addition, they are men so young or so new to the crisis-ridden field that practice has committed them less deeply than most of their contemporaries to the world view and rules determined by the old paradigm. How are they able, what must they do, to convert the entire profession or the relevant professional subgroup to their way of seeing science and the world? What causes the group to abandon one tradition of normal research in favor of another?

To see the urgency of those questions, remember that they are the only reconstructions the historian can supply for the philosopher's inquiry about the testing, verification, or falsification of established scientific theories. In so far as he is engaged in normal science, the research worker is a solver of puzzles, not a tester of paradigms. Though he may, during the search for a particular puzzle's solution, try out a number of alternative approaches, rejecting those that fail to yield the desired result, he is not testing the *paradigm* when he does so. Instead he is like the chess player who, with a problem stated and the board physically or mentally before him, tries out various alternative moves in the search for a solution. These trial attempts, whether by the chess player or by the scientist, are trials only of themselves, not of the rules of the game. They are possible only so long as the paradigm itself is taken for granted. Therefore, paradigm testing occurs only after persistent failure to solve a noteworthy puzzle has given to rise crisis. And even then it occurs only after the sense of crisis has evoked an alternate candidate for paradigm. In the sciences the testing situation never consists, as puzzle solving does, simply in the comparison of a single paradigm with nature. Instead, testing occurs as part of the competition between two rival paradigms for the allegiance of the scientific community.

Closely examined, this formulation displays unexpected and probably significant parallels to two of the most popular contemporary philosophical theories about verification. Few philosophers of science still seek absolute criteria for the verification of scientific theories. Noting that no theory can ever be exposed to all possible relevant tests, they ask not whether a theory has been verified but rather about its probability in the light of the evidence that actually exists. And to answer that question one important school is driven to compare the ability of different theories to explain the evidence at hand. That insistence on comparing theories also characterizes the historical situation in which a new theory is accepted. Very probably it points one of the directions in which future discussions of verification should go.

In their most usual forms, however, probabilistic verification theories all have recourse to one or another of the pure or neutral observation-languages discussed in Section X. One probabilistic theory asks that we compare the given scientific theory

Source: The Structure of Scientific Revolutions, Thomas S. Kuhn, 143–59.

with all others that might be imagined to fit the same collection of observed data. Another demands the construction in imagination of all the tests that the given scientific theory might conceivably be asked to pass.[1] Apparently some such construction is necessary for the computation of specific probabilities, absolute or relative, and it is hard to see how such a construction can possibly be achieved. If, as I have already urged, there can be no scientifically or empirically neutral system of language or concepts, then the proposed construction of alternate tests and theories must proceed from within one or another paradigm-based tradition. Thus restricted it would have no access to all possible experiences or to all possible theories. As a result, probabilistic theories disguise the verification situation as much as they illuminate it. Though that situation does, as they insist, depend upon the comparison of theories and much widespread evidence, the theories and observations at issue are always closely related to ones already in existence. Verification is like natural selection: it picks out the most viable among the actual alternatives in a particularly historical situation. Whether that choice is the best that could have been made if still other alternatives had been available or if the data had been of another sort is not a question that can usefully be asked. There are no tools to employ in seeking answers to it.

A very different approach to this whole network of problems has been developed by Karl R. Popper who denies the existence of any verificiation procedures at all.[2] Instead, he emphasizes the importance of falsification, i.e., of the test that, because its outcome is negative, necessitates the rejection of an established theory. Clearly, the role thus attributed to falsification is much like the one this essay assigns to anomalous experiences, i.e., to experiences that, by evoking crisis, prepare the way for a new theory. Nevertheless, anomalous experiences may not be identified with falsifying ones. Indeed, I doubt that the latter exist. As has repeatedly been emphasized before, no theory ever solves all the puzzles with which it is confronted at a given time; nor are the solutions already achieved often perfect. On the contrary, it is just the incompleteness and imperfection of the existing data-theory fit that, at any time, define many of the puzzles that characterize normal science. If any and every failure to fit were ground for theory rejection, all theories ought to be rejected at all times. On the other hand, if only severe failure to fit justifies theory rejection, then the Popperians will require some criterion of "improbability" or of "degree of falsification." In developing one they will almost certainly encounter the same network of difficulties that has haunted the advocates of the various probabilistic verification theories.

Many of the preceding difficulties can be avoided by recognizing that both of these prevalent and opposed views about the underlying logic of scientific inquiry have tried to compress two largely separate processes into one. Popper's anomalous experience is important to science because it evokes competitors for an existing paradigm. But falsification, though it surely occurs, does not happen with, or simply because of, the emergence of an anomaly or falsifying instance. Instead, it is a subsequent and separate process that might equally well be called verification since it consists in the triumph of a new paradigm over the old one. Furthermore, it is in that joint verification-falsification process that the probabilist's comparison of theories plays a central role. Such a two-stage formulation has, I think, the virtue of great verisimilitude, and

1. For a brief sketch of the main routes to probabilistic verification theories, see Ernest Nagel, *Principles of the Theory of Probability,* Vol. 1, No. 6, of *International Encyclopedia of Unified Science,* pp. 60–75.

2. K. R. Popper, *The Logic of Scientific Discovery* (New York, 1959), esp. chaps. 1–4.

it may also enable us to begin explicating the role of agreement (or disagreement) between fact and theory in the verification process. To the historian, at least, it makes little sense to suggest that verification is establishing the agreement of fact with theory. All historically significant theories have agreed with the facts, but only more or less. There is no more precise answer to the question whether or how well an individual theory fits the facts. But questions much like that can be asked when theories are taken collectively or even in pairs. It makes a great deal of sense to ask which of two actual and competing theories fits the facts *better*. Though neither Priestley's nor Lavoisier's theory, for example, agreed precisely with existing observations, few contemporaries hesitated more than a decade in concluding that Lavoisier's theory provided the better fit of thc two.

This formulation, however, makes the task of choosing between paradigms look both easier and more familiar than it is. If there were but one set of scientific problems, one world within which to work on them, and one set of standards for their solution, paradigm competition might be settled more or less routinely by some process like counting the number of problems solved by each. But, in fact, these conditions are never met completely. The proponents of competing paradigms are always at least slightly at cross-purposes. Neither side will grant all the non-empirical assumptions that the other needs in order to make its case. Like Proust and Berthollet arguing about the composition of chemical compounds, they are bound partly to talk through each other. Though each may hope to convert the other to his way of seeing his science and its problems, neither may hope to prove his case. The competition between paradigms is not the sort of battle that can be resolved by proofs.

We have already seen several reasons why the proponents of competing paradigms must fail to make complete contact with each other's viewpoints. Collectively these reasons have been described as the incommensurability of the pre- and postrevolutionary normal-scientific traditions, and we need only recapitulate them briefly here. In the first place, the proponents of competing paradigms will often disagree about the list of problems that any candididate for paradigm must resolve. Their standards or their definitions of science are not the same. Must a theory of motion explain the cause of the atrractive forces between particles of matter or may it simply note the existence of such forces? Newton's dynamics was widely rejected because, unlike both Aristotle's and Descartes's theories, it implied the latter answer to the question. When Newton's theory had been accepted, a question was therefore banished from science. That question, however, was one that general relativity may proudly claim to have solved. Or again, as disseminated in the nineteenth century, Lavoisier's chemical theory inhibited chemists from asking why the metals were so much alike, a question that phlogistic chemistry had both asked and answered. The transition to Lavoisier's paradigm had, like the transition to Newton's, meant a loss not only of a permissible question but of an achieved solution. That loss was not, however, permanent either. In the twentieth century questions about the qualities of chemical substances have entered science again, together with some answers to them.

More is involved, however, than the incommensurability of standards. Since new paradigms are born from old ones, they ordinarily incorporate much of the vocabulary and apparatus, both conceptual and manipulative, that the traditional paradigm had previously employed. But they seldom employ these borrowed elements in quite the traditional way. Within the new paradigm, old terms, concepts, and experiments fall into new relationships one with the other. The inevitable result is what we must call, though the term is not quite right, a misunderstanding between the two competing schools. The laymen who scoffed at Einstein's general theory of relativity because space could not be "curved"—it was not that sort of thing—were not simply wrong or mistaken. Nor were the mathematicians, physicists, and philosophers who tried to develop a Euclidean version of Einstein's theory.[3] What had previously been meant by space was necessarily flat, homogeneous, isotropic, and unaffected by the presence of matter. If it had not been, Newtonian physics would not have worked. To make the transition to Einstein's universe, the whole conceptual web whose strands are space, time, matter, force, and so on, had to be shifted and laid down again on nature whole. Only men who had together undergone or failed to undergo that transformation would be able to discover precisely what they agreed or disagreed about. Communication across the revolutionary divide is inevitably partial. Consider, for another example, the men who called Copernicus mad because he proclaimed that the earth moved. They were not either just wrong or quite wrong. Part of what they meant by "earth" was fixed position. Their earth, at least could not be moved. Correspondingly, Copernicus' innovation was not simply to move the earth. Rather, it was a whole new way of regarding the problems of physics and astronomy, one that necessarily changed the meaning of both "earth" and "motion."[4] Without those changes the concept of a moving earth was mad. On the other hand, once they had been made and understood, both Descartes and Huyghens could realize that the earth's motion was a question with no content for science.[5]

These examples point to the third and most fundamental aspect of the incommensurability of competing paradigms. In a sense that I am unable to explicate further, the proponents of competing paradigms practice their trades in different worlds. One contains constrained bodies that fall slowly, the other pendulums that repeat their motions again and again. In one, solutions are compounds, in the other mixtures. One is embedded in a flat, the other in a curved, matrix of space. Practicing in different worlds, the two groups of scientists see different things when they look from the same point in the same direction. Again, that is not to say that they can see anything they please. Both are looking at the world, and what they look at has not changed. But in some areas they see different things, and they see them in different relations one to the other. That is why a law that cannot even be demonstrated to one group of scientists may occasionally seem intuitively obvious to another. Equally, it is why before they can hope to communicate fully, one group or the other must experience the conversion that we have been calling a paradigm shift. Just because it is a transition between incommensurables, the transition between competing paradigms cannot be made a step at a time, forced by logic and neutral experience. Like the gestalt switch, it must occur all at once (though not necessarily in an instant) or not at all.

How, then, are scientists brought to make this transposition? Part of the answer is that they are very often not. Copernicanism made few converts for almost a century after Copernicus' death. Newton's work was not generally accepted, particularly on

3. For lay reactions to the concept of curved space, see Philipp Frank, *Einstein, His Life and Times*, trans. and ed. G. Rosen and S. Kusaka (New York, 1947), pp. 142–46. For a few of the attempts to preserve the gains of general relativity within a Euclidean space, see C. Nordmann, *Einstein and the Universe*, trans. J. McCabe (New York, 1922), chap. 9.

4. T. S. Kuhn, *The Copernican Revolution* (Cambridge, Mass., 1957), chaps. 3, 4, and 5. The extent to which heliocentrism was more than a strictly astronomical issue is a major theme of the entire book.

5. Max Jammer, *Concepts of Space* (Cambridge, Mass., 1954), pp. 118–24.

the Continent, for more than half a century after the *Principia* appeared.[6] Priestley never accepted the oxygen theory, nor Lord Kelvin the electromagnetic theory, and so on. The difficulties of conversion have often been noted by scientists themselves. Darwin, in a particularly perceptive passage at the end of his *Origin of Species,* wrote: "Although I am fully convinced of the truth of the views given in this volume . . . , I by no means expect to convince experienced naturalists whose minds are stocked with a multitude of facts all viewed, during a long course of years, from a point of view directly opposite to mine. . . . [B]ut I look with confidence to the future,—to young and rising naturalists, who will be able to view both sides of the question with impartiality."[7] And Max Planck, surveying his own career in his *Scientific Autobiography,* sadly remarked that "a new scientific truth does not triumph by convincing its opponents and making them see the light, but rather because its opponents eventually die, and a new generation grows up that is familiar with it."[8]

These facts and others like them are too commonly known to need further emphasis. But the do need re-evaluation. In the past they have most often been taken to indicate that scientists, being only human, cannot always admit their errors, even when confronted with strict proof. I would argue, rather, that in these matters neither proof nor error is at issue. The transfer of allegiance from paradigm to paradigm is a conversion experience that cannot be forced. Lifelong resistance, particularly from those whose productive careers have committed them to an older tradition of normal science, is not a violation of scientific standards but an index to the nature of scientific research itself. The source of resistance is the assurance that the older paradigm will ultimately solve all its problems, that nature can be shoved into the box the paradigm provides. Inevitably, at time of revolution, that assurance seems stubborn and pigheaded as indeed it sometimes becomes. But it is also something more. That same assurance is what makes normal or puzzle-solving science possible. And it is only through normal science that the professional community of scientists succeeds, first, in exploiting the potential scope and precision of the older paradigm and, then, in isolating the difficulty through the study of which a new paradigm may emerge.

Still, to say that resistance is inevitable and legitimate, that paradigm change cannot be justified by proof, is not to say that no arguments are relevant or that scientists cannot be persuaded to change their minds. Though a generation is sometimes required to effect the change, scientific communities have again and again been converted to new paradigms. Furthermore, these conversions occur not despite the fact that scientists are human but because they are. Though some scientists, particularly the older and more experienced ones, may resist indefinitely, most of them can be reached in one way or another. Conversions will occur a few at a time until, after the last holdouts have died, the whole profession will again be practicing under a single, but now a different, paradigm. We must therefore ask how conversion is induced and how resisted.

What sort of answer to that question may we expect? Just because it is asked about techniques of persuasion, or about argument and counterargument in a situation

6. I. B. Cohen, *Franklin and Newton: An Inquiry into Speculative Newtonian Experimental Science and Franklin's Work in Electricity as an Example Thereof* (Philadelphia, 1956), pp. 93–94.

7. Charles Darwin, *On the Origin of Species* . . . (authorized edition from 6th English ed.; New York 1889), 2, 295–96.

8. Max Planck, *Scientific Autobiography and Other Papers,* trans. F. Gaynor (New York, 1949), pp. 33–34.

in which there can be no proof, our question is a new one, demanding a sort of study that has not previously been undertaken. We shall have to settle for a very partial and impressionistic survey. In addition, what has already been said combines with the result of the survey to suggest that, when asked about persuasion rather than proof, the question of the nature of scientific argument has no single or uniform answer. Individual scientists embrace a new paradigm for all sorts of reasons and usually for several at once. Some of these reasons—for example, the sun worship that helped make Kepler a Copernican—lie outside the apparent sphere of science entirely.[9] Others must depend upon idiosyncrasies of autobiography and personality. Even the nationality or the prior reputation of the innovator and his teachers can sometimes play a significant role.[10] Ultimately, therefore, we must learn to ask this question differently. Our concern will not then be with the arguments that in fact convert one or another individual, but rather with the sort of community that always sooner or later re-forms as a single group. . . .

Probably the single most prevalent claim advanced by the proponents of a new paradigm is that they can solve the problems that have led the old one to a crisis. When it can legitimately be made, this claim is often the most effective one possible. In the area for which it is advanced the paradigm is known to be in trouble. That trouble has repeatedly been explored, and attempts to remove it have again and again proved vain. "Crucial experiments"—those able to discriminate particularly sharply between the two paradigms—have been recognized and attested before the new paradigm was even invented. Copernicus thus claimed that he had solved the long-vexing problem of the length of the calendar year, Newton that he had reconciled terrestrial and clestial mechanics, Lavoisier that he had solved the problems of gas-identity and of weight relations, and Einstein that he had made electrodynamics compatible with a revised science of motion.

Claims of this sort are particularly likely to succeed if the new paradigm displays a quantitative precision strikingly better than its older competitor. The quantitative superiority of Kepler's Rudolphine tables to all those computed from the Ptolemaic theory was a major factor in the conversion of astronomers to Copernicanism. Newton's success in predicting quantitative astronomical observations was probably the single most important reason for his theory's triumph over its more reasonable but uniformly qualitative competitors. And in this century the striking quantitative success of both Planck's radiation law and the Bohr atom quickly persuaded many physicists to adopt them even though, viewing physical science as a whole, both these contributions created many more problems than they solved.[11]

The claim to have solved the crisis-provoking problems is, however, rarely sufficient by itself. Nor can it always legitimately be made. In fact, Copernicus' theory was not more accurate than Ptolemy's and did not lead directly to any improvement

9. For the role of sun worship in Kepler's thought, see E. A. Burtt, *The Metaphysical Foundations of Modern Physical Science* (rev. ed.; New York, 1932), pp. 44–49.

10. For the role of reputation, consider the following: Lord Rayleigh, at a time when his reputation was established, submitted to the British Association a paper on some paradoxes of electrodynamics. His name was inadvertently omitted when the paper was first sent, and the paper itself was at first rejected as the work of some "paradoxer." Shortly afterwards, with the author's name in place, the paper was accepted with profuse apologies (R. J. Strutt, 4th Baron Rayleigh, *John William Strutt, Third Baron Rayleigh* (New York, 1924), p. 228).

11. For the problems created by the quantum theory, see F. Reiche, *The Quantum Theory* (London, 1922), chaps. 2, 6–9. For the other examples in this paragraph, see the earlier references in this section.

in the calendar. Or again, the wave theory of light was not, for some years after it was first announced, even as successful as its corpuscular rival in resolving the polarization effects that were a principal cause of the optical crisis. Sometimes the looser practice that characterizes extraordinary research will produce a candidate for paradigm that initially helps not at all with the problems that have evoked crisis. When that occurs, evidence must be drawn from other parts of the field as it often is anyway. In those other areas particularly persuasive arguments can be developed if the new paradigm permits the prediction of phenomena that had been entirely unsuspected while the old one prevailed.

Copernicus' theory, for example, suggested that planets should be like the earth, that Venus should show phases, and that the universe must be vastly larger than had previously been supposed. As a result, when sixty years after his death the telescope suddenly displayed mountains on the moon, the phases of Venus, and an immense number of previously unsuspected stars, those observations brought the new theory a great many converts, particularly among non-astronomers.[12] In the case of the wave theory, one main source of professional conversions was even more dramatic. French resistance collapsed suddenly and relatively completely when Fresnel was able to demonstrate the existence of a white spot at the center of the shadow of a circular disk. That was an effect that not even he had anticipated but that Poisson, initially one of his opponents, had shown to be a necessary if absurd consequence of Fresnel's theory.[13] Because of their shock value and because they have so obviously not been "built into" the new theory from the start, arguments like these prove especially persuasive. And sometimes that extra strength can be exploited even though the phenomenon in question had been observed long before the theory that accounts for it was first introduced. Einstein, for example, seems not to have anticipated that general relativity would account with precision for the well-known anomaly in the motion of Mercury's perihelion, and he experienced a corresponding triumph when it did so.[14]

All the arguments for a new paradigm discussed so far have been based upon the competitors' comparative ability to solve problems. To scientists those arguments are ordinarily the most significant and persuasive. The preceding examples should leave no doubt about the source of their immense appeal. But, for reasons to which we shall shortly revert, they are neither individually nor collectively compelling. Fortunately, there is also another sort of consideration that can lead scientists to reject an old paradigm in favor of a new. These are the arguments, rarely made entirely explicit, that appeal to the individual's sense of the appropriate or the aesthetic—the new theory is said to be "neater," "more suitable," or "simpler" than the old. Probably such arguments are less effective in the sciences than in mathematics. The early versions of most new paradigms are crude. By the time their full aesthetic appeal can be developed, most of the community has been persuaded by other means. Nevertheless, the importance of aesthetic considerations can sometimes be decisive. Though they often attract only a few scientists to a new theory, it is upon those few that its ultimate triumph may depend. If they had not quickly taken it up for highly individual reasons, the new

12. Kuhn, op. cit., pp. 219–25.

13. E. T. Whittaker, *A History of the Theories of Aether and Electricity,* I (2d ed.; London, 1951), 108.

14. See ibid., 2 (1953), 151–80, for the development of general relativity. For Einstein's reaction to the precise agreement of the theory with the observed motion of Mercury's perihelion, see the letter quoted in P. A. Schilpp (ed.), *Albert Einstein, Philosopher-Scientist* (Evanston, Ill., 1949), p. 101.

candidate for paradigm might never have been sufficiently developed to attract the allegiance of the scientific community as a whole.

To see the reason for the importance of these more subjective and aesthetic considerations, remember what a paradigm debate is about. When a new candidate for paradigm is first proposed, it has seldom solved more than a few of the problems that confront it, and most of those solutions are still far from perfect. Until Kepler, the Copernican theory scarcely improved upon the predictions of planetary position made by Ptolemy. When Lavoisier saw oxygen as "the air itself entire," his new theory could cope not at all with the problems presented by the proliferation of new gases, a point that Priestley made with great success in his counterattack. Cases like Fresnel's white spot are extremely rare. Ordinarily, it is only much later, after the new paradigm has been developed, accepted, and exploited that apparently decisive arguments—the Foucault pendulum to demonstrate the rotation of the earth or the Fizeau experiment to show that light moves faster in air than in water—are developed. Producing them is part of normal science, and their role is not in paradigm debate but in postrevolutionary texts.

Before those texts are written, while the debates goes on, the situation is very different. Usually the opponents of a new paradigm can legitimately claim that even in the area of crisis it is little superior to its traditional rival. Of course, it handles some problems better, has disclosed some new regularities. But the older paradigm can presumably be articulated to meet these challenges as it has met others before. Both Tycho Brahe's earth-centered astronomical system and the later versions of the phlogiston theory were responses to challenges posed by a new candidate for paradigm, and both were quite successful.[15] In addition, the defenders of traditional theory and procedure can almost always point to problems that is new rival has not solved but that for their view are no problems at all. Until the discovery of the composition of water, the combustion of hydrogen was a strong argument for the phlogiston theory and against Lavoisier's. And after the oxygen theory had triumphed, it could still not explain the preparation of a combustible gas from carbon, a phenomenon to which the phlogistonists had pointed as strong support for their view.[16] Even in the area of crisis, the balance of argument and counterargument can sometimes be very close indeed. And outside that area the balance will often decisively favor the tradition. Copernicus destroyed a time-honored explanation of terrestrial motion without replacing it; Newton did the same for an older explanation of gravity, Lavoisier for the common properties of metals, and so on. In short, if a new candidate for paradigm had to be judged from the start by hardheaded people who examined only relative problem-solving ability, the sciences would experience very few major revolutions. Add the counterarguments generated by what we previously called the incommensurability of paradigms, and the sciences might experience no revolutions at all.

But paradigm debates are not really about relative problem-solving ability, though

15. For Brahe's system, which was geometrically entirely equivalent to Copernicus', see J.L.E. Dreyer, *A History of Astronomy from Thales to Kepler* (2d ed.; New York, 1953), pp. 359–71. For the last versions of the phlogiston theory and their success, see J. R. Partington and D. McKie, "Historical Studies of the Phlogiston Theory," *Annals of Science*, 4 (1939), 113–49.

16. For the problem presented by hydrogen, see J. R. Partington, *A Short History of Chemistry* (2d ed.; London, 1951), p. 134. For carbon monoxide, see H. Kopp, *Geschichte der Chemie*, 3 (Braunschweig, 1845), 294–96.

for good reasons they are usually couched in those terms. Instead, the issue is which paradigm should in the future guide research on problems many of which neither competitor can yet claim to resolve completely. A decision between alternate ways of practicing science is called for, and in the circumstances that decision must be based less on past achievement than on future promise. The man who embraces a new paradigm at an early stage must often do so in defiance of the evidence provided by problem solving. He must, that is, have faith that the new paradigm will succeed with the many large problems that confront it, knowing only that the older paradigm has failed with a few. A decision of that kind can only be made on faith.

That is one of the reasons why prior crisis proves so important. Scientists who have not experienced it will seldom renounce the hard evidence of problem solving to follow what may easily prove and will be widely regarded as a will-o'-the-wisp. But crisis alone is not enough. There must also be a basis, though it need be neither rational nor ultimately correct, for faith in the particular candidate chosen. Something must make at least a few scientists feel that the new proposal is on the right track, and sometimes it is only personal and inarticulate aesthetic considerations that can do that. Men have been converted by them at times when most of the articulable technical arguments pointed the other way. When first introduced, neither Copernicus' astronomical theory nor De Broglie's theory of matter had many other significant grounds of appeal. Even today Einstein's general theory attracts men principally on aesthetic grounds, an appeal that few people outside of mathematics have been able to feel.

This is not to suggest that new paradigms triumph ultimately through some mystical aesthetic. On the contrary, very few men desert a tradition for these reasons alone. Often those who do turn out to have been misled. But if a paradigm is ever to triumph it must gain some first supporters, men who will develop it to the point where hardheaded arguments can be produced and multiplied. And even those arguments, when they come, are not individually decisive. Because scientists are reasonable men, one or another argument will ultimately persuade many of them. But there is no single argument that can or should persuade them all. Rather than a single group conversion, what occurs is an increasing shift in the distribution of professional allegiances.

At the start a new candidate for paradigm may have few supporters, and on occasions the supporters' motives may be suspect. Nevertheless, if they are competent, they will improve it, explore its possibilities, and show what it would be like to belong to the community guided by it. And as that goes on, if the paradigm is one destined to win its fight, the number and strength of the persuasive arguments in its favor will increase. More scientists will then be converted, and the exploration of the new paradigm will go on. Gradually the number of experiments, instruments, articles, and books based upon the paradigm will multiply. Still more men, convinced of the new view's fruitfulness, will adopt the new mode of practicing normal science, until at last only a few elderly hold-outs remain. And even they, we cannot say, are wrong. Though the historian can always find men—Priestley, for instance—who were unreasonable to resist for as long as they did, he will not find a point at which resistance becomes illogical or unscientific. At most he may wish to say that the man who continues to resist after his whole profession has been converted has *ipso facto* ceased to be a scientist.

RICHARD RORTY

"Postmodernist Bourgeois Liberalism"
1983

The degree to which truths and rights derive their status from some foundation above or beyond culture has long been a matter for debate among intellectuals. During the 1970s and 1980s, the philosopher Richard Rorty (1931–) established his leadership among those American thinkers inclined to doubt that truths and rights could claim a foundation outside the particular cultural tradition that had generated and sustained such truths and rights. In arguing for a pragmatic outlook, Rorty drew explicitly and repeatedly on William James, John Dewey, and Thomas Kuhn. In the essay of 1983 that follows, Rorty addresses sympathetically the notion that morality is not a transcultural and ahistorical universal, but is instead "the interest of a historically conditioned community." Rorty insists that it is a mistake to dismiss this position as a form of relativism. Rorty's most important works are *Philosophy and the Mirror of Nature* (Princeton, 1979), and *Consequences of Pragmatism* (Minneapolis, Minn., 1982). Of the many critiques of Rorty, an especially lucid and accessible one is an essay-review by Robert Schwartz, *Journal of Philosophy,* 80 (1983), 51–67.

Complaints about the social irresponsibility of the intellectuals typically concern the intellectual's tendency to marginalize herself, to move out from one community by interior identification of herself with some other community—for example, another country or historical period, an invisible college, or some alienated subgroup within the larger community. Such marginalization is, however, common to intellectuals and to miners. In the early days of the United Mine Workers its members rightly put no faith in the surrounding legal and political institutions and were loyal only to each other. In this respect they resembled the literary and artistic avant-garde between the wars.

It is not clear that those who thus marginalize themselves can be criticized for social irresponsibility. One cannot be irresponsible toward a community of which one does not think of oneself as a member. Otherwise runaway slaves and tunnelers under the Berlin Wall would be irresponsible. If such criticism were to make sense there would have to be a supercommunity one *had* to identify with—humanity as such. Then one could appeal to the needs of that community when breaking with one's family or tribe or nation, and such groups could appeal to the same thing when criticizing the irresponsibility of those who break away. Some people believe that there is such a community. These are the people who think there are such things as intrinsic human dignity, intrinsic human rights, and an ahistorical distinction between the demands of morality and those of prudence. Call these people "Kantians." They are opposed by people who say that "humanity" is a biological rather than a moral notion, that there is no human dignity that is not derivative from the dignity of some specific community, and no appeal beyond the relative merits of various actual or proposed communities to impartial criteria which will help us weigh those merits. Call these people "Hegelians." Much of contemporary social philsophy in the English-speaking world is a three-cornered debate between Kantians (like John Rawls and Ronald Dworkin) who want to keep an ahistorical morality-prudence distinction as a buttress for the institutions and practices of the surviving democracies, those (like the post-Marxist philosophical left in Europe, Roberto Unger, and Alasdair MacIntyre) who want to abandon these institutions both because they presuppose a discredited philosophy and for other, more concrete, reasons, and those (like Michael Oakeshott and John Dewey) who want to preserve the institutions while abandoning their traditional Kantian backup. These last two positions take over Hegel's criticism of Kant's conception of moral agency, while either naturalizing or junking the rest of Hegel.

If the Hegelians are right, then there are no ahistorical criteria for deciding when it is or is not a responsible act to desert a community, any more than for deciding when to change lovers or professions. The Hegelians see nothing to be responsible to excpt persons and actual or possible historical communities; so they view the Kantians' use of "social responsibility" as misleading. For that use suggests not the genuine contrast between, for example, Antigone's loyalties to Thebes and to her brother, or Alcibiades' loyalties to Athens and to Persia, but an illusory contrast between loyalty to a person or a historical community and to something "higher" than either. It suggests that there is a point of view that abstracts from any historical community and adjudicates the rights of communities vis-à-vis those of individuals.

Kantians tend to accuse of social irresponsibility those who doubt that there is

Source: Journal of Philosophy, 80 (October 1983), 583–89. Footnotes omitted.

such a point of view. So when Michael Walzer says that "A given society is just if its substantive life is lived in . . . a way faithful to the shared understandings of the members," Dworkin calls this view "relativism." "Justice," Dworkin retorts, "cannot be left to convention and anecdote." Such Kantian complaints can be defended using the Helelian's own tactics, by noting that the very American society which Walzer wishes to commend and to reform is one whose self-image is bound up with the Kantian vocabulary of "inalienable rights" and "the dignity of man." Hegelian defenders of liberal institutions are in the position of defending, on the basis of solidarity alone, a society which has traditionally asked to be based on something more than mere solidarity. Kantian criticism of the tradition that runs from Hegel through Marx and Nietzsche, a tradition which insists on thinking of morality as the interest of a historically conditioned community rather than "the common interest of humanity," often insists that such a philosophical outlook is—if one values liberal practices and institutions—irresponsible. Such criticism rests on a prediction that such practices and institutions will not survive the removal of the traditional Kantian buttresses, buttresses which include an account of "rationality" and "morality" as transcultural and ahistorical.

I shall call the Hegelian attempt to defend the institutions and practices of the rich North Atlantic democracies without using such buttresses "postmodernist bourgeois liberalism." I call it "bourgeois" to emphasize that most of the people I am talking about would have no quarrel with the Marxist claim that a lot of those institutions and practices are possible and justifiable only in certain historical, and especially economic, conditions. I want to contrast bourgeois liberalism, the attempt to fulfill the hopes of the North Atlantic bourgeoisie, with philosophical liberalism, a collection of Kantian principles thought to justify us in having those hopes. Hegelians think that these principles are useful for *summarizing* these hopes, but not for justifying them (a view Rawls himself verges upon in his Dewey Lectures). I use "postmodernist" in a sense given to this term by Jean-François Lyotard, who says that the postmodern attitude is that of "distrust of metanarratives," narratives which describe or predict the activities of such entities as the noumenal self or the Absolute Spirit or the Proletariat. These metanarratives are stories which purport to justify loyalty to, or breaks with, certain contemporary communities, but which are neither historical narratives about what these or other communities have done in the past nor scenarios about what they might do in the future.

"Postmodernist bourgeois liberalism" sound oxymoronic. This is partly because, for local and perhaps transitory reasons, the majority of those who think of themselves as beyond metaphysics and metanarratives also think of themselves as having opted out of the bourgeoisie. But partly it is because it is hard to disentangle bourgeois liberal institutions from the vocabulary that these institutions inherited from the Enlightenment—e.g., the eighteenth-century vocabulary of natural rights, which judges, and constitutional lawyers such as Dworkin, must use *ex officiis*. This vocabulary is built around a distinction between morality and prudence. In what follows I want to show how this vocabulary, and in particular this distinction, might be reinterpreted to suit the needs of us postmodernist bourgeois liberals. I hope thereby to suggest how such liberals might convince our society that loyalty to itself is morality enough, and that such loyalty no longer needs an ahistorical backup. I think they should try to clear themselves of charges of irresponsibility by convincing our society that it need be responsible only to its own traditions, and not to the moral law as well.

The crucial move in this reinterpretation is to think of the moral self, the embodiment of rationality, not as one of Rawls's original choosers, somebody who can distinguish her *self* from her talents and interests and views about the good, but as a network of beliefs, desires, and emotions with nothing behind it—no substrate behind the attributes. For purposes of moral and political deliberation and conversation, a person just *is* that network, as for purposes of balistics she is a point-mass, or for purposes of chemistry a linkage of molecules. She is a network that is constantly reweaving itself in the usual Quinean manner—that is to say, not by reference to general criteria (e.g., "rules of meaning" or "moral principles") but in the hit-or-miss way in which cells readjust themselves to meet the pressures of the environment. On a Quinean view, rational behavior is just adaptive behavior of a sort which roughly parallels the behavior, in similar circumstances, of the other members of some relevant community. Irrationality, in both physics and ethics, is a matter of behavior that leads one to abandon, or be stripped of, membership in some such community. For some purposes this adaptive behavior is aptly described as "learning" or "computing" or "redistribution of electrical charges in neural tissue," and for others as "deliberation" or "choice." None of these vocabularies is privileged over against another.

What plays the role of "human dignity" on this view of the self? The answer is well expressed by Michael Sandel, who says that we cannot regard ourselves as Kantian subjects "capable of constituting meaning on our own," as Rawlsian choosers,

> . . . without great cost to those loyalties and convictions whose moral force consists partly in the fact that living by them is inseparable from understanding ourselves as the particular people we are—as members of this family or community or nation or people, as bearers of this history, as sons and daughters of that revolution, as citizens of this republic.

I would argue that the moral force of such loyalties and convictions consists *wholly* in this fact, and that nothing else has *any* moral force. There is no "ground" for such loyalties and convictions save the fact that the beliefs and desires and emotions which buttress them overlap those of lots of other members of the group with which we identify for purposes of moral or political deliberations, and the further fact that these are *distinctive* features of that group, features which it uses to construct its self-image through contrasts with other groups. This means that the naturalized Hegelian analogue of "intrinsic human dignity" is the comparative dignity of a group with which a person identifies herself. Nations or churches or movements are, on this view, shining historical examples not because they reflect rays emanating from a higher source, but because of contrast-effects—comparisons with other, worse communities. Persons have dignity not as an interior luminescence, but because they share in such contrast-effects. It is a corollary of this view that the moral justification of the institutions and practices of one's group—e.g., of the contemporary bourgeoisie—is mostly a matter of historical narratives (including scenarios about what is likely to happen in certain future contingencies), rather than of philosophical metanarratives. The principal backup for historiography is not philosophy but the arts, which serve to develop and modify a group's self-image by, for example, apotheosizing its heroes, diabolizing its enemies, mounting dialogues among its members, and refocusing its attention.

A further corollary is that the morality/prudence distinction now appears as a distinction between appeals to two parts of the network that is the self—parts separated by blurry and constantly shifting boundaries. One part consists of those beliefs and desires and emotions which overlap with those of most other members of some community with which, for purposes of deliberation, she identifies herself, and which contrast with those of most members of other communities with which hers contrasts itself. A person appeals to morality rather than prudence when she appeals to this overlapping, shared part of herself, those beliefs and desires and emotions which permit her to say "WE do not do this sort of thing." Morality is, as Wilfrid Sellars has said, a matter of "we-intentions." Most moral dilemmas are thus reflections of the fact that most of us identify with a number of different communities and are equally reluctant to marginalize ourselves in relation to any of them. This diversity of identifications increases with education, just as the number of communities with which a person may identify increases with civilization.

Intra-societal tensions, of the sort which Dworkin rightly says mark our pluralistic society, are rarely resolved by appeals to general principles of the sort Dworkin thinks necessary. More frequently they are resolved by appeals to what he calls "convention and anecdote." The political discourse of the democracies, at its best, is the exchange of what Wittgenstein called "reminders for a particular purpose"—anecdotes about the past effects of various practices and predictions of what will happen if, or unless, some of these are altered. The moral deliberations of the postmodernist bourgeois liberal consists largely in this same sort of discourse, avoiding the formulation of general principles except where the situation may require this particular tactic—as when one writes a constitution, or rules for young children to memorize. It is useful to remember that this view of moral and political deliberation was a commonplace among American intellectuals in the days when Dewey—a postmodernist before his time—was the reigning American philosopher, days when "legal realism" was thought of as desirable pragmatism rather than unprincipled subjectivism.

It is also useful to reflect on why this tolerance for anecdote was replaced by a reattachment to principles. Part of the explanation, I think, is that most American intellectuals in Dewey's day still thought their country was a shining historical example. They identified with it easily. The largest single reason for their loss of identification was the Vietnam War. The War caused some intellectuals to marginalize themselves entirely. Others attempted to rehabilitate Kantian notions in order to say, with Chomsky, that the War not merely betrayed America's hopes and interests and self-image, but was *immoral*, one which we had had no *right* to engage in in the first place.

Dewey would have thought such attempts at further self-castigation pointless. They may have served a useful cathartic purpose, but their long-run effect has been to separate the intellectuals from the moral consensus of the nation rather than to alter that consensus. Further, Dewey's naturalized Hegelianism has more overlap with the belief-systems of the communities we rich North American bourgeois need to talk with than does a naturalized Kantianism. So a reversion to the Deweyan outlook might leave us in a better position to carry on whatever conversation between nations may still be possible, as well as leaving American intellectuals in a better position to converse with their fellow citizens.

I shall end by taking up two objections to what I have been saying. The first objection is that on my view a child found wandering in the woods, the remnant of a slaughtered nation whose temples have been razed and whose books have been burned, has no share in human dignity. This is indeed a consequence, but it does not follow that she may be treated like an animal. For it is part of the tradition of *our* community that the human stranger from whom all dignity has been stripped is to be taken in, to be reclothed with dignity. This Jewish and Christian element in our tradition is gratefully invoked by free-loading atheists like myself, who would like to let differences like that between the Kantian and the Hegelian remain "merely philosophical." The existence of human rights, in the sense in which it is at issue in this meta-ethical debate, has as much or as little revelance to our treatment of such a child as the question of the existence of God. I think both have equally little relevance.

The second objection is that what I have been calling "postmodernism" is better named "relativism," and that relativism is self-refuting. Relativism certainly is self-refuting, but there is a difference between saying that every community is as good as every other and saying that we have to work out from the networks we are, from the communities with which we presently identify. Postmodernism is no more relativistic than Hilary Putnam's suggestion that we stop trying for a "God's-eye view" and realize that "We can only hope to produce a more rational conception of rationality or a better conception of morality if we operate from within our tradition". The view that every tradition is as rational or as moral as every other could be held only by a god, someone who had no need to use (but only to mention) the terms "rational" or "moral," because she had no need to inquire or deliberate. Such a being would have escaped from history and conversation into contemplation and metanarrative. To accuse postmodernism of relativism is to try to put a metanarrative in the postmodernist's mouth. One will do this if one identifies "holding a philosophical position" with having a metanarrative available. If we insist on such a definition of "philosophy," then postmodernism is postphilosophical. But it would be better to change the definition.